Trouble in Paradise

Trouble in Paradise

Globalization and Environmental Crises in Latin America

J. Timmons Roberts and Nikki Demetria Thanos

With a Foreword by David Helvarg

Routledge
New York and London

Published in 2003 by
Routledge
29 West 35th Street
New York, NY 10001
www.routledge-ny.com

Published in Great Britain by
Routledge
11 New Fetter Lane
London EC4P 4EE
www.routledge.co.uk

Printed in the United States of America on acid-free paper.

10 9 8 7 6 5 4 3

Library of Congress Cataloging-in-Publication Data.

Roberts, J. Timmons.
    Trouble in paradise : globalization and environmental crises in Latin America / by J. Timmons Roberts
and Nikki Demetria Thanos ; with a foreword by David Helvarg.
        p. ; cm.
Includes bibliographical references and index.
    ISBN 0–415–92979–2 (HC : alk. paper) — ISBN 0–415–92980–6 (PB : alk, paper)
    1. Sustainable development—Latin America. 2. Pollution—Latin policy—Latin America. 5. Latin
America—Environmental conditions. I Thanos, Nikki Demetria. II. Title.
    HC130.E5R63 2003
    338.98'07—dc21   2003011577

CONTENTS

CHAPTER 4

Hazards of an Urban Continent 95

CHAPTER 5

Bio-Splendor, Devastation, and Competing Visions
in the Amazon 129

CHAPTER 6

Indigenous Peoples, Development Megaprojects,
and Internet Resistance 165

CHAPTER 7

Building a Global Civil Society:
Living What We Know 193

CONTENTS

When the People Lead
by David Helvarg

I was traveling through Guatemala's Alto Plano in the bloody winter of 1980. We had just hitched a ride on a truck out of the town of Nebaj, where three days earlier the army had killed eight Mayan Indians, shooting into a crowd of demonstrators in the town square. "What did they want?" I asked one of the troops who'd opened fire on them. "Who knows?" he said in Spanish. "They don't even speak our language."

As we drove along the dark switchbacks of the steep unpaved road we came upon a convoy of open trucks full of Indian campesinos guarded by army troops carrying Israeli assault rifles and wearing black woolen Balaklavas to hide their identities. Their "recruits" were the Mayan army of labor who would be used as seasonal pickers in the cotton fields of the Atlantic lowlands. They would have a month's long reprieve from the brutal repression in the mountains only to face pesticide poisoning and back-breaking wage slavery harvesting an agro-export crop that at the same time was eroding and drying out what had once been lush coastal rainforest.

It was during the five years I covered civil and highly uncivil conflicts in Central America, amidst the bombs, bullets, mutilated death-squad victims, coffee fincas, DDT-scented cotton fields, crowded barrios, and burned-over forests, that I came to appreciate the close connections between issues of war, development, population, poverty, and natural resource management.

Trouble in Paradise, J. Timmons Roberts and Nikki Demetria Thanos's fast-paced, complex, challenging, and important work, takes me back to numerous scenes I encountered while covering Central America's wars, the U.S. border region, and, more recently, environmental conflicts throughout Latin America.

Roberts and Thanos have traveled the muddy forest trails as well as the diesel- and dust-choked barrios of our hemisphere to track the issues and connections that link the impoverishment of many of Latin America's people with the degradation of their environment. They provide social and historical context from the post-Columbian colonization and plunder of South America to the most recent conflicts over indigenous rights in the globalized Latin markets of the early twenty-first century. While not denying the possibility of change and betterment, neither do they insult us with easy answers to complex questions about resource development, democracy, and sustainability.

Mostly theirs is an exploration of biological and social complexity. In setting the scene they argue, "To become sustainable, Latin America needs real democracy to create the leverage for its citizens to demand a cleaner environment and the services they need to survive."

The linkage between democracy and environmental protection is critical and dynamic. It could be argued that democracy is a precursor to significant environmental change and yet, in visits to places as diverse as Poland and South Korea, I've also seen how militant environmental protests have set the stage for popular democratic uprisings.

Roberts and Thanos point out the contradictions between U.S. and other developed nations' demands that Latin America protect its forests and biodiversity while at the same time, through multilateral lending agencies, imposing economic austerity that denies Latin American governments the means to pursue these goals. The North demands repayment of huge debts built up under a generation of (U.S.-backed) military dictatorships while ignoring how debt repayment has become a driver of the short-term liquidation of Latin America's natural resource base.

In expanding on these and other themes, the authors take us on a bottom-up tour of the post-NAFTA free-trade environment along the United States–Mexico border. They guide us into the war-ravaged and deforested heartland of Central America's chemically dependent "green revolution" and Cuba's forced shift to organic farming. They explore the urban heat of a continent 75 percent of whose people are now city-bound and take us across the vast Amazon basin, whose diversity is both human and biological and whose problems are as convoluted as a mating ball of anacondas. They explain the "Fourth World" of indigenous peoples who are using every available tool

from arrows to the Internet to reclaim their power as users and protectors of the natural environments that sustain them. And finally they give us a practical vision of an engaged civil society at the local, regional, and global level that must come to fruition if the eco-crisis of Latin America is to be reversed.

It's an expansive but well-documented journey that frequently recalled my own moments and memories and confirmed many of their key observations. After describing the state of pollution and poverty along the border the authors quote a UN report that suggests that the maquiladora assembly industry that defines NAFTA production on La Frontiera "specializes in cheap labor and does not constitute a motor for sustainable growth with more social equity." I recall a visit to a computer chip assembly plant in Tijuana that had a production line made up entirely of "maquila girls," young women in industrial smocks working nine-hour shifts. "With their smaller hands, they're much more dexterous workers than the men," the plant manager explained to me with a straight face (they were also paid less and were harder to unionize at the time). Years later I heard the same comment from a supervisor at a factory farm in rural Maine where over 150 Mexican women work the egg-packing line. The inequalities that global capital imposes on Latin America seem to provide a secondary benefit to corporations by driving cheap immigrant labor into both traditional and formerly unionized sectors of the U.S. economy. At the same time free-trade environmental standards are neither harmonized nor predictable. At that factory farm in Maine, eggs bound for Canada are separated out for a more rigorous health inspection process than those headed to U.S. store shelves.

And for those imagining hardy Latin peasants getting their own fresh eggs from the chickens in the yard, Latin America, Roberts and Thanos point out, is the most urbanized part of the developing world, with 380 million of its 507 million residents now living in cities, including fifty-two cities with populations of over 1 million.

"Ecology in the Third World," they quote a Brazilian expert, "begins with water, garbage, and sewage."

Certainly, traveling through the "Ciudades Perdidos," the lost unnamed tin and junk wood barrios on the sprawling edge of Mexico City, the hemorrhaging heart of a nation rapidly running short of the essentials of life, including water, light, and breathable air, it is easy to despair. Nor has my faith in urban restoration been inspired by the sight of children picking through burning mountains of garbage on the edge of Tegucigalpa, Honduras, or armored tanks guarding the entrances to the hillside favelas we visited during the 1992 Earth Summit in Rio, or El Alto, the cold-blasted stone hut barrio of displaced Indians that sits above La Paz, Bolivia. Here at thirteen thousand feet above sea level it is the poor who live on the heights while the rich live down below in the warmer, thicker air.

Despite a thorough investigation of Latin America's festering urban ills, the authors manage to make a good case for the efficacy of civic action. They present options from the Living Bay Movement, which has fought to clean up Rio's world famous waterfront, to the city of Curitiba, Brazil, which has become a kind of international model of ecologically livable design, its city planning compared favorably with that of Portland, Oregon. Finally and convincingly they argue the case that "democratic participation and transparency are central to the long-term political sustainability of urban environmental reform."

Their analysis of the broad-scale of loss and biological decline occurring in the Amazon basin, and the factors driving it, are as stunning as any I've read. Still they argue for the necessity of distinguishing the types of habitats, microclimes, and ecosystems within the basin in seeking area specific solutions, and also for the necessity of incorporating the millions of people already settled there in the search for sustainability.

Along with identifying the links between oil and war, and profiling different models of rural development, the authors are able to provide useful and contrasting examples of how the still mostly rural Indian peoples of Latin America (some 10 percent of the population) have carried out their campaigns for autonomy. They also highlight the affinity between these campaigns and environmental activists' demands for ecological sustainability.

Finally, the authors examine a range of positive activities, none of which they admit provide a silver bullet (or native arrow) solution to the question of how we secure a more equitable and ecologically sound future. Still, you can see the first building blocks of a new social order in the relative costs and benefits of organic farming, ecotourism, certification of extractive products, green/blue (collar) labeling, globalized standards for transparency and "fair trade," an end to toxic dumping and the "circle of poison," defense of environmental victims and indigenous rights, and development programs based on local needs and initiatives.

In Bolivia I reported on the efforts of a U.S. archaeologist who, working with his Bolivian colleagues, was excavating the ancient civilization of Tiwanaku. In the course of their work they were also helping local Aymara Indian villagers return to the ancient farming methods of their Tiwanakan ancestors. Having identified a pre-Columbian hydrological system from an aerial survey, they encouraged villagers to begin excavating three-thousand-year-old canals connected to Lake Titicaca and to use the dirt to build up raised fields in between them. The water from the canals acts as a thermal blanket for these fields on cold nights, and the canals attract waterfowl and provide nutrient-rich bottom muck that villagers can then use in place of costly synthetic fertilizers. Once they abandoned the flat field agriculture introduced by Spanish colonialists four hundred years ago, the villagers saw their raised field harvest of potatoes and other crops increase sixfold and eightfold. They also took new pride in their cultural heritage, while not forgetting to make new *pagos*, or payments, of thanks to Pachamama, Mother Earth.

The key to finding these types of practical, culturally based solutions may require a recognition of our interdependence in a global system not just of the market, but of the spirit. We need to recognize the practicality of altruism, of human solidarity, and the benefits derived from being part of something larger than ourselves. Simply put, we need to secure our niche in the larger community of life. Roberts and Thanos quote polls that find the citizens of the poorest cities of Latin America expressing the same opinions as those living in the richest cities of the United States and Europe, that we have to do better by the environment, even if it means sacrificing economic advantage.

Most people I've met in my travels seem to have this commonsense understanding that our economies are functions of our environments and must operate in harmony with the world's natural cycles of biological productivity. Clean air, clean water, rich soil, and wild places are not luxuries to be deferred during a process of rapid integration into the world market, but the essentials of life. It's only when people organize into coercive institutional structures, be they nation-states or global corporations, that they seem to lose track of these simple truths. But that's why we have majorities and political democracies, to act as correctives.

After finishing *Trouble in Paradise* I was reminded of a long-ago night at the Rio Earth Summit, when thousands of social and environmental activists from across the city and the globe took to the streets marching behind a group of Buddhist monks with cell phones and a banner that read, "When the People Lead, the Leaders Will Follow."

Read the following. It will help you to lead.

David Helvarg is the author of *The War Against the Greens* and *Blue Frontier—Saving America's Living Seas*.

PREFACE

Pleas from rock stars, environmental groups, scientists, and schoolteachers have amplified attention to environmental destruction in Latin America since the early 1980s. The volume began to crescendo when space shuttle astronauts photographed five thousand fires on a single night in the Brazilian Amazon state of Rondonia in 1985, and grew shrill when rubbertapper Chico Mendes was shot in 1988 trying to stop ranchers from clearing forests near his home in Acre. The 1992 Earth Summit Rio de Janeiro broadened the issues and capped a wave of environmental organizing around the world.

Turning the millennium, concern is growing again among a new generation of students and activists, but they confront a literature on the environment in Latin America that is either descriptive, dated, or exceedingly technical. Most general books and articles in English were written around 1990 and were based on research conducted in the 1980s. Beyond newspaper articles and fund-raising mailers from environmental groups, there have been a few compilations/readers with uneven and often disjointed chapters. We have used several of these books in courses and assembled clippings in course-packs, but students often find themselves wishing to know more about environmental issues in the Americas and needing a more coherent structure with which to understand them.

We have sought in this book to tie some of the cases we hear so much about—and some others we do not—to the economic and cultural forces driving global change. Among these is a cycle of debt drowning Latin

American nations in a struggle to generate hard cash by exporting raw materials. There are many misunderstandings and generalizations about globalization, and we explore the term by examining how it is creating very different results for environments and people in Latin America. Much more, any discussion of the effects of globalization must include an understanding of how the region's colonial history—of staggering inequality, racism, and exploitation of nature for quick profits—has led it to its current crises and limited options for survival in the global economy.

We are not saying that history cannot be overcome—far from it. But we share with the Latin American school of thinkers called the "structuralists" the belief that action must be taken with an awareness of the constraints operating and the forces that created them. Change is possible in the poorer nations of the world, but all change is not possible, and we are doing no one a service by blaming those who are effectively victims when they do not seem to rise by themselves out of the chronic problems that have plagued the region for centuries.

Trouble in Paradise examines five topics in what we hope is a readable format and includes an introduction and conclusion that tie the chapters together. Our organization is essentially north to south, but the chapters are organized around themes as much as places. The chapters cover pollution and health on the Mexican border with the United States (Chapter 2); agriculture, parks, and ecotourism, focusing on Central America (Chapter 3); urban pollution and environmental movements in the cities of the continent (Chapter 4); Amazon deforestation (Chapter 5); and indigenous peoples and development "megaprojects" in the rainforests (Chapter 6).

We attempted to shape each chapter along roughly similar lines. Each begins with one or two vignettes detailing the real stories of people dealing with an acute environmental problem. Next, each chapter looks broadly to grasp the current extent and depth of the problem. The following section explores the historical roots of the problem and describes the conflicting political and social groups in the conflict. A section examines prevailing theories on the causes of the problem and what is at stake in each position. Then we turn to the local and international implications of proposed and existing state policies. Each chapter ends with a summary and conclusion, emphasizing the importance of social analysis and the prospects for positive change. The book, however, attempts to dissuade students from the typically North American belief that we can immediately solve any problems we set our minds to; we need to put forward and support nuanced and long-term solutions to the environmental problems in Latin America. In some cases what is needed is *less* involvement by overbearing outsiders, not more, and many problems must be addressed here—in the "global North."

Rather than attempting to present both sides in polarized debates over these cases dispassionately, in the theoretical debates and policy sections of each chapter we take sides and strongly argue for one position. We believe many commonly held positions are misguided and dangerous. For example, in Chapter 4 we take on the World Bank and its economist researchers in their proclamations that environmental issues will improve with economic growth (what has been called the "Environmental Kuznets Curve"). In Chapters 3 and 5 we argue against Malthusians and the logic that population growth is an inevitable cause of land degradation and deforestation. The political and economic context is pivotal in determining that relation.

On the other hand, in Chapter 2 we argue against the simplistic rhetoric of environmentalists and "Cassandras" who claim that most U.S. and European firms have moved to Mexico to find a "pollution haven" in which to act in a sloppy fashion. Evidence suggests that pollution control is a minor cost for firms and that cheap labor was Mexico's main attraction. On the other hand, we argue that firms will not consistently "police themselves" when it comes to polluting in the Third World, again taking on the current push by the World Bank's environmental research arm. On the Amazon, we argue both against "fence it off" preservationism and against those social ecologists who believe that addressing inequality alone will solve the problem. Addressing inequality is a crucial but rather tough beginning; agricultural extension, ending legal impunity, and land reform are practical short-run approaches. In the concluding chapter we propose that real environmental solutions must deal with the critical issues of poverty, corruption, democracy, and legal impunity. We seek to bring the issues back to the choices we readers in the Northern wealthy nations make on a daily basis.

We hope that *Trouble in Paradise* will be useful to general readers and in courses in environmental studies, geography, Latin American studies, political science, sociology, and earth sciences. It could be adopted for teaching the booming field of globalization studies. It is designed as either a core text or supplemental reader.

Who are we? First of all, we are interdisciplinarians. Roberts was first trained as a field biologist, conducting field research in Costa Rica and the United States for five years until the events described at the beginning of the first chapter led to a switch to the study of the political and social and economic causes of environmental issues in the region. He thus changed fields in 1986 to study the sociology of international development. His research since then has been focused on Brazil, a huge nation that is sometimes called a "bellwether" for Latin America but that is poorly understood outside its borders. Clearly the stakes in rural and urban environmental issues there are huge, and attempts at resolving them reveal many paradoxes and difficulties at work everywhere. Roberts also has conducted research and traveled in Mexico, Nicaragua, Peru, Bolivia, Argentina, and Uruguay. He has learned about diverse issues from coediting the Environment in Latin America Network (http://csf.colorado.edu/elan) for seven years and helping organize the environmental section of the Latin American Studies Association. Thanos was trained as a true interdisciplinarian, designing her own course of study in environmental policy and Latin American studies at Tulane University. She has conducted research and traveled during extended stays in Costa Rica, Cuba, Guatemala, Mexico, and the Andes.

Second, we are outsiders; since we are not from Latin America and although we have lived and traveled extensively in the region, we cannot know firsthand what it is really like to deal with these issues on a daily, long-term basis. More insider perspectives are badly needed in this field, but we hope to add to the discussion and make the most of our outsider status by looking broadly across the region and across classes, groups, and perspectives.

Third, we are North Americans. While reporting the pivotal roles of European environmentalists and governments in these struggles, we also have chosen to direct some key examples to North America, since we believe readers here will most benefit from understanding the connections between their own lives and the future of the planet outside their borders. We regret any parochial feel this has created. We also need to apologize for the holes here—it simply was not possible to cover everything and still keep the book lively and brief.

We need to thank the countless people across Latin America who helped us when we needed it, welcoming us and answering our tiresome and some-times silly questions. For comments and assistance we would also like to thank Jim and Gann Roberts, Canaan Silveira, Maria Julieta Vaughn Menezes, David Barkin, Tom Rudel, Terri Thanos, Gus Thanos, J.J. Thanos, Craig Humphries, Loraine Bishop, Caroline Beal, Peeps Medow, Chris Mercer and Rachel Breunlin, Kristen Traicoff, Jennifer Bickham-Mendez, Tom Linneman, Gul Ozyegin, Sal Saporito, Elizabeth Ransom, Deenesh Sohoni, Kelly Joyce, Michael Lewis, David Grover, Donna Lee Van Cott, Amy Hite, Paulo Martins, Brad Parks, David Robinson and Henri Acselrad. Of course they bear no responsibility for any errors in the book. Leo Gorman deserves special thanks for his editing work and contributions to

Chapter 6 and Forest Bradley-Wright for his research on Chapter 3. Holly Flood provided endless support and typed revisions just as the project needed a final push. Thanks to Quinn Roberts for sharing his father with the greedy book. The Global Environmental Issues class at William and Mary was blessedly patient as a test audience for the book and provided us with excellent feedback. Some early funding came from John McLachlan and the Center for Bioenvironmental Research at Tulane University, with budgeting assistance from Donna Listz. Kate Stevin and Dianne Gilbert at William and Mary also provided generous funding, space, and assistance. Eric Nelson at Routledge has been remarkably patient as the project has sputtered along. We want to thank Amelia Janes at Midwest Educational Graphics for the wonderful mapping work, and Nicole Ellis at Routledge for the skillful production. And finally and maybe most importantly, thanks somehow must be sent out to the cultivators of all that fine dark roast coffee that made finishing this book happen. May their product someday be organic, shade-grown, and fair trade.

Latin America: major geographic features and political boundaries

CHAPTER 1

The Scene, Its Problem and Roots

Hiking across the Osa Peninsula in Costa Rica in early 1982, I (Roberts) spent a night at the guardhouse of the Corcovado National Park, one of the most remote and best-protected pieces of old-growth tropical rainforest in Central America. Sleeping in a crumbling hut, I was warned by the guards of the parasites that can fall from the thatch roofing and burrow into the skin of unsuspecting sleepers. I did not sleep much anyway, with the machine gun–like sounds of chattering toucans battling for territory like the Contra guerrilla "freedom fighters" on the border of Nicaragua, not so far away.

To celebrate one guard's birthday, the guards, cook, and I ventured out of base camp in the pitch darkness up a creek with flashlights and machetes. We stunned huge shrimp with the flashlights and then simply pinned them to the creekbed with our machete blades. We all knew that this kind of shrimp hunting was illegal inside the national park, but the birthday called for something special, for a delicacy.

There was another risk in the endeavor: snakebites had nearly killed researchers and guards at Corcovado before, and the effectiveness of the anti-venom vials we carried in our packs was a source of frequent debate. Survival often depended on whether or not a bush plane happened to be at the landing strip back in camp. They rarely were. "Stay in the creek and try not to touch the trees" was the advice of my guides as we splashed along. I stayed in the creek.

I needed to get back to my field research in another national park, Santa Rosa, in the dry Guanacaste province at the other end of the country. The only way out was to walk across the Osa Peninsula to the ferry. Somehow I strayed off the main trail, coming across two "invaders" on side trails in the otherwise pristine rainforest park.

Juan Luís, a sun-rutted, fifty-something gold miner, was panning for nuggets in a creek inside the park, his scrawny horse tied to a tree. Like artesinal miners I would meet years later in the Brazilian Amazon, the *Tico* (Costa Rican) miner used mercury and arsenic to separate gold from the other rocks, burning it off with a gas torch. We have known for hundreds of years that mercury causes brain damage, and when Japanese fishermen were poisoned by mercury pollution from the Chisso Chemical Company at Minimata Bay in the 1950s we learned how it also contaminates the ground and waters and fish downstream. We will return to this issue in our exploration of the struggle over the Amazon in Chapter 5, but mercury's use continues across Latin America as a key part of the cheapest way for miners to search for riches in the rainforests.

Continuing on down the trail, wide-buttressed, vine-covered, towering rainforest trees and howler monkey calls gave way to a bright clearing in the forest where chainsaw teeth revealed the intricate star shapes of the stumps of enormous trees. Trunks of dozens of the elaborate trees lay among ashes of a tiny "slash-and-burn" farm, the second "invader" of my hike. José and Maria Carmen and their five children were scratching out a living from their small clearing on the rolling hills. As I sat down to talk, the rain began. All seven of them slept in one bed, barely out of the rain. Their four chickens pecked at seeds on the bald, clay-eroded dirt floors around the tiny house. The downpour was visibly washing away their soil.

The family told me they had moved to the rainforests of the Osa from the dry, cattle-ranching province of Guanacaste. It was reported at the time that much of Costa Rica's beef exports were supplying McDonalds hamburgers for a corner of southwest Florida. This fact was a source of pride to some Costa Ricans I met, but of grave concern for others who worried about the rapidly falling Central American rainforest, who dubbed it "the hamburger connection."[1]

José and Maria Carmen had come to the Osa a year before, and said they liked it.

"Why did you come?" I asked innocently.

"Because there's more to eat here."

I was staggered. For years, environmentalists had been saying that population growth and slash-and-burn agriculturalists were the main cause of rainforest destruction in Central America. I'd had no reason to question that explanation until I looked in the eyes of José and Maria Carmen, people who had known dire hunger looking for food in a nation whose relative prosperity and peacefulness earned it the nickname "the Switzerland of the Americas."

My training as a biologist and the explanations offered by environmental groups did not address the deeper problems driving deforestation. This book is the result of two decades of trying to understand the nature and extent of these problems, their historical roots, and how they are driving rational people to damage the environment. More recently, I have sought to understand how shifting forces outside of the region are changing the nature and direction of environmental problems within the region.

Our first point in this book is that there is not one environmental crisis in Latin America: There are many. Most international attention to the region, however, has focused on the rainforests, especially after the murder of rubbertapper and labor leader Chico Mendes in his Amazon town of Xapurí just before Christmas back in 1988. There is a telling expression in Brazil, that people's concern for the destruction of the Amazon is directly proportional to their distance from it. There is some truth and some untruth in this generalization, as we will discuss later, but the point here is that the rainforest is just one of many environmental issues facing the people of Latin America. More basically, most people are forced to worry about their economic survival, safety from crime, stability of the political scene, and finding good health care and education for their children. Eighty percent of Latin Americans are now urban and many millions are poor, so safe food, drinking water, and breathable air are also pressing concerns. With four in every five Latin Americans now living in a city, people there are understandably frustrated when outsiders devote more attention to the cute fuzzy creatures of the jungle—what cynics call the "charismatic megafauna" you see on the wall calendars, insignias, and fundraising letters of many environmental groups—than to people struggling to meet their basic needs.

We seek here to examine a broader spectrum of issues, incorporating urban "brown" issues such as pollution and sewage, as well as traditionally "green" issues of deforestation, habitat loss, and agricultural change. In doing so we examine whether these environmental challenges have the same root causes, and whether attempts to address them face the same obstacles to change.

As a visitor to Latin America, environmental issues seem to lie all around you, in nearly all settings. Squalor, too, seems to be everywhere: Even the roads from many international airports to their city centers are lined with squatter shacks and grimy informal restaurants, bars, and vendor stalls.

But as a resident, this is the reality: There is no alternative place to live, nor any reason to believe things will change anytime soon. New economic plans are proposed by each new president but usually founded on deep structural problems and corruption scandals. Politicians use poor people when it is time for elections, campaigning into their neighborhoods on sound trucks with promises of new roads, electricity, health clinics, and schools. The elections come and soon after there is no money to staff and maintain the new buildings; the cheaply built roads crumble into perilous obstacle courses; sewer projects lay unfinished.

Here precisely is the reason why we believe a broader approach is needed. To become sustainable, Latin America needs real democracy to create the leverage for its citizens to demand a cleaner environment and the services they need to survive.[2] Without democracy there is no due process of law against those who degrade the environment. In turn, to be democratic, Latin America needs to address the widespread and "savage" inequality between rich and poor; between whites, Indians, mestizos, and blacks; and between men and women. This is not merely hyperbole or the use of environmental concern to argue for socialism: Based on the experience of other countries, environmental movements have relied upon relatively highly educated urban middle classes who will fight for the welfare of the country as a whole. These movements are stronger in times of stability and redistribution.

We examine what we believe are five of the most serious issues that threaten the region's very survivability in the not so long term. Moving roughly from north to south, first we look at the maquiladora industries along the United States–Mexico border, and what they can teach us about how free trade is affecting environmental protection. Next we look at how pesticides and poverty are determining the fate of Central America's lands. Chapter 4 focuses on urban air and water pollution, and the solutions that have been attempted to clean them up. Next, we turn to the complex Amazon. In Chapter 6 we look at indigenous peoples on the Amazon/Andes edge and how they are being confronted with perplexing opportunities and risks of huge development "megaprojects." Many other issues will come up along the way.

To understand the critical environmental crises in Latin America, we will argue here, one needs to grasp the extent of poverty and inequality that characterizes the whole region. And a novice needs some history, politics, and economics. Addressing these critical problems will also require much more: understanding the biology, sociology, economics, and culture. It will take informed citizens and researchers with an interdisciplinary background addressing policy questions. It will take cooperation in teams of researchers and policymakers from the global North and South. It will take attention to the local issues but also their global links. We need to know what improvement efforts succeeded or failed in the past and why.

We must also understand globalization—how the logic of the increasingly worldwide system of investing, trading, and political and cultural interactions is reshaping all the places on the planet. But we also need to understand the limitations of globalization, and why it is not creating a uniform social and environmental landscape.

Globalization and these environmental crises create new opportunities, with risks and pressures that require very strategic action on the parts of individuals, groups, states, corporations, and international agencies. There is hope for the region. The stories in this book show that there are indeed very deep historical roots to Latin America's social problems. But they also show the difference one group or individual can make. In the language of social science, there are structural constraints but ample room for "agency," even in times of powerful globalizing forces. Some hopeful signs:

- Members of a cooperative in Peru have found a way naturally to stimulate forest growth with pruning and selectively to harvest wood in a way that does not damage the forest. The wood is labeled as sustainably produced, which brings a premium from savvy European consumers.

- In Curitiba, Brazil, dozens of low-cost, low-tech innovations have been implemented that help poor people and the urban environment. Buses are fast, clean, and affordable; recycling rates are among the highest in the world; and by addressing environmental problems thousands of jobs have been created for the chronically unemployed.

- Solidarity groups throughout Latin America use the Internet to disseminate information about local environmental struggles to partner groups around the world, whose letters, phone calls, and faxes have influenced the outcomes of some of these struggles. For example, Mexican peasant environmentalists Rodolfo Montiel and Teodoro Cabrera were released from jail in 2001 after an international campaign by human rights and environmental groups put pressure on the Mexican government.

- In Costa Rica, small farmers have organized production and marketing cooperatives to sell organic coffee and fruit on the international market. These farmers are able to reap greater profits by skipping the "middle man" and, at the same time, to invest in long-term, ecologically sustainable agriculture.

Even lost struggles to improve environmental and social ills can provide opportunities to learn for the next ones. This is our hope then for this book: to look more broadly at the region and its environmental issues, draw some of what we see are the most important lessons from them, and finally attempt to sew them together into a bigger picture of what is possible.

We begin where we must begin, with a very brief history to understand how we got where we are today. We will not overwhelm readers with details about the tremendously rich history of Latin America: We commend to you several excellent books we cite along the way. However, our history pays mind to two areas: economic arrangements and how they shaped society and the environmental effects of those arrangements. Turn your watch back.

Two Worlds Collide: A Brief Social Ecology of Colonization

When Columbus stepped ashore on the Caribbean island of San Salvador in 1492, among his first words were, "Where is the gold?" He came, like the other conquistadors and adventurers after him, bearing cross and sword. Spain and Portugal had just "reconquered" the Iberian Peninsula of Europe from the Muslims, and they took the strategy and mentality of military occupation as they approached the new land they had found. Columbus sought to convert the "heathens," certainly, and to find the "fountain of youth." But more urgently, he needed to find precious metals and land to grow valuable commodities to sell in Europe in order to pay his debt to Isabelle and Ferdinand, the financers of his trip. Of the natives he met on his first landing, Columbus wrote in his logbook,

> I was very attentive to them, and strove to learn if they had any gold. Seeing some of them with little bits of metal hanging at their noses, I gathered from them by signs that by going southward or steering round the island in that direction, there would be found a king who possessed great cups full of gold, and in large quantities. [For] of gold is treasure made, and with it he who has it does as he wills in the world and it even sends souls to Paradise.[3]

Likewise, Hernán Cortés, conquerer of Mexico, told the messenger of the great Aztec king Montezuma: "I and my companions suffer from a disease of the heart which can be cured only with gold."[4] In 1519 Cortés pillaged tremendous treasures in Montezuma's Aztec capital; likewise in his conquest of the mighty Inca empire of the Andes in South America, Francisco Pizarro got for Spain one roomful of gold and two of silver for the return of the ransomed king Atahualpa. In just two decades the conquistadors looted and melted down the gold the natives had spent centuries mining and crafting into artifacts, pressing the Indians into slavery and demanding ever more gold.

The frantic search for gold led to the rapid exploration of the Americas. The Spanish and Portuguese were convinced they would find gold in the rivers and creeks of America's lowland rainforests, but the Americas were most generous in silver. Latin America's cold remote mountaintops at their highest altitudes—over ten thousand feet in the Andes and over six thousand feet in New Spain (what would later become Mexico)—yielded copious amounts of silver. Gold and silver flowing from the Americas exceeded all the reserves in Europe, and many scholars argue that it financed sixteenth-century European development.[5] The precious metals flowed quickly through Spain to its creditors, the Germans, Flemish, and Genoese.

The richest veins of silver were at a remote place called Potosí, 15,700 feet up in what is now the Andes mountains of Bolivia. After its discovery in 1545, forty thousand semi-enslaved Indians could be found there each day carrying sacks of ore weighing up to three hundred pounds out of hundreds of tunnels just wider than a man.[6] Their passage was lit in the dim, dusty tunnels by a candle tied to the forehead or little finger of the front man. They were at first there as part of their *mita*, the ancient Inca tradition of working a few weeks a year for the emperor. But as time went on, the mines demanded more labor, and so Don Francisco de Toledo forced them to stay for a year, working dawn until dusk on five-day turns.[7] Just to keep the ore and machines moving at Potosí required a rotating forced draft of all working-age men from an area of the Andes 800 miles long and 250 miles wide.[8]

Travel to the mine to serve one's time could take as long at two months, and men often brought along their families. In this way, traditional subsistence agriculture was entirely disrupted. Women were particularly affected by this shift as their traditional household responsibilities gave way to supporting new foreign economic interests. Furthermore, women often bore the brunt of the ecological damage that resulted as production became concentrated in remote areas, like the mountainous areas around mines, and the far-

away lowland colonial plantations near the coast. The mines required charcoal and timbers, which led to rapid deforestation. Women, usually charged
with collecting firewood and water, found their jobs becoming more time-
and labor-intensive as local forests were systematically decimated.

Many Indians were sickened and died from the extremes in temperatures: the six-hundred-foot-deep tunnels were hot from the earth's core, but
the outside air was near freezing. Dust from the digging caused silicosis and
other respiratory diseases. Many fell to their deaths or were crushed when
hastily constructed tunnels collapsed. But most insidious were the neurological effects from the mercury used to separate precious ores from the worthless rocks around them. By 1600 Potosí had 65 refineries; New Spain had
370.[9] Rocks taken from the mountain were ground down to sand, with the
power of water, horses, or Indians. In stone tanks or on stone patios, large
heaps of ore were piled up, and salt, copper pyrites, water, and pounds of
mercury were squeezed on them. Then the Indians were used as mixers:
They would stomp on the mosh for six to eight weeks until the master said
the mix was ready for separation. Finally, the mercury was squeezed out
through cloth and the excess burned off, leaving pure silver. This process was
used for two hundred years at Potosí.

The idea here is not to villainize Columbus, Cortés, and the others who
followed them, but to try to understand how they saw the land they discovered and how that influenced the way they treated that land and the people
who were part of it. Historian Warren Dean summarizes the Portuguese attitude toward this new world of Nature they encountered in their new land,
Brazil: "[U]nable to grasp intellectually the magnitude of their discovery, the
Portuguese stumbled through half a continent, driven by greed and right-
eousness, unmoved by pity or even curiosity. The magnificent Atlantic
Forest left them unmoved and uncomprehending."[10] He continues that this
depredation "reveals an entirely pragmatic attitude toward the natural world:
When in doubt: burn it. These were hearts ruled not by wonder or panic,
but by caution and thoroughness."[11]

The enterprise was not solely built on gold and silver, of course, but on
anything that could be sold back in the old country. Finding no gold on his
first trip, in 1493 Columbus came back to America with seventeen ships,
twelve hundred men, and seeds and cuttings for the planting of "wheat,
chickpeas, melons, onions, radishes, salad greens, grape vines, sugar cane,
and fruit stones for the founding of orchards."[12] These men set out to re-cre-
ate the Europe they knew, but the grains, olives, and grapevines all failed on
the Antilles. They resisted eating unfamiliar local American species used by

the Indians, and only did so when their own plants would not grow. Some imported plants thrived—most notably, sugar.

Sugar cane plantations and sugar mills were founded almost everywhere the Spanish and Portuguese landed, and sugar produced the first profitable crop to send back to Europe. Sugar reshaped European diets and powered workers and trade around the world.[13] The English and French followed suit in search of the sweet profits in their colonies around the Caribbean. Beyond claims for immense fields whose soil was worn out by the intensive production, sugar milling required huge volumes of firewood to boil down the cane, as Lisbon observed in 1786.[14] Tobacco, cotton, and coffee were likewise pivotal in colonizing huge swaths of the best lands in the newly opened territories. Alfred Crosby calls their success in replacing one continent's species with another's "probably the greatest biological revolution in the Americas since the end of the Pleistocene era."[15]

Portuguese King Manuel demanded that the sailors that set out for the East in 1500 and 1501 repay him in goods that could be harvested on the new land. America's land and its products, however, were entirely strange to the foreign colonizers. One tree used by native Tupí Indians to dye cotton was exported in large volumes; the *pau-brasil* tree gave the nation its name. Millions of trees fell to brighten European vestments and adorn their cabinetry in the 1500s alone.[16] The biological sacking continued—for example, just one ship in 1532 brought back three hundred live monkeys, six hundred parrots, and three thousand leopard skins.[17] To meet the demand for these trade goods, Indians had to scour thousands of square kilometers of forests, creating biological shock waves far beyond the areas actually colonized by whites. This collecting for trade also created political tensions among Indian nations over disputed hunting lands. And from 1511 at least, colonizers also hauled Indians back to Europe as slaves. When they fell ill by the millions from the imported European diseases, Africans were brought over to work the mines and plantations.

The Europeans established mines and plantations all over the Americas, from the vast empires of the Spanish and Portuguese to the smaller (but more intensively devastating) claims on the Caribbean islands by the British, French, and Dutch. Latin America was thus "inserted" into the European dominated world economy in 1500 as a place to make quick money and get back home. Luís Vitale made the bold and brilliant assertion two decades ago that South America's sad fate when compared to North America's was due precisely to the surpluses of gold and enslavable Indians that colonists stumbled upon there. And the point makes sense: The first English landing in North America, for example, had to put their own hands to work when the local Indians were relatively few in number and often impossible to control.[18] Latin American Indians were organized in much larger societies and friendlier at contact with the Europeans. They were already so advanced in technology in agriculture and mineralogy that profitable colonization was easy. By contrast, in Jamestown, the first surviving settlers sent in 1607 by the Virginia Company nearly starved in their desperate mud encampments and then were almost annihilated in 1622.[19]

The "pillage" mentality and extractive economy would shape Latin American society forever: Mines and plantations provided products for an overseas market, while mining and port towns created a new demand for textiles, tea, firearms, and overseas luxuries. Export "enclaves" also created a demand for some products that were produced in the Americas: Grain was cultivated in Bajío and Michoacán in what is now Mexico, wine was made on the Chilean and Peruvian coasts, and cattle and mules were raised on the Rio de la Plata, in what is now Argentina, Uruguay, and Paraguay.[20]

In a fiery 1884 speech, the most famous Brazilian abolitionist intellectual, Joaquim Nabuco, went further by arguing that slavery tainted everything it touched, both social and environmental.[21] Historian José Padua documents how a series of authors and social critics in Brazil have argued essentially that: that slavery allowed the nation's agricultural elite to continue using outdated techniques and defer innovations that would have conserved soil fertility. This and a huge open frontier allowed slave-equipped plantations to spread "almost nomadically" continually westward away from the coast, until three centuries later when slavery was abolished in 1888. Nabuco argued that "where it [slavery] arrived, the forests are burned, the soil is dug up and wasted, and when the tents are taken up, a devastated country is left behind." Brazil received 4 million of the 10 million Africans who survived passage to the Americas,[22] so it is especially important in this regard. However, the points apply elsewhere: The plantation system had the same ecological and social effects in the Caribbean islands, in coastal Central America, and to some extent the U.S. South.

Money, men, ships, and other resources were always scarce for the colonizers, who attempted to control an empire the size of a continent with a handful of sailboats and small numbers of soldiers, missionaries, and administrators. Communications were extremely difficult, especially inland and on the Pacific side of South America: instructions from the king could take months or years to arrive, and replacement administrators often took years to be installed. The Spanish, controlling by papal fiat a massive area from what is now Canada all the way to Argentina, installed four local mini-kings, called "viceroys," and gave them almost absolute power. There were also regional courts, local governments, and surprisingly powerful missions and priests. The Portuguese sent over Pombal, a viceroy, to run their vast empire in Brazil.

Together, these politicos made up a nobility, along with the religious leaders and the economic elite of conquistador heirs and friends, attorneys, miners, traders, and plantation and ranch (*hacienda*) owners. Race, place of birth, and occupation were the keys to the system of inequality, with those born in Spain and Portugal getting the most power, and *criollos*—nobles born in the New World—just below them. Below the criollos were the free but poor workmen, small farmers, and craftsmen, usually of mixed blood, often from European men impregnating Indian and African slaves. At the bottom of the pile were African slaves and natives, who broke their backs and lost their lives working the conquistador mines, haciendas, and plantations.

We are going to argue here that this system of oppression based on race and occupation is a root of many of the environmental problems we will be looking at through the rest of the book. For example, poor people are often forced into the rainforest because they lack better alternatives. Their desperate actions create cycles of devastation that can last for generations and that usually fail to lift them out of poverty. Meanwhile, to show their social positions, wealthy elites imitate foreign tastes by consuming lavishly and purchasing abroad. These elites often come to identify more with foreign peoples than with their poorer neighbors, and thus, the wealthy and powerful often do not see the problems of the poor as their own.

There are many parallels in the way Spanish, Portuguese, English, and Dutch colonizers treated the people they conquered. The Europeans used force as well as feigned friendship to quickly replace native empires with the Spanish crown and the Roman Catholic church. As we'll see in the next section, finding allies "among the locals" was an important part of the way many foreign powers came to exploit effectively the greater numbers of Latin Americans and their resources.

Another tradition that was, in varying forms, passed on from pre-Colombian and European societies is a system of authoritarian governance. After the conquest, Latin American authoritarian (nondemocratic) regimes were aided by foreign militaries and military aid, first from Spain and later from the United States. This legacy has had crucial environmental implications as many Latin Americans lacked the democratic space for citizens to exert pressures on their rulers to protect the environment. Political changes in the last two decades give us reason to hope that Latin America may continue to be democratized. Changes in the racist and elitist history that forged a culture, however, are inevitably slower coming.

From the beginning of the conquest, Latin America's mining and plantation agriculture were directly linked with the world economy. This new economic system sent out waves of influence that eventually reshaped local economies, societies, and ecosystems. Even in port towns where the Iberians spent little time, the emergence of overseas trade radically altered the New World's culture and environment. Because Latin America since 1500 was a place to make quick money by selling products back home, the economy was in many ways "globalized" from the start.

Were Pre-Columbian Peoples Living Sustainably?

The original discovery of America of course occurred sometime long before Columbus, somewhere between thirteen thousand and fifty thousand years ago. Most estimates are that people came across the Bering Straights from Asia into what is now Alaska and Canada about thirteen thousand years ago and reached the southern tip of South America about nine thousand years ago. This may seem like a long time, but in what is now the subcontinent of Brazil, Warren Dean calculates about four hundred generations of *Homo sapiens*, which is extremely brief compared to the sixteen hundred generations of fire-wielders in Australia and just a tenth as long as the four thousand generations in Africa.[23]

The human and ecological devastation wrought by the arrival of European colonists around 1500 raises many questions about those who came before them. How many people did the lands of Latin America support before the arrival of the Spanish? Were pre-Columbian peoples adapted to the land in a different way; that is, did they manage to live here without destroying the land as did those who came later? Do we need this indigenous knowledge to better use Latin America's land, plants, and animals?

The honest answer to all three of these questions is quite simple: We do not know. There were many hundreds of different cultures that lived here before Columbus's arrival. Some very tiny hunting-and-gathering groups made a modest impact on the land where they fished, collected fruits and roots, and trapped and hunted wildlife. Their skills were great, and their knowledge of the ways of nature were by necessity highly developed. In some places, living this way was relatively easy, such as in tidal areas and along mangrove tree-lined coasts, where there were plentiful oysters, clams, and fish. Huge mounds of oyster shells can be found around the Americas, some seven stories (twenty-five meters) high and three hundred meters long. Along major rivers, and the muddier the better, protein was plentiful. In the Amazon basin, archaeological evidence indicates that the rivers' fertile lowlands may have supported as many as 5 million to 15 million people.[24]

From the simple small bands of a few family groups that probably spread across the continents, more complex, hierarchical societies began to emerge with the advent of more advanced agriculture. The Inca empires of Quechua and Aymara speakers at their peak under Huayna Capac (just before the conquest) stretched from north of Quito, Ecuador, across Peru, and down the coast of Chile almost to Patagonia.[25] Their languages had nearly three million speakers.[26] The Olmecs, Toltecs, and Aztecs developed elaborate societies in what is now Mexico, building temples, roads, grain storage towers, and the massive capital city of Tenochtitlán. Tenochtitlán dwarfed the largest European city of the time, London, in population and, according to Spanish diaries, in beauty. The Yucatan peninsula in what is now southern Mexico at one time had 2.5 million speakers of Maya and Nuhatl languages.[27]

The first real inequalities in burials between different families date back to around 2500 B.C. in coastal Peru. This site shows the evidence of the beginning of hereditary leaders. Before that, and still in smaller hunter-gatherer groups, power within native societies was probably based largely on one's age, sex, and abilities.

In Peru, "chiefdoms" emerged when abundant fishing supplied a sufficient surplus to stay in one place. In Mesoamerica, sedentary villages and their chiefdoms came a thousand years later and were based on a crop that had been bred from scrawny weeds into bigger and bigger harvests by careful selection over millennia: corn. Another millennium later, about 500–250 B.C., the cultivation of corn, gods, and pottery had fostered the growth of major cities and civilizations in Mesoamerica, the largest being Teotihuacán, which managed to sustain somewhere near 150,000 people. In the Inca and Maya cases it appears there were different, "empty cities," serving largely as ceremonial and government centers, surrounded by agricultural households.[28]

On the question of the long-term sustainability of these pre-Columbian peoples, the literature is quite disputed. Many cultures survived for centuries on almost exclusively local resources, something we cannot claim for ourselves. However, many great civilizations, such as the Maya builders of the glorious Chichén Itzá pyramids and the Incas who built the engineering marvel Machu Picchu, quickly disappeared for mysterious reasons. Some archaeologists argue that they overtaxed the land, but some further studies suggest that they may have fallen as the result of intertribal warfare and other cultural conflicts.

The diversity of species the "indigenes" utilized deserves our attention for a moment because it has fascinating ecological implications. After burning a patch of tropical forest and planting a few seasons of maize (corn), manioc (cassava), beans, potatoes, squash, or other species in the fertile ashes, the soil became poor and weed seeds invaded. Instead of fighting the inevitable, Indians planted or transplanted many species of trees to the clearing, which provided fruits or materials for housing or other uses. These were helped along and protected from shading trees. As the weeds and more shade-tolerant trees came in, these recovering forest gaps were revisited again and again for their products. Some anthropologists argue that virtually all of the Amazon, for example, was this kind of "managed succession" and that the current distribution of major species like rubber trees and Brazil nuts are largely the result of these human uses, even in what we call "virgin" forests. Finding evidence that 192 kinds of fruits were gathered in the Amazon, Paulo B. Cavalcante estimated that the actual number was closer to 300:[29]

> There were fruit bearers, among them guava, papaya, cahew, soursop, Surinam cherry, and—lacking an English equivalent because they were neither exported nor cultivated in the English-speaking tropics—*jabuticaba, grumixama, araçá, cambuçi, cambucá, sapucaia, and pacova*; fiber and seed-bearing palms; canoe-wood trees; and the prized genipap and annato, which yielded black and red skin paints that also repelled insects and blocked the sun's rays.[30]

The same people, the Tupí, whose traces have been discovered in over one thousand sites in the lush Atlantic Forest of eastern Brazil, used dozens of species of wild game. For example, they ate over thirty-five species of fish and shellfish and hunted, "deer, marmosets, turtles, crocodiles, monkeys, sloths, peccaries, agoutis, armadillos, capybaras, tapirs, pacas, and otters—among larger animals—while their children raided birds' nests, caught rats, lizards, land crabs, snails, and small birds, and foraged for insect larvae and honey."[31]

But successful use of natural resources led quite naturally to populations that overgrew the ability of their surroundings to provide firewood, construction materials, fish, meat, and grains to support them. In search of these essential goods, villages had to move or take over other villages. Elaborate training of warriors and religions of war and sacrifice developed to support the expansion of some cultures, like the Tupí and the Aztecs.[32]

Between clearing and burning forests and roaming widely from settlements in search of wildlife, early peoples of Latin America had severe impacts on the ecosystems that supported them. There is (debated) evidence that humans decimated a whole series of large species that once roamed the Americas—the so-called megafauna that disappeared about twelve thousand years ago: large sloths, ox-sized armadillos, rhinoceroslike beasts called toxodons, huge mastodons, horses, and the saber-toothed tiger.[33] Although the disappearance of these megafauna coincided with a huge temperature and climactic swing, humans are probably culpable for their extinction, as they were easy prey for hunters with even the most basic stone tools.

So we leave the initial questions of this section with mixed answers: Indians used and sometimes overused and destroyed the lands of Latin America. Their impact, however, was much more localized and the forests tended to recover more rapidly than with European styles of land use. Even in areas of great dependence on corn, they planted or husbanded a vast diversity of species. Many cultures did live at sustainable levels of land use. Clearly we ignore the lessons of their economy and culture at our grave peril. It is disconcerting that the people who may hold the keys to crafting a sustainable society in the Americas are seeing their cultures vanish so quickly, as we will see in Chapter 6. In the meantime we return to the chain of events after colonization, with the shifts as Latin American colonies became sovereign states in the early 1800s.

National Liberation and New Dependencies

In a brave military campaign that altered the history of the continent in the 1810s and 1820s, Simon Bolivar helped free Spanish America. However, the new nations of Venezuela, Colombia, Peru, and Bolivia quickly ended up in the arms of new powers, ones inside and outside their borders. But by ending the Spanish monopoly control on trade, Bolivar also opened up the region to British and U.S. businesses: Today, striking busts of Bolivar still adorn boulevards in port cities along the U.S. eastern and gulf coasts. It was not long before Latin America's streetcars, lights, mines, and plantations were run by British and U.S. corporations.

The special role of the United States in the new world order that developed requires mention, since it has a lot to do with the particular legacy of relations between both government and civilian groups (including corporations and environmentalists) to this day. In the 1840s under President Polk, half of Mexico's land was taken to increase the size of the United States (by a third). In 1898, President William McKinley sent U.S. troops into Cuba, and after Spain quickly withdrew, the U.S. militarily imposed a new government. Several years later, President Teddy Roosevelt became furious when Colombia turned down a $10 million offer to purchase land for a canal across the Isthmus of Panama. So Roosevelt cooked up a fake rebellion and threatened the Colombian army if they interfered. As Roosevelt said bluntly, "I took Panama."[34]

Time after time Washington supported companies that would take the risk of moving into the region. In efforts to defend these economic interests, the United States intervened in the tiny nations of Central America and the Caribbean dozens of times in the 1900s, beginning in Nicaragua and the Dominican Republic. When Latin American governments did things that threatened the wishes of American plantation and mining firms, the United States could and often did "dispose" of unfriendly governments and install others. This was the case in 1954 when the United States overthrew Guatemala's democratically elected president Arbenz, who was considered a threat to the United Fruit Company's banana plantations. The CIA supported Brazil's 1964 military coup. Later, the United States intervened in Chile at the request of U.S. mining companies that feared President Allende would nationalize their operations. And the United States made life miserable for successful revolutionary governments, such as those that came to power in Cuba in 1959 and Nicaragua in 1979.

Elite Latin American "insiders" adapted quickly to the New World order without much consideration for the needs of their fellow countrymen.[35] These "Lumpenbourgeoisie" nationals, in the words of Andre Gunder Frank, acted as go-betweens developing relationships between foreign transnational firms and Latin American governments. These elites benefited from the cheap sale of state goods and imitated the consumption habits of the European, Miami, and New York bourgeoisie. In many ways, the Latin American elite held on to policies that kept their nations underdeveloped. The noted historian of the national period Bradford Burns explains:

> Since the elites had benefited handsomely from the colonial institutions, they were loath to tamper with them. . . . The economy after 1825 remained as subordinate to the economic needs of Europe as it had throughout the long colonial period. . . . They exported the raw materials required in Europe and the United States and imported the manufactured goods pouring from the factories. . . . Of all the elements of society, the governing elites profited most from growth, and the immediate advantage they reaped wed them to their policies. Furthermore,

development would have required changing some basic institutions—those governing land and labor, for example—from which the elites drew immediate benefits. . . . Economic changes were few. Agriculture and the large estate retained their prominence, and the new nations became as subservient to British economic policies as they once had been to those of Spain and Portugal.[36]

Before long, a new wave of nationalism spread across the region as state "progress" became a source of pride for Latin American elites. With a weak class of local businessmen, to achieve progress Latin American governments had to interfere more in state economies. Nations soon became known for the specialized products they supplied for the global markets: "For Brazil it was coffee; for Chile, nitrates and copper; for Bolivia, tin; for Argentina, beef and wheat; for Peru, guano."[37] Central America specialized in coffee and bananas. The export sector became extremely modern, with electrified railroads and modern plantation techniques. Policies on currency valuation and taxes were tilted heavily toward exporters. The rest of the economy languished and food production declined. Land and the benefits of its "development" became concentrated in fewer and fewer hands; exports drove opulence and misery:

> For the majority of the Latin Americans, progress resulted in an increased concentration of lands in the hands of ever-fewer owners; falling per capita food production, with corollary rising food imports; greater impoverishment; less to eat; more vulnerability to the whims of an impersonal market; uneven growth; increased unemployment and underemployment; social, economic and political marginalization; and greater power in the hands of the privileged few.[38]

Latin American slaves, Indians, and peasants did not simply submit to the European invaders; protests, escapes, rebellions, and less reported "weapons of the weak" such as sabotage, small strikes, work slowdowns, and even suicide were common occurrences. Heroic slave rebellions spread from Haiti throughout the Caribbean sugar islands into Brazil and Dutch Guiana (Suriname). In the aftermath, slave leaders were often sold, mutilated, burned alive, or crushed between cane-milling cylinders.

The slave trade cemented Latin America's connection to the world economy. It is no surprise that this human trade combined with the overseas sale of Latin America's raw materials laid the foundation for a region beset by racial tensions, environmental degradation, and social inequality. Latin America's link to the world economy as its "extractive periphery" has driven several different types of environmental impacts. An economy dependent on the export of natural resources left precious little by way of an integrated social infrastructure capable of absorbing the impact of subsequent waves of capital expansion, extraction, and contraction.[39] Concern was seldom paid to the sustainability of production and new technologies.

Around the turn of the twentieth century, Latin America began to become more urban, and while many poor peasants fled rural desperation to the cities, there was also a huge flow of immigrants from Europe and urban commercialists, who helped create a new middle class. Through their backgrounds, studies, and travels, some of these middle-class Latin Americans became familiar with Europe and the United States and began to emulate their industrialization programs. The Great Depression and World War II sent shock waves through Latin America and sharply reduced demand for its raw materials. As the global financial system collapsed, the world's attention became focused outside the region.[40] With few basic products being imported during these crises, Latin America's own entrepreneurs stepped in to produce goods for which there was a local demand, creating a new era of industrialization across the region. This later became known as the first stage of "import substitution industrialization," or ISI.

Import substitution provided jobs and progress never seen before in the region, and the ISI model was popularized in the 1950s by a UN-chartered group of economists and planners called CEPAL, or the Economic Commission on Latin America (ECLA in English). Led by Chilean economist Raúl Prebisch, the group proposed that Latin American nations should continue and expand ISI by producing more goods that had previously been imported from overseas, including the tougher products like steel, chemicals, and cars. Recognizing this period as a turning point in Latin America's history, these leaders directed Latin American governments to build huge steel mills, oil refineries, and assembly plants to eliminate the region's dependency on imported industrial goods like cars, large appliances, and machinery parts. Brazil had already dove into ISI programs during World War II, playing the Germans against the Americans to gain the technology and aid it needed to build the giant Volta Redonda steel mill. This mill and others later enabled the nation to use its iron deposits and charcoal to build a series of metalworking plants in the ABC districts of São Paulo state. The forests and mines of the Minas Gerais state were devastated, while São Paulo became the continent's industrial powerhouse.

Pollution controls and environmental impact considerations were often neglected during the pursuit of national development programs. Subsidized energy prices were kept so low that they eventually favored terrible ineffi-ciencies.[41] Where they were implemented, ISI policies were also heavily urban biased, buying "labor peace" by underpricing agricultural products and other basic needs. This kept wage labor cheap in the cities, but stifled any innovation in the fields. The prices for machines for the factories were kept inexpensive by keeping the local currency overvalued. However, this in turn made exporting agricultural products more expensive overseas. So in order to continue exporting agricultural commodities, plantation and ranch owners resorted to oppression of peasants and payment of wages below what was necessary for workers' survival. Governments and even urban labor unions looked the other way.[42] Many of these policies were possible because of a surplus of workers. So in many places the shift to ISI built upon and worsened the legacy of poverty, exploitation, deforestation, and soil erosion in the rural environment. Desperate to escape and pulled by the improve-ments in the cities, many countries saw huge migrations into the urban cen-ters. As Orlando San Martín points out, "the social costs [of ISI] that caused higher levels of income concentration [also] encouraged short-sighted approaches to resource exploitation by the rural poor."[43] And many urban environmental issues we will explore in Chapter 4 were worsened: Since a country's internal market was concentrated in the capital city, most compa-nies located in or around an already huge "primate" city, which quickly spi-raled out of control.

Back to the Future? Debt, Crisis, and the Reglobalization of Latin America

Much of the import substituting development that reshaped Latin America's landscape and economy was built on money borrowed from overseas. Mexico led the way, optimistically projecting its tremendous oil income surge in the 1970s into the future. But when the price of oil collapsed in the early 1980s, Mexico was forced to default on its loans. Brazil was close behind, defaulting on its loans in 1983. Although the process has been slow, the spreading "debt crisis" sent most Latin American nations into economic recessions that lasted for years. Inflation was one core problem, worsened because countries often spent more than they took in in taxes. Banks that stepped in to bail out these unbalanced economies demanded that nations drastically cut government spending. Basic social services like health, trans-portation, and food price subsidies were cut back, and the big industries run by governments were left to rust for lack of new investments. Import substitution policies were largely abandoned in the 1980s and 1990s as countries scrambled to increase exports to pay back skyrocketing loans or at least make payments on the interest.

Loans and debt impacted the environment in Latin America both directly and indirectly, in small and large ways. Large loans from foreign banks and multilateral agencies, such as the International Monetary Fund (IMF) and the World Bank, often went to fund development megaprojects. One dramatic example of the relation between megaprojects and debt was the massive Itaipú dam in Brazil, which cost Brazil U.S.$20 billion, or one-fifth of its foreign debt at the time.[44] Megaprojects have also included airports, highways, industries, and mining, colonization, agribusiness, lumbering and ranching projects. Many of these projects combined an export orientation with essentially ISI objectives such as opening bottlenecks in national infrastructure or heavy industry.

Megaprojects are relatively easy to begin but often spin out of control as weak states struggle to manage the financial, environmental, social, and regulatory challenges of such enormous projects.[45] Many megaprojects have had devastating environmental consequences as nations, such as Brazil in the Itaipú case, took the liberty of exempting themselves from preparing legally mandated environmental impact statements. Corruption as well as class and urban biases have also accompanied many megaprojects and often benefit political elites and well-connected government subcontractors, especially in construction. The environmental and social impacts of these megaprojects will be seen in the chapters throughout this book, especially Chapters 5 and 6 on indigenous lands and the Amazon. When Latin American nations are in the throes of a severe economic crisis, environmental enforcement is often considered a luxury that will have to wait until the day-to-day "firefighting" of dealing with the crisis subsides. In many of these cases, strong political pressure from environmentalists was necessary for any credible impact analyses to be carried out.

So will reglobalization help or hurt the environment in Latin America? Many optimistic observers predict that globalization will lead to increasing efficiency and environmental protection in the region. We will see by looking at specific cases and broadly across this world region that the relationship between globalization and environmental improvement is far from automatic. To minimize their imports (even as they shifted away from ISI) Latin American governments often continued to employ inefficient, domestically produced technologies long after "cleaner tech" versions were available elsewhere. So the hope is that today, some foreign investment is helping to bring new efficiencies to some outdated industries.[46] However, many of the ecological impacts of these projects, including those for internal and export markets, are difficult to measure and are hidden by the kinds of indicators for which we actually have data.[47]

Throughout Latin America, export-oriented plantation agriculture often forced peasants out of fertile lowlands into cities or marginal rural soils. The region became attractive as a site for U.S., European, and Japanese firms to avoid labor and environmental regulations and to penetrate new markets. Environmentalists have increasingly tied foreign direct investment (FDI) to air pollution, toxic contamination, and worker exposure throughout the region (Chapter 4). They have also criticized chemically intense agriculture, sloppy oil extraction, mining, lumbering and ranching projects, and highly polluting factories in the region's cities and across the maquiladora belt along the United States–Mexico border (see Chapters 2 and 3).

With this in mind, it can be said that in the post–ISI era, Latin America's relationship with the world economy is becoming both more intense and more complex. Some countries have diversified their export profiles to include "nontraditional" products such as grapes and cut flowers, but small nations have been far less able to substitute manufactured imports and most continue to be dependent on a fairly narrow range of "traditional" exports such as coffee, bananas, cacao, oil, and minerals. By 1990, two-thirds of Latin America's exports were still fuels, minerals, metals, and other primary commodities; only 30 percent of East and South Asian countries' were.[48] More than their Asian counterparts, then, Latin American nations have struggled to ascend in the global system of stratification of wealth because of a continuing reliance on export commodities. This emphasis on primary commodities and raw-material exports raises important long-term sustainability questions.[49]

The question of why some countries stay poor while others rise brings us to a long-running debate in the field of development. For decades the most common belief propagated around the world by U.S. foreign service experts and many university professors was that all countries, if they followed the steps and stages taken by Europe and the United States, would one day reach a similar level of development.[50] These were called the "modernizationists" because they believed that cultures and economies changed from traditional, backward, and primitive to more modern, industrial, urban, and dynamic.[51] Since the changes were being seen in people in nations under Soviet control, they believed it was not merely Americanization they were observing, but something universal, inevitable.

The U.S. government's Cold War era (1950–1989) foreign policy in the Third World was to fight Soviet communism directly with soldiers, and indirectly through exports of U.S. culture and products. The goal was to convince nations that they would reach the U.S. standard of living (in material terms at least) if they would just follow the U.S. lead and suggestions on how to run their countries. Poorer nations were told to utilize their "comparative advantages," that is, to specialize in only what they did best. Specifically, they were told to produce and sell only what they could sell competitively on the world market, such as cheap raw materials, tropical agricultural commodities, and cheap manufactured goods assembled with cheap labor. The United States sent billions of dollars in aid and loans around the world, but much of it was explicitly designed to create markets for U.S. products like wheat, rice, and machines.[52] Just after World War II, the World Bank for Reconstruction and Development (now called simply the World Bank) was set up to help Europe recover from the war. When Europe had been rebuilt, its focus shifted to the poor nations of Africa, Asia, and Latin America.

ECLA, mentioned in the previous section, adopted an opposite approach to the modernizationists. They argued that poor countries were poor not because of internal problems but because they were kept dependent on the expensive imports from the rich countries and were getting very little value for all the commodities they were exporting. These ideas caught hold in Latin America and Africa, and eventually in some circles in the rich countries, to a variety of degrees. But two camps developed. The more radical "dependency" group held that poorer nations like those in Latin America needed to cut themselves off as much as possible from the wealthy countries, since they would always be in disadvantageous trading relationships as long as they stayed connected.[53] The more moderate "structuralists" agreed that poor countries were caught in a larger cage of a world economy, but that with some strategic actions nations were able to move up in the global class hierarchy.[54] Still there was substantial agreement: Authors such as Andre Gunder Frank (a more radical dependency author) and Fernando Henrique Cardoso (a more moderate structuralist) wrote how the wealthy nations developed precisely because they "underdeveloped" the poorer nations. Both groups agreed that Latin American nations had been "globalized" from the beginning and that the only way to truly improve was to cut themselves off somewhat from the unfair external influences, in effect, to deglobalize. The debate was about how much.

American historical sociologist Immanuel Wallerstein took the main ideas of the structuralists/dependency group, combined them with the insights of Italian historian Ferdinand Braudel, and developed a global theory called World System Theory.[55] He argued that there were not individual nations developing, but one global economy that created wealth and poverty in different places as it changed. He saw the world as divided into a hierarchy with three main groups: the wealthy "core" nations, the poor "periphery" nations, and the in-between, the "semi-periphery." While a few countries can move up or down in the world stratification system, he argued, the structure itself remains largely unchanged. The core nations use modern technology and political power to control and reap profits from the poor periphery nations. Based on the hundreds of countries and hundreds of years of history, Wallerstein's theory was far more pessimistic than that of the modernizationists and Washington-led development experts about the chances for major improvement in the lives of the billions of people who live in poor countries, at least under the current dominant economic system.

However, Wallerstein described an important group of countries, the semi-periphery, who benefited from exploiting the poorer nations around them and yet had some of their features. There is some disagreement on where nations in Latin America fall, but most writers place Argentina, Chile, Venezuela, Brazil, Mexico, and Columbia into the semi-periphery.[56] Nations at the bottom of the pile would be called "peripheral" and seem to be Bolivia, Nicaragua, Guatemala, Honduras, and the poorest Caribbean island nations. The semi-peripheral countries had some hopes of "dependent development," but it was seen as limited and probably would only be possible with the intervention of the state in the economy and some serious protectionism from imports from the rich nations.[57]

This kind of protectionism ran directly counter to the "free trade" ideologies being promoted by Washington D.C. and Wall Street. As mentioned earlier, when Latin America's big nations imposed high import tariff tax walls within which they hoped to build industries, large foreign corporations adopted an important strategy: They bought up local firms or built "turn-key" factories to do the final assembly of products in high-tariff nations. Now when you buy a GM, Ford, Volkswagen, or Nissan car in Brazil or Mexico, it probably was assembled in São Paulo or Monterrey. Colgate Toothpaste is U.S.-owned, but it is produced in a dozen capitals around the region. Most VCRs sold in Latin America are Japanese Sonys or the Dutch brand Philips, but they are assembled in Manaus, Brazil, or Tijuana, Mexico.

Both the U.S. and Russian "models" for how to become "developed" were based on one core belief: that *industrialization* would create jobs, income, international power, and a high quality of life. Those countries in Latin America who were big enough to do so tried to go industrial: Mexico, Brazil, and Venezuela focused on areas that promised to create spin-off industries that would modernize the nation, such as forging steel and auto industries. Brazil and Mexico developed electronics production centers, assembling TVs, VCRs, and computers. Brazil carefully fostered an industry of arms and other military equipment, focusing on aircraft. Chemical industries grew in Brazil, Mexico, Venezula, and Argentina. As these national economies shifted in new directions, the countries themselves teetered on economic disaster. Today Latin American and many peripheral states are exporting more high-end transportation and electronics products, but the relative value of their exports remains low because they continue to be largely excluded from the more profitable research, innovation, and marketing stages of global commodity chains.[58]

Another response by Latin American countries to U.S. and European economic domination has been to create regional trading blocks. These blocks, such as Caricom (in the Caribbean island states), the Central American Common Market, the Andean Pact, and Mercosur, give preferential treatment to member nations by eliminating import taxes on products from other block nations. These pacts have often had slow start-ups and mixed success. The problem is that the less industrial nations are experiencing the same problems they did before regarding their local products competing with imports. Local industries often suffer, and unemployment can rise, at least until people shift to other industries producing goods for export. Another limiting factor has been the attempts to develop a hemispheric trade block, called the Free Trade Area of the Americas (FTAA), which the United States is pushing despite resistance from Brazil and a few other nations.

Debt remains an ominous threat to Latin America's economic and social progress, and indirectly to the state of its environment. Latin America's collective debt now exceeds $800 billion, or roughly 40 percent of its total gross domestic product (GDP).[59] Mexico's $160 billion debt and a bailout in 1995 by the World Bank/International Monetary Fund provoked a "Tequila Effect" of fiscal shock across the entire region. When Brazil's $232 billion debt sent it into crisis in 1998, the IMF responded with a "rescue" package including $2 billion in loans. To tame inflation, Argentina in 1991 tied its currency to the dollar, making it more difficult for the country to stimulate the economy or to increase exports through price deflations.[60] Argentina had a debt upward of U.S.$130 billion in late 2001, over half of its GDP. The IMF demanded cuts in state spending to pay the interest on the debt, and huge protests broke out, leading to a series of presidents resigning under pressure in December and January 2002. Even the threat that Argentina might default on its debt raised interest rates in Brazil, Mexico, and South Africa, sending their economies down as well.[61]

These instabilities indicate that Latin America's link with the global economy has gone beyond the old days of dependency when the prices of the region's important commodities were set at the exchange in downtown Chicago. Today, we can also see dependencies on the politics and cultures of the wealthy nations. Aid packages from the IMF, often in the tens of billions of dollars, usually come in the form of loans. These loans are supposed to help nations protect the value of their currencies, but they often serve more to the benefit of the international investors withdrawing from the country.[62] Aid packages come with "strings"—an almost universal condition is that governments cut state spending to pay back their debts. Just paying the interest on these loans forces many countries to focus on products that will provide quick returns, and natural resource exploitation is an obvious choice for governments in tough spots. The role of debt in driving environmental problems in the region will be discussed again in Chapters 3 and 4, and efforts to push for debt relief for the poor countries will come up again in the book's concluding chapter. Efforts to trade debt-for-nature preservation, once a popular idea for addressing deforestation, will be addressed in Chapters 3 and 5.

Beyond debt, economic globalization itself is causing a series of new risks and pressures for Latin American countries that may affect their ability to protect the environment. The same investors are now sending their money into all the major stock and bond markets in the world, and "the same global banking firms make loans in all the major economies. And what happens in one place affects the way investors and lenders behave everywhere else."[63] The rise of multinational firms who produce products with parts around the globe makes nations very vulnerable to economic problems a half a world away. "When a multinational firm begins to feel beleaguered because several divisions are in trouble, there is a tendency to pull back across the board."[64] This makes it more difficult for nations to do long-range planning, again favoring policies that provide quick returns, such as some types of natural resource exploitation. Some "cleaner technology" solutions that require greater start-up cash would likely be passed over during these times.

After the "lost decade" of debt crisis and recession in the 1980s, the region's economies (with a few exceptions) have grown in absolute terms over the last fifteen years, albeit sporadically. In the final chapter we return to the current economic picture and some surprising twists, but this growth

raises a question we take up in Chapter 4: Will growth allow the region to
attend to cleaning up the environment? To anticipate, we will argue that
while a point may be reached at which Latin American countries can afford
greater pollution controls, it appears that for most nations economic growth
will pose a multitude of urgent environmental problems with little evidence
that substantial improvements will be forthcoming. Several authors also
argue that increasing openness to trade is likely to intensify precisely the *type*
of growth that is driven by foreign productive technologies and brings with
it unsustainable imported consumption values.[65]

The Remains of Globalization

The term "globalization" is getting thrown around a lot these days, often
without clear definition. When we talk about globalization in this book, we
are referring to the ever-increasing economic and political connections
between nations and global forms of government, the space and time altering advancements made possible by new technologies and global communications networks, and the spread of global cultural interchanges. So globalization is a multifaceted phenomenon: We can speak of economic
globalization, political globalization, and cultural globalization. So far in this
chapter we have emphasized the economic dimensions of globalization
because we believe they have the most direct environmental impact.
However, to fully understand economic globalization, we must understand
the globalization of cultures and values that provide the base of support for
state and corporate economic policies. These environmental implications are
less discussed, but they are serious.

For many people, globalization implies the homogenization of world
culture and the spread of big corporations around the world. Coke,
Baywatch, Britney Spears, and CNN are today available across the hemisphere. News media and entertainment networks travel to places like Latin
America along with pitches for consumer products: Hollywood and the rest
of the American media industry have been extremely effective in selling the
U.S. model of consumerism, and advertisers support the industry's shows
and movies. Around the world, evidence of cultural homogenization extends
into the domain of food preferences, fashion styles, music, and architecture.
Even leisure activities, language, and humor have been globalized in many
ways. Many Latin American experts lament this kind of cooptive cultural
globalization—it is seen as an attempt to substitute local diversity for one
plastic world culture.

But any discussion of cultural globalization must recognize that there are still enormous gaps in the global distribution of communication, technology, and ideas. There are still significant, although shrinking, portions of the world untouched by global technology. Internet access in 2001 was limited to fewer than 5 percent of Latin Americans, and these are mostly upper- and middle-class urbanites.[66] In late 2001 a U.S. Christian group sponsored airdrops of transistor radios into isolated Mexican indigenous communities.[67] For decades Wycliff Bible Translators (among others) has sought to contact every human group on the planet, providing them the written Word in their own language. And at the other end of the scale, much of the "proof" of an emerging global culture that is widely cited is evident mostly within a relative elite of wealthier, socially dominant population groups: corporate and political leaders, cultural icons such as TV, movie, and rock stars who travel the world. So while there are increasing numbers of "global (non)places" such as airports, office buildings, international fast food chains, and hotels that are homogenous around the world, large numbers of Latin Americans have never been to them.

But chances are that they have "been there" through TV. Today, U.S.-led mass culture is directly influencing consumption patterns and demands throughout Latin America. Most of the new products being marketed on TVs across the continent are nonlocal, which reduces opportunities for national and local self-sufficiency. This in turn creates a need for countries to acquire quick cash to balance their trade with the world. Because often more imports are brought in than can be balanced with export sales, many Latin American nations are in a sticky foreign exchange situation. As is the case with international debt, this can cause nations to turn to their natural resources to generate quick money to balance import demands.

Cultural globalization has not occurred only because of the "natural" appeal of U.S. popular culture abroad, which "diffuses" across borders as inevitably as water during osmosis. During the 1930s and the Cold War, the U.S. government provided subsidies to U.S. firms for the exportation of advertisements, shows, and movies and for the purchasing of newspapers and TV stations covertly and overtly across the region.[68] Herbert Hoover made a direct plea to Hollywood movie directors in 1927, asking them to use their medium to aid in the "penetration of intellectual ideas and social ideals" to Latin America, and by the mid-1930s the U.S. government was working with the major U.S. radio networks in an escalating propaganda war against the Germans.[69]

Historian James Schwoch reports that the transition to television in the region was dominated by U.S. corporations, whose activities included "direct ownership of stations, investment in production companies, assistance in drafting legislation, massive exports of television programming, and extensive consulting." They worked with and were favored by the totalitarian right-wing regimes of the region: In Brazil, Time/Life secretly and illegally bought a stake in the massive Globo TV network, which rose to dominance in the 1970s with the help of the military regime.[70] And in times of "special insecurities," the CIA has covertly bought up newspapers and TV stations, such as in Costa Rica during the Contra war in neighboring Nicaragua.

Our point here is to deny that cultural globalization is entirely natural and inevitable; rather, it has been used historically as an important part of the U.S. wars on Nazism and communism. Before and now it has been a way to expand markets for U.S. products. It is not inevitable since it does not compete fairly, but seeks the aid of overt and covert intervention by the U.S. Department of State.[71]

Thirty years ago critics in Latin America dubbed this effort "cultural imperialism," the intentional control of another society's culture, which seems to be what many people mean today when they say "globalization." Most of those critics included commercial culture that came without government backing as well, as seen in the critique *How to Read Donald Duck*, penned by Ariel Dorfman and Armand Mattelart in 1975.[72] Today we can see that less extreme but certainly more prevalent and perhaps more devastating to local culture has been the virtual "carpet bombing" of Latin Americans by advertising, much of it by foreign firms.

But the pattern is more complex. The pattern that World System Theory described for the economic domination of large rich nations over smaller and poorer ones, and the exploitation of the hinterlands in each nation by the cities, is repeated throughout Latin America on a smaller scale, and on the small screen. The cultural industries of Mexico City and Rio/São Paulo are now responsible for the vast majority of the content on television screens across Mexico and Brazil. And in the smaller Latin American nations, much of what is not imported from the United States is imported from these three megacities. *Telenovelas*, or soap opera series that run an hour a night six nights a week for months on end, are produced in each nation and are especially popular cultural exports from Brazil and Mexico. These have been critiqued widely as reflecting an extremely urban and wealthy picture of life and as encouraging lifestyle choices outside the reach of the vast majority of Latin Americans. We documented this process in the Amazon of Brazil, where for years in the remotest towns of the Pará state one could get national and international TV by satellite but could not get news of one's neighbors just down river.[73] As Edna Castro and Rosa Acevedo have pointed out, products produced locally in the Amazon thrived only while the Amazon region was cut off from national products, and this provided the basis for a more integrated local economy.[74]

At the same time, some cultural imports certainly have positive environmental impacts. For example, it is commonly noted that with televisionization of remote villages birth rates tend to drop quickly. This is usually explained by the too simple observation that "now they have something else to do on those long evenings," and there is probably some truth in this. But rising education and the improvement of women's work opportunities often accompany televisionization, so it is difficult to say what is causing what. Women are more likely to migrate to cities, and in many places actually have a greater educational attainment than men.[75] Although we have never seen it documented, favoring imposed cosmopolitan products may decrease pressure on local resources, especially game species whose meat might be replaced by beef or chicken from elsewhere. However, the beef is likely produced by cutting down the whole local forests, a far worse prospect. In the eastern Amazon we found that preferences for higher quality rice than could be produced locally decreased the need to produce locally, and therefore conceivably might have lessened the reasons to cut the rainforest. But this positive potential is outweighed by the demand for beef and milk, which are produced locally. As we will be examining in Chapter 5, this is causing widespread clearing and prevention of forest recovery.[76] It is also causing profound inequalities of landholding and violence, unsustainable land use at both ends of the inequality scale.

As we have mentioned, cultural globalization does not always homogenize; sometimes it does the opposite. It can simultaneously polarize the world's wealthy and poor, as some places gain its benefits and others pay its costs.[77] It also sometimes creates backlashes: It is said that commercial modernization breeds fundamentalism, a point brought home by the September 11, 2001 terrorist attacks.[78] Some individuals and groups specifically fight globalization by reinforcing their own local cultures in more subtle and less violent ways. We need to remember that globalization does not homogenize as much as many people initially assume because different elements of global culture are adopted differently in different places. People may be wearing the same Nike clothes and even singing the same U2 song, but they often mean quite different things in doing so.

Looking over the broad sweep of things, the world is globalizing more quickly in some ways than it is in others. We have discussed how trade is opening up rapidly and how countries that for a time were producing for local markets are trying to shift to exporting abroad. The shoes and cars and computers we use are increasingly produced on a "global assembly line," utilizing cheap resources and parts from around the world, assembled where labor is cheapest.[79] Investors in stock markets and currencies can put their money into nations around the world at the click of a mouse, and corporations can move in with a new factory or, even more easily, buy out and take over a local firm. There is a lot for sale since debt and poor revenue have forced many Latin governments to sell off huge state-run monopolies, such as telephone and utility companies, mining firms, steel mills, and chemical plants.

On the other hand, labor moves far more slowly, with national boundaries and poverty impeding the flow of migrants. Some "sending" nations wish to slow the outflow of migrants; but virtually all "destination" countries limit the inflow. Laws and the extent to which they are enforced vary tremendously across the political boundary lines arbitrarily on the globe: They are simply not yet globalized. These make conditions very different for workers, employers, and the environment in different places. Third, unlike assembly factories, natural resources such as minerals, climate, and tropical soils cannot be relocated from one location to another, making the conditions of their extraction apparently nonglobalizable. And finally, communities are built on a sense of place and a sense of connection to others, something that cannot be (at least immediately) reconstructed in a new place.

So to sum up here, we believe that globalization has some positive as well as negative prospects for the environment in Latin America. Both are usually the case. All the issues we examine in the chapters of this book are laced with contradictions. For example, Costa Rica is held up as a positive case of globalization in that the conservation of its extraordinary park system and creation of its robust ecotourism industry. However, between those parks and destinations the land is being pressured by large- and small-scale agriculture. Costa Rica has one of the highest deforestation rates in the world, and as we perceived long ago, the parks are becoming islands. The bad is coming with the good, and vice versa.

Wrapping Up, Looking Ahead

Among the ads from military contractors and other lobbyists trying to grab the attention of the *Washington Post*'s influential readers as they drank their Monday coffee on July 9, 2001, was one ad that played on its own quirkiness. Over a photograph of a statue of Latin America's liberator Simon Bolivar ran the headline, "Welcome Back from the July 5th Recess!" The subtitle reflected the ad's savvy: "That's not a typo. In Venezuela, we celebrate our Independence Day on July 5th." The ad went on to describe how the two nations' destinies were inextricably linked in the past, present, and future, thus reflecting the reglobalization of Latin America today:

> Simon Bolivar and the first Venezuelan patriots were deeply influenced by the United States' crusade for national independence and development of a free and democratic society in the New World. Just after the United States won her independence, Venezuela's Francisco de Miranda took an extended tour of the new republic. His widely read travel journal was full of praise for the United States' free government and civic virtues. So in 1811, Venezuela's first Congress originally planned to declare our independence on the 35th anniversary of the United States' move for freedom. But the official declaration didn't actually occur until July 5th.
>
> Now, after nearly two centuries of friendship, shared democratic values, investment and trade, Venezuela is the United States' most reliable energy partner. Venezuelan oil, gas and refined products are a mainstay of the U.S. economy, and our energy reserves will be available for centuries to come. . . . Venezuela: Energizing the American Dream.[80]

The ad suggests the strong but starkly different influence of the United States over the region today from that of the national period of the 1800s, quietly skipping over tensions and interventionist years between. An expensive public relations firm and a carefully placed ad were purchased also to calm U.S. fears as populist president Hugo Chavez moved in late 2001 to renationalize much of the oil industry. But the ad also suggests how much, even in doing so, Latin America has shifted back to exporting. Venezuela, for example, has always exported raw materials: Today, four-fifths of its imports are manufactured goods, but only one-fifth of its exports are.[81] By contrast, in high-income countries around the world, four-fifths of all merchandise exports tend to be manufactured goods. Venezuela is in a risky position familiar to Latin America through its history: The price of manufactured goods tend to be stable or rise over time, while prices of raw materials like oil tend to fluctuate wildly and drop over time.

Of the two countries (Brazil and Mexico) that most actively adopted ISI, Mexico managed the largest shift toward manufacturing, which now accounts for nearly 90 percent of its exports, far more than the United States and the wealthy countries as a whole.[82] Brazil, by contrast, has a split economy, with 43.7 percent of its exports coming from primary and natural resource–intensive goods and 55.1 percent in manufactures. Looking more broadly across South America but excluding Brazil, two-thirds (68 percent) of exports are primary goods or natural resource–intensive goods such as petrochemicals, paper, cement and base metals.[83] For the Central American nations south of Mexico, over half (50.6 percent) of exports fall in these risky, low-benefit categories.

The riskiness of building a nation around heavy dependence on revenues from exporting, especially from exporting raw materials and agricultural commodities, was brought home after the 2001 terrorist attacks on the United States, which has long been the largest market for products from the region. It used to be that when the U.S. [economy] sneezed, Mexico got the flu. Now much of the world gets the flu.[84] For Latin America, globalization is back to the future.

Wrapping up the key elements of an environmental history of Latin America, historian Guillermo Herrera describes six features that distinguish the region's past.[85] First, the economy was based on plundering or, as we have said, on extraction of natural and human resources. Second, the region's development has been dominated by foreign firms; after liberation from the Spanish it was the British and then, from around 1920, firms from the United States. More recently, it has included the United States, Japan, Germany, Korea, and others. Third, local people who were wealthy and powerful, especially landowners and government officials, used their power over those resources as a "commodity and a guarantee" to keep themselves wealthy and in power, and this was usually at the expense of local people and lands. Fourth, because of the history of large land grants to a few rich individuals, and because peasants were expropriated in the mid-1800s, there was never any small and medium class of rural capitalist producers. Furthermore, there was never a middle class of urban intellectuals, who have made up the bulk of (at least early) environmental activists in the wealthier countries.

Fifth, while there were internal battles for control of these nations, both the political left and right accepted a vision of development as the taming of the "savage" natural world. As Herrera points out, to mobilize all the natural resources that have been exploited from Latin America over these five hundred years has taken authoritarianism and violent oppression of groups with alternative relationships with nature. Only recently, just a decade or two ago, has mainstream society in Latin America expressed the possibility that the example by which they were guiding their national planning and individual lives might be unsustainable.

The very real crises that are the subject of the following five chapters in this book are among those that have driven the beginning of a shift in people's attitudes and behaviors. Being able to express themselves politically without fearing imprisonment or worse has been critical in allowing Latin Americans to participate in what we recognize as "environmentalism."

The roadmap begins at the border between one world and another, between the United States and Mexico, and the environmental crises of industrial pollution and shantytown housing in a belt of maquiladoras, or factories. Examining the problems of the border allows us to enter an area of great debate and discuss whether companies are heading to poor countries to take advantage of loose environmental enforcement and regulations. In Chapter 3, we look at the problems of pesticide poisoning and deforestation on plantations and peasant farms in Central America's rainforests.

We shift gears in Chapter 4 with a look at some of the least studied of the region's environmental problems: the urban issues of air pollution, sewage, population growth, and trash. Chapter 5 brings us to the Amazon rainforest, as we discuss its amazing ecological and social diversity and highlight the different groups struggling to control its future. Indigenous peoples have most directly experienced the devastating effects of huge "megaprojects" like powerlines and oil drilling, and Chapter 6 ties their plight and recent political mobilizations to the fate of the ecosystems in which they live.

The book wraps up with a look at the prospects for the future of the environment in Latin America. To that end, Chapter 7 reviews the common threads that seem to run through these five cases, considers our own responsibilities as Northen consumers, and assesses whether the new international networks of environmentalists and social justice activists have the potential to dramatically shift the "corporate-led globalization" in a direction that will more directly concern the needs of people and the land of Latin America. We begin by very briefly looking across the landscape, at current issues and indicators, to gain a broad picture of where Latin America is today. But we begin at the edge.

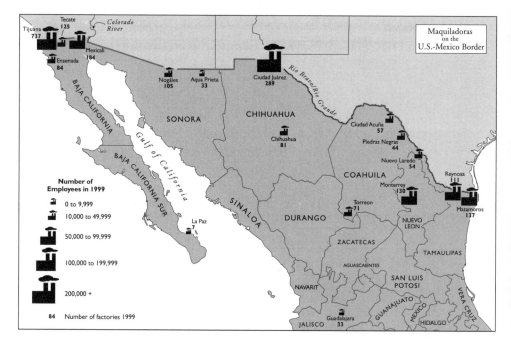

Maquiladoras (export processing zone factories) on the U.S.–Mexico border. Numbers below symbols are the number of factories; size of symbols represents the total number of employees working in maquiladoras in 1999.

CHAPTER 2

Pollution Havens on the United States–Mexico Border? NAFTA, Free Trade, and the Environment

A border patrol of five brown pelicans cast prehistoric shadows as they scan the confusing landscape of the lower Rio Grande Valley of Texas. A quick survey of the sprawling suburban developments—"Luxury from the $70,000s!", tire stores, U-store-its, taco and burger drive-thrus, free-trade warehouses, dollar-a-gallon drinking water windmills, and Home Depots—reveals how much has changed in just the past twenty years. Brownsville, Texas is the tenth fastest growing city in the United States; just upriver, McAllen is the third.

The troop wings over neighborhoods better hidden from those on the ground: Mexican migrants in shacks and mobile homes, with dozens of dogs and cats roaming the streets, cars in front yards, Virgin Mary icons, and homes with signs for their services: "Tamales: Call an Hour in Advance."

Heading toward the center of Brownsville just blocks from the border, the pelicans cock their heads over mission-style general stores from the Wild West era. Today, these historic buildings have been replaced in function by "casas de cambio" moneychangers, clothing and sporting goods stores, *taquerias,* and immigration lawyer shops. *"Se habla español"* say the signs in all the windows.

The pelicans search for natural habitat and open water to hunt for fish, but over 90 percent of the river valley's ecosystem has been destroyed by agriculture, urbanization, and suburban sprawl.[1] The U.S. and Mexican governments are working on an "Emerald Necklace" of parks along the river, but many wildlife species' populations are dipping dangerously low, losing habitat and confused by roads, noise from the "NAFTA trucks," and the blazing lights and tracking dogs of the U.S. Border Patrol.

The river—ironically named the "Wild River," or *Rio Bravo,* in Spanish—is itself now a sad joke. Having traveled hundreds of miles from the canyons of the deserts, by the time it arrives at these lower reaches it is hopelessly polluted with pesticides, fertilizers, sewage, heavy metals, and silt. Its flow is diverted to so many places along its voyage for agricultural, municipal, and industrial water supplies that sometimes the river runs dry. So weak is the Rio Bravo that recently its mouth was sealed off from the Gulf of Mexico by a sand bar.[2]

Sailing across the border without even the cursory check Mexican officials conduct on those with the magic blue and gold American passports, the pelicans catch a dusty inland wind and an updraft over Matamoros, Brownsville's Mexican "sister city." If these are sister cities, they were raised by vastly different parents. Today the two cities provide different functions: One is cheap and poor, the other cleaner and better developed.

Matamoros is a flurry of anarchic traffic, street vendors selling fruit and newspapers, blowing dust, and garbage. There are middle and upper-class neighborhoods to be sure, but a visit to the *colonias* (shantytowns) reveals what happens when too many people come to live in a poor and poorly planned city. Many colonia houses are shacks made of cheap local materials or leftover scraps of lumber. The streets are rutted mud, some with open ditches used as common sewers for human excrement. When the wind is from the wrong direction, and it always is for someone, the stench is beastly. The pelicans veer away.

The colonia streets are plied by "pumper trucks" and horse-drawn wagons collecting garbage for a fee. Pumper trucks suck out septic tanks and dump the sewage into nearby canals, transferring wastes in tanks sometimes used to haul hazardous industrial chemicals.[3] The horse carts haul the trash to a transfer station under an old "martini glass" broken water tower, where winds blow plastic grocery bags across the semidesert urban landscape until they are caught on barbed-wire fences. From the transfer station, trash is hauled by trucks out to the city dumps. One "NAFTA dump," a sanitary landfill built under new guidelines, has been on fire for months, generating wafting clouds of smoke and mobilizing airborne contaminants. At another, older dump, barefoot children play through piles of fetid cattle skulls in open hills of squalid refuse. The year is 2001 and we are less than ten miles from the United States, but the scene is something out of Dante. These scenes are why parts of the border have been characterized as "an American Calcutta."

Finally on their way heading out to the polluted Gulf of Mexico, the pelicans veer over "Chemical Row," a strip of foreign, U.S., and Mexican factories. These plants have been linked to devastating illnesses of workers and residents on both sides of the border. The most dangerous plant is probably Quimica Fluor, which makes HF—anhydrous fluoride for high-octane gasolines and etching metals. One accident at the plant could kill thousands of people if the wind was just wrong; nine people have already died from an accident at the plant in the 1980s. In the early 1990s, twenty-eight families filed suit against Quimica Fluor and some forty other Brownsville maquiladoras (factories), including General Motors, Magnatek, and Kemet Electronics. Residents alleged that these corporations were responsible for the anencephalic deaths of their children. Children born with anencephaly "look like frogs" with concave skulls and die within several hours of delivery. From 1990 to 1991 there were between thirty-one and thirty-three anencephaly cases in Texas's Cameron County—rates three times the national average.[4]

The North American Free Trade Agreement (NAFTA) went into effect on New Year's Day 1994, integrating Canada, the United States, and Mexico into a huge area without tariffs. NAFTA was promoted in Mexico as a way to create thousands of jobs exporting to its northern neighbors; for the U.S. and Canadian firms the treaty represented new markets to develop for sales and cheaper production. U.S.- and Canadian-based environmental groups and labor unions were alarmed at the possibilities that firms could flee the hard-earned regulations in wages and pollution control that they had fought for for decades. Critics predicted a "race to the bottom" in wages and worker and environmental protections, as nations and states had to reduce those protections to keep jobs. And so amended to the NAFTA treaty was language in its preamble about attention to sustainability of development, and two "NAFTA Supplemental Agreements" between the three governments, on environment and trade.

The "Environmental Side Agreement," as it came to be called, was the world's first such formal agreement linked to a trade treaty. It affirmed the interrelationship of the three nations' environments, but also the "sovereign right of States to exploit their own resources pursuant to their own environmental and development policies."[5] The question was whether protections would "harmonize upward," as proponents claimed, or downward, as opponents feared. The side agreement created three important institutions to deal with the environmental issues of the trade integration, which we will be returning to at the end of the chapter. One of the central and recurring arguments for NAFTA was that it would provide Mexico with the ability to bring its laws and enforcement up to the levels of the United States and Canada. The U.S. Council of the Mexico–U.S. Entreprenurship Committee of the Council of the Americas wrote in a 1994 *Business Mexico* editorial that "NAFTA makes the legal commitment and economic growth needed for environmental progress feasible and probable."

In this chapter we first travel from east to west following the paths of rivers that mark most of the United States–Mexico border. We review some of the history of earlier plans to spur growth along the border and how they evolved into the NAFTA initiative. The border region has become in many ways the test site for claims on both sides about the effects of globalization and free trade on the environment. We consider why borders remain important and how biological and geological systems of watersheds and airsheds have very different boundaries. We review claims about links between border pollution and illness and claims about the production of hazardous wastes and its transport across the line. We spend a moment reviewing how environmental groups in the early 1990s split on whether to support NAFTA or oppose it and how cross-national coalitions have formed among national and local groups. Finally we review how cooperative, binational, and trinational initiatives are beginning to address border environmental and health issues and what might be done to improve their impacts. Running through all these issues is one question: Is Mexico becoming a "pollution haven" for dirty Northern industries?

The debate about free trade and the environment on the border is extremely polarized, to the point that it is difficult to be sure what is true and what is exaggeration. As border journalist Ron Mader wrote in 1997, reporting on the border

> gets pigeon-holed . . . in one of two fashions—1) Great strides are being made or 2) All hell is breaking loose. The "progressive" magazines run toxic ravine and health risk stories, but rarely any positive stories. On the other hand, business magazines love Happy Maquiladora stories. Mainstream reporting fares no better.[6]

So completing their morning flight over the confusing border landscape, the pelicans reach the ocean, swoop low over the cresting waves of South Padre Island National Park, and settle in the waves, scarcely noticing the oil platforms behind them. Many species that cross these borders are losing habitat and numbers rapidly, but with the banning of DDT and the protection of nesting sites, the pelicans are mounting a comeback.

Borders versus Watersheds: A Journey from East to West

We are daily bombarded with news that we now live in "a world without borders." The United States–Mexico border seems a case at least where the border has been blurred: For years authors and local boosters have been proclaiming that a new hybrid Tex/Mex culture was emerging along the border that was unlike the mainstream culture of either nation. With unique food, music, and a huge number of bilingual residents who commute across the line each day, there seems to be a new and dynamic world unlike anywhere else. "You can almost say [the border] is a different country—different than the U.S. and different than Mexico," said Carlos Vasquez, president of the San Ysidro Business Association.[7] A 1996 article argued that beyond a common history, kinship ties across the border, common language, and integrated economies have created a new culture there:

> Border culture provides a further unifying influence. The U.S.–Mexico border
> region combines the characteristics of Anglo, indigenous, and Latin cultures in a
> mix that is dissimilar to and richer than that of either country alone. The special
> character of the border is recognized by others in both nations. El Norte is
> believed to be practically a different nation by many Mexicans, and U.S. citizens
> visiting border towns [on the U.S. side] often describe them as more Mexican
> than American. Bolstering and transmitting this separate culture are a number of
> border institutions, including cultural centers, historical societies, research organi-
> zations, newspapers and electronic media, and social organizations. An optimism,
> flexibility, and creativity often found on frontiers characterizes the border and
> leads to accommodation of interests.[8]

Twelve million souls now live in the counties and *municipios* (municipalities) along the two-thousand-mile (3,140-km) border separating the United States and Mexico, with close to 6 million on each side.[9] This number is projected to double by 2020 to some 24 million, if migration rates stay near those of the 1990s. In many senses, however, there still exists a social grand canyon between those who inhabit the two sides of this political line. By any statistical measures, on the Mexican side the residents are on average much poorer, less educated, and most are only Spanish speakers.[10] The average person south of the border earns one-half to one-seventh of the average of those on the U.S. side.[11] They are also much younger, since they came for work, whereas many on the U.S. side came as "snowbirds," to retire in warmth. The result is that the population will grow much faster on the Mexican side.

An innovative 2001 survey conducted on both sides of the border shows that people on the two sides hold vastly different opinions on social issues like immigration and NAFTA. "There is a cultural separateness" across the border, says Irasema Coronado, political scientist at the University of Texas at El Paso, "but also a vast class difference."[12] Many project that the border is creating a new type of polarization, which is starker because of the closeness of the juxtaposition. So two things are true: The binational border region is different culturally but that line still matters profoundly. As we will be seeing throughout this chapter, it may matter more and more in the age of free trade.

Three quarters of a century ago Paul Lapradelle said, "All boundaries are by their nature artificial and can only be viewed as an invention of the human mind. Lines may be a topographical convenience, they are not natural facts. Nature abhors lines."[13]

The border is marked and crossed at each end by important rivers. At its eastern end, the border follows the Rio Grande/Rio Bravo for hundreds of miles, all the way up from the Gulf of Mexico to El Paso. Here the border between Mexico and the Republic of Texas was disputed, and the more southerly river only became the border after the United States provoked its neighbor into the one-sided Mexican-American War (1846–1848). The tide turned quickly for General Zachary Taylor, and finally, with the U.S. Navy blockading its major ports and U.S. troops occupying the capital Mexico City and all significant military installations in the nation's north, Mexico finally negotiated. Mexico gave up 40 percent of its land in exchange for five annual installments of U.S.$3 million, each to be paid in Mexican gold and silver coins.[14]

Article V of the Treaty of Guadalupe Hidalgo that ended the war stipulated, "The boundary line established by this article shall be religiously respected by each of the two republics." Beyond the Rio Grande, the middle section of the border was to be a straight westerly line from El Paso, then north to the first branch of the Gila River, which it followed to the Colorado River. From there the border headed due west again to the Pacific Ocean. The western end of the border was redrawn five years later in the Treaty of Mesillas (The Gadsden Purchase), when the United States needed a level railroad route to the Pacific Ocean and was willing to pay for it. In California the Tijuana River and its dozen tributaries crisscross the border.

These four border rivers reflect how political lines are biologically meaningless. While the trunks of the rivers made convenient lines after the wars and treaties to mark the land of nations, their tributaries reached up into huge areas on both sides of the border. These "watersheds"—the area of land drained by a river and its tributaries—bring together the accumulated results of land and water use in all the areas they drain, regardless of nation. The pesticides applied to crops and the silt from farm runoff north of the border, for example, drain into the same river that is utilized as a drinking water supply by those living south of the border. The lack of sewage treatment for cities on the Mexican side upstream pollutes the irrigation and urban water of everyone downstream.

Beginning six hundred miles north of the border in the San Juan Mountains of Colorado, the Rio Grande/Bravo cuts into a eight-hundred foot deep gorge and then is siphoned off for "irrigating chiles, cotton fields, and pecan groves."[15] In much of the semi-desert that makes up the Grande/Bravo watershed, irrigation water is the only thing separating valuable from commercially worthless land, so getting access to water can make a speculator rich overnight. Meeting the border, the river divides the 1.6 million people in the twin cities of El Paso on the U.S. side and Ciudad Juarez in Mexico. With over a million people, Juarez had never had a public sewage treatment plant, but these are finally under construction within the environmental program of NAFTA, which will be discussed at the chapter's end.[16] In a typical year, following a 1906 compromise between the nations, Mexicans withdraw 14 percent of the water for irrigation; U.S. users get 79 percent.[17] That leaves only 6 percent left to flow downstream, so the "Wild River" occasionally runs dry over the next three-hundred-mile stretch.

The struggles over the river's precious water repeatedly become a source of international tension. Below El Paso/Juarez tributary, the Rio Conchos brings 75 percent of the river's water down from the Sierra Madre mountains in northern Mexico, and the Rio Grande runs through the steep walled canyons and mountains of national parks on both sides of the river: Big Bend in the United States, Boquillas del Carmen in Mexico.[18] This is strikingly beautiful and remote land, with several species found nowhere else on earth. One also hears rumors of drug trafficking and illegal migration through the remote mountains and plains. Roadrunners, kangaroo mice, peccaries, and dozens of species of birds inhabit the chaparrals up higher, with the few bear, javelinas, and ocelots who are left staying closer to the river.[19] Fish such as the phantom shiner and the "Amistad gambusia" are entirely extinct. Droughts and booming human demands from farms, sprawling cities and factories have cut river flows so dramatically that farmers on both sides are shifting away from certain profitable crops, and environmentalists are calling for just 10 percent to be left in the river to maintain habitat for the rare species.[20]

Down river, below the Amistad International Dam, the river cuts through the border transshipment sister cities of Laredo/Nuevo Laredo. There much of the water is pumped out for household, farm, and industrial water use, and water quality worsens again. A thirteen-year-old boy died in 1993 from a fatal inflammation of the brain caused by an amoebic infection called naegleria, contracted while swimming in the river near a water treatment plant.[21] Around and below the Falcon Dam the river flows through the Lower Rio Grande Valley, with 1.5 million people, and irrigates and drains millions of dollars in agricultural products on both sides of the borders.

The troubled river's problems get still more complex the further it goes. The already slightly salty water gets saltier as it evaporates in hot irrigation ditches and fields, and desalination plants are expensive to build and operate. In 1996, seven pesticides were found by Texas health officials to exceed federal health guidelines.[22] Three of them were ones used on lawns and gardens, suggesting that both urban and rural sources have to be addressed to solve the problem. Finally, besides all the toxins, two invading species of plants, the hydrilla and hyacinth, jam up the river, "plugging pumps and clogging irrigation canals."[23] "The ecological health of the Rio Grande/Rio Bravo is critically injured and in imminent danger of collapse," said Karen Chapman, assistant director of a watchdog group the Texas Center for Policy Studies.[24]

Finally, where the river meets the ocean has always been a "diverse estuary for blue crabs, redfish, spotted sea trout, snook and several varieties of shrimp."[25] The river is key to bringing freshwater to create the brackish estuaries for these commercially important species to hatch. One Texas fisher complained, "When they don't release enough water, it messes up the nursery area. We're farmers. We just don't plant the seed."[26] Of course when the river does run well there are other problems that are not well studied: the heavy metals, organic chemicals from pesticides, and siltation.

On the western half of the border, the Gila and Colorado rivers have some of the same problems, but the rivers' watersheds are largely in the United States, and Mexico is left downstream. Millions of "acre feet" of water (the amount of water required to cover an acre of land with a foot of water) are diverted from the Colorado, through pharoic aqueducts to Los Angeles, San Diego, and now to Central Arizona.[27] Where the Colorado River crosses the border, at the Arizona city of San Luis and the Sonoran city of San Luis Rio Colorado, the disparity in water issues is stark. On the U.S.

side, groundwater wells and adequate sewage treatment provide safe drinking water for the eleven thousand residents. On the Mexican side, the sewage collection system was built in 1967 for a population one-seventeenth the current 170,000 people, many of whom work at the thirty-two new maquiladora plants there.[28] This system just *collects* the sewage, to be dumped by gravity, into the Colorado River. The rest of the community's sewage goes into cesspools and septic tanks, some of which leach into ground water. Part of the sewage canal is unlined and leaks, contaminating agricultural groundwater wells.

Helmintiasis, affecting the intestines, is the world's most common disease. Irrigating crops with diluted sewage "increases risk to the public health . . . due to the potential of transmitting parasites and protozoa such as helmint eggs and fecal coliforms to agricultural workers as well as consumers."[29] Another concern expressed by U.S. public health officials is that 2.8 million pedestrians crossed the bridge there in 1999, as did another 2.8 million cars, and human contact can spread these diseases.[30] But the suffering in Mexico is cause enough: Thousands of cases of intestinal infections are diagnosed each year in San Luis Rio Colorado, where residents are three times as likely to die from communicable diseases as residents of Yuma, Arizona, just twenty-six miles away.[31]

Where the Colorado meets the Gulf of California, it spreads across a huge delta of marshes. The problems are remarkably like those in the Rio Grande/Bravo:

> River flows to the delta have been reduced nearly 75 percent during the 20th century. Consequently there is less silt, fewer nutrients, higher salinity, and higher concentrations of pollutants. Today less than five percent of the historic ecosystem remains. Still, the delta is the largest remaining wetland system in the American southwest.[32]

Not far from San Luis, the next set of twin cities on the border were created literally from the minds of U.S. land speculators, who saw that with water millions could be made. In 1900 the California Land Company opened the region north of the border with a canal and water, and the rush was on. In 1901 the company began digging a diversion ditch away from the Colorado River to the named-to-sell "Imperial Valley." In just four years, "100,000 valley acres were irrigated, with 10,000 people settled on the land and harvesting cotton, fruits, and vegetables."[33] In 1905 Harry Chandler, then publisher of the *Los Angeles Times*, and his Colorado River Land

Company dug a ditch on the Mexican side to bring water to 800,000 acres he controlled. After heavy rains the river broke through the barrier and jumped into the ditch and the old river bed, creating a "New River" (called Rio Nuevo on the Mexican side) running back north into the United States, and filling an ancient dry lake bed there some thirty-five miles long and twelve miles wide, now called the Salton Sea. At times the "All-American Canal," located just miles from the border, diverted 90 percent of the river's waters before letting them pass across the border to Mexico.[34]

The speculators used the newly irrigated valley as the site for two towns with opposite names fabricated from the state and nation on whose border they sat: Calexico in California and Mexicali on the Mexican side. In 2000 Mexicali had nearly a million residents working in 184 maquiladora factories. The cities are each bisected by the Rio Nuevo/New River, flowing north into the United States. The story repeats those told earlier, but with a graphic and macabre new twist since it flows straight into the United States, told here by a *Boston Globe* reporter:

> An hour past sunset, the nightly ritual begins. Naked except for their underwear, ten people wade into the river, each one clutching an inflated inner tube in one hand and a black garbage bag of belongings in the other. Hiding behind greasy mounds of foam that collect on the New River's surface, they form a human raft . . . past [the border]. . . . The New River, which carries raw sewage from Mexicali's one million residents, is such a disease-ridden, toxic cesspool that U.S. Border Patrol Agents have been ordered to stay out. Nearly 30 viruses have been documented in the river from hepatitis A to polio, as well as caustic chemicals from the region's maquiladora factories and pesticides from local farms.[35]

The extreme measures these immigrants take result from the crackdown on other border crossings elsewhere. Likewise, the twin cities both named Nogales, in Arizona and Sonora states, have a watershed flowing north into the United States and contaminating water supplies and a huge river system on the U.S. side.[36]

This acute and recurring problem of sewage and contaminants in the border rivers has inspired the United States and the new NAFTA institutions to spend more on sewage treatment plants on both sides of the border, in the realization that unserved migrant shantytowns in Mexico jeopardize the quality of life and even economic growth in the North.

On this point a final tale taking place at the border's western end is instructive, where the Tijuana River waters accumulates waste throughout the Chilpancingo *barrio* and flows directly back into the United States via San Diego and on to the prized beaches of southern California.[37] Almost 30 million gallons of raw and partially treated sewage flowed across the Tijuana–San Diego border every day, and decades of conflicts on both sides led to the expenditure of hundreds of millions of dollars on the construction of a huge International Wastewater Treatment Plant in the mid-1990s.[38] Just before Christmas 2001, the U.S. government lost a lawsuit brought by the twenty-eight-thousand-member Surfrider Foundation, a group "dedicated to enhancing wave-riding opportunities in ways which will not adversely impact nearshore ecosystems."[39] The two years of legal wrangling forced the government to study further the causes of and solutions to the sewage that was apparently escaping the huge treatment plant run by the U.S. Boundary and Water Commission.[40] Piping its partially treated water 3.5 miles offshore didn't stop the contamination of the beaches, which were closed thirty-nine days in 2000. It appears no one along the border is satisfied with solutions that have been developed so far, but the story also highlights an issue we will return to several times through the book: that legal strategies play an important role in strategies of citizens groups. It also raises an often-uncomfortable point: The solutions are often not cheap.

So with the complexity and difficulty seen on our watersheds/sewage tour of the United States–Mexico border, one may be tempted to stop there. However, there are three equally complicated, important, and poorly understood transborder environmental issues: underground waters in aquifers, the flow of airborne pollutants, and the circulation of migrant species. Aquifers and airsheds we will treat a bit later, when we discuss fears of health effects from the boom in maquiladora factories on the border. For now let us note on migratory species with the example of birds: 1,400 species of birds live in North America, 250 of which are migratory.[41] Many of those crossing from critical wintering grounds in Mexico and Central America into the United States also cross into Canada for summer breeding. Overall, seven hundred species of animals are now known to migrate across the border each year.[42] Only in 1975 was it discovered that all 60 million Monarch butterflies in North America migrate across the border to a tiny and threatened patch of mountain oyamel fir forest seventy-five miles west of Mexico City.[43]

Like sewage and pesticides flowing in border rivers, migrant species flow across these artificial lines that "Nature abhors"; it is up to us to develop solutions that are not limited by these artificial lines. As border experts Ingram and Varady aptly noted, borders "separate problems from solutions, create perverse economic opportunities, marginalize the interests of border residents in national policy making, and erect barriers to grassroots problem-solving."[44] We'll get to these issues as we move along, but the message to us from migrants and sewage and pesticides in the cross-border watersheds is clear: We must understand and attend to the needs of environments and living things on both sides of the border. Among those living things needing attention are the basic public health and service needs of the "talking fauna" who have flocked to the promise of jobs in the maquiladoras. But first we need to understand why the border was targeted: first by planners and politicians in Mexico City and Washington, then by global corporations to set up thousands of factories, and finally by the millions of migrant workers from all over Mexico.

Building a Border Boom, Promoting NAFTA

In 1965, facing a stagnant economy, inflation, and high unemployment, Mexican president Gustavo Dìas Ordaz declared the start of a bold new initiative to transform the sleepy, remote northern border of his nation into a massive export-processing zone. "In-bond" factories called maquiladoras, or maquilas for short (from the Spanish word for workshop), were established to assemble products sought after by American consumers. The scheme, expanded from earlier programs limited to the western end of the border, rested upon tax breaks for anyone who was willing to invest in the barren region within 20 kilometers of the border and take advantage of cheap Mexican labor.[45] The U.S. government supported this Border Industrialization Project (BIP) because it believed that the building of a series of factories along the border would stem the tide of poor migrants who were streaming into the country, burdening social services and testing tempers in California, Arizona, New Mexico, and Texas.[46] It was especially concerned with controlling immigration since it was terminating a long-running farm labor program that was about to leave 180,000 Mexicans in the United States jobless. Industrializing the border gave the United States and its companies the best of both worlds: labor that could be paid far less than would be necessary in the United States and none of the responsibility for employees' welfare, which would have to be budgeted if they were brought into the United States.

Since 1965, American and other foreign companies have been able to truck parts across the border, pay Mexican workers U.S.$4–$10 a day to assemble the goods, and then export a finished product back—all without paying any taxes except on the value added to the product (i.e., the value of the Mexican labor). This was a huge savings, and after a slow start in the 1960s, U.S. firms realized they could generate far greater profits and take away an advantage of foreign competitors, using this cheap labor source very close to home. Soon clothing manufacturers, television and stereo companies, car parts makers, and chemical companies were shutting down their factories in New York, Michigan, California, North Carolina, and Pennsylvania to set up plants in Mexico. The rule of thumb was that if "unskilled" or "semi-skilled" labor was a significant part of the costs of your product, you had to move offshore. Many started by keeping plants open on both sides of the border producing the same product, threatening workers at both with closure if they didn't produce as well and cheaply as the other. When the collapse of the Mexican peso caused wages to drop by two-thirds in 1982, the outcome was foregone, and the U.S. plants are still closing today.

Several of these sharp peso devaluations have sparked extraordinary maquila booms—from 1983 to 1988, the maquila sector grew by 19.7 percent annually. This new wave of border growth drew more capital intensive (and pollution intensive) maquilas, including high-tech chemical and electronic facilities. After leveling off from 1990 to 1994, the sector boomed again from 1995 to 2000. During this time the number of plants nearly doubled, from two thousand to thirty-five hundred, with the majority concentrated in the industrialized border cities of Tijuana, Mexicali, Ciudad Juárez, Matamoros, and Reynosa. Employment doubled to around 1.2 million workers.[47] Remarkably, in 2000 Mexico beat Singapore, Taiwan, and Malaysia as the host of among the most assembly plants in the world.

But there is constant pressure to keep Mexican wages low, as firms now leapfrog the border to venture further south and east into Guatemala, Honduras, and El Salvador—not to mention Sri Lanka and China and a dozen other "pajama republics" across the globe. In the late 1990s boom, demand for labor pushed up wages. In late 2001, some calculations put total labor costs when benefits such as transportation and food are included between $2 and $3 an hour. This was a huge savings over the United States, but still about five times higher than in China, where total costs, with benefits, were only 43 cents an hour.[48]

To compete and keep labor cheap, the Mexican state has sometimes resorted to repressive techniques against worker efforts to increase wages.[49] The ability to do so has rested in part on the use of young women laborers, many from rural backgrounds. For decades a typical maquila laborer was young (between the ages of sixteen and twenty-four[50]), female,[51] single, and nonnative to the border. Small, female hands were perceived to have a greater dexterity for the high-speed handiwork necessary to assemble garments, textiles, and electronic accessories.[52] These trends are shifting somewhat, as the industry includes more "heavy industry" plants such as those for chemicals and car parts, not just "light assembly" plants for textiles and electronics.

Women workers facing perilous working conditions for survival pay without the ability to organize are forced to perpetuate two environmental crises. First, they often face immediate environmental dangers to their health on the job and that of their offspring. Second, they are largely unable to address wider issues in their communities to improve air, water, and soil contamination. So the conditions of their work need understanding: Some companies are reported to pack hundreds or even thousands of workers into maquila warehouses with one exit and insufficient ventilation. In some factories without air conditioning or ventilation, the sizzling border climate combines with machine-generated heat to produce indoor temperatures that creep well above 100 degrees Fahrenheit. Forced overtime, sometimes as much as eighty hours a week, is not uncommon. Some workers have been refused bathroom "privileges," ordered to take birth control pills, and forced to endure "panty checks" during their menstrual cycles (to prove that they were not pregnant).

Through periods of rocky diplomatic relations, U.S. economic presence on the Mexican border has remained steady. Today, U.S. companies are reported to control 90 percent of maquila "mother" or "hub" corporations.[53] NAFTA proponents argued that the agreement would draw industries deeper into Mexico, away from the border, and reduce the overall concentration of maquilas so close to the line and its social and environmental ills. NAFTA has actually achieved some of this goal, but the picture is mixed: Only 60 percent of new maquilas are built on the border, down from 90 percent in 1995.[54] However, by helping stabilize the Mexican economy, NAFTA essentially created a climate that made maquila border development more attractive. What remains the billion dollar question is whether the border will remain one of the most efficient locations for American companies that want to assemble abroad. Since there are cheaper places to go for "low-skilled" assembly work, the border seems to be shifting to another niche, higher tech and heavier industry. This suggests new types of environmental and health impacts. With recession in the U.S. economy, and as evidence reported later suggests, there is the potential for severe pulses of unemployment, desperation, and new migrant flows into the United States.

Finally, an enduring and acknowledged problem and "challenge" for the maquiladoras is that so little—only 2 percent—of the $9 billion spent annually on raw materials comes from Mexican sources.[55] Everything else is imported—so everyone seems to agree that great opportunities for local and more integrated development are lost. Instead, the maquilas appear to repeat the history of Latin American development we discussed in the last chapter: modern enclaves surrounded by a sea of backwardness and poverty. This is what Latin American scholars call social exclusion and marginalization. Alejandro Nadal, an economist from the Colégio de Mexico, argues that maquiladoras cannot be "viewed as the villain or the hero of national development" because "the multiplier effects are being generated elsewhere."[56] Marco Antonio Valenzuela, president of the National Maquila Association, argues that the lack of linkages is "a positive challenge that we must all assume."

These are some of the downsides of BIP, NAFTA, and the maquiladora boom. But there are certainly positive sides that make the logic of the project almost unstoppable. The importance of border factories to the Mexican economy cannot be understated: The maquila sector is directly responsible for nearly half of all Mexican exports and is a significant source of employment in a job-hungry nation.[57] The maquila sector has created year-round employment for over one million Mexicans.[58] And maquila wages, although low by Northern standards, are better than in most places in Mexico. Many in the border's growing urban population are, in many ways, simply "very happy to have a job."[59]

Maquilas have been a central part of Mexico's wider policy shift to attempt to control inflation and get itself out from under a huge foreign debt. The country has gone rather quickly from greater state involvement in the economy—including huge government-owned monopolies in sectors such as oil and telephones—to increased private ownership, deregulation, and less public spending.[60] Foreign corporations were sent away after the Revolution years ago, but now they are welcomed: Almost $3 billion in foreign investment go into maquiladoras each year, which is one-sixth of the nation's total.[61] By generating $60 billion a year in exports, they have apparently helped to pay off part of Mexico's $100 billion debt and improved macroeconomic indicators. The $400 million in corporate taxes from maquilas are reported to make up about 2.5 percent of government revenues.[62] They are also reported to pay $1.3 billion in social security taxes.

Beyond the economic, there are some positive social changes brewing on the border. As the first site of U.S.–Mexican economic integration, maquilas were crucial to the formation of cross-border business relationships.

Binational economic development plans for the border have also, in many ways, helped to draw attention to issues such as the environment. The flipside of the earlier discussion about women workers is that the maquila sector has embraced women into the workforce, providing new economic leverage for nontraditional breadwinners.[63] Most writers see the double edge of their simultaneous inclusion and exploitation, and in this way women workers reflect the broader problems of the border: achieving measurable progress but at an unmeasured cost.

Disputed Links between Maquiladoras, Health, and the Environment

The cause (or causes) of the Brownsville infant deaths and anencephaly cases mentioned in this chapter's introduction is still an official mystery. Dr. Carmen Rocco, a Matamoros/Brownsville medic who worked on the case, says that instead of over thirty, there should have been no more than three cases of anencephaly for the population of the region.[64] Rocco found a correlation between the factories on the border and the rates of all birth defects in a study of Cameron and Hidalgo counties. A study by the Centers for Disease Control and Prevention (CDC) and the Texas Department of Health was less conclusive. Some scientists believe the defects may be caused by a lack of folic acid in the diets of pregnant women.

General Motors spokesperson Kyle Johnson said, "There is no causal link between the maquiladora operations and the birth defects."[65] Plaintiffs argued that toxins cannot recognize national boundaries and believe a highly toxic paint (90 percent xylene) used in GM's Matamoros plant may have been related to the anencephaly cluster. An internal GM company memo was turned up that said that the kind of paint used at the plant was "not allowed in Dayton." A senior environmental engineer for GM was quoted as saying, "In Mexico, we would never have been in compliance with the U.S. Clean Air Act."[66]

In 1995, families of afflicted children settled with dozens of companies for $17 million, claiming maquila pollution as a major factor in the infants' deaths. No companies have admitted liability, insisting like GM that the defects were caused by "a lack of sufficient folic acid in the diet [of the expectant mothers]." While the plaintiff's case was weak in terms of causation, the trial was a potential public relations nightmare—the story was covered throughout the United States including in a prominent 1993 piece in *Time* magazine—so they settled. Regarding one of its practices, the *Time* piece cited a GM internal memo that said, "This is in direct violation of the law."[67]

Time cited a GM study that found potentially carcinogenic solvents in the Matamoros plant's wastewater.

Birth defect rates in Cameron County dropped somewhat after the 1990–1991 outbreak, but neural tube defects in Cameron and other border counties of Texas remained twice the national average.[68] GM built a wastewater treatment plant, and other factories improved equipment. A few have simply cut back production of the controversial processes, and some have closed for various reasons. Still, in 1999 the Texas Department of Health declared that the entire border area remains a high-risk area (for neural tube defects) compared to the rest of the United States.[69]

Near Quimica Flor in the Privada Uniones colonia, residents discovered cancer-causing xylene at fifty-three thousand times the allowable U.S. level in a drainage ditch behind their neighbor, the Stepan Chemical plant.[70] Stepan, a Chicago-based multinational, said that the water and ground were already contaminated when they bought the plant in 1988.[71] However, the cross-border Catholic church–based group Coalition for Justice in the Maquiladoras (CJM) produced 1990 video footage showing Stepan workers dumping barrel loads of contaminants into open drainage ditches. After Stepan bulldozed the drainage ditches and presented proposals for a site assessment in February of 1993, CJM stopped circulating the video but the damage had already been done: Residents we interviwed in 2001 believed they still were living in a highly contaminated physical environment and distrust their industrial neighbors.

Workers who deal directly with chemicals often unknowingly carry contaminants into their home on their hair, clothes, shoes, or body. Pregnant women may also transfer pollutants directly to their unborn children. Although desperate for work, conditions are so bad in some maquilas that 15–20 percent of female maquiladora workers are estimated to leave their jobs over occupational safety and health concerns every year.[72] Like many such figures on the issue, this is a very difficult claim to confirm.

There is uncertainty and dispute on figures on the disposal side as well. Maquilas are responsible for several million metric tons of hazardous wastes per year, of which 40–70 percent is either disposed of in Mexico or unaccounted for altogether.[73] Under the LaPaz Agreement (discussed later),[74] any hazardous waste originating outside of Mexico is supposed to be shipped back to its country of origin for processing. Poor tracking and a lack of enforcement means that less than a quarter of hazardous materials are said to be returned to the United States.[75] Still, more than a fourth of the five thousand Mexican trucks that cross into Texas each day carry corrosives, chemicals, explosives, jet fuel, poisons, toxic waste, or pesticides.[76] The trafficking of hazardous wastes poses a non-zero risk to not only truck operators but also to any person that uses or lives along transportation routes.

Because legal dumping is expensive and enforcement is lax, illegal dumping on the Mexican side is reported to be common. Soil contamination on maquiladora sites is extremely common. Contaminated soil often leaks into groundwater aquifers or is mobilized after rains into nearby waterways. Very little reliable information is available, so we hear only about the most egregious cases. For example, in 1991 a fifteen thousand ton mountain of lead and arsenic was discovered at Alco Pacifico's abandoned Tijuana operation, after a chemical reaction triggered an underground fire at the site.

But there's another difficulty in tracking pollutants: Below the ground lie huge reservoirs of fresh water, a precious resource indeed in the arid Northern border region of Mexico and the U.S. Southwest. Both nations have been drawing down these aquifers, and much is still not understood about how long they will last, or about who has what rights to how much of the water. Aquifers are difficult to map, they take millennia to recharge with water, and they can be contaminated or damaged in other ways. El Paso and Ciudad Juárez pump 90 percent of their water from the "severely overdrafted" Hueco Bolsón and Mesilla aquifer, which may go dry by 2025, or even much sooner.[77] There were reports of wells dropping by ten meters a year in some parts of Juárez. There is fear also that drawing down the aquifers may cause them to draw in saltwater or, even worse, contaminants from maquiladora plants. Four other major aquifers along the border are also at risk.

A fairly new concept, air basins or "Airsheds," is even trickier to grasp and measure than watersheds. Roughly, airsheds are the area from which the air flowing over one point tends to come. Awareness of cross-border pollution drift is growing, since most of the border cities on the U.S. side struggle to meet the EPA's air quality standards.[78] Carbon monoxide, ozone, and particulate matter from chemical and electronic maquiladoras regularly gust across the border. A boom in electricity-generation plants just across the line in Mexico is expected to worsen the situation over the next decade.

Residents of El Paso, Texas, have long believed that their air was being polluted by industries in Juárez, Chihuahua, across the river. And now a few dozen scientific studies conducted under a new U.S.–Mexican university consortium are showing that in fact the two cities, like other twin cities along the border, are part of the same "Paso del Norte Airshed."[79] In 1992,

100,000 Mexican residents were evacuated after the Qomsa fertilizer company released a cloud of hydrochloric acid near the border; the EPA didn't even hear about it until two days later.[80] Now a Paso del Norte Joint Advisory Committee has been set up to address issues, including improving monitoring and research and speeding the flow of information across the border.[81]

The research has uncovered a lot of surprises in the early findings. For example, virtually every set of twin cities at the border saw statistically significant rises in the number of trucks and cars crossing the border since NAFTA came into effect in 1994, but airborne lead levels tended to drop, as Mexico began to remove lead from gasoline.[82] Closely watched by environmentalists and public health officials is ground-level ozone, which can cause asthma and other severe health effects by reacting with moisture, dust, and other airborne chemicals to create lung irritants, smog, and haze. Several studies have shown that visibility at the isolated desert Big Bend National Park in southwestern Texas is worsened by ozone, believed to be elevated because of emissions from maquiladoras, power plants, and vehicle traffic upwind.[83] But surprisingly, in most cities on the border, ozone levels have remained flat, not increasing with vehicular traffic, and not going up either with the increase in the number of maquiladoras.

A study of emergency room visits and hospital admissions in El Paso, however, uncovered a pattern of peaks of acute asthma cases in the spring and fall, two days after elevated levels of tiny airborne particulates (PM-10) were detected.[84] The Arizona Department of Environmental Quality conducted a study with U.S. and Mexican federal government assistance to estimate the health risks of air pollution in the two Nogales.[85] Using air testing, demographic data, and computer modeling, they estimated little increase in cancer rates, but an 8 percent increase in asthma episodes and respiratory illnesses from the same size (PM-10) particulates as the El Paso study. A substantial number of premature deaths from heart/lung complications were predicted: five in the Arizona twin city per year, forty-two in the Sonoran Nogales (4 and 11 percent increases). Many of the effects are turning out to be very localized: Pollution's toll kills many times more Mexicans than U.S. citizens each year.

Here's a twist: The pollutants and particulates were largely accounted for by vehicles and the dust from unpaved roads.[86] But about one-sixth of all PM-10 particulates turn out to be coming from the hundreds of "traditional" brick-making kilns, often in poor neighborhoods, on the Mexican side of the border.[87] Many of these kilns use whatever fuels they can, often burning old tires or dirty coal. The kilns vary tremendously, from rather crude family operations employing a few people to much larger and more sophisticated operations employing dozens. One intervention successfully moved the larger kilns to cleaner fuels like natural gas, but cleaning up the smaller semi-informal and quite marginal kilns promises to be extremely difficult, risking throwing many workers into unemployment. But the cost of inaction is substantial; forty people are estimated to die prematurely in Juárez alone because of the kilns each year, and the lives and productivity of thousands more are immiserated by chronic respiratory problems. The economic losses from their sicknesses and deaths have been estimated in the hundreds of millions of dollars per year.[88]

While it may seem obvious that there is a relationship between border health problems and a high concentration of industrial assembly plants, it is extremely difficult to link diseases to a point source contaminant. Afflicted residents who wish to hold a corporation accountable for a pollution-related disease must be able to empirically prove that their illness is a direct result of a particular pollutant. Unfortunately, there are little data with health demographics and a lack of independent monitoring systems (particularly on the Mexican side). At the same time, trackable medical reports are becoming less common as border industries internalize their health care systems and keep worker health issues off the public record. The question of links between maquilas and health and the environment may not be answered definitively—to the satisfaction of scientists or agencies or corporations—for a long time to come. Still, for those who have suffered and those who have seen the suffering, there is ample evidence.

Promise and Risk: NAFTA Institutions and FTAA Battles

In the years leading up to the NAFTA treaty signing in 1992, a profound split emerged among environmental groups in the United States over how to approach the impending huge free-trade zone from Canada to Mexico. The more "radical" groups, such as Greenpeace, Friends of the Earth, and the Sierra Club, opposed the treaty on the grounds that it would create a "race to the bottom" in environmental regulations, making it impossible for a nation to enforce stronger laws than its trading partners had.[89] Creg Merrilees of Fair Trade Campaign, an anti-NAFTA group, said "the question is how to hold on to U.S. environmental policies and labor standards, all of which are slipping away. If we continue to allow companies to escape the rules and regulations of national governments we will have an era of unregulated laissez faire."[90] Like other free-trade agreements, NAFTA's language

For example, the HAZTRACK program is trying to develop a system to identify, fine, and track hazardous wastes traveling between the United States and Mexico,[100] while the Border XXI Program is on its way toward identifying indicators to assess border environmental changes. Cooperation between the BECC and the NADBank has done a lot to improve environmental infrastructure. Environmentalists, however, are still fuming that the BECC operates behind closed doors. Although the organization has loosely enforced their rules, the public is still technically required to submit a request to speak at a public meeting fifteen days in advance and the board retains full discretion regarding whom may speak at meetings.[101]

A group of residents in Tijuana had hoped that NAFTA might be used to bring closure to an accountability struggle that has spanned almost twenty years. In 1994, the Mexican government shut down a lead, copper, and phosphorus smelter operated by Metales y Derivados (owned by the New Frontier Trading Corporation) for violating Mexican hazardous waste laws. The company has since been abandoned and its owner, José Khan, is reported to have "vanished" to San Diego where he continued to operate his $1 million a year business. In 1995, Mexico issued a warrant for his arrest and made some minor efforts to contain the estimated six thousand metric tons of lead, arsenic, cadmium, and sulfuric acid that remain on the site. A citizen enforcement submission complaint charging Mexico with failure to enforce its own environmental laws has been filed with the CEC by a Chilpancingo neighborhood association and the Environmental Health Coalition, but nothing has yet been done to clean up the site.[102]

Environmental groups on both sides of the border have given mixed, but largely critical, reviews of NAFTA's environmental agencies and programs. In many ways, the split that polarized "moderate" and so-called radical environmental organizations during the negotiations continues today. "Radical" groups, such as Greenpeace, Friends of the Earth, and Sierra Club, have remained active, although largely external, agitators. In 1997, for example, Public Citizen published a document entitled "NAFTA's Broken Promises: The Border Betrayed," chronicling NAFTA's environmental failures and even questioning whether NAFTA is doing "no further harm" to the region. "Moderate" groups, such as the National Wildlife Federation and the World Wildlife Fund, have been more accepting of NAFTA's slow progress and have tended to look for systemic/historical explanations of nonperformance. Environmental Defense has argued that its admittedly weak environmental record is simply a continuation of macroeconomic and socio-environmental stressors in place well before 1994.[103] For example, Mexico plunged into a major economic crisis in 1995, and environmental enforcement was set aside to address the dire needs of unemployment and a collapsing currency.

Proponents of border industrialization and the NAFTA treaty have argued hard against these environmental critics. Marco Antonio Valenzuela, the head of the National Maquila Association, believes that "a few bad apples have been used to spoil the image of the entire industry."[104] A 1997 editorial in the *Journal of Commerce* argued, "Border conditions are starting to improve, and NAFTA appears to be the reason. The current border conditions stem from a combination of factors that began decades ago."[105] Reporter Laura Carlsen specifies the bad apples argument: "Today there are more than 2,000 maquiladoras borderwide and they are frequently blamed for much, if not all, of the damage and disrepair to the border environment. Although some border operations have failed to address public concerns about environmental conditions at their facilities, many are adopting measures to improve their environmental practices." She ties the majority of border environmental problems to the booming population growth of border cities.

Roberto Salinas-Leon, the academic director of the Center for Free Enterprise Research in Mexico City, argues that the border and NAFTA are the *only* way to move Mexico to greater protection of the environment, and so must move forward. While the treaty was being argued in 1991 he wrote, "With a NAFTA Mexico will begin to generate the resources required to enforce existing environmental legislation and repair the ecological damage caused by excessive government control."[106] He sees the economic boost of free trade as allowing the nation to turn its attention to cleanup. "The logic is simple: more trade generates economic growth, which stimulates the demand for a healthier environment and thus leads to sustainable development."[107] George H. W. Bush said in 1991, "Such an unquestionably beneficial opportunity for a brighter commercial and economic future should meet with no rational opposition. What do anti-FTA people have against Mexican prosperity?" His son argued the same point after forty thousand people showed up in Quebec to protest the expansion of NAFTA in April 2001: "By failing to make the case for trade, we've allowed a new kind of protectionism to appear in this country. . . . It talks of the environment, while opposing the wealth-creating policies that will pay for clean air and water in developing nations."[108]

The "bad apples" and "develop first to clean up later" arguments contain some truth, but wider trends show broad-based problems. According to a January 2002 commentary, Mexico's census bureau INEGI has documented that "every major environmental problem has worsened since Mexico began liberalizing its trade policies."[109] Spending on environmental protection in Mexico has dropped 45 percent since 1994, the equivalent of $200 million, and inspections have dropped 45 percent. The report estimates $36 billion in hidden financial costs of environmental degradation to Mexico each year, some 10 percent of the GDP.

What is remarkable is that despite (or perhaps, because of) the split among environmental NGOs, the environment has been a serious issue in virtually all NAFTA debates. But in our evaluation of NAFTA it is important to remember that, from the very beginning, environment and labor concerns were textual appendices to a fundamentally economic agreement. Noneconomic concerns became important only when they became a real threat to NAFTA ratification. So while it is true that there is a sustainable development clause in NAFTA's preamble, and several articles mention environmental protection, eco-development did not serve as an ideological base in the drafting or implementation of the agreement.

Are Dirty Industries Fleeing to "Pollution Havens"?

Many environmentalists explain the blossoming of the maquila industry in terms that have come to be known as the "pollution haven hypothesis": Firms retreat to Southern pollution sanctuaries when Northern environmental regulations become inordinately expensive.[110] The idea of Mexico as a haven for dirty industries has been reinforced by several influential Mexicans, including former President Carlos Salinas. In an interview on U.S. Public Television's *The McLachlan Group*, Salinas reportedly explained that Mexico first needed to pollute itself in order to meet its basic development needs and that environmental concerns would come later. Trading environmental integrity for dirty development was, for people like Salinas, a simple economic decision to supply the free market with a coveted international commodity.

Yet while corporations may be enticed by the idea of escaping Northern environmental regulations, the most powerful lure to the South seems to be cheap labor. As we discussed earlier, the minimum wage in the United States recently stood at $5.15 per hour, while the Mexican minimum wage was $3–$5 per *day*.

Explaining the maquila boom as a simple extension of Mexico's past as a "raw material haven" (see Chapter 1) is attractive to environmentalists and green "Cassandras"; the idea of labor complicates an otherwise unicausal relationship. But recognizing labor as the border's central "comparative advantage" puts us in a better position to understand environmental challenges. "Upward harmonization" of Mexico's environmental standards would likely have very little effect on the nation's environment: We must remember that industrial pollution is only one stressor on the border environment—inadequate sanitation services, poor infrastructure, and widespread poverty are also important.[111]

Some industries may well be moving to Mexico to avoid pollution control. Battery metals recycling firms, for example, have largely moved across the border to escape California's tough regulatory climate.[112] But there is a large body of anecdotal evidence and several studies that have directly challenged the pollution haven hypothesis—specifically one well-cited 1988 study by Jeffery Leonard, which found no tendency of polluting industries to move across borders. Low and Yeats of the World Bank conducted a study showing that pollution control represents a tiny fraction of the costs of doing business in almost all industries. Only in cement manufacturing did it reach 1–2 percent of total costs. There are some terrible cases of firms seeking pollution havens, but the pollution haven hypothesis remains unproven overall.

One reason this may be so is that a few high-profile lawsuits such as those seen earlier in this chapter have made firms nervous about getting in trouble down the line, even if immediate enforcement is unlikely. Since the disaster at the Union Carbide plant in Bhopol, India, in 1984, larger multinational corporations also fear public relations nightmares if they were to cause a deadly disaster in Mexico.[113]

However, there are two other issues here. First, whether or not firms move to avoid regulation, they may decrease spending once overseas out of the control of U.S., Canadian, Japanese, or European regulators. There are some anecdotal reports on this for U.S. firms on the border. However, there are also some pressures on firms to maintain the same standards of production once overseas: Some "downstream" purchasers of products want to be assured that the components of products are being produced in an environmentally sound fashion. They therefore seek some labeling or formal certification (see Chapters 3 and 4).

Second, if Mexico were to ever reach a higher tier of international environmental and labor regulations, we have every indication to believe that firms would seek out another "salary sanctuary" elsewhere on the globe. "Salary sanctuaries" and "pollution havens" do not just exist in Mexico; so-called toxic colonialism is present throughout the world everywhere there is the right combination of social inequality, political cooperation, and public indifference.

We conclude, then, that although environmental considerations may not be the primary factor luring firms to Mexico, they may be a secondary motivator. For example, one study reported that 26 percent of companies that relocated to Mexico admitted that lax environmental regulation was an important factor in their decision to relocate.[114] As we can see, an examination of the factors motivating corporate decisions to head South quickly opens up a much broader discussion about the globalization of trade and economic interchanges, which will come up again in Chapter 4 and Chapter 7 to this book. Our point there will be that until labor, health, and environmental standards are globalized alongside free trade agreements, it seems we may forever be looking for corporations hiding the dirty "externalities" of their production in places with little government ability to control them.

Globalization from Above or Below? Social Movements, NAFTA, and the FTAA

"Justícia sin fronteras" screamed a banner during a 1998 demonstration against the Sierra Blanca nuclear waste dump, as 150 people joined hands in solidarity across the border Bridge of the Americas.[115] The idea of justice without borders has motivated people far beyond Ciudad Juárez and El Paso. Perhaps the most irrefutable effect of NAFTA on North America is the way it has brought the continent together toward a common, but not well-agreed-upon, goal of bettering our economies, land, and quality of life. NAFTA focused North America's attention on the border in a way no demonstration, public policy, or magazine exposé had been able to do. In a sense, NAFTA has united many policymakers, economists, scholars, and activists as a regional focus for debates and development dialogues.

Globalization assumes bright or dark shades for each of the many border stakeholders. What we see along the border is a fluid and ambiguous social phenomenon, something we would describe as a battle over whether globalization will be imposed from above or from below. Corporations and governments, through public policy and commerce, continue to globalize from "above," in the high-profile, high-stakes, and high-speed political/communications world. "Below," the rumble of cross-border grassroots networks organize workers and communities into a series of smaller groups linked at times with larger national and international environmental, labor, and human rights groups. What these groups oppose is not globalization per se; so-called anti-globalization activists protest the globalization of corporations, economic policy, and elite power structures without a corresponding globalization of labor, environment, and indigenous/cultural protection laws. These *globalfóbios* resist corporate-led globalization, arguing instead for more democratic power-sharing in the creation of international rules and links. There are some commonalties—the importance of the Internet, for example, for both sides of the globalization debate.[116]

NAFTA–based research has forged an uncommonly successful linkage between academia and the grassroots: Some universities and research institutions are playing an increasing role in working to understand border changes and document the effects of external influences on the region's environmental and economic stability. The Texas Center for Policy Studies, Arizona Toxics Information, and the Border Ecology Project have all assumed a major role in BECC policymaking.

A new development is that a diverse set of groups work together on specific issues, in coalitions that may be broadly categorized under the heading "environmental justice": maquiladora workers, labor activists, civil rights leaders, fair housing advocates, bird lovers, and people of faith.[117] Like African American communities in the Deep South of the United States, Latino communities in the border region face disproportionate impacts of toxins and disease. The Cross-Border Network for Justice and Solidarity in Kansas, for example, works with El Centro de Trabajadores y Comunidades de Nuevo Laredo. Groups like the Coalition for Justice in the Maquiladoras and the Environmental Health Coalition have found creative ways to operate on both sides of the border. Many of these are faith-based groups that have gone on to widen their membership.

The current battle between the two globalization camps surrounds government plans laid by U.S. President Bill Clinton in 1994 to extend NAFTA from Prudhoe Bay, Alaska, to Patagonia, Argentina. This "Free Trade Area of the Americas" (FTAA) would harmonize regional trade between all thirty-four nations of the Western Hemisphere (minus Cuba). Proponents see the FTAA as a tool to liberalize the region's economies, but support is far from universal—in April 2001 some sixty thousand[118] protesters traveled to Quebec to protest the fifth FTAA Summit of the Americas. They dubbed the FTAA "NAFTA on steroids."

We can now return to border specialist Ron Mader's point from the beginning of this chapter, that the literature is polarized between toxic ravine versus happy maquiladora stories. The National Toxic Campaign Fund in 1991 chose an absurd hyperbole when they called the border region a "2,000–mile-long Love Canal."[119] So if NAFTA is neither salvation nor destroyer of the border region where does the truth lie? Ultimately, we must begin a paradigm shift away from the logic that nations cannot simultaneously improve their economies and their environments. The idea that environmental protection should wait until after nations have developed has been disputed. Rather than a hindrance to economic growth, environmental regulations are generally a prerequisite to sustained economic growth and the creation of good jobs.[120]

From a historical perspective, the inclusion of an environmental side agreement in the NAFTA accord was a tremendous achievement in and of itself. The NAFTA text reflects an international recognition that free trade agreements affect, and should therefore include, noneconomic aspects of international commerce. And despite its shortcomings, the environmental side agreement created several agencies that are working to improve the border environment. As discussed in earlier sections, however, binational "green aid," regulation, and enforcement from the CEC, BECC, and NADBank are unlikely to provide meaningful changes until they are granted more political muscle, structural autonomy, and financial resources. Without these, they remain mere green window dressing.[121]

Recently, CEPAL came out with a statement that the maquiladora industry "specializes in cheap labor and does not constitute a motor for sustainable growth with more social equity."[122] Since NAFTA came into effect, border maquila growth has steadily increased and regional social indicators continue to tarry among the lowest in North America. In the ten years before NAFTA, the Mexican poverty rate remained constant at about 34 percent of the population, but by 1997 it had climbed to 60 percent. A decade after the agreement was signed, many of NAFTA's environmental and social promises have yet to be realized. NAFTA's Chapter 11 rule menaces our ability to improve environmental conditions. The "too soon to tell" explanation is losing legitimacy with each passing year, and many have been left wondering how bad it has to get before we reevaluate NAFTA's role in shaping our hemisphere's environmental and economic future.

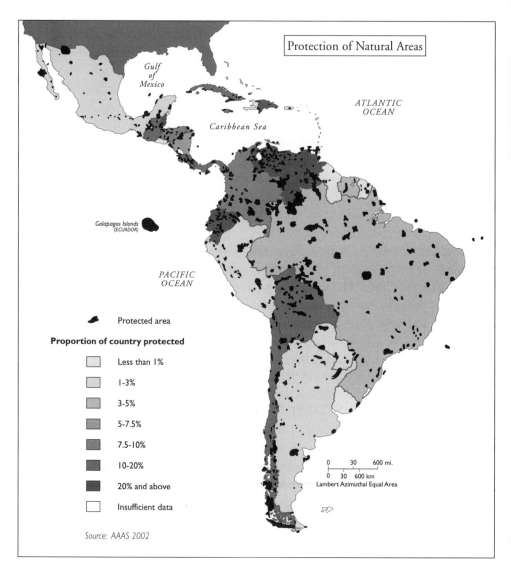

Protection of Natural Areas

Gulf
of
Mexico

Caribbean Sea

ATLANTIC
OCEAN

Galapagos Islands
(ECUADOR)

PACIFIC
OCEAN

Protected area

Proportion of country protected

Less than 1%

1-3%

3-5%

5-7.5%

7.5-10%

10-20%

20% and above

Insufficient data

0   30   600 mi.
0   30   600 km
Lambert Azimuthal Equal Area

Source: AAAS 2002

Officially-designated "Protected Areas" in Latin America. Protected areas are in black, and the proportion of the country in parks and other protected areas is represented by shading of countries. Source: AAAS 2002.

CHAPTER 3

Green Revolutions, Deforestation, and New Ideas

Two men, one morning. Reluctantly rolling off of his cotton sheets, Samuel groggily stumbles down the hall to the kitchen. The freezer door swings open to reveal a metal-wrapped half-pound bag of gourmet coffee. He gives it a shake and concludes there's just enough to make his morning pot. Samuel's practiced hands hardly require guiding as he pours the coffee into the grinder, presses the lid, and from there dumps it into the filter. The pot's in the sink filling, and then it's poured to the line in the maker and he's flipped the switch, taken out the sugar and cream. He's back down the hall to take a warm shower while it brews. Back from the shower the coffee and sugar are kicking in while he throws a premade smoothie mix of orange juice, bananas, mangos, and passion fruit into the blender.

Meanwhile a half-hemisphere away, the sun is already up as Claudio squints over seemingly unending expanses of humid banana plantations spread across the Caribbean coasts of Guatemala. As the pickup carrying six workers out into the fields bumps along a rutted mud road, there is little to distinguish the scene from plantations in Honduras, Costa Rica, Ecuador, or the Caribbean islands. The massive industrial enterprise is carved out of what were lush lowland rainforests—but now only hybridized, genetically identical banana trees grow on both sides of the road in monotonous rows for miles. Occasionally the vista opens up as a number of wood shacks for workers sit between the sea of banana trees and a small muddy soccer field.

Between the rows are "monorail" racks for moving the huge banana bunches from field to packing plant. The bunches are sprayed frequently in the field, then wrapped with plastic bags to hold in the chemicals. There are virtually no other living things among the banana trees. For twelve hours a day, for about U.S.$7 (a day), Claudio cuts the huge dangling bunches off the trees and pushes them along the tracks.[1] After a quarter mile, he reaches the "packing plant," a simple steel shed where women in the plant cut the plastic bags, which "serve as a reservoir on each bunch . . . when the women take the plastic from the fruit, they are drenched in the chemicals."[2] They use hooked machetes to carve the bundles into the bunches we see in the store, and on conveyor lines place them into the shipping crates that will be opened in the produce section or by the fruit vendor. They are picked green, and a new spray is applied in the box to cause them to ripen at the right time.

These are old secrets in the export plantations that send millions of boxes and bags of fruit North each month. And while newer "nontraditional" agricultural exports such as melons, grapes, cut flowers, snow peas, and broccoli have created a boom of interest in Latin American farming, many of the stories recall those of the old plantations. Workers on a Standard Fruit Company grapefruit plantation in Olanchito, Honduras, "speak of nerve problems and sterility. They display rashes that don't heal. Women carry ID cards of dead husbands and hold up children with deformities."[3] A study by the National University of Costa Rica reports that women working the packing plants "suffer double the average rate of leukemia and birth defects."[4] Children as young as ten or eleven work the banana fields of Ecuador for twelve-hour days handling dangerous fungicides.[5] Samuel doesn't know that ninety-four pesticides are allowed on coffee sold in the United States, or that sixty-six of those had no government guidelines.[6] Claudio doesn't know if he's among the 20 percent of male workers who is sterile from the chemicals.[7]

In late October 1998, Hurricane Mitch stalled and dumped a year's rain on Central America in forty-eight hours. Flash floods and mudslides down deforested slopes wreaked devastation on a vast scale, leaving ten thousand people dead, almost twenty thousand missing, and over 2.5 million people temporarily dependent on emergency aid. Honduras, the second-poorest nation in the Western Hemisphere, was the hardest hit. Almost six thousand people were killed and another eleven thousand declared missing, presumed dead, as communities, roads, bridges, and factories were swept away. Honduras had a population of 6 million. Of those, it was estimated that nearly 2 million were affected, 1 million made homeless, and 70 percent of the country's productive infrastructure damaged or destroyed. The government's initial estimate of the cost of reconstruction was $5 billion.[8] Ironically, since the disaster the national governments have been forced to seriously cut back expenditures for public services: Rural health care, rural roads, sanitation infrastructure, rural electrification, and telecommunications all have suffered.

The impact of the heavy rains from Hurricane Mitch was made much worse by the previous pattern of clearing the original forest of Nicaragua and Honduras. Many of the coffee plantations that spread across the mountainsides and the banana plantations carved out of the lush, coastal regions were financed by multinational companies. International markets for beef, bananas, sugar, cotton, and coffee have fed this displacement, while historic patterns of inequality in land access and political power absorbed and translated these forces into unsafe conditions at the local level. Poor and marginalized people live where they do because of macro forces in the history, politics, and economics of whole regions. They have no other livelihood choices. Both countries have been governed for many years by narrow oligarchies closely associated with the military and foreign corporations and the government of the United States.[9]

As UN Secretary General Kofi Annan said in 1999, "The term 'natural disasters' has become an increasingly anachronistic misnomer. In reality, it is human behaviour that transforms natural hazards into what should be called unnatural disasters." On some parts of its Pacific coast, the sea level landscape of Central America today bears a closer resemblance to a desert than a tropical oasis. A quarter of all land in the region is "severely degraded"— making it the most damaged region in the world.[10] Reshaped in each phase since Maya and Spanish colonization for timber, firewood, and plantations, land degradation in Central America and the Caribbean continues to be intimately linked to economies far away. This latest phase of "export or else" globalization is accelerating the "conversion" of tropical forests to farmland, pasture, and waste places. Despite increased national and international pressures, Central America has the highest average rate of annual deforestation in the hemisphere. Unless something changes, virtually all the existing forests will be gone in a generation.[11]

So it is important to understand the origins of the food we eat, to know something of the land and people on the other end of the commodity chains that links us. Traveling and studying in the banana plantations of Central America, as we did in the early 1980s (Roberts) and the late 1990s (Thanos), we ran across scenes and stories of pesticide poisonings and damaged lands. Claims by some authors about the frequency of pesticide poisonings are disturbing. The World Health Organization reports that there are 2–5 million pesticide poisonings a year around the world, of which about forty thousand are fatal.[12] Although 80 percent of all the world's pesticides are applied in the wealthy countries of the world's North, only 1 percent of these 2–5 million annual cases of pesticide poisonings occur in the North. Latin American farm workers are thirteen times more likely to suffer pesticide poisoning than U.S. farm workers.[13] This is an environmental injustice: We need to ask why and what is being done about it. But these numbers are disputed: Many manufacturers of pesticides claim that their products are safe when properly used and that many illnesses are being blamed on their product when they could be the result of many other factors.

This chapter examines the problem of lands in the region, focusing mostly on Central America. It looks at the problems as a series of solutions that have been proposed to solve the bitter poverty of the people in the region and to provide incentives for firms to come in and produce there. We rewind first to examine how the world's two major agricultural revolutions have played out in the region. First is the "Green Revolution," which drove the widespread adoption of pesticides and fertilizers in new chemical-intensive production technique, and second—going on today and very uncertain in its direction—is the rapid growth of biotechnology and genetic seed manipulations. We then turn our attention to debates about deforestation and discuss what is driving it: overpopulation, unequal distribution of wealth and land, or other factors. Then we move to evaluating some broad proposals for saving the lands of Central America: preservation initiatives including parks and biosphere reserves, "ecotourism," international agreements, treaties and judicial systems, and finally alternative production mechanisms such as social forestry, certified organics, and "fair trade" efforts. There's a lot of ground to cover.

The "First" Green Revolution: Chemicals and Central American Agriculture

Excited by post–World War II scientific and technological advances, farm seed companies, state university agricultural research departments, and the U.S. government led international efforts to "modernize" agriculture. This approach, designed by the United States and Mexico in order to boost agricultural production, advanced what was at the time a radical agricultural prescription: Replace traditional farming practices with mechanized single-crop production, construct massive irrigation systems, and use high-yielding hybrid seeds produced in research farms along with seed-specific agrochemicals to feed the plants and control pests. The program was exported as part of U.S. aid projects to "develop the Third World," to address poverty and economic stagnation, and to create markets for U.S. products.[14]

The Green Revolution was a success in that it transformed formerly inaccessible lands into productive fields and exponentially increased per acre/hectare crop yields. Traditional export crops like sugar and cotton propelled new Latin American economies: From the early 1960s to the mid-1970s the region achieved a 6 percent annual growth rate.[15] Heralded as a comprehensive remedy to alleviate technological, economic, and population stresses, the Green Revolution was seen as the quickest means of generating the capital necessary to drive modernization.[16]

It would be absurd to argue that pesticides have not advanced global agricultural capabilities in meaningful ways. Proponents of pesticide-intensive agriculture correctly point out the exponential increases in agricultural yields made possible by Green Revolution technologies. Global food production further increased as previously infertile or marginal lands came under cultivation. Central American nations enjoyed some of the highest increases in per hectare crop yields: In Nicaragua, for instance, cotton yields almost doubled in the 1950s.[17]

Yet the Green Revolution was not introduced into a social vacuum, and so it fell far short of delivering encompassing relief to poverty and famine in developing nations. First, the Green Revolution cemented Latin America's economic position as a supplier of raw agricultural goods and created a technological dependence on imported seeds, pesticides, and machinery. In many places food production was sidelined for export commodities. It also reinforced and worsened the economic and social cleavages that have divided Central American people for centuries:[18] Large landowners from the colonial elites and some few wealthier peasant farmers adopted new technology and rose in economic standing, leaving the poor to slip into marginality or wage laborer status. Both the large plantations producing for export and small desperate farmers "mining the soil" have pushed the lands of Central America and the Caribbean to terrible states of erosion and contamination. In Nicaragua's Pacific plains, for example, cotton land expanded 400 percent between 1952 and 1967 while peasant lands decreased by over 50 percent.[19]

One point is even more straightforward: The environmental legacy of the Green Revolution is a heavy reliance on agrochemicals. From 1970 to 1996, global pesticide use increased 3,300 percent. By 1997, pesticides globally were a $32 billion industry.[20] In Central America on average fifty-eight kilograms of fertilizer are applied on each hectare each year; in some highly competitive agro-export economies like Costa Rica's, the input numbers reach as high as 243 kilograms per hectare per year.[21]

Ironically, although pesticides are an integral part of modern agriculture, some estimates are that pests continue to destroy around 37 percent of the world's agricultural products. In 1940, before the onset of the Green Revolution, pests caused the loss of 35–40 percent of all global agricultural production.[22] If the percentage of crops lost to pests has remained invariable over the last sixty years, why have we remained committed to a pesticide-intensive development ideology?

While in the fields pesticides created ecological damages, in the political arena, the pesticide trade came with powerful backing as foreign firms and some locals profited on the pesticide trade. At the height of the Green Revolution, 40 percent of all U.S. pesticide exports went to Central America.[23] By the 1980s, aid packages from developed nations had grown to include donations of or funding for pesticides worth tens of millions of dollars.[24] Today, the unequal exchanges in the global market continue to be magnified in the technologies sector: Agricultural inputs, seeds, and machinery exported from rich nations are expensive, but the agricultural products are sold cheap, "at the price of bananas," as the Latin American phrase goes.

Latin America has historically served as both a testing ground and a dumping ground for pesticides banned or restricted in the United States. In 1951, for instance, the Bayer Corporation experimentally tested methyl parathion (a derivative of a nerve gas developed by the Nazis during World War II) in the area around León, Nicaragua.[25] Today, critics claim that the experiments continue with parathion, methamidophos, terbufos, aldicarb, endosulfan, mancozeb, captan, paraquat, and concoctions of several hazardous chemicals mixed together, called "toxic soup" by critics.

One of the best-known cases of pesticide poisonings is of a powerful chemical used to kill parasitic worms (called a nematicide) named DBCP. Because we have a longer history of the effects of this product and because the response by workers has opened new directions for recovery, it is a story worth recounting. Developed in the 1950s by Dow Chemical in conjunction with banana companies, the product was marketed as Nemagon and Fumazone starting in 1968.[26] The pesticide was first used by U.S. growers to eliminate agricultural pests in fruit and vegetable plantations. There was evidence that DBCP was dangerous, and so it was banned in the United States in 1979 after it was found to cause sterility in male laborers at an Occidental Petroleum Plant in California. The company commissioned studies as early as 1961 that suggested a link between sterility and the chemical.[27]

Not wanting to suffer the economic losses of backlogged inventory, DBCP producers turned to Third World markets. Although regulatory agencies and U.S. manufacturers were well aware of the dangers of DBCP, they continued to support the exportation and use of the pesticide in developing countries. According to Charles S. Siegal, a lawyer representing farm workers from Costa Rica, the Philippines, and ten other countries, "exports of DBCP to Africa and Ecuador continued at least until 1981 . . . and to the Philippines until 1986."[28] Worse, it is believed the DBCP was shipped without warning labels of its known effects.[29]

In the 1970s and early 1980s, an estimated 100,000 workers in Latin America and Southeast Asia were sterilized from exposure to DBCP. Sixteen thousand of them were contacted and joined a lawsuit filed in Texas against the companies who had produced and used the chemical: Dow, Shell Oil, Standard Fruit, and Chiquita the largest among them. Nearly half of the plaintiffs, about eight thousand, were in Costa Rica.[30] This terrible case of international environmental injustice provides a glimmer of hope, and we'll return to it later.

Because of shifts in export agriculture, pesticide contamination today may affect more diverse populations than before, and so efforts to prevent misuse must hit a moving target. Once concentrated largely among male laborers, pesticide exposure now poses substantial health risks to women and children as well. In some nontraditional agricultural sectors such as flowers and tropical plants, women comprise majorities of the workforce. Children meanwhile are exposed directly (as laborers), indirectly (when parents inadvertently carry pesticide residues into the home), genetically (as offspring), and accidentally (as neighbors of farm fields).[31]

By the 1980s, the effects of prolonged pesticide exposure had become too obvious to be ignored. A global movement gained speed calling for serious reform of pesticide policies. Before long, even the pesticide industry went public with statements calling for a review of the system. Many proposals grew out of this recognition, but it was the "Safe Use" approach, as proposed by the pesticide industry itself, which won acceptance in policy circles after heavy lobbying.[32] The industry proposed that educational programs, combined with improvements in registration processes, more thorough chemical risk assessments by regulatory agencies, and an improved labeling system, would significantly and sufficiently reduce pesticide hazards in developing countries.

In 1991, the pesticide industry spent just over U.S.$1 million to launch pilot projects in three countries to test the Safe Use plan—Guatemala, Kenya, and Thailand—and the development agency USAID pitched in another $4 million.[33] By 1994, the program claimed to have trained a quarter million Guatemalan farmers. Public health officials there reported that pesticide poisonings fell 90 percent by mid-decade. However, sociologists Douglas Murray and Peter Taylor believe the claims are reckless: The Guatemalan civil war at the same time caused all data collection to be abandoned in the areas with the greatest numbers of poisonings. Rather, poisonings were estimated to still be occurring at rates ten times those reported to officials. Many critics, such as Nick van der Graff of the UN's Food and Agriculture Organization, point out what they see to be an ironic claim of the initiative: that pesticides could simultaneously be proliferated and controlled and that pesticide industry representatives could be expected to do trainings that would include adequate education on ways to reduce pesticide use and about *alternatives* to pesticides. There is an assumption implicit in U.S. and international pesticide legislation that suggests that pesticides are not inherently more dangerous than any other technological product—if they are managed properly. Some have characterized the message reinforced by these policies as a directive to "use pesticides safely but by all means use pesticides."[34] This assurance is repeated by pesticide producers and backed up by scientific studies, often paid for or done by the pesticide companies themselves.

Safe Use programs are one step toward safer working environments in the developing world, but they are only one small part of the solution. It has been argued that the Safe Use initiative has served as a distraction from the creation of internationally binding laws and, more, the development of a new agricultural model that might reduce or eliminate the need for chemical inputs all together. There has been relatively little research into alternative agricultural technologies that reduce dependence on chemical inputs.[35] What's more, most large agricultural research centers, even in universities in the United States and Central America, are funded by the big seed and pesticide producers.[36] Rather, Safe Use initiatives need to be joined with other programs that fundamentally question the sustainability of worldwide pesticide use. Murray and Taylor call for elimination of the worst pesticides, substitution of safer products, training focused on applicators as opposed to buyers of pesticides, reorganization of production, and, as a last resort only, pushing the use of personal protective equipment such as masks and gloves. It is unrealistic, they argue, to expect owners to afford the equipment, and when available it is simply too hot in the fields of Central America to expect workers to consistently wear masks, skin covering, and gloves. American and European consumers of agricultural imports also have a role to play by supporting products that have less negative consequences on the environments and health of people in the developing world. Interestingly, some consumers are responding with far greater fear over a new threat, genetically modified food, in ways most never have to pesticide residues.

The "New" Green Revolution: Biotechnology and the Rise of GMOs

A new world of biotechnology is opening up in agriculture. Biotechnology includes the cloning of plants and animals, DNA typing, and, of most concern, the moving of genes from one species to another. On its Web site, the United Nations Food and Agriculture Organization (FAO) explains biotechnology as a process that has been used since people added yeast to bread or saved the seed from the pick of their crops.[37] Yet the pace, degree, and possibilities for gene manipulation today are hardly comparable to the modest, low-risk processes of previous centuries. Contrary to the FAO's explanation, biotechnology today is not an extension of a traditional farming or subsistence technologies but a radically new experiment testing the very limits of human science to police itself.

Many seed and "biotechnology" industries have been bought by chemical producers who can create species resistant to their own herbicides, so that all other plants die while only the modified species continues to grow after application of weed killers. This is the concept behind Monsanto's "Roundup Ready" crops. Biotechnology is a field in dispute, with huge economic and environmental stakes. In the United States alone there are 172 commercial biotechnology firms, 300 other related ventures, and billions of dollars in biotech investments.[38]

In 1992 the U.S. government ruled that food derived from gene-altered plants does not have to undergo any special tests. By 1994, the first genetically modified food to reach global markets, the FlavrSavr tomato, had secured a permanent position on supermarket shelves. This product was modified by inserting a gene into tomato cells from a salmon that can withstand freezing waters. By the late-1990s, fifty major plant species had been altered, including rice, wheat, potato, soybean, and alfalfa. By 2002, over 32 percent of U.S. crops were genetically engineered, including 35 percent of all corn, 74 percent of all soybeans, and 71 percent of all cotton.[39]

For some observers, biotechnology promises to be the answer to Central America's land crisis. In addition to boosting agricultural production, biotechnology could help reduce the spread of human diseases, improve the nutritional value of food, reduce dependency on pesticides, and even assist in oil spill and heavy metal cleanup efforts. To others, biotechnology is the greatest threat to global ecology and precisely the antithesis of sustainable development. Is there a middle ground in the increasingly polarized debate over genetically engineered foods?

The promise of biotechnology is challenged on theoretical, economic, and, of course, ecological grounds. Ecologically, there is the risk that traditional varieties of crop plants will become contaminated by cross-pollination with genetically modified strands. This has already been reported—in a controversial article in the top science journal *Nature*—to have occurred between genetically modified corn and traditional corn varieties in Canada and Mexico. It is possible that biotech genes such as those giving resistance to certain pesticides may actually spread to nearby weeds, creating "super weeds" or passing on other undesirable features. There is fear about the loss of genetic and biological diversity as fewer lines of each species are multiplied in their numbers while others go out of use. Lack of diversity can be riskier when conditions change or pests arise. Third, since biotech species carry pesticides within them, there is some fear of damage to water and land ecosystems. Concerns related to human health include the spread and introduction of food allergens, increased cancer risks, damage to human intestinal flora, and reduced effectiveness of antibiotics. Compared to Europe, the U.S. public has been much slower to show interest in genetically modified food, but there was some increased attention when a well-reported study linked genetically engineered corn to decreases in numbers of "America's favorite insect," the Monarch butterfly.[40]

Poor and rich nations have very different stakes in biotechnology: Although some authors believe Latin American universities could make some research contributions in the area, so far wealthy nations have been the principal beneficiaries of both the science and marketing revenues.[41] Industry giants like Monsanto, Novartis, and DuPont are all headquartered in the developed world. Even if one accepts the argument that the developing world needs biotechnology, the fact remains that Southern nations control very few processes in the development of these new technologies. Proposals to equalize access to benefits from new biotechnology, like the creation of a world gene bank, have been soundly rejected by developed nations, especially the United States.

The most well received genetically modified organism has been a rice engineered to include pro vitamin A (beta carotene) and iron, called "golden rice" by its supporters. Supporters hope the rice will save 350,000 children from vitamin A deficiency blindness and some 1 million malnourished children from death each year. Opponents charge that the rice is not representative of the kind of research being done by the genetically modified organism (GMO) industry. Because poor people are not wealthy consumers of biotechnology, corporations have no market incentive to develop products for the developing world. Genentech, for example, reportedly pulled out of a research project to develop a malaria vaccine when the World Health Organization refused to grant it exclusive marketing rights.[42]

A vocal grassroots opposition movement has grown up, especially in Europe and increasingly in some places in Latin America. Several Latin American nations have bans on planting GMOs, awaiting more definitive research. In Brazil, local Greenpeace activists blocked two ships from unloading what would have been the nation's first shiploads of GMO seeds. Greenpeace later sued the importing firm and forced Monsanto to postpone introducing the seeds in Brazil for at least two years. Throughout the 1990s, the Brazilian anti-GMO movement gained strength, spreading activism as well as a legal precedent to neighboring countries. In July 2000, Greenpeace Brazil launched its "Transgénicos no meu prato—Não!!" (GMOs on my plate—No!!) campaign in Rio de Janeiro. Meanwhile, however, farmers eager to use GMO technology, especially for soybeans and corn, are smuggling seeds across the border from Paraguay and Argentina.

The United Nations is looking into labeling initiatives and trying to develop international standards and guidelines for biotechnology. In 2000, member nations adopted the Cartagena Protocol on Biosafety, mandating that importing nations give their consent to trade in genetically modified organisms.[43] A "Code of Conduct on Biotechnology" is currently being developed by the FAO Commission on Genetic Resources for Food and Agriculture. In the future, there is a good possibility that some sort of international treaty might be signed to regulate the transfer, commercialization, and spread of biotechnology (several have already been proposed). There are other proposals on the table as well, including the prospect of developing bio-cooperation contracts to reward peasant farmers who preserve genetic resources by using traditional varieties.[44]

In the meantime, the unregulated spread of biotechnology continues even in some places where the citizenry is fairly well organized against it. We find it disturbing that this technological saturation has proceeded without much consensual approval from the scientific community, not to mention the global public. While making a huge contribution in the production of medicines grown in laboratories, putting genetically modified organisms in foods grown in open fields opens two new levels of risks with little way to control: Organisms can escape, causing unforeseen consequences for the environment and human health. A debate on this issue has been raging in Mexico since the study was published in *Nature* reporting that traditional varieties of corn had been contaminated with genetically modified pollen.[45] Even if they do work as crops, we believe that a full-blown new green GMO revolution is not a long-term, sustainable solution to global hunger or environmental degradation. This is because politics and economics determine the distribution of food—not human needs.[46] Today, global hunger problems continue to grow despite the fact that world food supply has outdistanced population.

Forests, Parks, and People

For centuries the forests of Central America were considered a place of danger and discomfort: It was something to get out of the way so that farming and ranching could be undertaken in earnest. Now that the forests are becoming scarce, there is more concern for their disappearance. There is also a multiplying set of ways people are trying to save them. The following sections describe some of these efforts.

For centuries, peasants across Latin America farmed for subsistence, trading or selling small surpluses in local markets. With the commercialization of agriculture as a commodity, many small-scale farmers found themselves unable to compete in a global market. Landless, many farmers became wage earners for the big ranchers and plantation owners, the *latifundistas*. The plantations, designed as enclaves for export and often owned by outsiders with few connections to the local needs, taxed their soils and sent peasant farmers to the mountains. Unlike the situation in Asia and Africa, land was first cleared in Central America for agricultural rather than timber purposes.[47] Bananas came first, followed by cotton, coffee, sugar, and oil. Large cattle ranches for beef export were also part of the conversion—today, pastures occupy nearly half of all the farmland in Central America.[48]

Latin American governments have instituted land use policies that have played a major role in contributing to clear-cutting and/or selective harvesting by undervaluing the real costs of timber and management of forests.[49] Some of the policies that have increased the attractiveness of cutting forests are log-export restrictions, subsidized harvests, transfer pricing (intentionally undervaluing or overvaluing timber), land tenure policies, and "blanket" policies that discount tree diversity (with regard to their species, size, or grade). First World consumers substantially contribute to deforestation: The United States alone imports some U.S.$4 billion in tropical timber products annually.[50] Virtually all the tropical wood sold in the United States is harvested unsustainably from virgin forests.[51]

Many environmentalists and academics have pointed out the link between environmental crises and poverty, a central tenet of this book.[52] However, it is important to explore the disagreements about what's driving key problems like deforestation and the poverty itself. Malthusians, building on the work of nineteenth-century economist Thomas Malthus, argue that deforestation is an inevitable result of growing human populations. Human populations, Malthus believed, inevitably increase exponentially while resources such as food can only be increased incrementally. Under this logic, each generational increase in human numbers places more and more demands on land and natural resources. In desperation, poor farmers either expand existing agricultural production ("creeping" further into already inhabited peripheral forests) or relocate to more remote pieces of forest.[53]

A large number of environmentalists and population control groups in the Northern countries hold this belief. The 1969 Soccer War between El Salvador and Honduras, which created 100,000 refugees and killed over two thousand people, initially appeared to be a classical case of overpopulation, with chronic land and food scarcities and an increasing reliance on food imports destabilizing the nations.[54] But economic rivalries, historic border disputes, and domestic political pressures all contributed to the evolution of the conflict, as did the the unequal distribution of land and the expansion of cotton, coffee, and other cash crops for export.[55]

Many Latin Americans bristle at the idea that their numbers need to be controlled, seeing such arguments as patronizing and frightening—especially when these arguments come from groups in the nation that acted for so long as Latin America's colonial power—the United States.[56] Eduardo Galeano begins his legendary book, *The Open Veins of Latin America,* by blasting the idea of population control, pointing out that with a few exceptions population densities in Latin America are among the lowest in the world.[57] Galeano attributes the popularity of population-based arguments to American squeamishness that masses of poor brown people will flow up the isthmus into the United States.

And yet deforestation continues to push the region's forests to the edge of disaster. One of the more successful tests of Malthusian and sociological theory in causing deforestation in the tropics is the political ecology framework proposed by Thomas Rudel and Jill Roper of Rutgers University.[58] Importantly, Rudel and Roper differentiate clearing practices in forests of different sizes. In countries with large forests, like Brazil and Nigeria, they propose that deforestation occurs first when "growth coalitions" of governments, entrepreneurs, companies, and small farmers open up frontier lands. By contrast, in countries with small forests like those in Central America, deforestation results from peasant population growth and agricultural expansion. They find that forest destruction accelerates as a result of population growth only when people already live around a fragmented forest (one with roads for access). Population growth, then, affects rates of deforestation more in small forests than in large ones.[59]

Thomas Reardon and Stephen Vosti have shed light on the problem, pointing out that there are important differences in types of poverty among rural poor in Latin America. Some people are struggling to meet their elementary needs, while others have enough to eat but lack consistent access to land, labor, or financial capital. Each type of poverty can drive different types of land degradation.[60] Some argue that outside financial interests, especially financial institutions such as the World Bank and International Monetary Fund, lend money for road, mining, and other development projects that open forests for "resource grabs." Foreign debt increases pressure on developing nations to expand export crops, which also influences small forests.[61] So there are no simple answers to these questions about the relationship between poverty, population, and environmental damage. There is some research that suggests that environmental degradation increases alongside increases in social inequality.[62] Individuals, "growth coalitions," social institutions, policies, and processes all affect the pace of rainforest destruction. As we discuss in the next two sections, parks and alternative forms of development such as ecotourism are part of the solution, but more attention must be paid to providing long-term economic stability to the poor.

How can we save the rainforests with their impressive variety of ecosystems, high biodiversity, and large numbers of endemic species and also help the people of Central America? Preserves are a key part of the puzzle. Just seventeen areas in Mesoamerica are believed to include 75 percent of the biological diversity in the region, so preserving these areas could go a long ways toward saving vast numbers of species.[63] For example, Mexico's Lacondona Forest is the largest single block of tropical rainforest in North America, with over three thousand plant species and eight hundred different butterflies. Although it occupies less than 1 percent of Mexico's territory, the Lacandona possesses 20 percent of the nation's biodiversity. Costa Rica, a nation the size of West Virginia, has more bird species than Canada and the United States combined. A look at the different conservation initiatives in Costa Rica, Honduras, Guatemala, and Mexico reveals the challenges of developing fair, effective environmental management systems.

Each Central American nation has an autonomous environmental ministry, park system, and enforcement mechanisms. Mexico has ten "biosphere reserves" and a loose network of protected areas; by contrast, Costa Rica is divided into nine "megapark" regional conservation areas (UCRs), two of which double as biosphere reserves. Costa Rica has an extremely well developed park system with 25 percent of all land falling under some kind of protection[64] while less than 5 percent of land is protected in Honduras and El Salvador.[65]

For decades, biologists and preservationists in the United States and Europe helped Latin American governments create national parks and wildlife preserves based on the model of protected lands in the United States. But the involvement was spotty: The transnational groups, such as the World Wildlife Fund, Conservation International, and Nature Conservancy, tended to send assistance and funds to nations that were politically "open" and where there were already active local conservation groups.[66] Early conservation initiatives were guided by an ideological emphasis on preserving "pristine" or "untouched" nature, so they tended to exclude humans and their activities from forest management plans. However, by forcing indigenous and nonindigenous residents to the peripheries of protected areas, local governments and conservationists created a climate of resentment and hostility.[67] Forest-dwelling people were relocated out of protected areas and treated as "poachers" if they continued to harvest fuel wood, wildlife, medicines, or other forest resources that had sustained them for generations. Since the first conservation initiatives began after World War II, many locals have come to believe that parks often serve the needs of "gringo" scientists and tourists at the expense of local populations.[68]

Preservationists, meanwhile, complained of "paper parks": areas so poorly secured and maintained that their park designation was practically meaningless. Limited financial resources, understaffing, and corruption make policing against human invasions and logging nearly impossible. In many ways, traditional conservation models pitted biologists and preservationists against local populations. As local people were left out of conservation initiatives, tensions over land and natural resources only intensified and neither party was pleased with the results.

Several contemporary management models are trying to address the shortcomings of the traditional park system. The United Nations Educational, Scientific and Cultural Organization (UNESCO) Man and the Biosphere's (MAB) World Network of Biosphere Reserves is by far the most internationally successful. Biosphere reserves are a management model of concentric zones, consisting of a human-free protected "core" area surrounded by a "buffer zone" for research, recreation, ecotourism, and environmental education and an outer "transition" area for human habitation, private enterprises, and so on. Intended to provide a space for both human sustenance and ecological conservation, since the project's inception in 1976 the network has grown to include some 337 reserves in 85 countries.[69]

Some creative ways have been designed by local populations to benefit from their natural resources without destroying them, while operating in the buffer and transition zones of Biosphere Preserves.[70] In the Montes Azules Biosphere Reserve in Chiapas, Mexico, for instance, over seven hundred local people sell preserved and handcrafted butterflies from a 326-hectare ranch. Proceeds from their operation help to preserve thirty-two hundred hectares of the Lacandona Rainforest. Reforestation and mixed use protect watersheds that supply the Huatulco tourist region of Oaxaca state. In the Las Chimalapas rainforest preserve a "peasant administered conservation program" in which community members are trained by scientific organizations and universities in forest and water management, peasants chose to begin developing ecotourism in the preserve.[71] Economist David Barkin argues that the key features of successful solutions for these innovations are autonomy, self-sufficiency, and diversification of their products.

Yet for all the successes of Biosphere Reserves, the model remains limited by its reliance on professional scientists, its almost negligible capabilities for enforcement, and its economic dependence on foreign tourists and funders from wealthy nations.[72] Both are at risk of disappearing when political or economic conditions become unstable.[73] Biosphere Reserve coordinators must find a way to both meet ecological objectives and engage local people in project planning.[74] True "community-based conservation" is a real challenge because environmental planning often remains centralized in the hands of national governments.[75] The result is that people living inside biosphere reserves often feel marginalized from the very program designed to ensure their integration. In one study of the El Vizcaìno Biosphere Reserve in Mexico, for example, 55 percent of interviewees were unaware they lived in a Biosphere Reserve and another 9 percent misidentified it as a national park.[76] The trend toward decentralization in government authority across the region suggests some new opportunities, and pitfalls, for protected area management.[77]

New programs must work to reestablish the trust that was lost during decades of highly confrontational clashes between conservationists and Central American miners, farmers, and ranchers. In the 1980s, Costa Rica called in the National Guard to evict miners (like Juan Luís from Chapter 1) from the Corcovado National Park. Mexico, too, has used force against "squatters" inside Biosphere Reserves.[78] Even when people are compensated for their land, the results are often unsatisfactory for those expropriated. When Costa Rica expanded Guanacaste National Park in the late 1980s, large landholders were reportedly paid up to seven times more for their property than small landholders and squatters were paid.[79] Small landholders generally do not receive enough compensation money to purchase land of equal value, let alone enough to cover a move and downtime as farmers struggle to get their new land producing at the level of the land they were forced to give up. Other costs are entirely uncompensated, including the insurance provided through social bonds and community ties.

Each nation has an international reputation—Costa Rica as an environmental safe haven, Honduras a deforester—but these international reputations are not always reflective of a nation's true preservation record. Costa Rica has enjoyed widespread international recognition for creative conservation initiatives,[80] but its unique position in the global economy calls to question the reproducibility of its model. For example, over $80 million of Costa Rica's debt was purchased in the early 1990s with $12 million in private grants and donations, under different "debt for nature swap" programs adopted by some Northern environmental groups, banks, and aid agencies. These funds generated some $42 million in local currency bonds that financed important parts of the national conservation system.[81] It appears doubtful that other Central American nations will have comparable access to foreign capital as they expand their national park systems.

A much larger concern is the fact that Costa Rica continues to have the highest deforestation rates in the entire region.[82] When Costa Rica privatized park funding in the late 1980s, it was seen as a way to escape the hiring freeze mandated by budget-cutting demands from structural adjustment programs imposed by its most important lender, the International Monetary Fund. But in the bargain, Costa Rica privatized formerly state-run industries as well.[83] Large, multinational corporations received permission from the Costa Rican government to lumber most of the forests outside of the "islands" of protected areas for which Costa Rica is famous.[84] Once the fifth largest exporter of hardwoods in Latin America, Costa Rica is today a net importer of wood.[85]

While the Costa Rican park system was developed under the guidance of foreign scientists and Northern conservationists, the Honduran park system grew out of an effort to regain control over foreign-owned forests.[86] Honduras took the opposite approach of Costa Rica and set aside very little

land in parks. Most Honduran forests were actively lumbered, first by foreign and later by local firms. This local industry developed longer-term
methods to manage the forests (including replanting and furniture work-
shops) in what appears to be turning out to be a rather sustainable system.[87]
While its parks are deficient, and reforested areas are often lacking in biodiversity, it is possible that more forests may be preserved in Honduras because
there is less pressure on the remaining tracts of virgin wood.

The point is that we must look beyond protected areas for a broader
view of how forests and wildlife are doing in Central America. In 1997, the
nations of Central America recognized the need to develop an integrated
regional protection system and established a Mesoamerican Biological
Corridor. As envisioned, this corridor would provide a cross-border green
space for migrating animals stretching from southern Mexico along the
Atlantic coast of Belize and Guatemala all the way to the Choco region of
Panama. In the meantime, however, national sovereignty remains a huge
obstacle to regional conservation initiatives.

Overall, the Biosphere Reserves in Central America can largely be considered successes in slowing, if not halting, forest destruction. However, the success of each Biosphere Reserve remains delicately hinged on maintaining local
participation and support—without this support, many wind up like the Rio
Plátano reserve in Honduras. Rio Plátano is the largest of all Biosphere Reserves
in Central America, but it lost 12 percent of its southern territory from 1980
to 1992.[88] La Macarena national park in Colombia, too, has lost one fifth of
its forest.[89] A sharp debate has developed between those who believe that parks
can protect both nature and provide livelihoods for locals and those who
believe that realistically people must be excluded from protected areas if they
are indeed to be protected.[90] Internationally, some scientists are concluding
that "sustainable use" by humans has had devastating impacts on biodiversity
conservation in many parks.[91] They complain that parks cannot be expected
to "cure structural problems such as poverty, unequal land distribution and
resource allocation, corruption, economic injustice, and market failure."

We believe that both sides need to be addressed: protected areas *and* the
needs and land use of the people who live outside of them. Local people continue to feel excluded from key decisions regarding protected areas in
Central America. International NGOs such as the Nature Conservancy,
Conservation International, and World Wildlife Fund continue to play a
critical role as project initiators, facilitators, and underwriters. Their literature describes new participatory relations with local people. But together
with state governments and outside scientists, these actors define much of

the agenda governing local environmental management. Local people—some of whom are most sensitive to the particularities of their local ecosystem—are often among the last to be consulted about new protection initiatives. Some groups gain "a place at the table" where decisions are made over local resources, while others are excluded.[92] We understand that many people from the scientific and environmental communities are willing to side-step the cumbersome procedures necessary to achieve multilevel stakeholder support in the name of ecological urgency. In our opinion, this strategy is a misguided gamble with unfavorable long-term consequences. It begs the question, who are we saving the forests for? If we succeed in "saving" an ecosystem but lose the people that are a part of it, what have we really won?

Ecotourism: Salvation or Dead End?

There is tremendous excitement about ecotourism as a new development model for Latin America. The idea is this: Tourists (perhaps domestic but often international) pay an indigenous community, government agency, or private enterprise to "experience nature." This ecotravel minimizes a foreigner's overall ecological impact, and their payments help to finance conservation initiatives. Ecotours are often led by local guides and include hikes, birdwatching, and visits to cultural sites. Lodging and other accommodations seek to minimize excess luxuries and impacts. Environmental education is a cornerstone of the ecotourism philosophy—organizers hope that tourists will take home what they learn about delicate ecosystems. Today, ecotourism is the fastest growing sector of the global tourism industry and an important source of revenue for many Central American nations. But does ecotourism provide long-term, sustainable economic alternatives for developing nations?

Ecotourism developed as a way to commercialize the existence value of sensitive ecological regions, protecting forests and generating employment and income at the same time. As Theresa Zuniga of the Mesoamerican Biological Corridor Project explains, "What good would it be for our developing countries that have many large immediate needs to conserve nature if we don't derive economic benefits from it?"[93]

In some ways it is difficult to evaluate ecotourism because it is not universally defined. Ron Mader, Webmaster of the world's largest ecotourism Web site, "Ecotourism in the Americas" (www.planeta.com), suggests that a real ecotour "provides for conservation measures, includes meaningful community participation and is profitable and can sustain itself."[94] But a wide range of enterprises are touted as "ecolodges," "ecotours," "ecoresorts," or "ecoadventures." These vary from camping-only backcountry areas of national parks and private rainforest preserves, to the 296-room Club Las Velas in Quintana Roo, Mexico (complete with an eighteen-hole golf course, disco, and multiple swimming pools). Some argue that the term has been co-opted by mainstream travel providers, eager to "green" their standard packages and tap into the market.[95] These environmental opportunists package the same travel that was once considered exploitative in a green ribbon, and travelers return home with the illusion that their luxurious vacation was actually good for the environment. The lure is ingenious—who doesn't want to save the rainforests and protect indigenous cultures by sipping poolside daiquiris after a round of golf?

Although tours may cater to the global traveler, ecotours are intimately tied to place.[96] Ecotourist destinations cannot seek out a cheaper labor force in another nation, expand peak bird feeding times, or "upgrade" wildlife diversity—unlike most other economic enterprises, ecotourism is directly dependent on preservation for its very survival.[97] However, even environmentally benign projects, like observing or feeding wildlife, can be incredibly disruptive when repeated by flocks of ecotourists every day, or even several times a day. In Brazil's Iguacedillacu National Park, dolphins are forgetting how to hunt after being handfed by the 1 million plus tourists that visit the park each year.[98] Even with strict controls, the huge number of tourists visiting Ecuador's Galapagos Islands are having worrisome impacts on the terrestrial and aquatic ecosystems there. To use an old phrase, some would say that the areas are being "preserved to death."

Conversely, when ecoventures eliminate excessive consumption from a tour package, what is left to generate revenue? Even the most successful ecotourism operations have yet to achieve a convincing level of economic sustainability. Ecuador and Costa Rica are the most successful: Costa Rica's U.S.$700 million nature tourism[99] industry has now surpassed coffee and sugar as the nation's largest source of foreign dollars. Yet because of enduring economic problems, the nation is still struggling to fund its national park system. Like other green enterprises, ecotourism is struggling to redefine the meaning of "successful business" by incorporating new pricing mechanisms and nonfinancial indicators into their evaluation systems.

Ecotourism still has a long way to go, but it does mark a shift from the ideology that governed development in places like Cancun. Built from scratch along Mexico's Atlantic Coast in the late 1960s, Cancun is today promoted as "Mexico's Caribbean playground"—a twenty-six-kilometer stretch of hotels, condominiums, bars, restaurants, and modern convenience stores. The project far exceeded its economic expectations (it is the largest source of revenue for the state of Quintana Roo, generating U.S.$3 billion annually), but it has been something of an environmental disaster. Unregulated construction along the coast damaged the area's mangroves, lagoons, sand dunes, and the animals that depend on them. In sharp contrast to the state-of-the-art facilities that characterize Cancun resorts, the stream of job-seeking migrants has overtaxed an inadequate sewage system and a chronic lack of housing and other urban infrastructure. Now, tourist spillover to the "Mayan Riviera" south of Cancun appears to be spreading Cancun's environmental legacy along the entire Atlantic Coast of the Yucatan Peninsula.

As sociologist Ken Gould devastatingly documents, class, race, and gender divisions are often reinforced at large ecoventures. At Barry Bowen's elite $350 a night Belizean Chan Chich ecoresort, for example, racist "master-servant" relationships persist between "white" managers and mestizo/Mayan workers.[100] Ecotourism does not directly challenge the inequalities inherent in the global tourism industry; it is unlikely that ecotourism will ever generate the salaries necessary to grant tour guides their own vacations as ecotourists in the countries of their guests.

Ecotourism is built on other paradoxes as well. Since it relies on exotic natural places that are a novelty for at least moderately wealthy travelers from Northern countries, ecotourism requires the burning of large amounts of jet fuel or tour boat diesel to get there.[101] Building docks and airports for the large jets and deep-draft oceanliners has severe local ecological impacts. It requires enough disposable income, notes Gould, that travelers probably have to have invested money in the stocks of firms that make money destroying natural landscapes elsewhere in bringing products to market. Finally, the more successful an ecotourism establishment is, the more likely it is to destroy the very resource on which it was built. And so on.

Like Biosphere Preserves, this glass is half full *and* half empty. Ecotourism cannot be dismissed in one summary statement. In our research, ecotourism seems to work best when it is autonomously controlled by a community cooperative (like the Achuar Indians in Ecuador's Amazon[102]), under consensual rule with full profit-sharing. The degree to which ecotourism affects local communities and cultures depends on many factors: the scale of the project, the level of planning and local participation, and whether the project is controlled by the government, private sector, or community.[103] "Ecotourism doesn't leave much for the locals except low-level jobs," says Mexican author and environmental activist Homero Aridjis.

"Before ecotourism, these people were dignified loggers or fishermen. We shouldn't be turning them into busboys."[104]

One challenge then is to preserve the dignity of the ecotour concept through some sort of rigorous, independent labeling or evaluation process.[105] The more sustainable ecotourism operations must restrain their visitors' consumption: ecotour packages that include one nature hike during a weeklong rendezvous at a mega-ecoresort are less environmentally sustainable than small-scale operations in which tourists more closely emulate the living conditions of their host community/nation. But as long as ecotourism remains dependent on the international economy it appears it will be influenced, and ultimately overpowered, by the corporations (and local elites) that dominate the industry.[106] It is unlikely these companies will downshift so drastically. And the burden does not fall exclusively on the supply side—consumers of ecotravel experiences also have a responsibility to research their travel destinations and support enterprises that reflect their convictions.

Contentious Globalization: International Law, Treaties, Green Labeling, and Human Rights

The case of DBCP poisoning described at the beginning of this chapter is a striking example of land-based problems in Central America, but it is also a fascinating case in international law. Recall that in the 1970s and 1980s tens of thousands of workers were sterilized by exposure to the nematicide DBCP. Also recall that U.S. firms continued to export the chemical after it was found to harm workers and after it was made illegal in the United States. Pesticide exporting firms did not bargain on winding up in court—and certainly did not expect to lose. The case suggests how recent advancements in international law may indicate that a new system of justice is opening up for the people of the developing world.

Between 1983 and 1991 approximately four hundred sterile workers sued plantation operator Standard Fruit as well as DBCP producers Dow Chemical and Shell Oil in U.S. courts for their negligence in failing to inform workers of the associated health risks. Workers also claim to have suffered emotional and psychological damage including mental depression, impotence, alcoholism, and increased divorce rates.

In 1992, 981 Costa Rican workers settled for $20 million with Dow and Shell companies, which after their legal costs netted them from $2,000 to $20,000 each.[107] By comparison, U.S. workers sterilized from DBCP have received over $1 million *each* from the defendants. And in 1993, another suit was filed in Texas, representing the sixteen thousand workers from around the world. Justice Lloyd Doggett's decision to allow the suit in a Texas court was a pivotal step in the international struggle to make transnational corporations more accountable to their employees.[108] In 2001, the law firm that helped in Erin Brockovich's famous case began taking three thousand Nicaraguan banana workers in a class-action suit against the banana and chemical companies, 130 plaintiffs at a time.[109] "We will file on a rolling basis," attorney Walter J. Lack was quoted as saying. "Every 60 days, there will be a new batch." These plaintiffs are suing for $1 million per person.

Their case proposes that the principal determinants in the case were political-economic and social factors—not technical or procedural factors as claimed by Dow and Shell. Specifically, the plaintiffs argued that the "dominance of profit interests, . . . [as well as] control over information and technology by the manufacturers (who concealed early toxicological research evidence of the reproductive hazards) and by the managers of the banana producer-companies" influenced and ultimately determined the case.[110] Although the scientific and regulatory system put in place by the U.S. Environmental Protection Agency (EPA) could have been extended to protect foreign workers, he argued, existing safeguards were overwhelmed by the interests of Dow, Shell, and Dole.

International treaties and agreements are also helping to slow land destruction and contamination in Central America. One of the three major treaties coming out of the 1992 Earth Summit in Rio de Janeiro was the Convention on Biodiversity, which attempts to value species preservation by providing a portion of the profits from the development of medicines and rainforest products to the producing nation. Another more recent treaty is the International Convention on persistent organic pollutants (POPs). Several of the toxic pesticides mentioned in this chapter are included in this new treaty and are scheduled to be phased out globally. However, there is an ongoing battle over how to add chemicals to the original list of just twelve with which it began.[111]

Internationally, there is also an agreement in discussion about the international trade in timber, which would make it more difficult to illegally harvest and sell lumber from areas in preservation. More consumers now are demanding to know that the wood they buy is not coming from the destruction of the rainforest. It is having an impact: the market for so-called green wood now represents 2–3 percent of all tropical hardwood imported into North America and Europe. This number sounds small, but after intense activist campaigns by the Rainforest Alliance and Rainforest Action Network, two of North America's largest lumber suppliers, Home Depot and Lowe's, agreed to stop buying wood from old-growth forests. Rainforest Alliance's "Smart Wood" program certifies U.S. timber importers, wholesalers, and retailers; "Green Cross" does life-cycle assessment of timber resources (affiliated with The Knoll Group, Westinghouse Electric). Pacific Certified Ecological Forest Products (Institute for Sustainable Forestry) is another licenser.

On the supply side, alternative organizations of harvesters, including indigenous groups and neighborhood co-operatives, have become global players in the timber trade. Traditional logging industries as well as this new breed of community harvesters have developed innovative harvesting methods in response to both dwindling forest resources and First World consumer demand. For example, the Yanesha Forestry Cooperative in central Peru naturally stimulates forest growth by permitting direct sunlight to penetrate the forest canopy through thirty- to fifty-yard strips of cut forest. This "strip shelterbelt" technique is one of several alternative harvesting techniques, along with directional felling, selective harvesting (removing trees of a certain diameter or species without disturbing surrounding trees), and natural forest regeneration (in which one or two trees are removed from each acre on a fifteen- or thirty-year cycle).[112]

Governments in Central America have tremendous power to reverse deforestation trends—in 1992, for instance, the Honduran government was reported to have rejected a proposal by Stone Container to construct a massive tree plantation in an area of virgin pine forest. Some state governments are increasingly prohibiting cutting in primary forests, opting instead to concentrate harvesting activity in expansive tree plantations. Stone Container, Scott Paper, Champion International, and other multinational logging corporations today operate small and medium-size forest plantations in previously damaged soils throughout Central America. These plantations may eventually relieve pressure on old-growth forests, but many argue that monoculture tree plantations, usually using fast-growing *gmelina* or non-native eucalyptus trees, are a tremendous threat to biodiversity, and do not address global overconsumption of forest resources. Plantations also have squeezed small farmers. Certainly these points have merit. Still, legal, treaty, and labeling efforts are promising uses of globalization to improve the conditions of Central American lands and people, if consumers are savvy and international institutions are strong.

Before leaving this topic, we must remember that there is a perilous local reality faced by those on the ground in Central America: private violence and government violations of human rights. In the mid-1990s, two peasant environmental activists from Mexico's Sierra de Petalàn mountains (near Acapulco), Rodolfo Montiel and Teodoro Cabrera, lead a movement to halt logging there. They successfully forced the U.S.-based lumber company Boise Cascade to withdraw operations from the region in 1998. The Oganization of Campesino (Small Farmer) Ecologists, with whom Montiel and Cabrera worked, believe that indiscriminate logging in the region has destroyed the forest and devastated yields for subsistence farmers. In May 1999, Montiel and Cabrera were arrested on trumped-up charges of firearm and marijuana possession. Two months later, the Mexico Commission on Human Rights reported that the men had been tortured into signing false confessions.[113]

Both men had been recognized internationally for their work and were declared "prisoners of conscience" by Amnesty International. From jail, Montiel received two of the highest environmental honors, the Goldman environmental prize and the Chico Mendes award. Under intense international pressure led by a joint Sierra Club–Amnesty International campaign (including a petition signed by over forty members of the U.S. Congress), in November 2001 both men were released from jail.

Not all Latin American environmental activists have been as fortunate as Montiel and Cabrera and many have lost their lives fighting for changes. Digna Ochoa, a well-known human rights activist who had worked on the Montiel-Cabrera case, was murdered in her law office on October 18, 2001. Medardo Varela, the leader of a Honduran struggle to seek compensation for banana workers sterilized from DBCP, was murdered in his hometown of Sava in 1998. In 1997, Guatemalan Carlos Catalan was murdered for his work (with Conservation International) to curb illegal activities such as logging and poaching in the Maya Biosphere Reserve. Three years later in February 2000 environmental activists Erwin Ochoa López and Julio Vásquez Ramírez were also murdered in Guatemala. Ochoa in particular was known for his pursuit of environmental lawbreakers, and both victims were employees of Puerto Barrios's protected areas council CONAP.[114]

The deaths of Gonzales, Varela, Ochoa, and Vásquez suggest that we must turn our focus to the social and political underpinnings of environmental violence. Their deaths, coupled with high deforestation rates, growing regional economic inequality, and acute and chronic pesticide exposures, raise important questions about the future of conservation in Latin America.

Envisioning Alternative Futures: Social Forestry, Fair Trade, and Organic Farming

There are three other positive trends for Central America's lands and people that we would like to discuss briefly, but their future is also uncertain. Traditional farming techniques provided a sustainable lifestyle for Central America's farmers until recently—in this sense, campesinos have been guided by the principals of sustainable agriculture for centuries.[115] Today, however, the concept of sustainable farming is much different than it was three hundred years ago. Cornerstones of traditional farming systems (such as rotating crops and long fallow periods) are often no longer socially or financially possible.[116] Today, land is extremely scarce in Central America, and agricultural policy is dominated by the profitable lure of export cash crops.

Subsistence farming became even harder as campesinos were pushed out of fertile lowlands onto hillsides, into steep, easily eroded soils and other marginal environments. In this context, the resiliency of native farming techniques and their campesino practitioners is remarkable. Many farmers have adapted traditional techniques to new markets and consumer demands. Traditional production cooperatives, still standard among many of Central America's indigenous peoples, are becoming popular with some other farmers (such as the huge landless workers movement in Brazil) as a way of gaining some autonomy and economic power in a world of big players.

A variety of methods fall under the umbrella of "alternative agriculture." Here we focus on *organic* food and plant production (produced without artificial pesticides), *social forestry* (extracting forest goods in a controlled, sustainable manner), and the *fair trade* way of marketing products (in which artisans/producers are paid a fair, living wage for their exported products).

It is important to understand how the traditional pricing system short-changes farmers: presently, for every $1 paid at a U.S. supermarket for a Guatemalan cantaloupe, 79 cents go to U.S. brokers, shippers, wholesalers, and retailers. Five cents are spent on chemicals, seeds, and fertilizers (all imported from the United States) and 4 cents go to domestically purchased inputs. Only 1 cent of every dollar paid for a cantaloupe goes to the contract farmer.[117]

Economic incentives for sustainable agriculture can be every bit as persuasive as social and ecological motivators. Organic farming relies more on labor (an abundant resource in Central America) rather than costly pesticides, seeds, and imported machinery. The one outstanding new cost required of all exporting producers—getting certified by a third-party organic agency—

might be creatively offset through marketing and production co-ops. Profits from shade grown coffee (which preserves some diversity and wildlife shelter in coffee groves), fair trade cacao (in which producers receive more of the profits than in traditional arrangements using middlemen), and organic bananas are funneled directly back into the hands of small farmers.[118] New research shows that consumers are often willing to pay higher prices for organic products, even if product quality and consistency vary.[119] "Farmers here [in the rural community of Cipreses de Oreamuno] have a different mentality," said Rafael "Macho" Coto, president of the Association of Organic Farmers of Cartago in Costa Rica. "Organic farming has changed everything."[120]

Fairtrade.org and other new networks market bananas in the United Kingdom from Costa Rica while considering the social conditions of workers. Fairtrade sets aside a "social premium" for community improvements, which are based on local decisions about priority needs.[121] FairTradeMark Canada licenses seals of approval on coffee and other products, costing about 16 cents more per three-hundred-gram package, or about a penny a cup. By 1996 fair trade seals covered 4 million pounds of coffee beans in thirty-five-thousand supermarkets. The groups suggest consumers ask about brands in supermarkets, coffee shops, and offices. The labels often cover whether the coffee was produced with traditional shade-grown trees or by new more chemical-intensive sun-grown varieties. After receiving negative reports on conditions at Guatemalan coffee plantations, activists in Seattle began a leafleting campaign at Starbucks to force the firm to screen its suppliers. The firm adopted a "Code of Conduct" and addressed several of the issues, leading to the lifting of the campaign.[122] On the positive side, Starbucks agreed to buy 1 million pounds of organic coffee over an eighteen-month period. On the negative side, this represented less than 1 percent of their coffee purchases.[123]

Overall, state support for sustainable farming techniques varies tremendously from country to country. El Salvador and Honduras have received very little state resources; Costa Rica, by contrast, has had a state-supported National Organic Farming Committee since 1995. By 1997, Costa Rica had passed an organic certification statute into law. In 1994, the U.S. EPA said it would spend U.S.$4 million in technical assistance to help developing nations reduce their use of pesticides.[124]

However, the most sweeping alternative agriculture programs in Latin America (and perhaps in the entire hemisphere) are happening in Cuba, where alternative agriculture lies at the core of national development schemes. With the fall of the Soviet Union in 1989, Cuba lost its primary source of food, pesticides and fuel imports, and market for its sugar. In des-

peration, Cuba rerouted its agricultural focus (from a petrochemical intensive monocrop sugar export economy) and almost overnight embarked on
the most widespread organic experiment in the modern world.
Agrochemicals were banned for use in the capital and have been significantly
reduced elsewhere in the country. While most sugar and tobacco are still produced with pesticides, more than half of the 6.2 million acres of nonsugar
farmland in Cuba are totally organic.[125]

Trained state agronomists, centralized control over agricultural inputs,
and, ironically, the U.S. embargo all helped propel Cuba's agricultural revolution. But because Cubans literally have no access to chemicals, critics fear
that organic production may end when money and petrochemicals become
available as the economy emerges from its current depression, euphemisti-
cally called the "Special Period."[126] State planners, however, insist that recent
agricultural changes are permanent and a natural extension of Cuba's forty-
year commitment to worker safety and environmental health. "These
changes [in Cuban agriculture] are not temporary. When a farmer learns a
better way to produce, this knowledge does not disappear. Here in the coun-
tryside we are sharing information that will sustain my children and my
children's children," Cuban Luís Sanchez told us in the spring of 2000.[127]

The massive food shortages that accompanied the initial stages of Cuba's
organic revolution hardly make it a blueprint for other nations, but its successes are truly remarkable—in just one year, Cuba was able to increase its
total food production by 30 percent and reduce its fertilizer use by 90 percent. Cuba has also successfully encouraged urbanites to grow their own food:
In the first half of 2000, some 100,000 urban gardens produced 690 tons of
fresh vegetables and spices.[128] Officials expect urban harvest yields to reach 2.3
million tons by 2005. In rural areas, state agronomists provide free trees to aid
in soil conservation and advise campesinos about ecological pest control and
organic fertilizers. Sales on Biasav, the line of completely biological herbicides
and pesticides made by Cuba's Institute for Crop Protection INISAV, were
reported to be doing well, but farmers had few options.

Cuba has been able to transform economic desperation and authoritarian
isolation into something of a model of sustainable agriculture. Delegations
from Britain, Italy, the United States, and almost all of Latin America have
traveled to observe Cuban production methodologies. But Cuba still has a
long way to go—it still imports almost half of its food and consumes $100
million worth of fuel, $80 million worth of chemical fertilizers, and $30 million worth of pesticides each year.[129] Cuba's unique history, geography, climate,
and political system call into question the reproducibility of the model.

Many nations (as well as conventional producers like Dole and Del Monte) have expressed an interest in alternative agriculture because they see it as a lucrative niche market. In this sense, the Cuban project is distinct from all the other alternative projects we've highlighted in this chapter. In Cuba, the need or desire to create a self-sustaining, *domestic* food supply, not the magnetism of world market forces, provided the major impetus for a shift to organics. Their road to organics in agriculture has been an anti-globalization road.

Finally, it is important to remember that *organic* and *sustainable* are not interchangeable synonyms. In examining the full "ecological footprint" of transporting an organic banana, Smart Wood 2×4, or hand-painted gourd from Central America to First World markets, it becomes obvious that we must rethink the sustainability of global agricultural trade altogether.

As we described in Chapter 1, land reform never was completed in most Latin American nations. Latin American countrysides are the site of old struggles over land in which small farmers have tended to lose out again and again to ranches and large plantations. Campesinos have been left with the discouraging options of migrating to a city (see Chapter 4), working as a poorly paid wage laborer at a plantation, or invading marginal environments like rainforests or hillsides. We'll see how this is also some of the story in Brazil's massive Amazon forest in Chapter 5.

Those farmers who are able to transition to medium or large-scale farming are pushed into the need to protect their investments in seeds and fertilizers with pesticides. This is when Latin American farmers begin to have similar environmental profiles as the large corporations who grow export crops in expansive plantations. Even under the "safest" of circumstances, Latin Americans are constantly at risk of being contaminated or poisoned by agropesticides.

We don't know how many human victims and how much ecological damage the incautious use of pesticides claims on each side of the North–South divide, but we do have a series of possible solutions to reduce the impact on Central American lands: addressing poverty and fertility control; developing Biosphere Reserves that truly incorporate local needs and aspirations; investing in community-based conservation and serious ecotourism, social forestry, and organic agriculture; and strengthening existing international mechanisms like fair trade, environmental treaties, and green labeling. There is no silver bullet for Central America, but rather, like so many other cases we discuss, a series of concrete and viable steps for change.

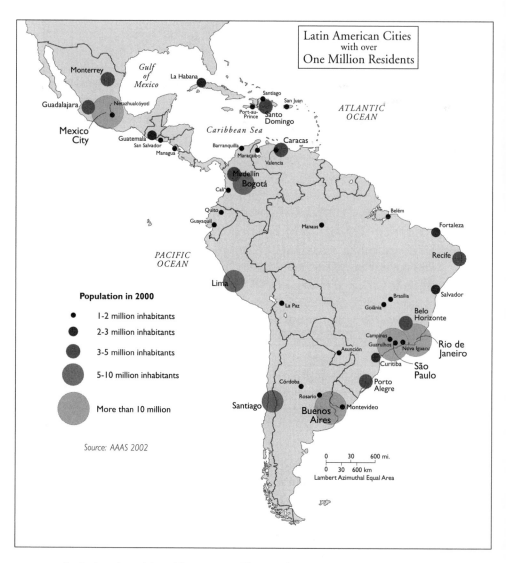

Latin American cities with over one million residents, 2000. Circle sizes represent number of residents. Source: AAAS 2002.

CHAPTER 4

Hazards of an Urban Continent

Monday afternoon, 5 P.M. The sun is dropping quickly, casting shadows across the graying apartment buildings and tropical palms of Copacabana, one of Latin America's most glamorous beaches. In the distance lie the Tijuca mountains and the remnants of the Atlantic Forest that once stretched for a thousand miles along the Brazilian coast, now 93 percent deforested. At the tallest peak stands the Corcovado, an enormous concrete statue of Jesus Christ with outstretched arms, and on the other side, the city's other signature, the Sugarloaf mountain. On its other side, the gorgeous white sand beaches that stretch between the stunning mountains form the edge of the Guanabara Bay, an immense body of water (381 square kilometers) that once made the city the key to controlling the Brazilian coast and trails to the gold mines, in struggles between the Portuguese, the French, and the Dutch.

Exhausted from a ten-hour day washing dishes and clothes and cleaning the apartment of a wealthy family two blocks back from Copacabana beach, Clede lifts her shopping bags off the black-and-white mosaic sidewalk, too tired to notice the striking patterns of tiles laid out for miles in the tourist districts. As she crosses the bike path that runs along the beach, two deeply tanned women in tiny bikinis wearing Walkmans and chatting nearly knock her over as they speed by on Rollerblades. Clede walks to a thatch-roofed beach bar/stall where a seven-foot-high cage holding coconuts advertises in a handwritten sign: "Coco R$1." She buys a tiny plastic cup of sweetened expresso and a *salgadinha* (a salty fried piece of bread stuffed with chicken) and turns back to wait for her bus. The noise of the traffic is growing to a deafening level as car horns, buses, and unmufflered motorcycles crowd the road.

Rio has some social similarities to Los Angeles: It is an intensely urban, beach society, with a large music, video, and film industry and an internationally sophisticated class of extremely wealthy residents. But the contrasts are even more stark: Chic apartment buildings occupy the dozen blocks closest to the beach, giving way as the hills begin to rise steeply to a sloping cascade of squatter shacks, called *favelas* in Brazil. Over time, most of these squatter shacks have slowly been upgraded to precarious brick houses, accessed along steep staircases that cut through narrow passageways along the hillside. During occasional torrential rainstorms, mudslides have washed away hillside shelters, taking with them their favela residents.[1]

Rio's downtown streets were cleaned up in 1992 for the UN Conference on Environment and Development (UNCED), known to the world as the "Rio Earth Summit," and to Brazilians simply as "Rio '92." During the conference, street people were hauled away, the area was spruced up, and military police were stationed on every corner. Motorcades of dignitaries and heads of states pulsed through the streets to the official meetings, while tens of thousands of environmentalists from around the world held a parallel "unofficial" meeting nearby. Hosting the conference was a way for Brazilian president Fernando Collor de Melo to rebuild the nation's green image and quiet criticism from foreign governments and investors about the destruction of the Amazon (see Chapter 5). Today, Rio '92 is a fading memory, and the city's tourism industry struggles in an area plagued by violent crime and environmental degradation.

Clede's bus finally comes, a hulking 1980s model with "740D—Niterói" in the window. She climbs in the back and hands the eighteen-year-old collector R$2.20 for the ride. She flops down in the plastic seat and the bus lunges forward, bouncing over the potholed roads and jerking her left and right as the driver speeds around turns like the late Brazilian racecar driver Airton Senna.

After traveling through the tunnel cut from the stunning mountains that connects Copacabana to the business center of Rio, Clede's bus passes the huge Flamengo Beach park. The water here is contaminated virtually every day of the year with the sewage of clandestine and broken sewers. Still, the park is a popular spot for jogging, beach volleyball, and soccer games that run all night long. Everyone once assumed the "black tongues" of sewage spoiling the beach originated from the favelas that lay behind the apartment buildings of Rio's upper class, but research showed that even some of the most deluxe towers were illegally dumping their sewage into the river.

A coalition of environmentalists and wealthy and poor neighborhood groups got together around the Earth Conference to stop the sewage or at least divert the "black tongues" away from the beach. However, the problems of Flamengo Beach recur frequently as construction projects are delayed by squabbles between the state and local government, as new clandestine hookups put sewage in the storm sewers, and as raw human waste washes up the beach from other parts of the Guanabara Bay.

Racing past the financial center of downtown, the bus passes enormous rotting port warehouses from before the era of containerization, spraypainted with revolutionary, electioneering, and adolescent graffiti: "Down with imperialism!" "Vote for Nelson #32154," "Bregazinho." Rising up on the overpass, Clede notices several colorful African-themed *carnaval* float heads and props in a warehouse, but the splendid decadent festival that transforms the city for five magical days and nights each Lenten Season is still months away. Beside the elevated highway, huge cranes work day and night loading steel coils and containers onto freighters, while thousands of General Moters cars sit waiting for export demand. Not far from the other side of the ramp to the Rio-Niterói Bridge, a small oil refinery adds to the city's ripe mix of smells and smog.

"Don't throw litter from the bridge" reads the sign, as the vista opens up over the spectacular Guanabara Bay. Despite contamination from sewage, oil production, urban runoff, sedimentation, and many other sources, fishing boats still can be seen plying the waters. "Artisanal" oyster fishers snorkel along the rocks, throwing their catch into floating bins. Huge tanker and freighter boats wait for their turn to load and unload as Navy cruisers stand guard at bases on both sides of the bridge. A 737 swoops down over the bus in its final descent into Santos Dumont airport, built, like Flamengo Beach park, atop landfill in the bay. Back behind the bay is the Angra I nuclear power plant, built by Westinghouse, which finally opened in 1985 after some fifteen years of delays due to cost overruns and technical problems.[2] Locally it's known as the "firefly" powerplant because it so frequently flickers on and off. At one point the plant was closed for six months to repair cracks, but after these repairs, on May, 28, 2001, it leaked twenty-two thousand liters of radioactive water. So as to "not alarm residents," the problem was kept from the public for four months.

Approaching the far shore, a regatta of picturesque sailboats plies the far shore near Niterói. Right next to the bridge stand three huge oil platforms undergoing repairs and construction. Since Brazil first discovered oil deposits off its coast in the late 1970s, it has become a world leader in deepwater drilling. The state-owned company Petrobras now produces 70 percent of the nation's petroleum needs. There are frequent leaks from drilling rigs and pipelines in the Guanabara Bay, including a leak in January 2000: 1.3 million liters of oil spilled from a pipeline from a tanker loading to the platform of the chronically polluting Duque de Caxias refinery.[3] The most famous disaster, however, occurred off the Brazilian coast in March 2001 when the world's largest oil platform, Plataforma 36, tipped slowly into the sea after an explosion in one of its legs caused the structure to collapse. Eleven workers died and the half-billion-dollar rig lay on the ocean floor under forty-five hundred feet of sea water.

Reaching the far shore, Clede's bus swoops down the off-ramp to the center of Niterói, a rather sad-looking fringe city of ten-story offices, apartments, and shops outside sprawling Rio. It is now home to one-fifth of greater Rio's 12.5 million people. Clede's bus pauses to let off about half of the passengers at the waterfront bus and ferry stations, then twists along the coastal mountains, passing poor women and children waiting for buses in front of a fence that separates them from the spectacular pools of the Praia San Francisco Beach Club and the Icaraí Yacht Club. Members at these resorts enjoy clean pool water to swim in and a spectacular view down the beach and across the bay to Rio. The annual membership starts around R$2,000, as much as Clede will make in eleven months in her job as a domestic servant.[4]

As the bus turns away from the bay toward the interior, Clede alerts the driver of her upcoming stop with a pull to the hanging cord and its brusque buzzer. Passing luxury homes in gated communities and clusters of shacks, gated communities and piles of garbage, Clede gathers her bags and navigates the moving bus as it lurches to a halt. As the bus roars away, Clede trudges past enormous mansions up a side path to her squatter-settled neighborhood behind. Every house here seems to be in a state of construction, with rusting rebar sticking out of concrete pillars on the roof and cheap orange bricks half covered with stucco. Clede is a single mother, and her home is a small place to raise her two children, eight and ten years old. She gathers her girls from her mother's house on the corner and brings them home for dinner. It's seven o'clock. She's spent almost half of her day's salary of R$9 on the bus, the *salgadinha*, and the expresso. The air is thick with the smell of some neighbors burning their garbage in small piles near the street.

An Urban Continent and Its Unmet Needs

Cities are of critical importance for the global environment: a recent report estimated that globally, cities use 60 percent of all freshwater and 75 percent

of all industrial wood and are the source of 80 percent of the main gas causing the greenhouse effect, carbon dioxide.[5] The figures would be higher if we
had data on other pollutants and garbage. As go the cities, so goes the earth.

Latin America is the most urbanized part of the developing world, with
380 million of its 507 million residents—three in every four Latin
Americans—experiencing their lives as urban.[6] This makes the region starkly
different from Asia and Africa, where only 30–35 percent of residents live in
cities.[7] There are now an astounding fifty-two cities in the region with populations over 1 million. And there are four megacities almost unimaginable
in their scale: 12.5 million in greater Rio de Janeiro, 13 million in the
Buenos Aires metropolitan area, 22 million in greater São Paulo, and 25.6
million in the sprawl of Mexico City, one of the largest cities in the world.[8]
Behind them are ten other cities with populations well over 3 million: Lima,
Bogotá, Santiago de Chile, Carácas, Belo Horizonte, Guadalajara, Porto
Alegre, Monterrey, Recife, and Salvador.

Urban environmental issues in Latin America are many and complex, as
Clede's commute from work only begins to suggest. Sometimes these environmental issues rise to the level of consciousness for urban residents, but
often they simply form the backdrop for their lives. Some of these issues
were long listed under the category of "public health" or basic sanitation, but
they have been "environmentalized" since the 1992 Earth Summit, which
sought to bring together environment and development issues.[9] The list of
urban environmental issues might vary depending on whom one consulted,
but it would probably include unsafe drinking water, untreated sewage, air
pollution from vehicles and factories, the illegal and improper dumping of
solid waste (trash), contaminated soils from sloppy industrial facilities, and
sprawling urban growth destroying drinking water supply reserves and other
protected areas. These are critical problems in virtually every major city from
the United States–Mexico border to the Southern Cone nations of Argentina
and Chile.[10] As Brazilian Carlos Minc puts it, "Ecology in the Third World
begins with water, garbage, and sewage. Here, the 'hole in the ozone layer' is
right on the surface, inside the house."[11]

To begin at the top, clearly the most important are sewage and water.
Some estimates are that up to 80 percent of illnesses in the region and one-
third of deaths are the result of contaminated water.[12] The World Bank dedicated its influential *World Development Report* in 1992 to addressing
"Development and the Environment" in order to express their position in
time for the 1992 Rio Earth Summit. At the top of their list of "priorities for
action" in the volume were urban environmental issues: For "the one-third

of the world's population that has inadequate sanitation and the one billion without safe water . . . providing access . . . would not eradicate all these diseases, but it would be the single most effective means of alleviating human distress."[13] The 1996–1997 issue of *World Resources*, a joint effort between the World Bank, the UN Environment and Development Programmes, and the World Resources Institute, focused on *The Urban Environment*, echoing this point and covered the issues in somewhat greater depth.

Looking around the region, it can be said that most houses, apartments, and office buildings in the big cities have running water and pipes taking sewage away. Official statistics report national averages of from 60 to 100 percent of homes having "access to sanitation services."[14] However, it is shocking to discover that a vast majority of the sewage is merely dumped downstream or out at sea without treatment. By the early 1990s, Santiago de Chile was still only treating 4 percent of its sewage, Buenos Aires only 5 percent, and São Paulo only 10 percent.[15] The sewage water is often dumped into open drainage canals that flow into urban rivers. In many cases the poorest people must build their houses along these rivers or drainage canals because it is the only affordable place they can live. They are also subject to periodic but unpredictable floods of the contaminated waters. Because of all the fatal and debilitating diseases caused by "fecal–oral" contamination, to say "human feces remain one of the world's most hazardous pollutants" is a fair portrayal.[16] But to say so raises a million questions about why the situation has been allowed to reach this point.

The case of São Paulo is striking. Probably the financial capital of South America, the city's four-lane highways, offices, and apartments stretch for miles along the Tieté River, which is both a drainage canal and an open sewer. Making matters worse, the river is pumped uphill to the Billings reservoir, the water supply for much of the city. In 1911 the Canadian electricity firm "Light" and U.S. engineer Kenney Billings suggested building a reservoir to generate electricity, by dropping the water a thousand meters down the steep hillside that separates the city from the ocean.[17] Being solely concerned with generating electricity, the firm bought only the lands that would be inundated by the dam's floodwaters, leaving the rest of its watershed to private ranchers. The reservoir served as a tourist attraction for decades, being an elite neighborhood called by some "the Brazilian Switzerland."

This was the case until the arrival of the automobile industry in the 1950s and 1960s. When thousands of migrants looking for work in the factories of the ABC districts of Sao Paulo were unable to find suitable housing elsewhere, they settled along the margins of the reservoir. These shantytowns lacked sewage treatment entirely, so the waste flowed directly into the reservoir. Often local governments did not want to "regularize" shantytowns by providing basic urban services like sewage and water, since by so doing they would be giving the squatters tacit permission to stay on the land they invaded without proper ownership. The cycle is perpetuated because local governments lack the resources to provide adequate housing and because squatters represent needed blocks of potential voters.

Laws passed in the 1970s to protect the Billings reservoir watershed were widely ignored, and the several municipalities that the reservoir crosses battle with the state to gain finances for the extremely expensive projects needed to pipe and treat the sewage.[18] Threats to the watershed continue as encroaching development and untreated water flow in: Touring the reservoir in 1993 and 2001 the smell of sewage was noticeable anytime we were downwind. In 2001 there was a nice new bike and jogging path along the shore, but hundreds of plastic bottles and other garbage had washed up just yards away.[19] More difficult still are conflicts between environmentalists attempting to protect the watershed and social justice groups and municipalities who see the need for more housing in the immensely crowded city.[20]

We in the wealthier nations take for granted that safe and plentiful drinking water will be just the turn of a faucet away. Much of Latin America has unpredictable water service, so those with plumbing and who can afford it design their houses to accommodate a five hundred or one thousand liter tank on the roof, which is filled when the water is running. But in the poorest neighborhoods, many families must seek out water by the bucket from a communal faucet or well, or pay a water truck to come deliver a barrelfull. In Lima, Peru, residents in the *pueblos jovenes* (young towns) shanty-settled neighborhoods pay up to twenty times more per liter than weathier customers because they have to have their water delivered by truck, something we witnessed in 1986.[21] Millions of people in various parts of the continent are still forced to bathe, wash clothing by hand, and collect water for household use from polluted wells and contaminated waterways.

So, behind the national averages of 60 or 90 percent of households having sewer pipes or drinking water lie extremely different experiences of life for the poor and for the wealthier residents. And these differences can mean life and death: globally 2–3 million children a year are estimated to die from diarrheal diseases; they cause almost 2 *billion* illnesses a year.[22] Latrines are still very common in poor neighborhoods, but to use them safely requires much better hygiene behavior than for people with piped water.[23] There are many places around Latin America that even lack latrines, so people urinate and defecate in the open. Ironically, this is often safer for the user than a dirty shared latrine.[24] The smell is distinctive, but you get used to it.

Air pollution is nearly as deadly: The World Bank calculated that "If emissions could be reduced . . . an estimated 300,000–700,000 lives could be saved each year, and many more people would be spared the suffering caused by chronic respiratory difficulties." The problems are driven by four main sources: industries, vehicles, power plants, and dust. They are worst in cities where mountains hold in warmer, polluted air: Santiago, Mexico City, Carácas. They are also the result ultimately of the forces that created such huge "primate" cities: Only Colombia and Brazil vary from the Latin American pattern of huge capital cities with large proportions of the nation's population and wealth. For example, Mexico City includes almost 20 percent of the whole nation's population, and one-third of the entire national GDP. (This would be the equivalent of New York City holding 60 million people.) This pattern stemmed originally from the way the continent was settled by the Spanish—with cities as points of military and administrative control for a vast unsettled area of empire. But the "primacy" was heightened when twentieth-century "import substitution" (ISI) policies (discussed in Chapter 1) favored production for the local market. Most of the suppliers of parts and nearly all the potential consumers for manufactured products were in the same primate city, so it paid to locate factories there.

Take thousands of poorly regulated and often inefficient factories and add a skyrocketing number of vehicles—automobiles have recently become affordable for significant proportions of the population—and you have a recipe for an air quality disaster. Because it is expensive and technically difficult, it was not until fairly recently that Mexico, Brazil, and Venezuela took lead out of gasoline and forced new car venders to install catalytic converters to control emissions.[25] Many other countries still use leaded gasoline, which can lead to devastating neurological effects in children from the dust it creates. Even with improving emissions controls, transport vehicles are estimated to cause three-quarters of the smog in Mexico City and over 80 percent of smog in other cities such as those of Central America.[26] The numbers are staggering: In 1994 (the last year for which data were available) Mexico City's air contained more than double the levels of total suspended particulates set by the World Health Organization.[27] Accordingly, some 2 million inhabitants of the Mexico Valley Metropolitan Area (MVMA) suffer from diseases caused or aggravated by air pollution.[28] Air quality alerts are frequent occurrences in Santiago de Chile, São Paulo, Carácas, and several other Latin American cities.

On April 23 and 24, 2000, smog put Santiago, Chile's, 5 million inhab-itants under an environmental "state of emergency."[29] This meant that the one thousand largest factories had to shut down, and 40 percent of the cars (those using leaded gasoline and without catalytic converters) were banned from the roads. In a controversial step, the National Environmental Commission (CONAMA) banned all vehicles except buses from Santiago's six major avenues, to speed travel for buses and encourage car drivers to use them. Mexico City has long used the *Hoy no circula* program, forbidding each car from driving one day a week in the Federal District, depending on its license number. Administrators have discovered, however, that these pro-grams have often been undermined by those who can afford it, who simply buy another car. The 1991–1992 smog seasons in Mexico City were among the worst, with twenty-eight days of a state of environmental emergency, forcing a PEMEX refinery and six hundred other plants to be temporarily or permanently shuttered.[30] The longer-term solutions are more expensive: For example, Chilean president Ricardo Lago put forward a plan developed by his predecessors that included relocating industries, expanding bus and metro systems, paving dirt streets in poor neighborhoods, and reforesting the city.[31] The mayor of Bogotá, Colombia, has gained international attention with his efforts to get people to get out of their cars and to commute by bicy-cle: One day he simply banned car usage.

Garbage is a major unresolved problem in much of the region, and it is linked in several ways to the problem of sewage. First, substantial propor-tions of city populations lack proper and frequent pickup of waste. In Guatemala City this is reported to be true for over a third of the residences, and this number may be reflective of many other cities around the region.[32] The situation is especially bad in poor neighborhoods, so residents often throw garbage in inappropriate places, such as drains, canalized rivers, parks, and empty lots. In the canals, plastic and other waste clog the flow of stormwater and create toxic flooding.

In many places, trash is burned in small piles in streets and empty lots. Because most of the region's sewage pipes are considered too fragile to handle it, the custom most places is to place used toilet paper in the garbage. When hauled off to the dump, trash is picked over by garbage pickers, who recycle substantial proportions of what would otherwise be wastes. Thousands live on or near dumps doing this work; others patrol neighborhoods and business dis-tricts for any recyclable materials. Elaborate organizations of these garbage-pickers exist in many cities, often controlled by political parties and sometimes linked to large transnational corporations who buy their product as cheap raw materials. There are a series of hazards for the sanitation workers and garbage-pickers, from infection to exposure to hazardous chemicals and high risks of accidents. Although neglected and marginalized, clearly their work is crucial for the viability and sustainability of the cities.

Which Issues Get Addressed and How? Opinion, Movements, Governments, and Foreign Attention

To understand whether the environmental and health conditions of the cities are likely to get the attention of local elites and international aid groups, it is useful to consider the extent to which those with power can ignore them. Some urban environmental issues are relatively "democratic," affecting the wealthy and the poor similarly. Smog and other air pollutants are often said to be democratic, and indeed these have been more aggressively addressed, since they are so difficult to escape.[33] The situation, however, is not so simple: Some wealthy residents can live quite far from polluting factories and highways, leaving poorer residents needing affordable housing close to work to live there. Wealthier residents have political connections to exploit when a hazardous facility might be planned for their neighborhoods. Middle- and upper-class residents can stay inside with air conditioning when smog alerts are announced, and many use additional indoor air filters.

By this token, water is less democratic still. Safe drinking water can be bought by the bottle almost anywhere in Latin America, and increasingly is. In Central America, watercoolers of purified water are now a fixture in offices and homes everywhere. Or one can install filters, which can be found under kitchen sinks in middle- and upper-class residences across the region. But both of these are substantial investments beyond the ability of many working-class and poor people to afford. Some families who lack filters boil their drinking water, but to do so requires a substantial amount of cooking fuel. Boiling water kills bacteria and other parasites, but it does not remove other contaminants. Regarding sewage collection and treatment, wealthier neighborhoods can more effectively lobby for their prioritization by local, national, and international agencies.[34]

This is another example of how environmental risks and the benefits from exploiting natural resources are distributed in an exceedingly unequal fashion. The concept of "environmental justice" was developed in the Deep South of the United States to describe how residents of minority and poor communities are forced to face more risks than those of wealthier and whiter neighborhoods.[35] The concept has been increasingly adopted around the world, quite recently in Brazil by a group of activists and academics to bridge the difficult gap between groups fighting for social justice and those working for environmental protection.[36]

At the heart of urban environmental challenges, they argue, lies the huge disparity between the rich and the poor. In income terms, Latin America has some of the most unequal societies in the world.[37] Just two figures: In Honduras, Nicaragua, Ecuador, and Guatemala, over half of all city-dwellers live in poverty, and throughout the region as a whole, nearly 60 percent of children under age twelve live in poverty.[38] Poverty is difficult to define, but minimum wages across the region range from U.S.$30–$200 dollars a *month*. Many households subsist on far less. It is difficult even to express in words the depth of the poverty many experience there: One would have to imagine losing everything one owned and living hand-to-mouth in a neighborhood of clapboard one-room shacks.[39] Often there is a racial side to the segregation, as those of Indian or African descent are excluded from wealth and, therefore, the ability to escape environmental risks.

Campaigns to improve *urban* conditions in Latin America were long ignored by international environmentalists because they lack the attractiveness of other environmental struggles: In cities there are no fuzzy wildlife victims to put on calendars, no pristine wilderness for ecotourists to explore, and no potential cures for cancer or AIDS.[40] But while attractive to some in the wealthy countries, globally these are probably unusual reasons to care about the environment. Indeed, environmental social movements in wealthy core nations have often been characterized as elitist, and while support for environmental causes crosses class lines, activists in the mainstream groups tend to be highly educated, urban, and of above-average income.[41] While Enrique Leff points out the complexity of the environmental movement in Latin America and its potential to bridge social classes, some of Eduardo Viola's early research suggested that, at least in Brazil, environmental activists tend to be urban professionals.[42] The groups are well connected with universities, government agencies, policy networks, and international financial institutions. Highly educated technicians and administrators are leading these advocacy and research organizations, making the movement increasingly a professional one.[43]

How widespread is environmental concern in the broader populations of Latin America? Cross-national research on environmental concern and participation in environmental groups has been scarce. Dunlap and the Gallup Institute's 1992 Health of the Planet Survey asked a series of questions to national samples in twenty-four nations, including Mexico, Brazil, Chile, and Uruguay.[44] Over the 1990–1993 period, the World Values Survey also asked a consistent battery of questions to national samples in forty-three nations, including the same Latin American countries as the Dunlap/Gallup study (except that Uruguay was replaced by Argentina).[45] Both studies were biased to the countries in the region with the highest average income per capita, and many have urban-based samples of respondents, but they provide the only existing cross-national data.

The surveys show that approval of the environmental movement and concern about the environment both reach levels that are in some places even *higher* than in wealthier countries. This is especially true for local environmental issues such as air and water pollution. According to the Dunlap/Gallup poll, the most serious local issue for respondents in all four countries was inadequate sewage treatment. That poll found that concern over global issues was at a level similar to that for the wealthier countries. A 1992 survey by the Brazilian polling agency IBOPE found that overall levels of *interest* in environmental issues did not vary significantly by class or education (although profiles of public supporters and activists do tend to differ). The IBOPE survey found that lower-education respondents are more practical and interested in conservation of local resources, while higher-education people are "more idealistic" and interested in national and international environmental issues.[46] Given the choice between placing a priority *either* on protecting the environment *or* on promoting economic growth, 64 percent of Chileans and Uruguayans and 71 percent of Mexicans and Brazilians chose protecting the environment, levels *higher* than those found in the United States.[47]

Surveys taken in Bolivia, Columbia, and Peru just weeks before the Johannesburg Summit on Sustainable Development (WSSD) in August 2002 found that twice as many people believed their country's environmental quality had "worsened over the ten years since the Rio conference, than said it had improved" (58 percent versus 30 percent).[48] A November 2001 poll in Venezuela, Chile, Mexico, Brazil, and Argentina had very similar finding: 60–70 percent of these urban respondents said their country's environmental quality had worsened over the past ten years. Argentineans were the most negative of any nation in the world: over six times as many people said things were getting worse (83 percent versus 13 percent).[49] Eighty-six percent of Latin Americans believed that access to clean drinking water should be a basic human right.

While these polls must be taken extremely cautiously, they do show that stereotypes of poor people being unable to attend to "higher" values such as quality of life are misguided, and probably elitist.[50] Jamie Anderson's 1994 survey in three favelas in Rio de Janeiro showed levels of concern about the environment above those in Europe to identically worded questions. In a survey of 225 residents in Campeche, Mexico, Marilyn Gates found that over half of urbanites were concerned about environmental degradation.[51]

These polls do show why environmental groups grew dramatically in number, and this is a crucial social change for the direction of these battles. For example, in Brazil in 1971 there were only two groups; this was up to about forty in 1980, but then by the early 1990s there were thousands.[52] Other nations have rates of growth in their environmental movements, and many countries have seen a significant decrease in environmental activism since its high-water mark in the early 1990s.[53]

Environmental NGOs in Latin America share a common problem. In North America and Europe, just by sending in their check each year hundreds of thousands of dues-paying members provide independence, power, and legitimacy to environmental group leaders. There is a much smaller potential constituency of dues-paying members in Latin America, and the culture is quite different with regard to membership in these kinds of organizations. So while the World Wildlife Fund in Britain in the 1990s had 1.2 million members, each donating varying amounts, the World Wildlife Fund in Brazil itself had virtually no dues-paying members.[54] A nationwide publicity campaign by Brazil's largest group, S.O.S. Mata Atlántica, only recruited one thousand new members, although this represented a doubling of the membership to two thousand.

Thus, Latin American NGOs are forced to look for other sources of funding, primarily from international groups, corporate sponsors, or government contracts. Each option opens new doors at the cost of a certain loss in autonomy.[55] Before 1992, U.S.-based groups involved in Latin America faced criticism from local activists that their approaches often excluded concern for the social side of conservation. These groups found that to make progress in their conservation goals they had to link their concerns to those of local people. An undeniable result of the Rio UNCED conference was the massive encounter of environmentalists from rich and poor nations at official and unofficial parallel events around the city. Many connections involved support from Northern nation groups, but in some cases they obliged Latin American groups to focus on issues outside their own priorities, namely, species or habitat preservation, instead of urban pollution and the environmental effects of poverty. But a different route has been followed by other groups, especially some northern European foundations, national aid agencies, and intergovernmental groups, which have sent consistent and substantial support to "social" environmental groups in the region that are focused on broader issues of poverty, injustice, health, and the environment.

A pivotal period in Brazil was the two years leading up to the UNCED conference in Rio in 1992, when there was a tremendous upsurge in coalition work. A vast "Brazilian Forum" network was created of these social and environmental groups, which met in eight huge conferences and "numerous state and regional preparatory NGO conferences."[56] The Forum grew to include twelve hundred organizations: "social movements of all kinds, unions, professional groups, and many more" before the Rio meetings.[57] Labor unions in the Amazon and the big cities, and the large Workers Party (PT) have played an important role in the framing of environmental issues in Brazil.[58] And with the first democratically elected president in thirty years beginning his term, the lifting of military repression on activists provided a political opening in which people could see some change as possible for the first time, and people felt greater safety in participation.[59]

There is a common sentiment in Latin America that environmental problems are a government responsibility, yet many doubt environmental regulations will be enforced (because of weak infrastructure and corruption).[60] As national and international environmental commitments have grown, and as more resources are "decentralized" down to local governments, much of the responsibility for deciding how to combat urban pollution has been placed in the hands of municipal regulators.[61] Many observers see this as a positive change since local governments are most in touch with such basic needs. However, there are problems of "joint irresponsibility," especially when problems like sewage and air cross political lines: for example, there are thirty-nine municipalities in São Paulo and fourteen in Rio.

Shifting coalitions of environmentalists and public health agencies have attempted to address urban environmental crises such as the "depolluting" of the Guanabara Bay, which is a fairly well studied and informative case. In the run-up to the Rio Earth Summit, both state and federal governments in Brazil faced tremendous debts.[62] Touring North America and Europe just before taking office in 1990, Brazilian President Fernando Collor became painfully aware that the nation was not going to receive financial help with those loans until it had improved its international reputation on the environment. He proposed and won the site of the Earth Summit to draw attention to his new effort, which would combine environmental improvement with his conservative agenda of privatization of state agencies and companies such as electricity, water, and sewage services. But he also understood that Rio's contaminated beaches would bring attention and almost certainly hundreds of millions of dollars of new loans to finance some new sewer projects. The administration let it be known that groups should organize proposals for projects to address issues in their neighborhoods or area of expertise.[63] Dozens of groups got together to form the "United Peoples of the Bay" (União dos Povos da Baía), composed of environmental groups, neighborhood groups, fishers, politicians, and other groups, finally settling on the "Living Bay Movement" (Movimento Baía Viva).[64]

Their goal was a clean bay without sewage, but the Collor administration announced a state-federal program that combined many ongoing and planned projects and took a centralized, top-down approach, setting up an Executive Group for the Depolluting of Guanabara Bay (GEDEG).[65] The group proposed to the Interamerican Development Bank (IDB) late in 1991 a vast fifteen-year, $4-billion project. The IDB approved a $600-million loan, mostly to pay for sewage work and digital mapping. Since these were to be loans, however, they would have to be repaid with users' fees for their new sewage service. However, studies showed that families with incomes below the $455 median per month were not able or willing to pay enough, and wealthy beach users were unwilling to pay for clean beaches. So part of the digital mapping was focused simply on assisting in the collection of these taxes.

Popular groups "felt deceived," as there was "little information available about the program and no way for society to participate, not even for the municipal governments affected by the program."[66] Baía Viva attempted to set up the Consortium of Bay Municipalities, but this was rejected, until 2000 after the Petrobras oil spill mentioned earlier in this chapter. One assessment concluded that after ten years, the Program for the Depolluting of the Guanabara Bay created "practically no benefits . . . the water works and sewage collection and treatment system have not been completed" because of poor materials and various project delays, leading to the damaging of partially constructed works.[67]

During the high-visibility cleanup of the Carioca River's "black tongues" that reached the Flamengo Beach, architectural firms went out of business and engineering and construction firms had their assets frozen.[68] The state environmental agency nearly disappeared from the scene, as salaries collapsed when state budget allocations were cut and withheld.[69] Returning after five years away, one American researcher concluded that neighborhood and grassroots environmental organizations such as those that came together back in 1992 to push for the cleanup are exceedingly fragile.[70] One neighborhood leader had died; another was elected to the city council but switched later from the Green Party to the conservative but powerful Partido da Frente Liberal (PFL) to have access to more political funding. One neighborhood leader in a poor area described the way his organization was treated:

"The municipal government came, they made a plan, and began to do the work." The state sewer and water agency Companhia Estadual de Águas e Esgotos do Rio de Janeiro (CEDAE) was almost entirely absent from the area since privatization was proposed but not finalized, a process that dragged on for years. As a result, inspections for clandestine sewer hookups have been neglected. As Looye describes it, "Government has found other ways to act in the city and citizens have followed the fragmented approach by making increasing demands for 'their neighborhood.'"[71]

The problem of people getting distracted by other demands is common to volunteer organizations such as these. But groups who have gotten further in professionalizing themselves with staff people who can carry the ball and attempt to maintain momentum during slow times appear to be doing somewhat better: In late 2001 we met staff people from a series of groups whose acheivements were substantial. For example, the Movement for the Defense of Life in the Greater ABC District (MDVGABC) has protested contamination in the Billings reservoir and continued to draw press attention to contaminated sites in industrial areas around São Paulo. The Federation of Social Assistance and Education Groups (FASE) and the Brazilian Institute for Economic and Social Analysis (IBASE) have been working with communities, universities, and others in long-term projects for decades.

For the run-up to the 2002 World Summit on Sustainable Development in Johannesburg, South Africa, the Brazilian Forum began to meet again. This time, there were five hundred groups registered in the Forum, of which about fifty were more active.[72] The most prominent groups were those who had been around from the start and who could create the electronic presence for the 2002 Forum: the World Wildlife Fund and the Amazon Working Group (GTA), with the support of the British Embassy and the German Technical Committee. Other Brazilian groups, such as ISA (Instituto Socioambiental), Vitae Civilis, Argonautas, and Vitoria Regia, were also active participants, along with representatives of the The Workers Union Central (CUT). The environmental movement put together a delegation of forty to fifty representatives to the Johannesburg conference. The Brazilian business community was expected to have 70 representatives. Many environmentalists in Brazil in 2001–2002 described the movement as going in "cycles," growing in strength and getting coordinated when necessary for events and larger struggles, then falling back into more modest and fragmented groups and projects between these times.

If environmental activism in cities remains fragmented or weak, it is not the only social movement to face this problem. In looking across Latin

American cities, Alan Gilbert provides several explanations for the relative lack of popular protest, including a lack of time and resources required for successful organizing, the high risk of repression for radical protestors, the role of clientelism (control of the poor by those with money and political power) in local development, and traditional urban political conservatism.[73] Urban environmental concerns remain one isolated component of both regional development planning and environmental organizing. Latin America's cities prove reflections of the region at large: In relatively few areas have environmental struggles developed into cohesive social movements.[74]

Finally, something needs to be said about why the big international lending agencies have suddenly become interested in urban environmental issues. An excellent and crucial example of this trend is the World Bank. The Bank estimates that health costs resulting from urban water, air, and solid waste pollution can reach up to 10 percent of urban income.[75] Since the early 1990s, the World Bank and its sister agency the IDB have begun shifting some of their loans to address urban environmental problems. The shift in these huge banks' attention to the public health and basic needs side of development is an extremely positive change. However, in so doing, they and the federal and municipal governments with whom they are working take a "technocratic" approach, attempting with good engineering to address what are deep-seated social problems.

As Henri Acselrad, professor of urban planning at the Federal University of Rio de Janeiro, points out, an inevitable problem is making these technological approaches bound to fail. He points out that globalization is driving cities to compete against one another to create a better "business climate" to attract investors from around the world. To draw investors, localities offer generous packages of tax incentives and subsidized infrastructure, such as industrial parks with utilities and even buildings provided by the city. However, in doing so they undercut their own ability to collect the taxes they need to take care of basic social and environmental needs, and thus create conflicts and environmental insustainability. Crime, bad health, and poor education all create poor business and human climates in the longer term, but to compete today for investors, nearly any incentives will be given. This goes on even in wealthy nations such as the United States all the time, but Latin American nations are even hungrier for development and must overcome greater disadvantages with even greater incentive packages they can less afford.

Thus the needs of cities to compete for investors, the ability of some citizens to escape the worst risks of water and air pollution, the difficulty of organizing and sustaining a fragile social movement, and the short-term and self-interested agendas of politicians together create and perpetuate environmental injustice in the cities. Even with strong public support for the movement, and some extremely high-profile international attention in 1992, a decade later the urban environment appears to be getting worse.

Curitiba: An Ecotopian Model for Urban Latin America?

About now, readers are probably sorely needing a positive case of urban sustainability in Latin America. Curitiba, Brazil, is by nearly all accounts a Latin American ecotopia. Designed around environmental ideas, the city is committed to addressing the basic needs of children and the poor. Curitiba's 1.7 million inhabitants enjoy an unusually breathable city, with fifty square meters of green space per capita. Traditional cornerstones of ecodevelopment such as recycling, reclamation, and waste reduction are complemented in Curitiba by a public transportation system that has proved to be both efficient and affordable. At the same time that the city's population doubled, traffic decreased by 30 percent. Two-thirds of all garbage is recycled, and the city has received dozens of awards for environmentally friendly design.[76] During the UN Earth Summit in Rio de Janeiro in 1992, over a hundred officials came to Curitiba to observe its innovations, including planners from New York City, Paris, Prague, Toronto, Santiago, and Moscow.[77] The pilgrimages and positive press reports continue.

The miracle of Curitiba is due in large part to the vision and work of one man: a young architect whose master plan for the city was adopted in 1968. That same year Jaime Lerner became the director of the City Planning Institute, and he was appointed mayor in 1971. Soon after taking office, Lerner faced a critical moment when plans to construct an overpass that would have destroyed the main historic street in the city were about to be acted upon. He took advantage of his executive authority by banning all traffic on the street and created a pedestrian mall, a decision that angered shopkeepers, motorists, and the construction company.[78] When the construction crew arrived to continue the demolition, they found the street lined with flowerpots and children painting murals. "And so Curitiba's historical pedestrian mall was born by executive fiat."[79]

Even more drastic was the way Lerner and his planning institute, the Curitibian Institute for Research and Urban Planning (IPPUC), reorganized the roads and land use in the city. To create an efficient bus and auto transit system, Lerner created a "spider web" system linking speedy bus routes along a series of concentric circles connected to five radial lines coming out of the city's center.[80] Like subway trains above ground, each radial line bus transports over two hundred passengers in its own dedicated traffic lane. Passengers pay before entering raised Plexiglas tube-shaped waiting stations, then board quickly and transfer for free to other lines. The system is extremely efficient and agreeable: Three-quarters of all commuters are estimated to use the bus system, which was built for less than one one-hundredth of the cost of a subway.[81] A tightly zoned stretch of dense urban housing lines the main bus routes, making it easy for workers to quickly reach jobs downtown or in the "Industrial City," where companies continue to operate under strict pollution emission standards.[82] The DáPedal (Starter Pedal) program encourages use of the largest network of exclusive bike lanes in the country by allowing commuters to buy bicycles by paying for them with their bus allowances.[83] Today, Curitiba's transportation system moves over 2.1 million passengers daily and serves many more on some 150 kilometers of bicycle paths. The system provides stable jobs funneled through eighteen private companies and thrives without any government subsidies.

In Curitiba, citizens sort trash into two bins: biodegradable and non-biodegradable. In the recycling plant (built of recycled materials), the handicapped, recent immigrants, and the poor are reportedly given work separating materials to be reused and sold to local industries.[84] "We transformed the garbage man into an environmental hero," said Lerner, who worked as a trash collector to kick off the program.[85] In squatter settlements without roads wide enough for garbage trucks, the poor bring in their trash to collection centers in exchange for eggs, milk, potatoes, and bus tickets. Lerner says the vouchers and food cost no more than hiring trash collectors, and World Bank officials comment that the program makes the city cleaner while improving nutrition among the poorest residents.[86] Instead of advertising to get people to change their habits to recycle, Lerner sent out people dressed as trees to the schools, teaching about "garbage that isn't garbage."[87] Environmental education is in every public school, as well as in a new Free Open University for the Environment, which brings community members together with city planners and officials.[88] The city's recycling rate is among the best in the world.

Lerner provided 1.5 million tree seedlings for residents to plant themselves.[89] Lerner is reported to have convinced every industry, shop, and institution to "adopt" a few homeless street children, who in exchange for doing simple cleaning or office chores receive a daily meal and a small wage.[90] Lerner organized street vendors into an open-air market that circulates through the city's neighborhoods. Aging city buses are converted into classrooms that go from neighborhood to neighborhood offering short courses training residents in basic skills like typing, hairdressing, and electrical repairs.[91] Rather than constructing impersonal homogenized housing projects for the poor, Curitiba provides subsidized loans and architects so that locals can build their own. This kind of decentralized development is reported to have another benefit: reducing the opportunity for corruption.

Curitiba is truly a world-class ecotopia, and we agree with Michael Cohen of the World Bank in his observation that "[Curitiba] is a model for the First World, not just the Third." Lerner is reported to be a "dynamic and charismatic" leader with an "optimistic vision of humanity."[92] Well-known environmental writers such as Bill McKibben and the late Donella Meadows have described Lerner and his planners in glowing terms as enlightened technocrats who "do not see despair and difficulty, but simply constraints around which to work."[93] And visiting Curitiba, even in a time of desperate inflation in 1990, we sensed a difference in its residents from most other cities in Brazil or Latin America, or for that matter in the Americas as a whole. The dire poverty of most Brazilian cities was less evident, and since many Curitibans have recently immigrated from Italy, Germany, Poland, Japan, and the Ukraine,[94] this cultural profile contributes to the European "feel" of the city, one that is reported to be more participatory and cooperative than most other places. Public opinion polls have at times shown some 99 percent of residents are satisfied with their city, and Lerner's approval ratings at 92 percent were by far the highest in Brazil.[95]

But as Rosa Moura and Kristin Traicoff point out, there are some major caveats to the Curitiba green dream. "Attributing the successes of Curitiba to the talents of the mayor and the perceptions of the populace towards their city begs the question as to how this culture was created and why it is absent in other Brazilian cities," says Traicoff.[96] First, the reorganization of the whole city along environmental lines was accomplished because of unique political arrangements made possible by a military dictatorship, under which Lerner served in two separate terms. Lerner rose to power during a period of Brazilian history in which state-controlled elections were frequently suspended, manipulated, and corrupt. Lerner's broad executive powers made it possible to push through the pedestrian downtown, the bus system, the land zoning, and the expansion of the public parks network.[97] People, including businesses and residents, were forced to take pro-environmental behaviors and deal with a master plan designed by the mayor and his planning institute, the IPPUC. The IPPUC is staffed by a diverse group of trained professionals, clustered into four largely autonomous departments that are given "complete legal, research, and coordinating responsibilities of urban planning and development, as well as the responsibility to revise the plan as necessary."[98] The culture described by some authors is a strong local "boosterism" that makes any critic feel a traitor to the cause.[99] Moura points to a lack of continual participation by locals in planning, making the city compare unfavorably to other ecological "model cities," such as Portland, Oregon.

It must be said that the mayor and the IPPUC constantly educated the populace about the design principles behind their plans and actions, and open debates were held on land use and other policies. In contrast to the models of democracy applauded elsewhere in the Americas, interest groups were excluded from watering down Curitiba's projects. Traicoff makes the point that as democracy continues to be "consolidated" in Brazil, it remains unknown if the success of Curitiba could be replicated elsewhere—or even if current Curitiba successes will be maintained. The experience of urban development elsewhere suggests that "growth machines," coalitions of developers, local businesspeople, builders, and real estate brokers, are often able take over local development to tilt development plans in the direction of rapid, uncontrolled growth that profits themselves more immediately.[100] Traicoff's projections on Curitiba's future are optimistic in the face of interest group pressures under democratization: She sees an environmentally educated populace supporting continuation of the policies of the Lerner years. But applying the Curitiba model elsewhere looks much more difficult.

Finally, is the reality that the area within the municipal lines are well planned, but surrounding Curitiba is a belt of poorer, and more poorly planned municipalities.[101] Moura reports that in them there have been over 180 land invasions, which now house 121,000 people, or 8 percent of the metropolitan population. These are "not mentioned in official discussions," so she is led to call this the "belt of non-citizens."[102]

The Curitiba case raises two points for discussion. First, Curitiba's success is in some ways similar to organic agriculture reforms in Cuba (see Chapter 3). Lerner's executive authority and the use of environmentally sustainable, low-budget responses to economic and social crises has much in common with many of Cuba's Special Period initiatives in organics. Curitiba's experience is also similar to that of Chile under the neo-liberal economic reforms of military president Augusto Pinochet. Chile has often been heralded as model for other Latin American nations struggling to cut down government spending and get inflation under control. However, the success of Chile in creating a vibrant export-based economy owes much to the fact that these reforms were carried out during times of strict military control. As Alejandro Portes points out, Chilean technocrats were at once free from pressures from industrialists (who had been weakened by the nationalization of key sectors), the landed oligarchy (who had lost power under previous land reforms), and civil society (especially unions, students, and neighborhood and rights groups, who were terrorized by the military).[103] Rather than restoring power to old elites, Chile sold off state enterprises to foster new commercial farming and industrial classes and then protected these new enterprises while they gained strength to compete internationally. As in Curitiba, Chile's "technocratic elite could sustain setbacks and failures that would have discredited their leadership had they occurred under democratic conditions." This is an important point that distinguishes Chile from places like Mexico (or current Brazil, Colombia, or Venezula), where there were powerful opposition movements.[104] Traicoff brings us to the core paradox of the Curitiba example, that the experiment has been positive "for the possibility of sustainable development in Latin America, but much less so for the consolidation of functional democracy."[105]

The struggling state of Latin America's cities is indisputable—the question then becomes, how will conditions improve? Is economic growth the answer to the region's environmental and social problems? What role can private transnational firms play in addressing them?

The Rise of Corporate Environmentalism in Latin America

At 10:30 A.M. on April 22, 1992, at least nine separate explosions in sewers under the streets of Guadalajara, Mexico, ripped a one-mile "jagged trench" through the city.[106] It looked like "it had been bombed."[107] At least two hundred people were killed and more than fifteen hundred were injured by the explosion of petrochemicals, which had leaked either from a refinery of the state-owned giant oil monopoly Pemex or from La Central, a small cooking oil company. Twelve urban blocks were almost erased from the map.[108] The event generated a wave of protests in the city, and the *damnificados*, or injured ones, have continued to put pressure on the government and firms to clean up their act. Pemex, the Mexican state-owned oil giant, was found at fault in a series of past explosions, including a 1984 explosion in Ixhuatepec that was reported to have killed more than five hundred people.[109]

On February 25, 1984, 700,000 liters of gasoline leaked out of a pipeline under the poor Vila Socó neighborhood of Cubatão, near São Paulo in Brazil, causing a fire that killed a hundred people and burned six hundred shacks to the ground.[110] Under skies smudged with smoke from billowing chemical, fertilizer, and oil refineries, Cubatão had already gained the reputation as the "Valley of Death," as one of the most polluted places on earth. Health problems that locals tied to pollution, including anencephaly (see Chapter 2), leukopenia (low white blood cell counts, tied to benzene exposures), asthma, severe bronchitis, and allergies, were seen in Cubatão residents at levels unseen elsewhere. From June 1982 to December 1986, for example, 150 children in the small city were reported to have been born with some kind of birth defect.[111] The pipeline leak and fire sent the story of poverty and death by petrochemicals around the world.

Later in 1984, halfway across the planet at the U.S.-based Union Carbide's battery and pesticides plant in Bhopal, India, a devastating leak of methylisocyanate wafted over squatter shacks killing somewhere between 2,000 and 10,000 people and injuring over 200,000.[112] The tragedy was tied to corporate neglect and a long history of cost-cutting plans that compromised health and safety precautions. Union Carbide eventually settled out of court with the Indian government for $450 million, but the victims received little, and the case drags on.

These events tarnished an already shaky image of the entire global chemical industry. Even the cleanest firms operating in the wealthiest countries began to face a new wave of tough and expensive regulations. The petrochemical industry learned in the wealthy countries from polling and focus groups and local community protests that their collective image was badly hurt by sloppy firms half a world away. Within months after Bhopal, the American Chemistry Council (ACC, at the time called the Chemical Manufacturers of America, or CMA) adopted an industrywide program named Responsible Care®, which had been developed in Canada to improve community relations by addressing the public's growing dread of chemical contamination and explosions.[113]

As we saw in the previous chapter, in the 1990s corporations around the world increasingly faced demands by consumers for products that are certified to have been produced in an ecologically sound manner. Examples include labels such as "postconsumer recycled paper" content, "dolphin safe tuna," or "certified plantation-grown tropical hardwoods." By 1994, there were already more than thirty national "green labeling" schemes instituted in as many different countries around the world.[114] In an era of increasing free trade and global production and marketing, the idea of having to be certified in dozens of countries under drastically different green labeling systems and industry programs soon became industries' worst nightmare.

As a response, industries of many types turned to the International Organization for Standardization (ISO), an industry/UN agency, to create one set of global environmental certifications. ISO is a nongovernmental, voluntary, private-sector specification standard for environmental management. Proponents of the system maintained that ISO represents a "new paradigm [in environmental policy regulation] that relies on positive motivation not punishment. . . . ISO transcends the regulatory compliance approach."[115] In contrast to "command and control" policies in which governments mandate environmental standards, ISO is a voluntary program that allows each member organization to independently establish targets for improvement.

Some very promising developments among Latin American corporations include the emergence of a sustainability discourse and environmental management plans within the corporate sector itself.[116] DuPont CEO Ed Woolard is credited for first promoting this concept, which he dubbed "corporate environmentalism." During a 1989 speech to the American Chamber of Commerce in London (and in the wake of the Exxon Valdez oil spill), he called for "an attitude and a performance commitment that place corporate environmental stewardship fully in line with public desires and expectations. . . . [T]he environmental groups cannot solve any of these problems. Governments can't do it. Corporations have to do it."[117]

Researchers in northern Europe have noticed a crucial shift in the actions of corporations with regard to the environment. Namely, they have reported that the goal of minimizing inputs and waste and maximizing outputs (eco-efficiency) is being incorporated into the internal decision-making of firms.[118] This process, called "ecological modernization," implies that countries can shift from the heavy state-directed "command and control" regulation of environmental issues to more voluntary approaches to problem-solving. When given flexibility to reduce pollution as much as possible at the lowest cost, it is frequently argued, firms find more effective ways than do regulators, who tend to apply "one-size-fits-all" standards. Similarly, the authors of the influential book *Natural Capitalism* argue that firms will have to make the shift to eco-efficiency or they will be forced out of business by those firms who do.[119]

Recent years have seen the emergence of a new breed of businesses, ethics consultants, nonprofits and how-to books that have popularized and developed the philosophy of corporate environmentalism. Paul Hawken's book *The Ecology of Commerce* made the bestseller's list, *Business Ethics* is now a popular magazine, and organizations such as the Social Venture Network, Business for Social Responsibility, the Coalition for Environmentally Responsible Economics, and the Council on Economic Priorities have enjoyed unimagined successes. Livio DeSimone, chairman of the Business Council for Sustainable Development, put it this way: "A paradigm shift has clearly taken place.

Business . . . used to be depicted as a primary source of the world's environmental problems. Today it is increasingly viewed as a vital contributor to solv-
ing those problems and securing a sustainable future for the planet."[120]

ISO standards are being adopted and firms are being "ISO 14001 certi-
fied" around the world. By June 2002 over forty thousand eight hundred
firms in 103 countries had gained the ISO "green label."[121] And Responsible
Care is spreading around the world with a substantial push from the
American Chemistry Council, the International Council of Chemical
Associations (ICCA), and now from regional and national chemical indus-
try groups in some forty nations. The Brazilian chemical industry association
ABIQUIM launched its first program in April 1992, and by January 1999
all 130–some ABIQUIM members agreed to a mandatory commitment to
the initiative.[122] Chemical industries organizations in Argentina, Chile,
Mexico, and Uruguay have adopted the Responsible Care program, and
Colombia, Ecuador, and Peru have gained approval from the International
Council of Chemical Associations to institute it.[123]

Beyond Responsible Care and ISO 14001, individual firms continue to
make their own efforts at pollution reduction and public relations, thus
attempting to set themselves apart from their competitors in the eyes of customers and environmentalists as they attempt to bring up their industry's
public image. Environmental cleanups and emissions reductions are often
complemented by individual firms setting up or supporting nature preserves
or zoos near their factories, running or supporting environmental education
efforts, and supporting cultural activities and universities in the cities of their
headquarters and operations. Big companies usually take this dual approach,
supporting industrywide public relations efforts while not abandoning their
own corporate image-care.

Critics argue that many of these initiatives are merely "corporate green-
washing," efforts designed to silence potential critics and boost polluting
firms' corporate image without them doing signficant pollution reductions.[124] A stark example is one ad for the chemical refining complex Copesul
from southern Brazil that featured a photograph of a wild bird on a mani-
cured grass foreground with a chemical facility in the background. The text
includes the following: "There are 68 hectares [about 170 acres], adjacent to
the Copesul industrial area, totally protected from the predatory actions of
man. There, innumerable species of birds, fish, mammals, reptiles and
insects live together. To hear the applause and thanks of nature requires only
you look at the quero-quero bird in the photo."[125] Author Joel Hirschorn,
one critic, reflected, "Most of these companies are green the way an apple is

green: on the outside, where you can see it."[126] Still, it is not always clear what proportion of corporate environmentalist initiatives can be discounted as greenwash and which are likely to improve its sustainability. Copesul's more recent environmental reports for 2001 show significant accomplishments: Most air pollutants are reported to be down by half or more of 1996 levels, but "volatile organic compounds" were up 26 percent.[127]

Activist author Joshua Karliner of Corporate Watch and others have expressed concern that programs such as ISO may some day be used by corporations as ways to block stricter environmental requirements in national laws as "barriers to free trade."[128] There is much concern that they are being offered as substitutes for strong government oversight: In 2002 the Mexican industry organization National Association of the Chemical Industry (ANIQ) has reportedly "begun lobbying the government to credit Mexico's Responsible Care program . . . as an offical management system."[129] Other critics note that ISO is not a binding agreement and that its "global" span today only includes corporations large enough to pay for the certification analysis.[130] Consumer activists worry that ISO and other self-regulated programs may actually make it more difficult for citizens to hold corporations accountable. And, there are many important management issues that Responsible Care and ISO does not address, including, most evidently, working conditions and labor rights, such as the right to refuse unsafe work.

To return to the arguments of ecological modernizationists, it is true that some industries are cleaning up their acts, but some nations are doing better than others. Two comparative studies have documented that Mexico is improving more quickly in its corporate environmental behavior than are Brazil and Argentina.[131] One study in Brazil found European firms taking more seriously their environmental efforts than U.S.-owned firms.[132] But many times the industries and companies chosen for study are those who are making the most progress. Another problem with some studies is that they are done by interviewing only plant managers and the manager for "health, safety and environment" at those plants, without much contact with other workers, unions, neighbors, and local environmental groups. Two recent studies of the steel and leather industries suggest some terrible environmental behavior continues in the region, and in particular, firms are avoiding places with higher concern about the environment by simply moving to more desperate and poor parts of the nations.[133]

These studies raise serious doubts about claims that one global level of environmental performance will emerge in this evolving era of globalized production. Rather, they portray a highly heterogeneous and fragmented field with "global class companies" acting at a high level with a mass of smaller, local firms highly resistant to change. Are we witnessing a "Swiss-cheese" situation with modern pollution prevention and other proactive environmental management the norm while resistance is unusual, or are we looking at "islands of (ecological) modernity in a morass of traditional thinking"?

We attempted to answer this question by looking for patterns among the 619 chemical firms in Brazil. We found that the typical Brazilian chemical firm that subscribes to the Responsible Care environmental program is a foreign owned, publicly held, professionally managed firm that exports about $6 million a year and has 237 employees. Nonparticipants in the program, by contrast, tend to be far smaller, nationally owned firms who sell none of their products outside Brazil, and half of these firms are managed by the owner's family. Similarly, a study of the Mexican chemical industry found that small firms were less than half as likely to bother with environmental investing as were large firms.[134] One widely stated hope (which we share) is that if they are given access to information about their pollution emissions, plant neighbors and local and national environmentalists will pressure firms to behave better. A World Bank–sponsored study set out to test this hypothesis, but reported that local environmentalist pressure was not directly changing the performance of corporations in Mexico.[135] Our own study found no difference in participating in the Responsible Care and ISO 14001 programs between two parts of Brazil with high and low levels of environmental group activism.[136]

Returning to the Cubatão story, in 1983 state technocrats and community leaders teamed up to develop a comprehensive Cubatão Pollution Control Project (CPCP)—the beginning of Cubatão's transformation from the "Valley of Death."[137] By 1992, 228 of 320 identified air, water, and soil pollution sources had been controlled.[138] The cleanup in Cubatão received support from the World Bank, but in a unique departure from Brazilian politics, industries were ordered to pay the bulk of the costs of running the monitoring and cleanup programs. Political scientist Maria Carmen de Mello Lemos identifies three factors in Cubatão's turnaround: The state had a new pro-environment governor, a new generation of technical staff moved into a new department at the state of São Paulo's environmental agency CETESB, and there was public accountability and a strong local popular movement pressing for change.[139] The timing was good: After years of unsuccessful petitioning, community opposition groups gained ground as the nation began to transition out of a dictatorship into a more open democracy. The chemical industry tried to control and pacify the movement, but organizers established a powerful coalition of environmentalists, academics, and

Catholic church members under the umbrella of the Victims Association (AVPM).

The coalition was instrumental in securing the Cubatão cleanup plan but eventually demobilized, as occured in the case of the group which pushed for the Cariola River cleanup in Rio, the leaders either went into politics or went back to their lives. A key question then is the durability of the solution at Cubatão: interviews in October 2001 among environmentalists in nearby São Paulo found most extremely cynical about the state environmental agency CETESB, and many lingering contamination issues around Cubatão are still unresolved. Today, plans are in motion to site a large thermoelectric power plant in the city, a proposal strongly opposed by environmentalists, residents, and labor unions.

Is Cubatão trapped in a cycle of getting dirty and getting clean? The Cubatão story may be a timely example of the dangers of a fragile regulatory regime—even after decades of lawsuits, lobbying, and public protests, Cubatão may be heading back in the direction it started. Without effective state laws or public accountability provisions, even the best cleanup efforts are unlikely to be more than Band-aid solutions in the long term. Ultimately, the Cubatão example calls into question the reasoning of the Business Council for Sustainable Development that environmental problems can be ameliorated through a restructuring of current management and pricing systems. The need of corporations to turn short-term profits appears to make them as a whole unlikely to properly valorize environmental and human health over the longer term, especially in "weak regulatory climates." The current picture is uncertain and complex. We would certainly be pleased to be proven *wrong* in our conclusion and would be happy to find that voluntary environmental initiatives meant real and *enduring* progress in industrial environmental performance, in a broad range of firms across Latin America.

Few can contest De Simone's statement that businesses need to be integrated into global sustainability discussions. However, many environmentalists see the root of current environmental problems as "[a design] rather than a management problem, a flaw that runs through all business."[140] Corporate environmentalism continues to be approached with a great deal of cynicism from many environmentalists in the region. The core problem is that while corporations and international markets today operate across borders, regulatory laws remain largely limited to the traditional nation-state system. What global performance standards and international agreements do exist are painfully void of substantive enforcement mechanisms. National laws unfortunately lack the capacity to effectively address impending international regulatory needs. Although corporate codes of conduct, social responsibility platforms, and environmental management systems are progressive management tools that have the potential to improve company performance, these efforts are grossly insufficient in and of themselves.

Wealth and Health: Will Countries Clean Up as They Get Wealthier?

In 1992, the World Bank in its influential *World Development Report* proposed a theory for urban environmental issues that held out hope for the future of the world's poor countries. The theory was, essentially, that things will get worse for a while until people reach a certain level of development at which they can afford to switch away from only worrying about their daily survival. Only then, conditions will start to get better. The World Bank cited as evidence background papers by several economists that showed that for some pollutants, contamination levels were worst for countries with middle levels of income, and better in the richest and poorest nations.

The theory was dubbed the "Environmental Kuznets Curve," after the upside-down U-curve that Simon Kuznets saw and theorized back in 1954 on the issue of inequality of income.[141] Kuznets theorized that as countries move from poor and rural to more industrial and urban, some individuals move into the higher-paying jobs first. This increases inequality. The wealth will spread to a broader population later, after the original industries or new sectors of employment begin to hire more workers, or at least as they provide paid services to those employed in the more "modern" sectors.

There are a series of questions that motivate the environmental version of this theory, and they have key implications for every issue we discuss in this book, rural and urban. To quote three authors from the World Bank's Development Research Group, they are:

1. Does pollution follow a Kuznets curve, first rising and then falling as income increases?

2. At what income level does the turnaround occur?

3. Do all pollutants follow the same trajectory?

4. Is pollution reduction in developed economies due primarily to structural change or to regulation?[142]

This last question essentially asks, do rich nations simply move polluting industries offshore to poorer nations, or do they actually clean up those industries? That is, does the "structure" of the economy shift from industry-heavy to service-oriented?

Beneath all this debate is the core question that drives all kinds of strategies: Will things first get worse, and then get better? This issue of whether pollutants increase and then decrease as countries develop economically has critical policy implications. If the Kuznets curve is supported by the evidence, it suggests that current development policies are capable of being environmentally benign over the long term.[143] The problem would then become how best to *accelerate* those processes and policies so that all countries could experience production and living conditions found now only in the wealthy countries. If the curve trend is in error or misinterpreted and the most polluting technologies cannot be expected to disappear without explicit intervention, then policies promoting only accelerated economic growth might be a course for disaster.[144]

The World Bank and some influential economists have pointed to the fact that some cross-national, cross-sectional studies have found such an inverted U-curve in the relation between level of development and certain pollutants such as particulates, sulphur dioxide, toxic chemicals, and several water pollutants.[145] We need to pay close attention here, however, since T. Selden and A. Song found that only the most "in-your-face" pollutants tend to get cleaned up in wealthier countries. In fact, many continue to get worse. That is, the U-curve is valid only for types of pollution that have "local short-term costs (for example, sulfur, particulates, and fecal coliforms), not for the accumulation of stocks of waste or for pollutants involving long-term and more dispersed costs."[146] The total amount of garbage and carbon dioxide produced by countries tends to increase as they get richer: While they may become more efficient, richer countries consume more, and ultimately generate more waste.[147]

On the second question about where the "turning point" might be, one study claimed that this turning point for several pollutants tended to be before countries reach a gross domestic product of U.S.$8,000 per capita.[148] Using different measurements and techniques, other researchers have found turning points only at much higher economic levels.[149]

For Latin America and much of the Third World, data are spotty and often not comparable. For many good variables, we have no historical data to test whether and which countries move from worse to better. So we really are speculating from one snapshot of one historical moment. We did a historical analysis of carbon dioxide emissions, the most important greenhouse gas responsible for global warming for which we do have good data. The analysis showed that the intensity of emissions per unit of gross domestic product (what we called "carbon intensity") changed from essentially linear in 1965 to strongly curvilinear in 1990.[150] That is, an Environmental Kuznets Curve did emerge. However, the only group of countries showing a net improvement in CO_2 intensity over the period were the high-income countries. It also showed that ecological improvements in the high-income countries' averages began just *before* the oil crises of 1973 and 1979 and as a group, low-income countries have become steadily less efficient in carbon terms over the period. The middle-income countries worsened over the period but less severely than the poorer nations, with periods of increasing and decreasing efficiency. Finally, some countries are cleaning up quickly while others are lagging behind. This suggests that other historical, geographical, social, or political factors are increasingly important in determining which nations institute efficiency measures.[151]

All of this indicates that the relationship between economic growth and environmental protection should not be seen as stage-based or as a given. The history of the world economy (see Chapter 1) suggests that rather than passing through stages and eventually reducing their pollution through economic development,[152] only a few nations have ever successfully moved up substantially in the global hierarchy of wealth.[153] World-system analyses have supported the observation that most nations are structurally limited from ever ascending because of their colonial history as hinterlands for exploitation by the wealthy "core" nations. As we discussed for Latin America in the Preface, the continuing low prices of their exports, a history of unfavorable links with foreign corporations and banks, and their lack of geopolitical power all contribute to these limitations.[154] It is highly unlikely that poorer nations will repeat the history of European and North American development, particularly because these same world powers continue to dominate the world economy. Conventional theories involving stages of national development are unfortunately inconsistent with the historical record.

So we would argue that to deduce stages of development from present cross-sectional snapshots that look like an upside-down U-curve is irresponsible and potentially extremely dangerous. There is no reason to believe that most nations will ever reach the hypothesized "turning point" of pollution intensity, whether it be U.S.$8,000 GDP per capita or especially if it is higher. Rather, the curve of national pollution intensity established over the last twenty years is deepening and in all likelihood will persist. This raises the issue taken up in Chapter 2 concerning "pollution havens" and whether

wealthy nations are increasingly specializing in services while energy-inten-
sive industries such as the production of intermediate semiprocessed goods
tend to concentrate in middle-income countries.[155] And as we saw in the case
of the maquiladora industries, industrial relocations even of relatively clean
"assembly plants" do not necessarily mean upward economic mobility
toward the hypothesized turning point for nonwealthy nations. This is
because many industries move production facilities out of the wealthy
nations only in later stages of the product cycle at a time when competition
between producers is much greater. This ultimately keeps profit margins
low.[156] Industries in developing nations also often remain limited by subcontracting links to marketing and design firms in the wealthy nations, which
tend to garner the bulk of the profits.

Regardless of the evidence on the pollution-haven hypothesis, we have
seen that middle- and lower-income countries like those in Latin America
are usually less able to enforce environmental regulations effectively, and
may even see good reasons not to.[157] Further, even identical industries operating in nonwealthy countries face obstacles making them less efficient in
energy and carbon terms, such as poor roads, inefficient energy sources, and
local shortages of well-educated hi-tech workers, suppliers, and contractors.[158] Because nations often extend tax holidays to attract firms but benefit
very little from the low wages of the firms that do relocate, is it difficult for
developing nations to substantially upgrade infrastructure and human
resources. This is true in private industry, but especially true for government
agencies who are charged with enforcing environmental regulations.

Looking globally, the overall picture over the past thirty years that
emerges, we believe, is that although some wealthy nations are improving
their pollution intensity, conditions in much of the rest of the world may be
worsening. This suggests that if massive increases in pollution emissions in
rapidly growing nations are to be avoided, nations need a proactive and
explicit approach to environmental quality. These protections do not need to
come at the expense of solid economic growth, but sustainability must be
earnestly addressed at all "levels" of development. Firms and nations around
the world are discovering that it is far easier and cheaper to *avoid* environmental devastation than it is to clean it up later.[159] However, these firms and
nations need a level playing field so that short-term advantages will not go
to firms that don't comply—and poorer countries will need help and money
to ensure that environmental compliance does not drive firms out of business or drive them away. We come back to this question in the last chapter
of the book, but we are arguing here for a strong international reporting sys-

tem of pollutants, for some *international* environmental standards, and for stronger enforcement mechanisms.

So dealing with the dire environmental and public health issues in Latin American cities will require our attention to a series of very social issues. First, we must address the rural problems that are sending a stream of migrants into the overcrowded cities, as suggested by the previous chapter and the next. Second, the desperate conditions of sewage treatment, safe drinking water, sanitary garbage disposal, and air pollution suggest that foreign attention to the environment in the region needs to return to these basic public health issues, which largely were addressed long ago in most wealthy countries. Most urban Latin Americans say their environment is getting worse. Clearly more funding is needed from international agencies, but foreign NGOs need to be present and working closely with local NGOs and governments to make sure the money is being well spent. Many solutions, as seen in the case of Curitiba, are quite inexpensive and can provide rippling positive social effects if carefully planned and executed. But we would argue that democratic participation and transparency are central to the long-term political sustainability of urban environmental reforms. As the chemical industry study suggested, the business community must be incorporated into new urban solutions and monitored closely, a point we return to in Chapter 7. Latin America's desperate cities need economic growth, but growth alone is insufficient to improve the urban environment. Poverty and environmental issues must be explicitly addressed at all stages of growth, and they cannot be addressed without addressing social inequality and issues of participatory democracy.

In both urban and rural areas, our approach in this book has been to examine the extent to which poverty and social inequality are intimately tied to questions about environmental health and sustainability. This may seem a radical approach, but even the World Bank's Furtado and Belt commented in 2000 that distribution of wealth is a key to reducing pollution and other forms of environmental degradation and that economic development must be achieved in an environmentally sustainable manner.[160] But for now, we will leave the point there: Economic inequalities have created a situation in which Latin America's rich and the poor experience urban environmental problems in very different ways. Latin American cities are in trouble, and the question remains open of whether their problems will be addressed in a meaningful way or whether solutions will be limited to merely "restoring the postcard" of global cities like Rio de Janeiro[161] for the benefit of tourists and the wealthy, not Clede and other "marginals."

Clearing roads and pastures in Pará state, Brazilian Amazon, 1997.
Photo by J. Timmons Roberts.

CHAPTER 5

Bio-Splendor, Devastation, and Competing Visions in the Amazon

Immediately the day turns hot as the sun hits our canoe and the brown water of a small Amazon tributary. The deep brazil-nut wood canoe somehow fits eight of us, plus a solid hardwood bedframe that a squatter family plans to move into the forest preserve encampment today.

The muddy river provides a thin and inadequate buffer between the dusty boom town of Parauapebas (where Roberts lived in 1989–1990) and the largest preserved piece of the southeast Amazon, the Carajás mountains. Together with an indigenous reserve and three environmental protection units, a huge stretch of forested mountains here is controlled and guarded by a Brazilian mining corporation. These four units of preservation measure 2.5 million acres, an area which if square would measure sixty-two miles on each side. Its operator, the Vale do Rio Doce Company (CVRD), is the largest iron ore vendor in the world and one of the world's top five hundred corporations. Ironically, the heavily guarded entrance to the mine—an open pit (strip) mine that annually produces over thirty million tons of the world's purest iron ore for export—boasts only an enormous banner: "Carajás Ecological Preserve."

Squatters have been forcibly removed from this preserve dozens of times, but this time the group is larger, better-organized, and armed. Three weeks have tensely ticked away since three hundred families invaded the Carajás preserves. In that short period of time, the teams of workers have roughed out about fifty houses made of thatch, logs, and black plastic sheets just thicker than trash bags. "Living like Indians," they call it. Jutting out of the muddy bank, a small hand-painted sign in the yellow and green of the Brazilian flag reads: "We want land, not conflicts. Work, not hunger. Land reform now!!"

Reaching the bank, our canoe is pulled up by Alberto, a worried-looking farmer whose smile radiates the blasting sun amidst white stubble and deep suntan. The discussion comes around to ecology. "The real ecologists are the poor. We collaborate with the environment, we don't want to pollute. But we are preserving our bellies too, working to avoid starvation." Two chainsaws whine in the background as Alberto describes the work of a group of forty men and another of thirty women who set out along a freshly cut trail to help open up more land to plant.

If one were to believe everything one hears in the Amazon, one would conclude after talking with enough people that no one is responsible for the demise of the forest. Fingers are pointed in every direction by every Amazon "stakeholder" group, and no one wants to take the blame. Squatters like those in the Carajás preserve explain clearing as necessary for survival and cite the huge difference in their clearing sizes as compared to ranchers. Ranchers proclaim that it's the lumberers and the peasant farmers who are responsible. Lumber middlemen have told me, "It's not the lumberers who are destroying the Amazon, it's the clearing and burnings of the ranchers. When one mahogany comes down, a thousand come up in its place." The mining company cites figures that they have disturbed less than 2 percent of their forest preserve. Others cite the mercury contamination from the hundreds of thousands of artesenal gold miners who now pan and sieve the Amazon's creeks and rivers and gouge the occasional hillside. For others it is the dams, the roads, the legacy of the military regime, the politicians, the multinationals, the World Bank, the Americans, or the Indians who are to blame.

Meanwhile, courses of action taken in the developed countries to preserve the Amazon region have often had poor results. Protests in the Northern Hemisphere are closely watched by Brazilians and other Amazon nationals. Brazilians are cynical after decades of "gringo" interventions in the Amazon to extract rubber, minerals, lumber, and pharmaceuticals. Efforts to preserve the region are widely seen as attempts to prevent Brazil from gaining the superpower status it has long sought. Self-interest is always assumed to be the underlying motivation. After America's invasion of Panama, one local Amazon editorialist and politician even warned that the Amazon was going to be the site of the next Yankee military intervention.

Self-righteous postures north of the Caribbean have fostered these defensive ones to its south. Under pressure in the late 1980s over high releases of carbon dioxide from slash-and-burn clearing for farming and ranching in the Amazon, many Brazilian politicians reacted with proclamations that the pollution from U.S., European, and Japanese factories and cars was worse than the burning of the Amazon. A typical and very legitimate reaction to outside environmentalists is, "You cut your forests to build your world-power economies, how can you tell us not to cut ours?"

Misconceptions about the Amazon forest vary from pictures of a dark, savage jungle to idyllic scenes of a paradise on earth. Famous visionaries saw it as the next breadbasket to feed the world.[1] Many people believe the forests are the "lungs of the earth"—breathing in what our cars exhale—that prevent the acceleration of global warming through the greenhouse effect. Northern media commonly reduce the problem of rainforest destruction to peasants and their slash-and-burn farming techniques or blame ranchers raising cheap beef for American fast food companies.

While these images have some elements of truth, they are substantially false. Taken out of context, Amazon debates have largely resulted in impractical proposals and nationalist backlashes. Forty years after the first roads were built to link the poorly understood region to industrial centers of the continent, polemics about the Amazon have generated far more heat than light. What is needed is a step back to examine the area as a whole, the groups involved in the debate, and what's behind their positions. The more rational occupation of what all sides agree is the world's largest reserve of biological diversity necessitates a new posture of cooperation in the Amazon. This search for common ground must begin with a solid understanding of what "The Amazon" actually is, and what is really going on there. Some evidence of this new attitude is emerging.

This chapter takes on the enormous topic of the sociopolitical roots and solutions for the "Amazon Problem" in five steps. In the next three sections, we address some very basic questions: How big is the Amazon? Is it uniform? How quickly is it being torn down? How important is the forest, and why? Answers to many of these basic questions are surprisingly uncertain. Recognizing that Brazil hosts 60 percent of the Amazon forest, we focus on that nation, taking a quick look at the history of land and development in the Brazilian Amazon to understand how things got where they are. Next we examine the deep-seated conflicts between ranchers and poor peasants. Then we look to conflicts over trees themselves: between lumberers who want to cut them down, preservationists who want them fenced off, and the rubber-tappers, Brazil nut gatherers, and indigenous peoples who want to use them standing. Before concluding with an assessment of possible solutions, we examine the debate over and the effects of the U.S.-sponsored "Plan Colombia" drug war on the western edges of the Amazon rainforest. Readers looking for a simple solution should be forewarned, however: The Amazon is a fascinatingly complex place and solutions in the region have been difficult to come by. Clearly successful ones must be nuanced and supported with long-term commitments. We begin with the basics.

Grasping the Vastness

The Amazon River system contains an unbelievable one-fifth of all the freshwater on earth. Where the river meets the Atlantic near the city of Macapá, freshwater pushes back the ocean salt over one hundred miles. Even eight hundred miles up river from the sea it is difficult to see the other side of what locals call "the river-sea."

What is the "Amazon" region? Even defining what we mean by "The Amazon" is not as simple as it seems. The problem is that the Amazon River basin reaches into dry areas of savannas in Brazil and Venezuela and into subarctic habitats in the Andean mountains. Defining the region by types of typical rainforest plants or climatological conditions leads to various definitions of the area. Depending on your definition, the Amazon covers between 1.4 and 2.3 million square miles. To add to the confusion, each nation around the basin has a politically defined "Amazon" region.[2] But however one defines the region—indeed, even the lowest spatial estimates underscore the undebatable vastness of the Amazon—the region covers an area roughly the size of the continental United States minus Texas and Ohio.

The Amazon is the largest and oldest block of tropical rainforest on earth—over 60 percent of our planet's richest ecosystem. It is estimated to be home to between 1 and 2 million species, or about one of every five life forms on the planet. The forest tapestry is a dense weave largely uninvestigated by modern scientists. What we do know about the forest has come from satellite overflights, detailed studies of only a few groups of species, and comprehensive studies of several scattered corners. The vast majority of the Amazon's species have never even been identified.[3]

It has been estimated that one of these species—known or unknown—is driven to extinction every single hour.[4] This represents five hundred to one thousand times the natural extinction rate. The most recent (and highly debated) estimates are that 10–15 percent of Amazonia (440,000 square kilometers or 273,000 square miles) have already been deforested.

The Amazon basin is one of the longest stable geological regions on the planet, undergoing no major volcanic activity and little faulting or uplifting in the last 1.7 billion years.[5] This arcane fact is important—as a result of its geologic history, Amazon forest soils are also among the most "worn out" in the world. Over time, nutrients in the Amazon have washed off into creeks or been pushed deep underground by heavy rainfall.[6] Three-fourths of the region's soils are highly acidic and have high aluminum toxicity. Paradoxically, the world's richest forests live on the world's poorest soils.[7]

Compared to its geological history, the Amazon's climatic history has been far more tumultuous. Shifting air currents and fluctuating global temperatures have changed weather patterns and rainfall innumerable times in the basin. Still today, rainfall patterns vary tremendously from one end of the basin to another. Some places in the eastern Amazon have dry seasons that last for months, while just a hundred or two hundred kilometers away it may rain nearly every day, year round.

One controversial theory ties the tremendous diversity in species of animals and plants in the Amazon to its shifting and irregular climate. Developed in 1969 by Jurgen Haffer, the "refugia" theory suggests that drier periods in the past forced rainforests and their fauna to retreat to smaller pockets. Studies of fossilized pollen suggest that about ten thousand years ago the climate shifted to a more humid one, and the Amazon forest expanded far beyond its current range.[8] There is debate about whether those pockets were the wetter hills, as Haffer believed, or lowland areas, as proposed two decades later by Paul Colinvaux.[9]

The question of refugia is crucial, since it suggests where parks need to be set up if the most species are to be protected. Such parkland refugia may become the only islands of intact Amazon forest left in the coming decades, and choosing their location, size, and number now is a critical, if dismal, task. In 1979, Brazil established a set of thirty parks and preserves based in part on recommendations of the refugia theory. Parks in Suriname, French Guiana, Peru, and to a lesser extent in Bolivia and Colombia, have also been planned based in part based on the Pleistocene refugia theory.

Aerial cinematic views of the Amazon leave the viewer with the feeling that the forest is one huge unvarying carpet of green. Children's books and zoos educate about the "layers" of "the rainforest," but in so doing suggest that there is one type of rainforest in the Amazon. In truth, whole ecological communities differ in response to rainfall, temperature, and soil composition. Rolling hills, eroded ravines, occasional mountains, and shifting floodplains make vegetation patterns even more intricate. Even subtle differences in altitude and rainfall make huge differences in what is possible on a piece of land: Understanding the basic types of habitats in the Amazon is a first step to developing an appropriate development strategy.

The *terra firme* is upland, well-drained forest accounting for over 85 percent of the Amazon basin. Most highways built into the Amazon have sought these higher grounds to facilitate construction, and thousands of colonists have been settled there on farms by the government. However, attempts to farm along these upland roads have sometimes proven disastrous because the terra firme generally has very poor soils. In some lower-lying areas where nutrients have accumulated, farming is possible, but better-drained soils, on slopes and hills, have almost no agricultural promise.

By contrast, *varzeas* are floodplains of silt-bearing rivers, seasonally flooded with waters rich in nutrients, covering about 6 percent of the Amazon basin. The muddy, or "white," water drops its dissolved soil particles brought down from the Andes in predictable patterns. The heavier particles fall out first, along the riverbanks, forming levees that then create huge lakes along both sides of the river. Periodic flooding serves as weed and insect pest control, and Indian cultures have flourished on these habitats for millennia.

Archaeological estimates of human populations before Columbus's arrival and how they were distributed may indicate how many people the Amazon region can sustainably support. Geographer William Denevan estimated that over 4 million Amerindians inhabited the region before the arrival of Europeans, with the largest and most complex societies laying along the varzeas. These groups combined intensive agriculture in rich soil with fishing and gathering from other ecotypes.[10] These tribes, however, were most vulnerable to attack, slave raids, and exotic diseases brought by the Portuguese and Spanish. For this reason current Amerindian populations and distributions reveal a striking difference from the early days: Most existing reserves are located far from the main rivers on terra firme soils. Today, only about one-thirteenth of terra firme soils are fertile, although almost half of the floodplains are.[11]

The lower Andean slopes, or the *ceja de la montaña* (the "eyebrow of the mountains"), show some of the highest biodiversity in the world, with each altitudinal belt supporting a peculiar flora and fauna. World-famous botanist Alwyn Gentry reports that "the compaction of so many distinctive vegetational zones into such a small area makes the Andean slopes of special interest for conservation. . . . I estimate that approaching half of all neotropical plant species are found in the minuscule region.[12] These areas lie mostly in remoter regions of Colombia, Venezuela, Peru, Ecuador, and Bolivia.

Past the "Point of No Return"? Dissent on the Devastation

Around 1990, British rocker Sting appeared with Amazon Kayapó Indian Raoni, who wore a full white-feathered headdress and a disk in his lower lip, as they appealed to the Brazilian government and foreign funding agencies to get their reserves mapped. Grateful Dead and Phish acts were often dedicated to saving the rainforests. Shocking MTV ads told viewers that within the seconds it took to tell viewers about it, football fields of rainforests had fallen. In 2000 and 2001 Internet petitions circled the world explaining that the Brazilian Congress was considering a bill that would rapidly accelerate destruction of the Amazon forest. A direct mail plea from the Rainforest Alliance sent in 2000 alerted readers, "In the single minute it takes you to read this page, another 80 acres will vanish. By this time tomorrow, nearly 100 species of wildlife will tumble into extinction."[13]

These ads and pleas from rockers, environmentalists, academic researchers, and indigenous rights groups give what often seem to be apocalyptic visuals and statistics about the Amazon's fate, but they are highly disputed and cannot be accepted uncritically. How bad is it really? Will the Amazon forest soon reach a "point of no return" from which it could not recover? If so, how soon?

Two studies released in 2001 relit old wildfires of contention over how fast the Amazon forest is being destroyed, and how soon it might reach a point of instability. In 2000, a group of researchers led by Daniel Nepstad from Woods Hole Research Center and the Environmental Research Institute of the Amazon (IPAM) put out a report warning of the dangers of a new development push in Brazil, but got little publicity for their work.[14] However, January 19, 2001, the highest-profile outlet in American science, the journal *Science*, published a study by William Laurance of the Smithsonian Insitution and an international team of seven others.[15] TV film crews and national and international press flocked to the study's release in the remote Amazon city of Manaus.[16] "I've never been mobbed by the press before," said Laurance. The study was one of the first comprehensive analyses of the Brazilian government's seven year U.S.$10–$40 billion set of projects to boost its infrastructure and exports for the Amazon. The program, called Avança Brasil (Forward Brazil), called for the paving of thousands of kilometers of Amazon roads, the deepening and straightening of key rivers for shipping, and the construction of ports. Gas and oilfields, pipelines, power lines, logging concessions, and dams were also part of the project. Much of this development was geared to provide a cheaper outlet to the sea for soy farmers in Brazil's booming Center-

West agricultural belt.[17] Plans to pave the old rutted dirt roads that often become impassible in the rainy season were perhaps the most contentious part of Avança Brasil. Brazil heavily advertised the projects to overseas aid agencies and private investors, receiving some big promises from groups like the Japan Bank for International Cooperation (JBIC).[18]

The *Science* article was widely disseminated and featured two terrifying computer-generated maps of what the Amazon might look like in twenty years. Laurance and Colleagues's maps, detailing their "optimistic" and "nonoptimist" scenarios, showed deforested or heavily degraded lands in black, moderately and lightly degraded areas in red and yellow, and pristine forests in green. The computer models and maps were based on predictions about what might happen along the roads if they were paved and sparked a new wave of migration and land occupation. The "nonoptimistic" scenario had only a tiny bit of green left at all, indicating that only 4.7 percent of the Amazon would be left in its wild state in 2020.[19] The article stated, "Forest loss will be greatest along the southern and eastern areas of the basin, but there will also be extensive fragmentation and degradation of remaining forest blocks in the central and northern parts of the basin. . . . In all, nearly 42 percent of the region will be deforested or heavily degraded [by 2020]",[20] a shocking number three times the current amount estimated to have been cleared already.[21]

At the center of the controversy is the BR-163, a 1970s-era dirt highway that slices into the heart of almost intact Amazon forest from Cuiabá in soy-producing Mato Grosso state to Santarém, in Pará on the Tapajós River where it flows into the Amazon. There are estimates that the road will save soy producers in Brazil's Center-West U.S.$150 million per year in transport costs, and lumbermen another U.S.$50 million.[22] The muddy BR-163 and impassible side roads has long made it difficult for most farmers and small loggers to sell their products, even locally. The paving of BR-163 would change everything, for better and worse, bringing a better life for many or only quick profits for speculators and lumberers and a rapid decline, as has occurred along many other roads in the Amazon.

Santarém's vice-mayor, Alexandre Wanghon, favors paving the road for the economic and political benefits it might bring.[23] The road may very well create enough population momentum to create a new state of Tapajós, of which he would be a likely candidate for governor. "It [the road] will come like a hurricane. Our concern is to discipline the occupation that will follow." Citing Wanghon, the London *Guardian* reports that "speculators from all over Brazil are already buying up land along its route and oiling the chainsaws . . . a new port terminal in Santarem . . . has gone to Cargill, the world's largest soy exporter. ADM, another major agribusiness, is building local storage facilities."

The dire predictions of researchers are based on two deadly and synergistic changes for rainforests: fragmentation and fire. Laurance and two of his team members have worked on a huge research project examining what fragmenting forests does to the number of species they support.[24] That work suggests that forests along clearing edges are significantly altered and impoverished in species diversity. The team also looked at the effects of selective logging, which Penn State researcher Christopher Uhl had shown to damage significant proportions of the other nonharvested trees. Since ranchers and farmers use fire to make the nutrients from cleared trees available to their grasses and crops (the wood ash is rich in nutrients), the fires often escape control, as happened to forty thousand square kilometers in 1998.[25] "When you view these forests from a distance, they look OK," said Laurance's coauthor Cochrane, "but when you stand in them . . . you can see how they've been chewed up. It's like they have holes punched in them. These holes can make a rain forest dry out and be vulnerable to fire."[26]

The Brazilian government issued a swift and angry response to Laurance et al.'s report. Just five days after the *Science* article was published, Brazil's Secretary of Planning and Strategic Investments, José Paulo Silveira, held a press conference to say that Avança Brasil included not one kilometer of new roads and that waterways were chosen to be developed for their lesser impact.[27] Silveira said, "The predictions of deforestation are exaggerated and do not reflect a more careful analysis of future scenarios"; rather, they are based on data from 20 years ago before Brazil had environmental laws. He made the same points in a refutation published later in *Science*: "[S]ome 20 million people live in the Brazilian Amazon region, most of them very poor. We must offer these people a lifestyle better than hacking and burning. That is what Avança Brasil seeks to do, by steering development towards the appropriate and sustainable use of each individual area through correct zoning."[28]

Finally, about the time the comment was published, another study by geologist James Alcock predicted that the whole Amazon system could reach "the point of no return" in just 10 to 15 years and could "essentially disappear within 40 or 50 years."[29] His estimates are based on computer models of the feedback process of evapotranspiration, where rain that falls on forests is retained and later vaporized by heat back into the air to form more clouds.

Nepstad's group in Belém and Woods Hole described a similar set of factors leading to less rain coming off Amazon forests, altering local climates and making it more likely to be degraded and burn.[30] They chronicle three vicious cycles, driving the impoverishment of the forests and their imperilment. First, paving the Amazon highways will open up new areas to the "extensive" approach, creating quick-and-dirty approaches to ranching and slash-and-burn agriculture. Accidental fires also affect the selectively lumbered forests, multiplying the damage. Dark clouds of soot from forest fires have been shown to inhibit rainfall, and with less evaporation of rain from intact forests, rains decrease. They predicted some 25–35 percent of the forest would be destroyed in the next twenty to thirty years. Despite the similarities to the Laurance group's research, the two teams debated whose study was more complete and conservative in its estimates, and which was the most responsible science.

Ever since astronauts on the space shuttle in 1985 noticed thousands of fires in the state of Rondônia, the pressure has been on Brazil, the World Bank, and environmental groups to do something about Amazon destruction. However, people researching rates of deforestation in the Amazon often find themselves at the center of a political firestorm: If their estimates are high, they are considered alarmists who are anti-growth; if estimates are low, they are considered to be apologists for the government and the developers of the region. This was the case back in 1989 when three sets of estimates, all using satellite photographs, came up with different estimates of deforestation ranging from 5 to 12 percent.[31] The researcher with the middle estimate of 8 percent, Philip Fearnside of the National Institute for Research on the Amazon (Instituto Nacional de Pesquisa da Amazônia, or INPA) in Manaus, gained credibility for having what was the most acceptable number to both sides in the struggle.

In mid-2001, estimates of deforestation in the Amazon continued to vary widely. Estimates were as high as 20 or 25 percent, but the most widely accepted numbers were that 13 or 14 percent of the Brazilian Amazon forest (an area the size of France) has been completely cleared.[32] There is fairly solid agreement that annual clearing rates in Brazil range between sixteen thousand and twenty thousand square kilometers, with an average of around seventeen thousand.[33] These figures are down from the average for the period 1978–1990, which was around 22,500. This puts the rate of deforestation about 0.55 percent per year but there are still startling years, like 1995, when 27,100 square kilometers were destroyed, or 1998 and 2000, when a savage drought caused slash-and-burn fires to flare out of control and destroy significant forests in the western Amazon. The area denuded each year is often compared to Rhode Island for North Americans, Belgium for Europeans. Brazilians often bristle at the comparison of the areas of these tiny units, in comparison to the continental size of the Amazon rainforest. And they remind us that even the worst estimates leave 80 to 86 percent of the forest intact.[34]

So the Amazon, even as it falls, is full of uncertainties. We do know that it's getting worse and that there is a nonzero probability that something terrible could happen, such as a protracted El Niño drought and uncontrolled fires reaching larger swaths of dried-out damaged forests. But we don't know how likely that is. In the next section we consider some of the claims about the region's importance for humanity and the local and global environment. The stakes are tremendously high.

Contested Valuations of Amazon Forests

In the debate on what course development should take in the Amazon region, three main types of value have been placed on the forest itself:

1. As a source of exportable products and the site for economic expansion

2. As a "climate control" center for the world's atmosphere

3. As a massive library of genetic diversity and potential medicines for the future

In this section, we consider the claims heard most often in the press and examine some attempts made by scientists and economists to place an economic "value" on the Amazon. It will quickly become clear that there is no collective agreement of what the Amazon is good for—how you value it depends on where you stand, and what you stand to make from it.

The Amazon forest has real, direct economic value: Forest produce such as fruits, rubber, nuts, fibers, wildlife, and lumber are worth millions in internal production and exports for Amazon nations. Under the forests are billions of dollars worth of mineral deposits. Removal of some of these products, such as Brazil nuts and rubber, require that the forest remain sufficiently intact. Others like lumber, minerals, and farm products require removal or alteration of varying areas of forest.

A number of research projects have attempted to compare the economics of sustainable extraction versus more destructive land uses. The most publicized study, a 1989 *Nature* piece by respected botanists Peters, Gentry, and Mendelson, cataloged the marketable fruits, cocoa, oils, rubber, and medicines from tiny rainforest patches in the Peruvian Amazon.[35] The group reported that profits from harvests of these products are two to three times greater over time than logging or clearing the forest for pasture. Seventy-two species on the site yielded products with actual market values in the neigh-boring city of Iquitos, Peru.[36] Factoring in heavy transport costs and the cost of saving 25 percent of fruit harvests for regeneration, Peters et al. found that one plot could sustainably net U.S.$322 per hectare per year. Studies of Açaí palm fruit harvesting near Belém have also shown sustainable profitability without cutting forests.[37]

Sadly, virtually nowhere else in the Amazon basin are there urban popula-tions so willing to purchase the number of exotic forest products as are Iquitos residents. And many of the plots chosen for these studies are well situated in terms of transport to any potential markets. Lumbering and ranching often occur because they produce immediate income and are not perishable in trans-porting over long distances on terrible roads. Collecting forest products or growing perennial products that are less destructive produce income only over a longer term. Thinking long-term is a luxury for many people and next to impossible for almost everyone in times of economic or political uncertainty.

The Amazon's role in regulating the world's atmosphere continues to be given great importance in the popular press. But are Amazon forests really the "Lungs of the Planet"? Proponents of this theory believe the forest reduces excess carbon dioxide and produces enough oxygen to safeguard against the "greenhouse effect." Although this position served environmentalists as a shocking and effective political mobilizer, the "Lungs of the Planet" hypothe-sis appears to be largely incorrect. In truth, the forest fails to absorb any sig-nificant amount of carbon dioxide because it is a mature forest, and it recycles its carbon. Furthermore, the forest barely produces a surplus of oxygen. Rather, 90 percent of the world's oxygen is produced by underwater algae called phytoplankton. The algae are the real lungs of the world.

A more serious concern is that significant amounts of carbon dioxide are *produced* by rainforest burning. Tropical forest burning is currently the sec-ond leading cause of the buildup of greenhouse gas in the atmosphere, behind the burning of fossil fuels. At the peak of rainforest burning in the late 1980s, deforestation globally accounted for an estimated fifth of all global carbon dioxide emissions. Amazon burning was responsible for about 7 percent of worldwide emissions that peak year, and this number has dropped since then. By contrast, the United States emits 24 percent of all global warming gasses, year after year, from our addiction to fossil fuels.

The contribution of Amazon burning to global warming has become an extremely barbed political topic. In response to criticism from First World environmentalists, several Brazilian politicians and editorialists have pointed to the failure of these nations to control their own carbon gas emissions, or even deforestation or other environmental disasters. U.S. President George W. Bush has repeatedly said that he opposes moving forward on reducing greenhouse gas emissions without parallel efforts from developing nations. The issue is important, but the Amazon is not the site of the real battle.

Rather, the Amazon forest is extremely important in maintaining the area's climate, and it may affect global air flows. Because so much water is evaporated from forest trees, the water cycle of the region is being drastically affected by deforestation. Currently productive areas of Brazil, the south and Northeast are at risk of becoming desiccated as a result of disturbing the Amazon water cycles.[38] As mentioned in the last section, some recent climate models suggest some terrifying scenarios of deforestation driving devastating droughts and destabilizing the intact areas of forest. Brazil's 2001 energy crisis, darkening homes across the nation for rationing, was largely due to drought that sapped the hydroelectric supplies Brazil had come to rely upon. This ironically is causing Brazil to consider new dam and thermoelectric projects, some in the Amazon.

Is the Amazon the "Principal Genetic Bank of the World," the "Global Medicine Chest"? This point is often made in appeals from groups such as the Rainforest Alliance. "The active ingredient in 1 of every 4 prescription medications come from plants, many of which are found within the rainforest," reads an explanation on their Web site.[39] Despite years of teaching about the importance of rainforest species as a potential source of medicine, I (Roberts) remained somewhat skeptical. However, one of the first medicines my son received after being diagnosed with the usually fatal cancer infant leukemia was called Vincristine, derived from the whorled periwinkle plant, discovered in the disappearing rainforests of Madagascar. The drug is now used to treat non-Hodgkin's lymphoma, Hodgkin's lymphoma, rhabdomyosarcoma, Wilm's tumor, neuroblastoma, and multiple myeloma.

There does seem to be fairly wide agreement on the importance of Amazonia's biodiversity, as a massive store of genetic information and species diversity. As discussed earlier, the forest contains perhaps one-fourth of all species on the planet, and only a fraction of a percent of these have been analyzed for their potential uses. These uses include medicines, new fibers, food additives, new crops, and varieties of hardy wild stock for breeding with domestic crops to prevent diseases. What is *not* well agreed upon is who owns the rights to profit from those products, or who will pay for the lost opportunities taken away from Amazon nations for preserving them. Drug companies stand to benefit from "bioprospecting" in Latin America's rainforests, often without much benefit going to host nations or local populations. After they are discovered, new medicines are often synthesized in laboratories, leaving little need for the rainforest whence they came.

"To destroy even a hectare of tropical forest without studying it carefully is the same as tearing up a book without reading it," said biologist Daniel Janzen. "To destroy the entire forest amounts to burning an entire library."[40] Janzen works mostly in the tiny rainforests of Central America. Cutting and burning the Amazon might be better compared to burning the largest library in the world, the Library of Congress.

Finally, we must mention the importance of the forest as a refuge for some of the last remaining indigenous cultures, and for species and ecosystem types that have value of their own. We return to the issue of Indians in the Amazon shortly, and again at length in the next chapter. But first, we review who are the "stakeholders" in this massive struggle for the great prize: the Amazon. We've divided the seeming chaos into three parts, examining the struggles over land, subsoil, and trees. In each we contrast the interests and methods of large enterprises with those of small-timers, to get a picture of the struggle over Amazon development.

Just from looking at the types of habitats within "The Amazon," we can see the danger of a "one-size-fits-all" policy for the region. On top of that biological map we need to overlay the social story, the human history of who has done what, where, and why. It is crucial to recognize that there are indeed people—a lot of people—living in the Amazon. In Brazil alone, the population of the Amazon region has skyrocketed tenfold, from 2 million in 1960 to some 12 to 21 million today, depending on which definition of the Amazon one uses.[41] Some 70 percent of those people live in towns and cities.

Nine South American countries have boundaries within Amazonia, and each nation has a different pattern of forest colonization. Several nations, including Suriname, French Guiana, Guyana, and Venezuela, are just beginning to intensively exploit their Amazon territory. The most immediate threat to the integrity of ecosystems in these nations is probably tens of thousands of small-time gold miners crossing the borders from Brazil. The Surinamese government has been frantically leasing off vast tracts of its nation's forests to lumberers, and Malaysian firms have come in by the dozens.[42] Each nation is divided by conflicts among internal groups, and each stakeholder group has responded differently to the international furor over tropical deforestation. In the Amazon, there are virtually no constants. Therefore we should not be talking of "The Amazon," but of "The Amazonias."

If there is one constant it's that the desperation of Latin America's poverty and social inequality will continue to spread into the lush basin. In Peru, Bolivia, Brazil, and Equador, squatters and "homesteaders" follow new roads into the forest, invade a piece of land, and cut and burn a plot to plant. Poor Andean peasants plant coca in the Bolivian and Peruvian Amazons because it pays many times better than any other crop. Since 1960, Brazil, Peru, and Ecuador have used the Amazon as their main frontier for economic expansion—extracting petroleum, gold, and aluminum; logging its trees; and slashing-and-burning it for pastures and crops. Part of the foreign debt these countries now carry was incurred to build massive road, railroad, pipeline, mining, and hydroelectric projects to facilitate the development of this frontier.

Opening and Closing Frontiers in the Brazilian Amazon

Brazil accounts for 60 percent of Amazon forests and so it will be the focus of this and the following two sections. Economics, geopolitics, and a potentially explosive internal political situation have driven Brazil to develop its rainforest. Brazil's paranoid military government sensed an international covetousness of its natural resources in the Amazon, and has used landless settlers to secure its claims to what it called "a demographic vacuum" by offering rainforest plots to homesteaders along its borders.

Until recently the Amazon basin was protected by natural barriers to economic development—disease, temperature, heavy rainfall, difficult access—and its sheer size. Too poor to effectively protect the region, the Portuguese in colonial times prohibited the release of much information about the Amazon, for fear others would discover and seek out its natural wealth.[43]

In most of the Amazon, life until the early 1960s was a succession of booms in the extraction of spices, rubber, and Brazil nuts, each with their successive demise, as cheaper substitutes were found and prices dropped.[44] Local economies were never diversified to include significant processing of extracted materials: Profits were therefore shipped out with the cargo to national cities or across the ocean to the "developed" world. More lucrative processing jobs were created elsewhere.

National boundaries in the Amazon region have been a bone of contention between Latin American states since Spanish and Portuguese control reached the interior in the late 1700s. Boundary disputes continue to this day, especially between Peru and Ecuador, Colombia and Peru, and Venezuela and Guyana. The need for latex grew with the industrial boom in Europe and North America in the late nineteenth century, creating a sharp price rise and a boom in the Amazon—the sole global producer of rubber. The rubber boom reached its peak between 1880 and 1910, when rubber accounted for half of the exports from the Amazon region and a third of Brazil's total foreign exchange earnings.[45]

In Brazil, Peru, Ecuador, and Colombia, Indians were pressed into service collecting rubber from natural stands of *Hevea* trees scattered throughout the forest. In Brazil, poor from the country's northeast were also lured into the area with promises of work and fortunes. These collectors, or rubbertappers, were advanced the supplies they needed for a season in exchange for rights to collect on one parcel, and with the agreement to sell only to their distributor.

In those days, the only law in the isolated reaches of the Amazon was that of the rubber barons, and they kept their collectors in a state of perpetual debt by manipulating prices of supplies and the latex. While the system of debt slavery ("debt peonage," or *aviamento*) was used earlier in extraction of dyes, quinine, and rosewood oil, the rubber era was an especially brutal one. Imagine spending months on end walking the same soggy circuit trails through dark rainforests, visiting rubber trees, scratching grooves in the trunks to drain some sap, collecting that sap in tiny cups, and carrying the sap back to your campsite. Then firewood must be collected to slowly boil down the sap to make balls of rubber, which then are sold to the *aviador*, or middleman/boss. He tells you that the price is too low to pay for all the supplies you've used this year: gunpowder, soap, collecting tools, and your meager food. You must work again next year to try to pay your way out of debt. The rubbertappers were often forbidden from growing their own subsistence food, and the punishment for the sale of even a tiny portion of rubber production to anyone else or attempted escape was brutal torture or death.

The rubber boom ended almost overnight, when rubber seeds were smuggled out of the Amazon by the English to Malaysia, where plantation cultivation was possible because of the absence of a disease that killed the plants when planted densely in the Amazon. In 1910 the more efficiently produced East Asian rubber reached the market, and by 1911 the global price of rubber had plummeted. The deep economic depression that ensued left numerous rubbertappers in the area, and many reverted to subsistence farming while continuing to collect some latex. These peasants adopted at least some of the complex use of forest resources of the Indians, and many interbred with detribalized Indians. These longtime forest residents continue to specialize on a few products they can sell for some cash in addition to the subsistence use of the forest. Today, forest-dwelling groups continue to be called by their specialties: *Seringeiros* tap the rubber trees; *caboclos* live along the varzeas and farm and fish the riverbanks and floodplains; *riberenhos* also live on the varzeas but specialize more on fishing; and *castanheiros* gather Brazil nuts for cash. Estimates of how many people there are in any of these groups are entirely unavailable. World War II brought a renewed interest in Amazon rubber by the United States, but after 1945 the area went back into decline.

Dawning awareness in the 1950s and 1960s of the rich mineral resource wealth of the Amazon sparked the interest of the region's governments and businesses. In Brazil, President Jucelino Kubitschek's ambitious plans to move the capital to Brasília in the late 1950s signaled a new attempt to integrate the country's interior into the nation's largely coastal economy and polity. The completion in 1960 of a highway connecting the new capital to the Amazon port of Belém sparked a massive immigration by landless poor in search of farms. Large lumbering and ranching interests from the country's south often got there first, leveraging massive land purchases along the highway.[46] The Superintendency for the Development of the Amazon (called SUDAM) was set up in 1966 by presidential decree of the nation's military coup's leader, Castelo Branco, to spur regional development. According to the original charter, the role of the agency was to "support settlement plans and colonization designed to conquer empty spaces."[47]

Brazil's new military government made securing the nation's boundaries in the area a top national security priority in the mid-1960s.[48] By building highways, colonization projects, and military installations along key parts of its Amazon borders, Brazil began in 1964 what has become a continentwide land and resource rush. Peru, Venezuela, and Bolivia feared aggression by their much larger neighbor, and all have attempted to settle their own citizens on small farms along their jungle borders.[49]

In 1970, Brazilian President-General Emilio Medici was shocked by the poverty he saw on a visit to the country's drought-stricken northeast. Medici saw the Amazon as "a land without men for men without land." He offered land to dispossessed farmers to homestead in the jungle rather than undertaking the politically charged task of land reform (redistributing land from rich to poor) in occupied regions of Brazil. Soon thereafter, the government unveiled the Program for National Integration (PIN), which featured the construction of a two-thousand-mile Transamazonic Highway, bordered on both sides by small (one hundred hectares) subsidized homestead farms. The program promised to settle hundreds of thousands of families on these farms, with government loans, titling help, and guaranteed prices for their produce. Thousands of families migrated to the Amazon, but the government failed to provide the infrastructure and funding necessary for such a massive project.

Despite hopeful government reports, farming and ranching in the Amazon countries have been difficult at best. In most colonization projects, more than half of the government-settled colonists had abandoned their land by 1988.[50] World Bank–funded projects in the Brazilian Amazon worth $700 million reached only 16 percent of their original productivity targets by 1989.[51]

Problems with Amazonia settlement stem partially from the land itself, much of which is ill suited for farming and grazing. Imagine being settled on a farm that was laid out to make a nice rectangle on a land map back in the land agency office in Brasília, or in state or local offices in Belém or Marabá. One tiny corner might be on good soils, or none at all. Imagine clearing huge jungle trees, vines, and bushes with machete and chainsaw, carefully drying and burning the land, only to find out that the land was only good for a few years of productive harvests. Many cattle pastures and agricultural fields in the Amazon degrade, after just four years, into weedy wastelands with impoverished soils. Many colonization projects were quickly thrown together to settle farmers from other areas where there were conflicts over land. In this way, old problems were solved for the government at the same time that new problems were created for farmers.

Some experts have argued that blaming deforestation in the Brazilian Amazon on peasants is "blaming the victims."[52] Some estimate that these farmers only account for 10 to 20 percent of Amazon devastation. In Ecuador, Peru, Bolivia, and Colombia, small farmers are a much larger part of the cause of deforestation. More of the problem, however, may be attributed to the poor infrastructure and services provided to colonists once they reach the frontier. Many peasants promised land were never able to secure ownership because of the bureaucratic tangle and the isolation of the areas. Lacking title, they were unable to acquire the loans necessary to purchase seeds, tools, and fertilizers. The fact that most roads in the Amazon are unpaved and therefore impassible during the rainy majority of the year makes transporting crops to what are already distant markets nearly impossible. Cows, on the other hand, can walk out to market, even through roads impassable to trucks. Farmers arrived in the Amazon with little knowledge of appropriate farming techniques, and "agricultural extension" programs failed to provide adequate technical resources. Farmers in a colonization project in the southeast Amazon told us that *they* had to teach the government extension agent how to farm there. Peasant farmers also lacked the social services they needed to survive debilitating diseases such as malaria. Rural schools were horrible, forcing most farmers to maintain a house in the nearest town as well as one "in the bush."

Failing for one or some combination of these reasons, many small farmers sold their land to cattle ranchers and moved on to clear more virgin forest. Relocating was often more profitable than staying. In this way, small settlers literally prepared the ground for large enterprises. The land was concentrated into fewer hands and the forest never was given a chance to recover. Still today, thirty years after the building of the Transamazon Highway, small farmers are linked to deforestation, and controlling their land use remains difficult. In 1999 Brazil's environment ministry announced a limit on clearings by small farmers, to three hectares (seven acres) a year.[53]

Whereas farming continues to be a hardship for small farmers in the Amazon, ranchers, lumber companies, and construction contractors have the resources and power to make a better go of it. In Brazil's wealthier south and southeast, monied interests fought back against the 1970 incentives for small farmers by establishing a powerful São Paulo–based lobbying group, the Association of Amazonian Entrepreneurs, and pushed intensely for their own government subsidies.[54] They were quickly and immensely successful: in 1974 a new development program called POLAMAZONIA was unveiled, which was a virtual about-face in policy, featuring medium- and large-scale mining, lumbering, and ranching and massive hydroelectric projects. The new strategy attempted to maximize exportable production from the Amazon, and large-scale enterprises were seen as the most efficient means for doing this.

Tax breaks and direct subsidies financed by external loans and government largesse made ranching of immediate interest to powerful developers. Some of these ranches were enormous, the largest being Suia-Misu, occupying 625,000 hectares (over 1.5 million acres), and a huge ranch near the Transamazon Highway owned by Volkswagen, later sold to the Japanese group Matsubara. For the 549 early projects that were financed by Brazil's federal agency, SUDAM government subsidies averaged U.S.$2.5 million each.[55]

Many of Brazil's enthusiastic early proposals for utilization of the Amazon to expand cattle ranching were based on some overoptimistic reports—for example, that cattle actually improve the condition of the soil. These, however, were based on experience on other continents and were put forward because they provided rationale for the method of development favored by powerful interests in the south. A report by Yokomizoâ found that of the ninety such subsidized cattle ranches he surveyed, only three were profitable.[56] Overall they were producing only 16 percent of their projected profits, and herds were 40 percent of those expected.

Financially as well as ecologically, ranching in the Amazon appeared by the mid-1980s to have been a disaster. On average, many studies found that less than one cow could be supported by one hectare of pasture, and one for every two hectares may have been more common.[57] One calculation was that each 125-gram (quarter-pound) hamburger was produced at a cost of 75 kilos (200 pounds) of forest life being destroyed. Contrary to public conception, however, the beef did *not* end up in U.S. fast food: because of hoof-and-mouth disease, uncooked Brazilian beef could not be imported into the United States. Rather, Brazil's internal demand for beef was so strong and growing so quickly that the Amazon region and the country as a whole were reported to be actually net importers of beef.

Raising cattle also failed to provide employment: On average only one permanent job was generated for every one thousand hectares (five square miles) of pasture land. Instead, peasants are hired to clear forest on a temporary basis, and then laid off, causing them to move into the frontier to gain more work. Many ranchers are also responsible for the coercive removal of small farmers, forcing sale or abandonment with hired hit men called *pistoleiros*. Some of the most violent areas of the Amazon frontier have been the places most dominated by ranching.

While Brazil's fiscal incentives to cattle ranchers were largely cut in 1989 under the Nossa Natureza (Our Nature) program, at this writing existing projects continued to receive subsidies and tax holidays under grandfather clauses—some thirteen years later. But conversion of rainforests to cattle pasture can and does proceed in the absence of fiscal incentives.[58] Small and medium-sized farmers also keep cattle because cattle are good savings devices, since their value goes up with inflation and because they tend to appreciate in value. Because so much of the Amazon population is now urban, there is reliable demand locally for beef and milk. Brazil's annual estimates suggest that the numbers of cattle in the Amazon (north) region increased by 68 percent through the 1990s, from 13.3 to 22.4 million head. Thus it appears that older trends have continued even without the financing: Several experts have estimated that about 70 percent of deforestation in the Brazilian Amazon in its worst periods was due to cattle ranching.[59] Cattle ranching is almost without question the major cause of the problem, accounting directly for the deforestation of 21 percent of the state of Mato Grosso and 7.5 percent of Pará.

The fivefold increase in people in Brazil's Amazon has not been spread uniformly across the landscape.[60] As Amazon specialists began to note already by the late 1980s, the immense region so many imagine to be a never-ending forest or demographic vacuum is already a "closing frontier." My guide at the squatter camp, Alberto, with whom this chapter began, confirmed that the frontier was already closed for such impoverished farmers as these and that their occupation of the nature preserve was a truly desperate act. "We lost out in the other land distributions here, and only can find work clearing the land for the ranchers. Rent here in the city is two minimum salaries. Our jobs only pay one. The last chance we have is here." Economic and political power allows some individuals to lock up huge swaths of the forest and exclude others. Ranchers and other large establishments continue to struggle for land and access to natural resources with poor squatters while utilizing them as a cheap labor force. Like that battle between ranchers and small farmers for the Amazon's soil, *garimpeiros* (artisinal miners) have fought with huge mining corporations for what lies below the soil, and lumberers and those who survive on intact forests (rubbertappers and indigenous peoples) battle for the trees.

The Fight for the Subsoil

In attempting to prod the sleepy Amazon region into a dynamo for its national economy, the Brazilian government set out in the 1974 POLAMA-ZONIA development plan to gain benefits of grouped types of resource exploitation by funding enterprises around three "development poles." According to this thinking, each of these economic activities makes the other more viable since they share the most expensive infrastructure there: the roads and railroads. All three "poles" centered around large mineral deposits, especially massive iron and bauxite (aluminum) deposits discovered in the late sixties. "The time has arrived," said early documents of the plan, "to take advantage of the potential that the Amazon represents, principally to contribute significantly to the growth of the GNP."[61]

Suriname began mining its Amazon aluminum deposits in the 1970s, without fostering any associated development in its Amazon region. The same was true for development around the huge Icomi magnesium deposits that Brazil had opened up in Amapá state in the 1950s: Even three decades later only 2 percent of the state had been deforested.

But by the 1970s, the nation's attitude had changed, and Brazil had different plans for its massive Carajás mineral province of eastern Pará state, which had been discovered in 1967 by U.S. Steel. The story is a fascinating case of the struggle between foreign firms, the Brazilian government, and small artisanal miners over the massive wealth that lies under the rainforest shroud. Using helicopters for the first time in Amazonian mineral explorations and data from U.S. Air Force mapping and prospecting missions,

U.S. Steel's "Brazilian Exploration Program" crisscrossed the Carajás range and discovered what would turn out to be the world's largest deposits, 2 to 35 billion tons, of high-grade iron ore.[62] The message was telegraphed in code directly to Pittsburgh.[63]

Realizing the enormity of the discovery and finding borderline fraud by the American firm in staking its mineral claims, the Brazilian government forced U.S. Steel to accept a joint venture with its state-owned Companhia Vale do Rio Doce (CVRD).[64] But it was a classic case of global versus national priorities: U.S. Steel's own mines in Liberia and Venezuela stood to suffer from competition from Carajás, so the North American firm dragged its feet on the project.[65] The project was so huge that it could supply one-tenth of the entire world's demand for iron, some 50 million tons a year of a product whose price was already dropping with future demand uncertain. Reading World Bank predictions of a supply shortage coming up in 1985, CVRD pushed U.S. Steel to remove itself. After mysterious negotiations, the gringos accepted U.S.$50 million in payment for their investments to date.[66] Unable to find foreign partners for the immense venture in a time of a glut of iron and steel, CVRD then went it alone, as sole proprietor of the world's largest mineral province.

There is some irony in the fact that CVRD was closely linked to the country's military regime, which had overthrown the democratically elected João Goulart in 1964 with U.S. support in fear that he might nationalize American corporations in areas such as mining. After the 1977 departure of U.S. Steel, CVRD soon discovered excellent deposits of copper, manganese, and gold as well. However, U.S. Steel was in terrible financial straights, and observers speculated that its decision to withdraw was based on the realization that the main profits in steel were in the metallurgical stages, not the mining.[67]

CVRD's project at Carajás became a national priority after a visit to the barren mountaintops by President João Figueiredo in 1980.[68] The powerful Minister of Planning Delfim Neto designated an area 895,000 square kilometers—the size of France and Britain combined—around the mine and railroad for the Greater Carajás Project (PGC).[69] He formed a special interministerial committee and hired a Japanese consulting firm to strategize development.

Removing the minerals involved building an eight-hundred-kilometer railroad to the ocean, constructing a massive hydroelectric dam called Tucuruí, building cities and continental-scale highways from scratch, and raising over $3 billion in financing to do it. Federal planners reasoned, "Why not use this infrastructure to create a dynamic regional economy?"[70] This "growth pole concept" was adopted by the government and Japanese consultants proposed how it would work: To help create export products and hard currency for debt payments, an enormous incentive area around the mine and railroad would be created for lumbering, plantation agriculture, and a series of pig iron smelters.

A CVRD report apparently prepared by consultants from the Japanese International Cooperation Agency saw that the region around the mine could draw investment, "seeing as how the industrialized countries are facing growing costs of energy, labor, pollution, etc. and the conditions are extremely favorable to attract them." This suggests a somewhat cynical approach to the region's lack of environmental and labor protections, supporting the "pollution haven hypothesis" discussed in Chapter 2. One group of Brazilian academics saw the huge undertaking at Carajás as an attempt by the government to "create and manipulate a new perspective of a country with high development potential. [Carajás] contributes to rehabilitating the credibility of Brazil, to recreate the image of a frontier for the expansion of international capital."[71]

Under the plan, large areas of forest would be cleared for plantations, enormous lowlands would be flooded for hydroelectric projects, and twenty-three pig iron smelters (crude steel foundaries) would be fueled with charcoal from native forests.[72] European and U.S. environmentalists identified the project as potentially among the five worst disasters in the world. A member of CVRD's own environmental staff leaked a key document on the pig iron plants to international environmentalists and the press, and another publicly criticized the plans.[73] Studies estimated that it would only take about twenty years to entirely deforest the 980-kilometer belt along the railroad. As Amazon expert Phillip Fearnside commented at the time, "Brazil is violating it own laws."[74] A boycott on Carajás iron by the European Community eventually forced Brazil to cancel all but three of these plants.

Railroad and access roads around Carajás have opened the way to uncontrolled destruction as colonists, ranchers, lumberers, and gold panners rushed in. Our observations from the window of the train that we traveled between 1988 and 1991 confirm that the devastation was indeed vast.

With diligent environmental controls within its property, CVRD assured the banks, and the European Community consented to buy the iron. Today over 35 million tons of the red ore are carried by massive trains to the sea each year, where they are loaded on freighters bound for Japan, Germany, South Korea, France, Italy, and the United States. Many groups still believe mining to be the last hope for Amazonian development. Robert Goodland of the World Bank and the Brazilian newsweekly *Veja*, for example, have stated that mining will create the most income while destroying the least area of the forest.

Among those who rushed into the Carajás region were tens of thousands who came to work on the big construction projects: the roads, dams, mines, and oil fields. Others came hoping to set up a shop, bar, or restaurant in the hundreds of new Amazon frontier towns.[75] Hundreds of thousands of men have turned to small-time gold panning, silting up the creeks and rivers by running dirt through sluices, contaminating them with mercury used to separate dirt from the precious grams.[76] Brazil's devastating economic situation helped fuel a rush for gold by eliminating the poor's more secure options for survival.

A gold rush at Serra Pelada is the most dramatic example. The hill was just outside the Carajás preserve and was officially claimed by CVRD itself. But after one man discovered gold at the back of a ranch, tens of thousands of men raced to the remote hillside in search of fortune as rumors spread like wildfire of gold nuggets the size of baseballs. According to the unwritten but rigid laws of Brazilian garimpeiros, two-by-three-meter plots could be set up by claimants directly adjacent to another's pit, and a claimant could only hold as many plots as he could actively work at one time.[77] Plots multiplied in the areas that turned up the most gold, and the hill quickly became a hole. Gold was spotty and unpredictable, and because most "owners" of the plots went heavily into debt to hire workers to excavate the holes, ownership was quickly concentrated into a few hands. The mine gained fame for the thousands of mud-crusted men hauling sacks of mud out of the giant pit that grew to a mile wide and two hundred yards deep, an unbelievable site we witnessed in 1989.

The garimpeiros were unable to handle the problems that emerged at Serra Pelada as "the hole" deepened. By excavating only the nugget-rich pits, walls around the mine got progressively steeper and more precarious. The hole was the site of frequent accidents and dozens of miners lost their lives when mine walls caved in. The hole would fill with seeping groundwater, and even with a cooperative to pay for equipment like pumps and trucks, it finally filled up in 1990. Owning legal right to the site since 1974, CVRD looked enviously at Serra Pelada and speculated on what production it could sustain using more efficient mechanical mining. The garimpeiros, however, saw Serra Pelada as an important symbol of their national movement, and through repeated protests forced the federal government to reopen the mine again and again.

Most garimpeiros work in small teams in the creeks and rivers of the Amazon. Estimates have ranged as high as 1 million gold miners in the region, but the exact numbers will never be known. Other than the rich strikes such as that at Serra Pelada, where claims are just six meters square, two other types of *garimpagem* have far greater ecological effects: that in creekbeds and deep rivers. In creekbeds, miners work in small teams typically using two pumps and a sluicebox. One high-pressure pump is used to blast creek beds and banks with water, driving the dirt down into a stagnant pool they've created. Then the second pump pulls that water up into the felt-lined sluice box, where mercury is used to settle out the gold. Workers are advanced the tools and food by an "owner"; each takes a percentage based on the richness of the strike and on their skill, ownership, and bargaining ability.[78] Deeper river bottoms like the Tapajós and Xingú are mined with pump "dragons" mounted on rafts, which suck the silt off river bottoms into their floating sluice boxes.

While directly deforesting a very small area of the Amazon forest, garimpagem severely damages Amazon ecosystems. Siltation is tremendous, and the fish populations that were the sustenance of generations of Amazon inhabitants are totally devastated. Garimpeiros go everywhere, invading Amerindian and nature preserves near and far, traveling first with only a backpack loaded with food, clothing, a rifle, and a gold pan, then coming back later with hand equipment and, later, gasoline-powered pumps. Gold miners maneuver the Amazon's innumerable tributaries with powerboats and pontoon planes, and clear forests for simple airstrips and helicopter pads, to reach almost any location in the basin.

Mercury used in sluices and pans to fix the gold escapes by air and water to contaminate creeks and rivers. The contamination is endangering Indians, wildlife and the garimpeiros themselves: Ingesting mercury through the air, soil, or fish can lead to brain damage, death, and birth defects. The dispersal of miners throughout the enormous region has made control extremely difficult. It has also permitted the smuggling of vast quantities of gold to avoid taxation and export tariffs. Therefore the benefits to the society are limited. The Brazilian government is obviously very interested in increasing control of garimpagem, but the surprisingly good political organization of the garimpeiros and the fact that most are armed has led to something of a stalemate. Controlling garimpagem poses an immensely complex challenge on the order of controlling cocaine production in the region, to which we turn after considering the other battle—over the forests.

Which Way for the Trees and Waterways?

Lumberers have cut their roads into some of the remotest reaches of the forest, searching out mahogany and other valuable hardwoods. "Mahogany knows no distance," one lumberman told us in the remote town of São Felix do Xingú. "We will build a road any distance to get it."

The need of Amazon nations to bring in foreign exchange has favored "instant development" strategies such as lumbering the forest. Diminishing stocks in Southeast Asia's rainforests are also fueling the saws in the Amazon. This problem is worsening: Lumber production for export is increasing rapidly in the Amazon. A report by the International Tropical Timber Organization said that even though Latin America possesses 57 percent of the tropical forests and 27 percent of the forest reserves of the world, its share of the tropical wood market in world trade (excluding pulp and paper) is at present less than 5 percent. Brazil's forest product exports are only 1.8 percent of global exports.[79] Nevertheless, given the extent to which the forest reserves in Southeast Asia and Africa are being depleted, and the limitations of industrialized countries to significantly increase production, Latin America will undoubtedly have a much greater share of the international market in the near future. Commercial logging of virgin forests has been promoted by the national government as a low-cost way to boost exports— huge tax breaks and subsidies to lumbering firms were begun in the late 1960s and continued until 1987.

Unfortunately, reforestation efforts remain uncommon in the Amazon. Many of the most desired species, such as mahogany, are rapidly disappearing and regrow very slowly. One of the hopes is that the timber trade could be certified by savvy consumers, providing incentives for cutters to also take care of replanting and caring for the trees in a more sustainable way. Sustainable agroforestry could be viable in substantial tracts of the Amazon, but a number of factors make it unlikely to be adopted by small farmers.[80] As is the case with other protection issues, insecurity of income and land tenure leads to short-term planning by Amazonia's small farmers. Agroforestry requires long hours of tough labor, and no results come from tree crops such as cacao for at least five years. Fast-growing *gmelina* and eucalyptus take a decade or two to reach harvestable size. It has been difficult for small farmers to get bank credit for annual crops, let alone perennials that take years to bear fruit or lumber. Finally, rainforest pests are tough on trees, especially those planted in homogeneous plots.

Lumberers and ranchers often come in conflict with rubbertappers, Indians, and other "people of the forest." Rubbertappers and Indians fought between themselves for decades, but now frequently see their needs as overlapping and complementary. Rubbertappers, as described earlier, live a fairly sustainable existence bringing the boiled-down latex sap to collection points, work that requires that much of the forest remain intact. As we also discussed earlier, Amerindians have shown that the Amazon forest can support millions of people on a sustainable basis for thousands of years. Indians and later the rubbertappers have combined the cultivation of a variety of crops in small clearings with the gathering of forest products for food, medicines, and building materials. Indians' subtle manipulation of the forest environment includes planting fruit trees in old fields and promoting the growth of medicinal and food plants in the existing forest.

Today, however, even the indigenous preserves are the site of devastating lumber and gold extraction deals between Indian leaders and businessmen.[81] This topic is little discussed in the literature, perhaps because it is an uncomfortable one. While outsiders would prefer to believe that indigenous groups protect all the resources in their control, that is not always the case. Laurance et al. predict that as roads come closer to reserves "corruption of traditional lifestyles can occur, sometimes leading to a sharp increase in forest exploitation."[82] A recent *Newsweek* article reported that indigenous groups have illegally cleared protected lands, stopped firefighters, and "even assaulted government inspectors attempting to control illegal logging."[83] But as anthropologist Bill Fisher documents, Amazon Indians like the Kaiapó he studied have grown dependent on very basic "trade goods" they need even to maintain a relatively spartan forest existence (pots, pans, machetes, salt, and so on).

Indians have been mobilizing politically to defend their land and in Brazil have formed some important coalitions with their old enemies, the rubbertappers, to fight predatory development of the Amazon. Together they make a critical internal political alliance for preservation. The Indigenous Federation was formed to join all Amazon tribes as a political force in 1989, and the Amazon Alliance brings together Indians, rubbertappers, and ex-slaves living in "maroons" from all nine Amazon nations. At their Amazon Forum V, which we attended in Washington, D.C., in June 2001, they shared many of the same concerns: ranchers, lumberers, land demarcation, poverty, health care, and education. They strategized and built cooperative agreements on how to address these needs. Two examples of their cross-border organizing are featured in the next chapter.

Currently about five immense hydroelectric projects are on line in the Amazon. Each has similar problems: Huge zones of flooding cause destruction of habitat and native lands and farms, and the lakes have problems of siltation and a reduced useful life span. Because trees were sometimes not cleared before flooding, methane is produced as they rot underwater, which can damage the dam's turbines. Brokopondo dam in Suriname, 150,000

hectares in reservoir area, was in 1964 the first dam built in tropical rainforest without clearing, and it experienced numerous problems. Development
around building the dam can also engender an associated development boom.

Three huge projects in Brazil—Tucuruí, Samuel, and Balbinas—have
proceeded without heeding the experience of Brokopondo. Some harvesting
of wood actually went on underwater with new submersible chainsaws at
Tucuruí. Robert Goodland, from the World Bank, stated in 1985 that
smaller dams could have been built "at less environmental cost than the single high-head at Tucuruí."[84] A large number of dams have been planned for
the Brazilian Amazon, but because of the international uproar over the ecological and human costs of building them, there has been less talk of these
in the recent past and it is unlikely that more than a few more will be built.
Facing an international uproar, Sheldon Davis of the World Bank reported
at the 2001 Amazon Forum V that they are not funding any dams at present.[85] However, facing a damaging energy crisis that forced rationing and
hurt the president's popularity in 2001, Brazil is "dusting off" old hydro
projects abandoned twenty years ago for environmental reasons.[86] Brazil is
simply looking elsewhere for the funding: to private banks and its internal
funds. Among those most at risk of losing their land are indigenous groups
in the Amazon.

The Drug War and the Colombianization of the Amazon

Of the multitude of plants in the Amazon, coca has always distinguished itself
as special. Run off good soil by Spanish conquistadors and their descendents,
the Incas discovered coca in the jungle and celebrated the new crop as a gift
from the gods. The Incas, pioneers of advanced agricultural systems, found
themselves struggling for survival in a marginally inhabitable jungle—chewing
coca leaves not only alleviated their hunger but actually gave them an energy
boost. Elaborate rituals came to govern the production, harvest, and distribution of this sacred plant, still very much a medicinal and cultural staple of the
Andes. Today, however, indigenous coca rituals have been overshadowed by
another coca distribution network—a $5-billion international drug trafficking
labyrinth that supports a culture of violence, corruption, and abuse.

In August 2000, the United States approved a $1.3 billion aid package
to Colombia as part of the "War on Drugs" to get cocaine off American
streets.[87] This aid package, known as Plan Colombia, provided funding (funneled through the Colombian army) for a massive coca eradication offensive
designed to biologically destroy half of all Colombia's coca crops in two

years. Crop eradication efforts were concentrated in the Colombian Amazon, an area one-fifteenth the size of the legal Brazilian Amazon with close to equal its biodiversity. By May 2001, aerial sprayings of the herbicide glyphosate had successfully wiped out thirty-five thousand hectares of coca (almost half the annual goal of eighty thousand hectares).[88]

Here's how it is supposed to work: Glyphosate (better known by its trade name, RoundUp, a Monsanto chemical) penetrates plant's cells and within a few days, the plant completely shrivels up and dies. Glyphosate is marketed as a water-soluble herbicide that can "eradicate weeds and unwanted grasses effectively with a high level of environmental safety." It is the miracle silver bullet in weed eradication—after a couple of days at work wiping out unwanted plants (at a 90–95 percent effective rate), glyphosate "breaks down" and disappears.

The first problem is that glyphosate does not seem to be able to discriminate coca from legal agricultural crops. As Carlos Alberto Palacios, Secretary of Human Development in La Hormiga, Colombia, explains, "We believe we will go hungry. They've fumigated everything, fields and plantain rows and yucca and everything that people need to live on."[89] Colombia's indigenous communities like the Cofán people in Putumayo have watched their harvests, including sacred ceremonial crops such as yagè, shrivel up. In Putumayo (the center of Plan Colombia's "push into southern Colombia"), where the initial spraying has been concentrated, cows and other mammals are reported to be turning up dead.

Government officials are correct in their assertion that illicit coca production can be environmentally destructive. First, land must be cleared, and every small coca monoculture requires some 1.3 tonnes of imported chemicals.[90] This intensive production exhausts delicate soils, and every year some sixteen thousand hectare of coca plantations are abandoned because of low productivity.[91] Processing coca leaves into cocaine paste requires even more chemicals, which also contaminate regional ecosystems. Eventually (either from overproduction or aerial spraying) land becomes infertile, and many small farmers see no economic alternative but to seek out virgin forest, clear it, and begin planting a new harvest. As this cycle continues, farmers are pushed further into the Amazon. Meanwhile, the more coca is destroyed, the more profitable coca production becomes.

Critics of Plan Colombia charge that the fumigations are causing coca production, military violence, and guerrilla violence to spill over across Colombia's borders. Glyphosate contamination and fumigation refugees seem to be spilling over, too—already, some eight thousand Putumayo farmers are reported to have been displaced by aerial sprayings.[92] Peru, Venezuela, Ecuador, and Brazil have all expressed concern about the plan; many, like Brazil, are beefing up their own military presence along the border.[93]

The militarization of the Amazon is a central concern of the plan's opponents. One U.S. civilian pilot was killed by guerrillas from the Armed Revolutionary Front of Colombia (FARC) during a routine fumigation run in 1998.[94] The recent fumigations in Putumayo (previously a FARC stronghold) have met surprisingly little opposition, thanks to (depending upon who you talk to) the success of U.S.-funded Colombian ground units or paramilitary violence in the months preceding the flights. Given the complexities of the Colombian Civil War, many are concerned about the United States aligning itself with the Colombian military, especially in light of its human rights record. The United States has already committed helicopters, arms, and counternarcotics training to the military—a signal, for some, of the beginnings of the "Vietnamization" of Colombia. According to people like Venezuelan president Hugo Chavez, the fumigation strategy (and the proposed use of the *fusarium oxyporum* fungus as an herbicide) amounts to biological or "green" warfare—a twenty-first-century version of the Agent Orange used against North Vietnam.

Plan Colombia does include money to assist over twenty-five hundred families who agree to voluntarily pull out their coca crops in exchange for around U.S.$1,000 in direct economic aid and technical assistance. These crop substitution plans are crucial in working toward a more socially sustainable Colombia, but alternative development schemes only work when peasants trust the state. Furthermore, crop substitution incentives must be supplemented with a broader regional development scheme to improve rural education, infrastructure, and access to health care. This is a basic lesson from the failure of countless small farmers in Brazil's Amazon.

In May 2001, Colombian indigenous leaders visited the U.S. Congress to protest Plan Colombia's damage to the environment and their traditional way of life. These protests built on earlier actions, including a series of marches from July to September 1996 in which some 240,000 coca farmers participated.[95] Already, 12 percent of Colombia's Amazon is reportedly degraded, much of it from coca farming and coca eradication.

Weighing Proposed Solutions: No Panacea, but Guarded Hope

After just three days in the Amazon on my first trip there in 1988, it was clear to me that the world's vastest forest was not going to be preserved intact. After a year there I realized the absurdity of the Amazon debate as it was often conducted. It became difficult to resolutely say that the ranchers and lumberers, gold miners, and government official were wrong for wanting to bring "light" to their frontier and to earn money for themselves and their families. They too have moral intelligence, but as we do with things we're frightened to see in ourselves, we've projected onto these Amazon entrepreneurs the image of evil: selfish, destructive, and heartless murderers of cuddly forest creatures and harmless Indians. We can point to their wrong without examining the contradiction of our own lifestyles. Meeting and living with the characters involved, however, complicate the issue.

There are already over 20 million people living in Brazil's Amazon region and another 2–5 million in the eight other nations that house the other half of the Amazon forest.[96] These 22–25 million people need livelihoods, and they and their fellow nationals become understandably apprehensive when they sense that foreigners are threatening their sovereignty by proposing the fencing off the rainforests for parks. Back in the 1980s Brazil's president and the military regime used foreign environmentalists as targets for nationalist rhetoric, saying they were stifling the nation's hopes for development.[97] This sentiment lives on: For example, in 2000 and again in 2001 an e-mail hoax went around Brazil with an attached file of a page from a supposed geography textbook from the United States, "widely used in Junior High school classrooms." The map showed an enormous area called the "Amazon Forest Preserve" set up by Americans to protect the region from the irresponsible and corrupt peoples who live around it. Thousands of Brazilians believed the hoax and were outraged at what seemed like a typical American approach toward the region: arrogance and bullying, lacking of respect for sovereignty and local people.[98]

Steadily, it seems, the political scene is shifting. In the last fifteen years, Amazon Indians and their once rivals the rubbertappers have come together in Altamira, Belém, Brasília, and Washington, D.C., to fight the destruction of their domain. The World Bank has been forced to respond to pressures by international environmentalists and indigenous rights groups to cease funding projects that cause large-scale damage to the forest. They have over a decade of experience now with designating some entire projects to conservation. The debate is moving into new territory as a broader consciousness emerges over the need for sustainable development: Local populations have a growing awareness of the risks of deforestation. A 2001 study of opinion leaders in the Amazon and a random sample of the population in three Amazon states of Brazil found that the forest was highly valued and deforestation was a great concern, that ecological zoning was a popular idea, and that the goals of environmentalism that also addressed social needs were strongly supported.[99] After nearly a decade of very little action on environmental protection, the Brazilian government announced at the World Summit on Sustainable Development in September 2002 that it would triple the size of protected areas in the Amazon.[100]

Several strategies that we discussed in Chapter 3 to address problems of the Central American forests apply in the Amazon as well: agroforesty, ecotourism, debt relief and ecological zoning, and sustainable, managed extraction of resources.[101] Each has possibilities and limitations, but each also deserves serious consideration and continued funding by international aid and lending agencies and environmental and social NGOs. Zoning is a good idea to help control land use in rainforests and more generally in Latin America, although site-level specifics about soil quality and microclimatic shifts need to be considered in deciding what should be done where.[102] To be successful, such zoning cannot be done without concern for the social and political landscape.

Pharmaceutical prospecting among indigenous medicine men and women is worthwhile, if there is a way to ensure that the benefits of these hugely profitable products are shared justly with those who are the stewards of the resource whence they came—the forest. Otherwise outside bioprospectors are little better than the gold-seeking garimpeiros.

Throughout the 1980s, state policies that promoted lumbering and ranching drove much of the worst destruction of the forests, although these enterprises generated little economic benefit. At a minimum, subsidies and tax breaks that encourage environmentally devastating land uses should be avoided. However, it is now clear that both lumbering and ranching can be profitable even without subsidies, so they cannot be expected to disappear when subsidies are cut. The other side of the new consensus in the Amazon is that those interested in solutions to protect the region are seeing that both can now be done in less environmentally damaging ways. This will require serious state presence in law enforcement to allow the environmental agency IBAMA to levy the serious fines and imprison violators who illegally clear, burn, and log the forest, as allowed under Brazil's 1998 "environmental crimes law."[103]

Since we in the North have already cut much of our forests, we can indeed not tell those in South and Central America not to use theirs. We cannot and should not propose "fencing it off." Without seeking to rebuff all the proposals set forth in the ominous Avança Brasil program which caused the firestorm of debate in 2001 (now called the PPT), then, we remain seriously concerned about the environmental impacts of the new plan. Probably oil drilling and mining, if carefully done, will impact the forests the least. Today there are many alternative extraction methods to minimize the spilling of oil-field wastes, and some even avoid building the roads that attract migrants. Dams and other megaprojects often cost billions of dollars and have dire environmental and social consequences (see also the next chapter). The long-term viability of dams remain uncertain in areas deforested by the waves of colonists that destroyed regional watersheds and silt up river basins. Rather, we join with the Woods Hole/IPAM Belém group's proposal that agriculture needs to be *intensified* in the areas now under extensive production, rather than undertaking another wave of extensive, sprawling growth based around cattle ranching and newly paved roads of Avança Brasil. Such intensification must take care with the effects and risks of dependency on increased fertilizer and pesticide use. Finding a way to expand the use of the Amazon's tremendous rivers is probably a more appropriate transportation solution than paving roads, if it can be done safely.

Is land distribution the solution? We believe that land reform must be undertaken in earnest, with real reorganization of the rural landownership patterns. However, equally important are the resources that small farmers need to succeed: markets for their products, with reliable roads, medical care, malaria prevention, technical assistance, transportation, educational opportunities, clear title to their land and access to bank credit to buy seeds, pest control, fertilizers, and food for their families.[104] Farming, especially in rainforests like the Amazon, is far from a simple or certain business. The people are there, so the economy needs to work.

Perhaps the grimmest problem in Amazonia is impunity of environmental criminals and murderers alike. The struggle over the Amazon has long been a violent one, most dramatically seen in the December 1988 assassination of Chico Mendes, leader of the rubbertappers union, by ranchers. Mendes's death was a rare glimpse into the innumerable confrontations on the land, in the frontier towns, in courtrooms, in IDB headquarters, and in the halls of Congress as the struggle for control of the Amazon shifts, ebbs, and advances. In 1992, the international group Human Rights Watch reported that of the homicides committed in the Amazon region of Brazil, few were ever brought to trial, and virtually none were convicted.[105] In more recent land struggles, fewer peasant farmers are dying in the conflicts, as they have become better organized into larger land invasions. But the violence continues. Eduardo Martins, the president of IBAMA, admitted in 1997 that "practically 100 percent of the fines applied against those who destroy fauna and flora are never collected."[106] Most are not even investigated—this seems to be true for many assasinations of labor and farmer organizers. A first step in improving the situation in the Amazon, therefore, is helping Brazil build a functioning policing and judicial system that will slowly improve the rate of corruption and bias in the current system. International groups can be important in supporting these efforts, a point we take up in our concluding chapter.

Addressing the problem of the hundreds of thousands of renegade garmipeiros and illegal loggers roaming the region invading every preserve and indigenous area is a daunting task, but national governments, especially Brazil, must seriously engage themselves in working toward solutions. Foreign aid may also be crucial in this process. Some very basic remedies could spark an almost immediate upswing (although these certainly are not simple to distribute deep in the rainforest). For example, miners can purify their gold by burning off mercury in simple recapture vessels, which cost maybe U.S.$40 and can pay for themselves quickly, since the captured mercury can be saved for reuse. They are reported to reduce mercury emissions to the envionment by 99 percent. It is imaginable to see some aid group distributing the recapture vessels for free, along with a technical and educational outreach program to help miners to understand why they are necessary. More complex mercury-free methods could come later. This could be coordinated with the work of a well-funded and well-staffed malarial control program, which is desperately needed as part of an improved public health network in the rainforests of the region. A low-cost program could be designed to combine medicinal malarial control measures with disease prevention (to minimize miners' permanent disturbance to creek beds, and so on). Again, there need to be environmental agents with police support to allow them to fine and control miners, lumberers, and ranchers in remote regions; scenes of IBAMA agents in bullet-proof vests jumping off of helicopters and doing exactly that sort of thing have appeared periodically on Brazilian television since about 1990. That year President Collor took a military approach in bombing illegal mining airstrips in the Yanomami indigenous preserve, also in an attempt to stop drug trafficking through the region.

The problem of artisinal mining in the Amazon waxes and wanes: The allure of the garimpeiro gold rush grows and shrinks with gold prices and is largely driven by unemployment and desperation elsewhere. The migrant sending regions, especially the desperately poor and drought-stricken areas in northeast Brazil, need sustained attention to providing appropriate development there. And here is another lesson from many issues in this book: The dynamics driving environmental crises are often far outside the regions most affected.

The Amazon shares with the rest of Latin America the issues of how to create sustainable parks and biosphere reserves that serve the needs of local peoples while stabilizing their borders from invaders. Biosphere Reserves and fair trade efforts described in Chapter 3 are a start. Certainly the marketing of products that valorize the forest in its uncut state are worthwhile small steps. Examples are Rainforest Crunch ice cream from Ben and Jerry's, Brazil Nut lotion from The Body Shop, and so on. The Ben and Jerry's case, however, had some ironic twists that are quite instructive for our goal of suggesting viable, non-naïve solutions. The Brazil nuts for the ice cream were initially provided through cooperatives and indigenous groups organized by the nongovernmental group Cultural Survival. However, demand soon outstripped supply from these "fair trade" sources, so the company ended up buying nuts for a time from the Mutran family, one of the most exploitative of the old "Brazil Nut Baron" oligopoly.[107]

International support has an important role to play in most of these proposed solutions. It cannot set the direction, but it can support worthy initiatives. There are many existing local groups with long track records of involvement in these socio-environmental issues. The next chapter on indigenous issues is a continuation of these debates and will raise more policy issues for the region. Those concerned about the environment will have a very difficult time gaining support among the population of the Amazon if they are, as one environmental group puts it, "mindlessly against growth." However, they can be "against mindless growth," if they can provide viable alternative solutions. To summarize our approach, we argue for an eco-social approach that seeks to address social needs and environmental protection at the same time.

Shuar/Achuar demonstration against Houston-based oil and gas
company, Burlington Resources. Macas, Morana Santiago,
Ecuador—April 11, 2002. Photos by Leo B. Gorman.

CHAPTER 6

Indigenous Peoples, Development Megaprojects, and Internet Resistance

With Leo B. Gorman

About four hundred years ago Spanish conquistadors penetrated northeastern Colombia, pushing a large group of indigenous U'wa people to the upper limits of habitable forest, just below tree-line at twelve thousand feet. According to U'wa oral tradition, a portion of the tribe committed mass ritual suicide rather than submit to enslavement. Thousands of U'wa placed their children in ceramic pots and threw them off a fourteen-hundred-foot cliff; the adults then walked off the edge backward.[1]

Modern U'wa leaders threatened to repeat the same fate if Los Angeles–based Occidental Petroleum was to go through with plans to drill for oil on U'wa sacred land, stating, "We would rather die, protecting everything that we hold sacred than lose everything that makes us U'wa."[2]

On November 16, 1999, over two hundred U'wa marched onto Occidental Petroleum's planned oil well, Gibraltar-1. There, within their legally recognized territory, the U'wa set up a permanent camp to block the drilling slated to begin in the following weeks. About two months later Colombian police, under pressure from Oxy,[3] used tear gas and physical blows to disperse more than 450 U'wa (including women, children, and elders) who were blockading the road leading to the drilling site. In the aftermath of the chaos, three children were reported to have drowned and two were missing and presumed dead.[4] A week and a half later, more than twenty-five hundred Colombian supporters arrived in the small community of Gibralter. Campesinos (peasant farmers), students, and union members in solidarity with a well-organized support network in Europe and North America joined U'wa groups in resuming the blockade of the road.[5]

Just two months earlier along the Venezuela–Brazil border, Pemon and other indigenous groups tore down four huge electrical towers supporting the Guri Powerline, an industrial megaproject linking the two countries and which will bisect indigenous ancestral lands. Two hundred Venezuelan National Guard members surrounded the protesters and warned there would be physical retaliation if they downed more towers.[6]

According to a 1995 U.S. State Department Report, "Where indigenous people clash with development projects, the developers almost always win."[7] No longer, however, are state and multinational developers finding it easy to simply ignore indigenous demands to ancestral territory and culture. With the globalization of investment capital has also come the globalization of communications and human rights law. In the past two decades, national laws and international conventions on indigenous rights have increased space for indigenous groups to maneuver. Through e-mail, the Internet, telephone, fax, photocopies, and international conferences, Latin American indigenous peoples are establishing unprecedented links with other regional indigenous organizations and environmental/human rights activist communities in North America and Europe. As a result, native communities and their supporters are now waging persuasive transnational campaigns in the name of self-determination, cultural survival, and ecological stewardship.

These conflicts raise a series of questions that will guide our brief analysis of contemporary indigenous groups' struggles. How are industrial megaprojects impacting Latin American indigenous communities? What are the historical and contemporary roots of conflicts between megaproject developers and forest-dwelling indigenous groups? What are the economic, political, social, and cultural factors that shape current indigenous–developer conflicts? How are indigenous groups (and their growing support networks abroad) confronting frontier forest development policies? And finally, what are the short- and longer-term prospects for change?

Often when Westerners conjure up images of rainforests they picture pristine forest landscapes lost in time, bright green tropical vegetation wet from a recent shower, squirrel monkeys swinging on liana vines, and multicolored toucans and macaws flying gracefully above the towering canopy. Seldom do we envision the native inhabitants of these fragile ecosystems and the sight of oil wells, gold mines, logging camps, and electric power lines that have now become part of their forest habitat. Yet the struggle for indigenous rights is inextricably linked to the environmental sustainability movement.

In the words of Ryser and Karn, the earth's biodiversity "is mirrored by the diversity of cultures humans created over great lengths of time."[8]

In this chapter, we seek to address the changing dimensions of Latin American indigenous struggles in the midst of national economic liberalization and the rise of transnational social movements. To grasp the extent of this conflict, we first examine the colonial, postcolonial, and modern roots of indigenous land/resource disputes and review the analytical tools offered by Fourth World Theory. Later, we follow the U'wa and the Pemon in two case studies of indigenous–developer conflicts. We then turn our attention to the resistance strategies adopted by Latin American indigenous people, highlighting the importance of cross-border organizing. Finally, we address both short- and long-term proposals for conflict resolution and sustainable development, such as land demarcation, environmental law enforcement, community-based economic endeavors, indigenous autonomy, and debt relief. We begin with the big picture, putting the two cases into perspective of struggles around the region.

Evolving Assaults on Indigenous Lands

Since the arrival of the Spanish in the fifteenth century, indigenous peoples in Latin America have consistently come in conflict with Westerners over land and natural resources. The precious natural resources extracted by the Spanish and Portuguese in Latin America came from indigenous lands. Deforestation, soil degradation, disease, indigenous territory loss, and cultural erosion followed. Unfortunately, the same pattern continues five hundred years later, with a variety of state, national, and transnational actors as the resource extractors.

Throughout Latin America and the Carribbean there are some 40 million indigenous people, more than 10 percent of the region's total population. In places like Bolivia, Guatemala, Peru, and Ecuador more than 40 percent of the population is indigenous. There is tremendous diversity within Latin America's estimated four hundred ethnic groups, but most share one important characteristic. Ninety percent of all Latin America's indigenous people are subsistence farmers, and most continue to depend very directly on the environment for basic survival.

Contemporary indigenous–developer conflicts begin to shed light on a belief held by many economic planners in both developing and developed countries, that protecting indigenous land interests will impede economic development. "You can't compare the interests of 38 million Colombians

with the worries of an indigenous community," said Rodrigo Villamizar, former Colombian Minister of Mines.[9] From the other side, Pemon Indian
leaders from San Rafeal de Kamoirán in Venezuela articulate a different
point of view: "[These megaprojects] will impose a model of development
contrary to our harmonious relationship with nature. . . . They will attract
to our territories large non-indigenous populations that will strip us of our
territories."

Groups like the U'wa and Pemon are calling into question the dominant
development paradigm of Western-led economic growth through big development projects like resource extraction and the building of roads and dams.
Instead, they argue for true self-determination, autonomy, and traditionally
based economic initiatives.[10] Governments, as the Amazon Alliance's director David Rothschild explains, often side with big developers because "in
each case the government feels like the country is dependent on the project
going through."[11] In the 1970s and 1980s, state developers and multinational banks promoted a modernization model based on megaprojects.
These megaprojects, such as the Three Gorges Dam in China and the
Brazilian Carajás project discussed in Chapter 5, were multibillion-dollar
ventures with massive environmental, social, and human rights concerns.

We have made this point before, but it has special meaning for indigenous people across the region. Facing great pressure from runaway inflation
and economic instability, most Latin American governments in the last
twenty years attempted to pay the interest on their foreign debt and so
needed hard currency reserves. Together, these needs have placed heightened
pressure on Latin American governments to extract and export whatever
valuable natural resources they could find within their tropical forests. This
"economic progress" has often become a direct threat to indigenous groups
who depend on the forest for survival.

To understand the roots of current development policy, we must look
back to a long history of territorial and cultural colonization in Latin
America. Conflicts between oil interests and native Colombian peoples, for
instance, date back almost a century. In 1916, the Colombian government
granted the U.S.-based Tropical Oil Company a thirty-year exclusive contract to the Mares Concession, in the area known as Barrancabermeja in the
department of North Santander—just north of U'wa territory.[12] The oil concession led to the Yarigue indigenous people's "rapid extermination." In
1931 the Barco Concession (North Santander) led to the passage of Law 80
by the Colombian government, which put "all the protection needed to repel
attacks by the Motilon savages" at the disposal of the oil companies.[13] Sixty

years later, the Motilon people had lost over two-thirds of their ancestral territory and more than half their original population.[14]

In the 1960s in southern Colombian department of Putumayo (near the Ecuador border), Texaco (Texas Oil) and Ecopetrol began constructing access roads and pipelines and drilling for oil. Land-seeking peasants swarmed into the region, and rivers, creeks, and groundwater were often contaminated due to oil development. Such impacts lead to the displacement of Inga, Siona, Kofan, Huitoto, and Coreguaje indigenous peoples. In less than two decades, these indigenous groups lost 84 percent of their legal territory, which facilitated the gradual loss of food self-sufficiency, traditional political organization, language, and customs. During the mid-1980s, a string of British Petroleum oil discoveries in the municipalities of Yopal, Tauramena, Monterrey, and Aguazul in Cansanare province sparked a wave of colonization that tripled the area's population. Thousands of indigenous people were displaced in the process.[15]

Today, oil remains one of Colombia's most important commodities. In 2000, the oil sector represented more than 15 percent of the nation's GNP and was a leading national export, ahead of coffee, bananas, and cut flowers.[16] According to the Colombian Ministry of Mines and Energy, Colombia would have to begin importing crude oil by the year 2004 if significant explorations are not made. "This situation underlies a concern that state responsibility for minority rights and environmental protection must not block economic development," noted the *Oil and Gas Journal*.[17] But the more Colombia becomes limited by structural finance reforms, the more important rapid oil development has become for the Colombian government.

Ultimately, land used by many native communities for subsistence is considered "undeveloped," and thus in need of economic modernization. Land conflicts emerge as these two development ideologies intersect—indigenous people on the one side and economic "progress," "modernization," or "development" on the other.

"The same situation is happening at over 100 other localities in South America—a conservative estimate—some slightly better, some very much worse [than the U'wa]," says the director of one indigenous support network.[18] A brief look around the continent confirms this. A project mentioned in the last chapter, the Brazilian Tapajós Waterway, an industrial route for large ships exporting grains from northern Mato Grosso to the Amazon River, has faced opposition from Munduruku and Kaiaibi indigenous groups whose reserves would be affected by dredging, canal and lock construction, and road construction.[19] Plans have also been delayed in Brazil on the construction of the Belo Monte or Cararão Dam on the Xingú River. This controversial infrastructure project would flood a portion of the Kayapó indigenous reserve and cause irreparable damage to the local ecosystem. In 1989, the project lost World Bank funding due to environmental and indigenous opposition, but the Brazilian government continues pursuing the project.[20] As a Kayapó Indian told representatives of the World Bank, "In the old days, my people were great warriors. We were afraid of nothing. We are still not afraid of anything. But now, instead of war clubs, we are using words. And I had to come out, to tell you that by destroying our environment, you're destroying your own."[21]

The reports come like a drumbeat. Ecuador's Cofan people once numbered fifteen thousand. After Texaco moved into their territories and constructed 200 oil wells and a 315-mile pipeline, their numbers dropped to barely 650. One report from the late 1980s documented more than 3.2 million gallons of toxic waste spilling from Texaco's operations every day.[22] The Trans Ecuadorian pipeline alone has "leaked" 16.8 million gallons of crude into the Amazon River—one and a half times more than the Exxon Valdez spill.[23] Today, Texaco is facing a $1.5-billion class action lawsuit filed against the firm in the United States and a consumer boycott organized by the Rainforest Action Network and Acciòn Ecologica. In June 1994 Ecuador's twelve indigenous groups united to shut down the whole country for two weeks. These groups protested, among other things, decades of environmental destruction and social irresponsibility by Texaco.

In 2000–2001, indigenous communities and farmers in Brazil and Bolivia mobilized against a 630–kilometer gas pipeline, sponsored by U.S.-based Enron International and Shell International Gas Ltd., which would cut through tropical forest in both countries.[24] Indigenous people in the community of San Matias (near the Brazilian border) have experienced water and air pollution, soil degradation, and a growth in crime and prostitution from new neighboring worker towns.[25] The pipeline was completed despite the protests, and most of the worst fears of environmental groups have occurred.[26]

In 1982, Shell Oil discovered South America's largest gas field in the Camisea area of the Peruvian Amazon. Camisea was supposed to propel Peru into a net exporter of hydrocarbons and generate billions in tax revenues. Indigenous groups report that pollution, social unrest, and increased rates of infectious disease have accompanied the project.[27] In 1998 Shell pulled out its $250 million investment in the project, and the gas field went up for auction.[28]

In many other places around Latin America, the situation varies only in details. In Guyana in 1995, a tailings pond at the foreign-owned Omai gold mine gave way, spilling over 800 million gallons of wastewater laced with cyanide, cadmium, mercury, arsenic, and copper. In March 1997, three Guyanese citizens filed suit in a Montreal court for some twenty thousand people, many indigenous, living near Omai River. The suit attempts to hold the companies responsible for cleanup costs and $69 million in damages—damages that, as Moody argues, could have been avoided if the company had only built a second tailings dam.[29]

In Panama, the Kuna Indians are battling a proposed copper mining facility. Donald McInnes, president of the Canadian company Western Keltic Mines, was quoted as saying, "They have explained to me that the Kunas have not permitted us to enter their territory, but I like challenges."[30] The argument that resource exploration projects like Western Keltic will "bring economic development to the natives" and help to "modernize the savages" raises centuries-old concerns about rights, racism, and the nature of progress. It is too easy to write them off as inevitable, but such mineral extraction claims often ignore the cultural and spiritual richness of the indigenous people and undermine the basic human rights principals guaranteed under international law.

Internal Colonies and "Fourth World" Theory

How do indigenous worldviews, religions, dress, music, and organizational structures fit into contemporary political and theoretical frameworks? Most frameworks divide the world into threes: There are the "First World" capitalist nations, the old Soviet-bloc socialist nations of the "Second World," and the "underdeveloped" poor nations of the "Third World," over which the first two battled. Others, such as the World Bank and left-leaning academic world systems theorists, also have three categories: high-income or "core" countries, middle-income/"semiperipheral" nations, and low-income/"peripheral" nations. While these categories do not perfectly correspond, they overlap significantly. In the late 1970s, indigenous scholars began responding to the limitations of these models, arguing that cultural and spiritual understandings of space and power should be incorporated into our theoretical arrangement of the world. They conceived of another world, a "Fourth World" of indigenous nations comprised of aboriginal people who have "special non-technical, non-modern exploitative relations to the land in which they still live and are disenfranchised by the states within which they live."[31] These poor and disenfranchised "Fourth Worlds" exist within other nations.

For proponents of Fourth World Theory, theoretical structures based around the economic wealth of nation-states are inadequate to explain patterns of violence and "ethnocide" perpetrated upon the world's indigenous people. University of California–Berkeley anthropologist Bernard Nietschmann, after working for decades with Miskito Indians in Atlantic Coastal Nicaragua, questions whether aboriginal nations can be squeezed into the European model of a nation-state. He argues that

> states and nations represent two seemingly irrepressible forces in collision: states, with their large armies, expansionist ideologies and economies, and international state-support networks, and nations, with their historical and geographic tenacity anchored by the most indestructible of all human inventions—place-based culture.[32]

This is, of course, a core battle in the era of globalization. Fourth World Theory reasons that modernization, capitalism, industrialization, and globalization have alienated people from land and nature—today, indigenous nations are threatened by a new pattern of recolonization. They argue that this "Third World colonialism" or "internal colonialism" continues the rape-and-pillage patterns established by European colonialists by robbing Fourth World nations of their resources and pushing indigenous peoples off their ancestral land.[33]

Fourth World theorists are working to reclaim indigenous history through their work and activism in solidarity with the international indigenous rights movement. This movement is intimately linked with some environmental groups and advances the idea that biological and cultural diversity are often mutually supporting. Closer study of the U'Wa and Pemon cases reveals some of the complexities of these relationships.

The Thinking People: The U'wa of Colombia

The U'wa, known in their language, U'wa ajka, as "the thinking people," are a semi-nomadic hunting-and-gathering group numbering approximately five thousand. They inhabit the cloud forests of northeastern Colombia, in the north Santander province near the Venezuelan border. The U'wa believe that the earth granted them life, and, as such, their ancestral territory, Kajka Ika, or the "Heart of the World," and the resources it possesses are sacred.[34]

The U'wa occupy an oil-rich region known in the industry as the "Samore block," which is estimated to hold around 1.5 billion barrels of oil—about three months' supply for U.S. consumers.[35] The original consortium to drill for oil in the area consisted of OXYCOL (Occidental of Colombia) with 37.5 percent of the market share; Royal Dutch/Shell (37.5 percent); and Ecopetrol—the state-owned oil company (25 percent).[36] In February 1998, because of a variety of political, economic, and public relations reasons, Shell withdrew its commitment to drill in the Samore block. The current Gibralter project investors are OXYCOL, Ecopetrol, Occidental Andina (an Occidental subsidiary), and Cia De Petroleos Cordillera, a Venezuelan firm.[37]

On August 24, 1999, U'wa leaders and the Colombian government signed an agreement that nearly tripled the official size of the U'wa Unified Reservation to 534,000 acres.[38] Since then local campesinos aided their U'wa neighbors by selling them two farms that encompass the Gibralter 1 site, bordering the U'wa Unified Reserve.[39] Although the current Gibralter exploratory area falls within U'wa traditional lands, it falls outside their legally recognized territory. Under Colombian law, Occidental was not required to even consult the U'wa people when it purchased exploration rights in April 1992.

Because of their relatively remote location in the mountains, the U'wa were seldom contacted after Spanish engagement, and by 1940 they subsisted on lands stretching to southern Venezuela. During the 1940s and 1950s, the first road was constructed into their territory. Displaced campesinos from Colombia's civil war settled on U'wa lands, igniting cultural friction and competition over resources. To accommodate white/mestizo colonizers and Catholic missionaries, the Colombian government ceded more than 85 percent of U'wa traditional subsistence territory between 1940 and 1970, reducing U'wa lands to just one-sixth of their former size.[40]

Colombian courts have not been of much help to the U'wa, issuing a series of contradictory rulings regarding U'wa legal rights. In January 1995, two government-sponsored consultation meetings were held between U'wa representatives and Oxy. Although the U'wa leadership was not given sufficient time to discuss the meetings and clearly opposed the project, the Ministry of the Environment interpreted the meetings as adequate consultation and granted Oxy the environmental license for seismic exploration.[41]

In August of the same year the U'wa filed suit against the Ministry of the Environment in the Superior Court, arguing that Occidental failed to properly consult with the U'wa about the project. The U'wa won, but the ruling was soon overturned by the Supreme Court in favor of Oxy. This decision was again reversed in February 1997 by the Constitutional Court, citing that the U'wa had not been properly consulted and the exploration license threatened their ethnic, cultural, social, and economic integrity.[42] However, in March 1997 the Council of State, by a vote of 14 to 7, gave Occidental the green light to proceed in their exploration, ruling in favor of "the general interest of the Colombian people, the dominion of the State over the national territory and the State ownership of the subsoil above all other considerations, including the rights of indigenous peoples protected under the National Constitution, as one critic put it."[43]

The U'wa presented colonial land titles from 1661 in which the king of Spain recognized both the surface and subsurface land rights of Colombia's indigenous people.[44] In an 1873 supreme court decision, the Colombian government said that all subsoil mineral rights belonged to the state except for those granted to parties under the "Royal Land Deed" law. This finding has tremendous legal implications for both the U'wa and other Colombian indigenous groups, given that in the past Colombian courts have consistently upheld colonial law.[45]

The U'wa contended that Occidental had (1) not properly consulted the legitimate U'wa leadership, a right guaranteed under the 1991 state constitution; (2) not fully disclosed pertinent environmental and social impacts of the proposed projects; (3) consciously attempted to undermine U'wa credibility by linking them to guerrilla activities;[46] and, in their overall negligence, (4) violated national and international legislation on indigenous and human rights. Occidental stated that it had complied with all existing Colombian indigenous consultation and environmental laws.

The year 2001 was a rough one for Occidental in Colombia—in the first six months of the year, its pipeline was bombed more than 110 times, rendering its Cano Limon field inoperable. Occidental made headlines again when its private security contractor, AirScan, was implicated in an attack on the small community of Santo Domingo in which twelve people, including nine children, were murdered.[47] Then, in August 2001, as many U'wa were in the middle of a three-month spiritual fast in which U'wa shamans prayed to Sira, their God, to "hide" petroleum from the company, Occidental issued a statement that it was unable to find oil on the Gibraltar 1 site.[48] The news of U'Wa celebration traveled around the world in hours. While the U'wa consider this a tremendous victory, they caution that Gibraltar 1 is but one of several Occidental operations on U'wa traditional territory. With oil in its known reserves running out, Colombian Senator Hugo Serrano said, "This is very bad news for the country."[49] U'Wa leader Daris Cristancho said, "We plant to continue our struggle with the help of international non-governmental organizations so that Occidental leaves our territory for good."

The Pemon and Other Southeastern Venezuelan Indigenous Groups

In the southeastern Venezuelan state of Bolivar in the Guyana region, the Pemon and several other indigenous groups (Karina, Arakawa, Akawaio, and Warao) are confronting two specific development issues. Decree 1850, declared by former President Caldera in April 1997, opens up to large-scale logging and mining concessions 40 percent of the Imitaca Forest Reserve, much of which indigenous groups claim as ancestral territory. The second controversial issue is a binational project, signed in 1996, between the Venezuelan and Brazilian governments. The Venezuelan state-owned electric company, Corporaciòn Venezolano de Guyana (CVG-EDELCA), is planning to sell hydroelectric power to Brazil via a 470-mile-long powerline. A $110 million project, the Guri Powerline would cut across indigenous ancestral lands in the Imitaca Forest Reserve and the Gran Sabana in Canaima National Park, a World Heritage Site.[50]

The Guri Powerline route falls within various protected areas: 80 percent of that in Canaima National Park (60 percent of this within the strict protection zones), 15 percent in the Imitaca Reserve and 5 percent in the Sur del Estado Bolivar Protection Zone.[51] The project would clear a twelve- to thirty-three-meter-wide service corridor from the Guri Dam near Puerto Ordaz in northern Bolivar State to Boa Vista, Brazil.[52] Decree 1850 and the powerline would impact over twenty-four thousand people in more than thirty indigenous communities. The powerline and future binational development projects in the Guyana region stem from Venezuela and Brazil's eagerness to boost their economies by integrating them more closely. In April 2000, Venezuelan president Hugo Chavez and then Brazilian president Fernando Henrique Cardoso met to discuss possible binational business endeavors and reaffirm existing ones such as the Guri Powerline. Both presidents considered it a necessity to (1) stimulate bilateral relations; (2) promote an agreement between the countries of the Andean Community (CAN) and those of the Common Market of the Southern Cone (MERCOSUR); and (3) propel the energetic and physical integration "that should be understood as the fundamental pillars of the Brazilian-Venezuelan approach."[53] In a joint declaration the two heads of state also said that it is a priority to "create an effective association of interests" between the petroleum companies Petrobas of Brazil and PDVSA of Venezuela, who are interested in constructing a gas pipeline linking the two countries.[54]

The Pemon and other native groups contend that they were not consulted about either issue and believe that the Guri Powerline, if allowed to proceed, would attract more mining and logging into the region. Indigenous communities are concerned about the following threats: (1) destruction of the forest and plains ecosystem;[55] (2) loss of biological diversity; (3) mercury and cyanide poisoning in water sources (from gold processing); (4) the invasion of independent gold miners; (5) the increased crime, violence, and prostitution that accompany mining towns; (6) increased rates of malaria; (7) safety issues concerning the close proximity of an electricity powerline; and (8) further erosion of indigenous control over land, resources, and culture.

As in Colombia and other Latin American countries, economic restructuring has accelerated penetration into Venezuela's frontier forests. With world oil prices in constant fluctuation and a national poverty rate exceeding 50 percent, diversification of the economy is a top priority for economic planners in Carácas.[56] The largely "undeveloped" forests south of the Orinoco River, identified by the World Resource Institute as "Venezuela's last large block of intact forest," contain unexploited natural resources such as gold, timber, and hydroelectric power—making the region very attractive to national and multinational developers.[57]

Bolivar state indigenous groups have responded primarily through direct action (protests, blockades, etc.) and national legal campaigns (lawsuits), in addition to modest transnational mobilization. Attossa Saltani, director of the Los Angeles–based Amazon Watch, has commented that the indigenous struggle in Bolivar state against Decree 1850 and the Guri Powerline "became the posterchild for indigenous people [in Venezuela] gaining territorial rights" during the drafting of the 1999 Constitution. Their opposition, Saltani suggests, was pivotal in putting indigenous land issues on the national agenda.[58]

On August 26, 1998, indigenous representatives and government officials came to a breakthrough agreement. The government stated that it was prepared to recognize indigenous property rights and would suspend all work on the powerline until the question of land title was resolved. Despite these negotiations, the following day near the Pemon village, where the talks were held, Indians continued their monthlong blockade of crews attempting to clear land for the pipeline. National Guard troops were reported to have assaulted several of the village residents with rubber bullets and tear gas.[59]

Several days before the April 2000 meeting between Venezuelan President Chavez and Brazilian President Cardoso, the Indigenous Federation of Bolivar State (FIEB) signed a preliminary agreement with the Venezuelan government allowing the powerline to continue under two key conditions: (1) that indigenous lands in Bolivar State be demarcated and legally recognized and (2) that no industrial development receiving energy from the Guri Powerline would be permitted within Canaima National Park in the future.[60] But there are deep splits between different indigenous groups on the process and what is acceptable development in their territories: The final agreement that was officially signed by FIEB in July 2000 worsened a sharp division between the organization and its twenty-nine supporting communities on the one hand and the sixteen impacted indigenous communities who are still opposed to any major development projects on their ancestrally claimed lands.[61]

Anti-powerline indigenous leaders voiced that the agreement violated their indigenous rights and customs. They maintained that FIEB's decision to sign the preliminary agreement with the Chavez administration was made by a majority vote, and not by consensus—an action that the communities in resistance contend does not reflect their traditional decision-making process. Anti-powerline indigenous communities also have stated that the Federation did not consider that their communities, although the minority in the voting process, will be the most affected by the construction of the powerline.[62] They argue that despite the conditions of the agreement, the powerline will obstruct visibility of their ancient landscape, violate sacred places, and lure industrial and commercial development to the Gran Sabana.[63] According to Jovencio Gomez, a Pemon leader,

> We have taken action into our own hands, and exercised our rights in the supreme court of justice. We have had protests and specific marches, but we still weren't listened to. We are clear about what specialists say will happen to our community if this project goes through. That is why we take these kinds of actions, acting to tell Venezuela, the world, and our government that the indigenous people exist and we have rights, and we must be taken into account. Our culture and traditions have a right to exist and be taken into account just like any culture.[64]

The Shape of Transnational Indigenous Rights Activism

At the annual Amazon Alliance meeting in Washington, D.C., in June 2001, indigenous leaders mingled with North American supporters, the conference room a mix of bright batiks, conch shell jewelry, macaw feather headdresses, and jeans. I (Thanos) promise to call one Pemon man soon for an interview and he says with a nod of the head, "Better to e-mail."

Resistance strategies frequently take aboriginal groups "across worlds" into high-speed communications networks where information sharing, urgent e-mail actions, and cross-border coordinating are accessible with a click of the computer mouse.

Here we review and compare indigenous activist strategies as they have emerged in the Colombian and Venezuelan cases, briefly comparing them to the larger indigenous-based Zapatista movement in Mexico. Of course each conflict has its own unique circumstances, but we will argue that activist responses to indigenous land threats depend on a number of common factors. The shape these struggles take are determined by a series of factors, which give different constraints and possibilities for leverage to indigenous groups:

1. The type of developer—whether state or multinational—and its investors/funders

2. The amount of political and legal space Indians have to maneuver in

3. The economic situation of the country

4. How citizens both at home and abroad respond to the struggle

We return to the three struggles and recount the shape cross-border organizing has taken, focusing on the most successful case, the U'Wa.

Transnational organizing around Latin American indigenous rights and the environment began to converge in the mid-1970s when many Northern conservationists began to pay closer attention to the native peoples that lived in and around the nature parks they wanted to establish. Later, in the 1980s, Northern cultural survival and human rights groups established greater links with indigenous organizations by providing funding, technical resources, and advocacy support.[65] Among the most famous efforts was the work of anthropologist Darryl Posey and the Environmental Defense Fund and Conservation International, who brought Kayapó Indians from Brazil's Amazon to Washington, D.C., to meet with congressional leaders and World Bank leaders to attempt to stop the construction of a series of huge dams along the Xingú River. Cross-border alliances organizing around a specific indigenous issue can be thought of as transnational social movements— "closely interrelated groups and organizations belonging to more than one country that sustain interaction for coordinating mobilization to reach common—but not necessarily transnational—goals."[66]

Transnational advocacy campaigns on behalf of indigenous rights have been significant in other development conflicts, such as those of the Brazilian Yanomami and the Ogoni in Nigeria. The U'wa struggle has similarly been supported by a strong network of international allies who have mobilized important economic and political resources. Strong leadership within the U'wa Traditional Authority by Berito KuwarUw'a, and its current leader Robert Perez who won the distinguished Goldman Award for environmental activism, have further empowered local U'wa resistance.

Organized international support for the U'wa began in September 1996. Responding to a National Indigenous Organization of Colombia (ONIC) request to support the U'wa cause, the Amazon Alliance for Indigenous and Traditional Peoples of the Amazon Basin issued an "action alert" over the Internet, which addressed the U'wa's claims of Oxy violating their rights.[67] Support within Colombia for the U'wa emerged: In addition to the legal suits filed by ONIC, in August 1996 Senator Muelas organized the U'wa Forum for Life at the entrance to the main U'wa reservation; Colombian citizens, international journalists, and NGOs attended. In April 1997 (before the May Council of State court ruling in favor of Occidental), three thousand students, environmentalists, and journalists marched to the Ministry of Environment in Bogota to demonstrate their support for the U'wa.[68]

Growing awareness about the conflict in the United States propelled the *New York Times* and AP–Dow Jones News to release news stories about the issue the following month. A coalition of U.S.-based NGOs that includes Amazon Watch, Rainforest Action Network, Project Underground, and the Earthjustice Legal Defense Fund—called the U'wa Defense Working Group—was formed in July 1997 to "publicize the U'wa struggle and mobilize international support by organizing institutions and people in defense of the U'wa."[69]

Other transnational actions have followed. In January 1998 the Rainforest Action Network began a campaign that targeted Shell and Occidental for their involvement in the Samore block. The U'wa Defense Working Group took out a full-page ad in the April 14, 1998, edition of the *New York Times* headlined, "Why Occidental's Oil Project Is a Death Sentence for the U'wa People."

International mobilizations moved to another level in March 1999 when three U.S. indigenous rights activists, Ingrid Washinawatok, Lahe'ane'e Gay, and Terrence Freitas (one of the founders of the U'wa Defense Working Group) were murdered in Colombia by FARC guerrillas.

Controversy mounted as several early reports linked the U.S. government to the killings, through aid money to guerrillas and arms sales.[70] That two of the activists were U.S. Native Americans suggests how solidarity was being built between these indigenous communities.[71]

Continuing to raise awareness about the now sensationalized conflict between a "pristine indigenous culture" and the powerful oil industry, Amazon Watch and Action Resource Center organized a nonviolent direct action against Occidental's headquarters in Los Angeles; protesters "installed" a twenty-three-foot-long mock pipeline in Occidental's lobby.[72] On October 12, 1999 (Columbus Day and a day of international U'wa solidarity), five activists rappelled from the Colombian Consulate in Beverly Hills and unfurled a banner in Spanish that read "Colombia: Invest in Peace, Not Oil."[73]

In the spring of 1999, celebrities such as Bonnie Raitt, Martin Sheen, and Cary Elwes and Congresswoman Cynthia McKinney (D-GA) helped as environmentalists and indigenous rights activists targeted Vice President Al Gore, then running for president, who had inherited from his late father $500,000 of Occidental stock held in a blind trust.[74] They attempted to make the U'wa case a presidential campaign issue as U'wa activists from Boston to L.A. staged vocal demonstrations in Gore campaign headquarters and speech sites and at the Democratic National Convention, calling on Gore to cut his family ties to Occidental. He did not.[75]

The U'wa campaign effectively targeted another key Occidental investor, Fidelity Investments. After activists waged over seventy-five protests at its offices around the world from February to October 2000, Fidelity sold 60 percent of its Occidental shares, totaling more than $400 million in value.[76] According to Simon Billenness, senior analyst at the Boston-based "socially responsible investment" firm Trillium Asset Management Corporation, "Fidelity is between a rock and a hard place, since they don't want to set a precedent by taking a stand on drilling, but also don't want to lose investors who are concerned about where their money goes."[77] A Fidelity spokeswoman said that the divestment was "based solely on the merits of the company, and was not connected in any way to the U'wa campaign."[78] Activists, however, claim that world's largest investment firm's divestment was a result of an intensive activism campaign.

Shell and Occidental, two of the most powerful oil conglomerates appear to have demonstrated substantial sensitivity to transnational U'wa campaigns. The same day that an OAS/Harvard team issued their recommendations, Shell abandoned the Samore project altogether, and Oxy decreased its original concession by more than 75 percent. Although Shell cited financial reasons for the pull-out, the public relations "black eye" they received for drilling in Nigeria,[79] coupled with the possibility of another human rights disaster in Colombia, leave the question open.[80]

Shell's pull-out in February 1998 from the Samore block and Fidelity's divestment are significant events, as corporate fear of possible human rights and environmental disasters appears to have taken precedence over their potential earnings there. A November 29, 1999, *Oil and Gas Journal* article read, "The continuing standoff with the U'wa has escalated to a critical mass, to the point where the next step by either side could put the white-hot spotlight of the world on a single well . . . tantamount to another Brent Spar or Exxon Valdez."[81]

For the Pemon in Venezuela, the situation has been quite different. One key difference is the *target* of their campaign—the Venezuelan state-owned electric company makes a much more difficult target for transnational organizers than does a high-profile multinational corporation. Still, indigenous organizations in the Gran Sabana and Chiapas have also established cross-border links with North American NGOs. These Northern groups help to raise awareness about the conflict via advocacy campaigns and also provide crucial financial and technical resources to which indigenous groups would otherwise have little access. In 1997, for instance, the Alliance for Indigenous and Traditional Peoples of the Amazon Basin sponsored meetings between Pemon and Karina leaders and U.S. government officials. Los Angeles–based Amazon Watch trained Pemon leaders to document firsthand their struggles through the use of video equipment, photography, and the Internet.[82] Other U.S.-based groups, such as Global Response, have organized Internet action alerts and letter-writing campaigns aimed at applying pressure on Venezuelan governmental officials to act on the behalf of affected indigenous groups.[83]

However, it has been activism *within* Venezuela's borders, comparatively, that has elicited the most significant legal and political changes. Since April 1998, affected indigenous communities and their supporters in Caracas have mobilized against Decree 1850 and the Guri Powerline. In June 1998 the Indigenous Federation of Bolivar State (FIEB), an organization representing the region's native peoples, filed two lawsuits against the national government: one contesting the legality of Decree 1850 and the other challenging the powerline. As mentioned earlier, a series of anti-powerline direct actions materialized between July 9 and September 1998. Supported by the Indigenous Federation and national environmental groups, the Pemon and other native groups initiated a blockade of the El Dorado highway, the access road for the Guri Powerline. On July 27 over one thousand indigenous people from Pemon, Karina, Arawaco, and Akawaio groups rolled several massive logs onto the only highway linking Venezuela and Brazil. On August 12, the eleventh day of the blockade, the National Guard forceably dispersed eight hundred protesters. One observer described the tense scene: "The National Guard came at dawn in riot gear with orders from Carácas to remove our blockade. Using a military tank they removed the logs we had used to block the road. The soldiers forced our people out of their tents, some still sleeping or half-dressed, and continued to aggressively disassemble our camp."[84]

In Mexico, the southern state of Chiapas has vast natural resources, including valuable untapped oil and natural gas reserves and kilometers of untouched forests, but remains desperately poor. A guerrilla group called the Zapatistas (the Ejercito Zapatista de Liberación Nacional, or EZLN) formed in the mountains of Chiapas, staging an uprising that began on the day the NAFTA went into effect, January 1, 1994. The group sought to represent the needs of the poor and the hundreds of thousands of indigenous groups living in Mexico's Fourth World: 300,000 Tzotziles, 120,000 Choles, 90,000 Zoques, and 70,000 Tojalabales.[85] Significantly, the first recorded clash between the Mexican Army and the EZLN took place on May 21, 1993, before the uprising, in the Ocosingo canyons off a road leading to an important natural gas site, the Nazareth 101–104 wells.[86] Later their movement would grab the attention and support of millions of Mexicans and, through sophisticated use of the Internet, people around the world.

Unlike the U'wa and Zapatistas, the evidence suggests that transnational activism has not been the deciding means of resistance for the Pemon and their indigenous counterparts in the state of Bolivar. Rather, direct action tactics such as civil disobedience and infrastructure destruction coupled with domestic legal advances seem to have created the most leverage to negotiate with the Venezuelan government. Granted, the U'wa struggle is eight years older than the Pemon conflict and theoretically has had more time to attract concerned First World activists. However, other attempts by Colombian Indians to draw in international support have met little success; Van Cott notes that international supporters promoted a very "romanticized" portrait of the U'wa in contrast to the public image of FIEB, the national indigenous organization, which was more professional and less "primitive."[87] In the Venezuela case, the fact that the developers were Venezuelan state-owned companies, rather than transnational U.S. corporations, inherently makes the conflict less of a transnational issue. This suggests why international activism has been more intense and successful in the U'wa case. The successful internationalization of resistance campaigns also hinges on the promotion of a central figure or idea that can capture the imagination of foreign journalists and support networks. The U'wa threat of collective suicide attracted considerable interest, as did the emergence and mystery of the Zapatista Subcommondante Marcos, a charismatic leader who has a keen understanding of Mexican history, guerrilla theory, and contemporary politics, as well as effective public relations strategies.

Prospects for Change: Short- and Long-Term Solutions

To address solutions to indigenous–developer conflicts in Latin America, we must first acknowledge that both short- and long-term solutions are required. Here we first address short-term solutions including indigenous land demarcation, strict environmental law enforcement, moratoriums on industrial development, "surgical" drilling (in the U'wa case), and locally based indigenous economic projects like the sustainable harvesting of non-timber forest products and ecotourism. Long-term alternatives include measures such as formalizing indigenous autonomy, investing in peace (specifically in Colombia), and alternative energy sources. At the end of the section, we also call for a reassessment of values for ecosystems and cultural diversity.

True indigenous autonomy may lead to clashes even with traditional allies. For example, "surgical" drilling—in which drilling pipes reach diagonally from disturbed areas underneath parks and reserves without damaging the surface—has recently won support from both oil companies and some environmentalists as a "lower impact" alternative to conventional extraction methods. In Ecuador, monorails have been used for transporting equipment and oil company workers to rig sites, to avoid creating roads that can be followed by peasant farmers and lumberers looking for forestland to clear. Helicopters are now increasingly being used for mining operations. For groups like the U'wa, however, cultural and spiritual beliefs often supercede the "ecological benigness" of technological innovations. Oil for the U'wa is more than a natural resource; *Ruira*, U'Wa for oil, is sacred and any type of Ruira extraction is a violation of sacred rules.[88]

Establishing indigenous property rights and demarcating indigenous ancestral territories are essential first steps in the effort to protect ecosystems and traditional cultures. Attossa Saltani, director of Amazon Watch, notes, however, that a major obstacle to land demarcation is the small capacity of indigenous groups to prepare land claims. Proving such claims often requires anthropological studies of traditional oral histories and the use of satellite mapping technology such as the global positioning system (GPS) to establish the boundaries of ancestral lands.[89] Nonindigenous third-party claims to land from many small farmers and others make demarcation of indigenous ancestral land more complicated. Additionally, governmental policy toward indigenous peoples is subject to change, depending on political and economic circumstances. Unfortunately, establishing indigenous territories is not only politically difficult but also time-consuming and expensive.

The enforcement of environmental and indigenous rights legislation is another fundamental first step to ensuring a healthy future for native peoples. In the past decade, Mexico, Argentina, Nicaragua, Colombia, Peru, Brazil, Honduras, Guatemala, and, most recently, Venezuela have passed constitutional laws that for the first time recognized indigenous cultural and territorial rights. In 1991, Colombian indigenous groups won the right to a bilingual education, the right to control the (terrestrial) natural resources of legally demarcated land, and the right to a legitimate formal consultation process regarding development projects.[90] On November 3, 1999, the National Constitutional Assembly of Venezuela (charged with drafting a new constitution for Venezuela) voted to include provisions that set forth legal rights for the country's indigenous peoples in accordance with Convention 169 of the International Labor Organization on Indigenous and Tribal Peoples. This legislation would guarantee "the right to exist as indigenous peoples and communities with their own social and economic organization, their cultures, and traditions, and their language and religion."[91]

Unfortunately, gains in the creation of indigenous laws have been overshadowed by their lack of enforcement throughout the region. "In the 1990s we saw constitutions [in Latin America] that give indigenous rights; rights have been won. What hasn't been won is the ability to exercise them," said David Rothschild, director of Amazon Alliance.[92] Murillo remarks that "indigenous activism is met with negotiations and agreements on paper that are ultimately ignored once the dust has settled."[93]

International laws that protect indigenous rights, such as ILO Convention 169 and the United Nations and Organization of American States Declarations on the Rights of Indigenous Peoples, have strengthened indigenous legal claims to land and culture in the international legal arena. International laws regarding indigenous rights, however, have been similarly difficult to implement, and are also frequently ignored.[94]

Securing full autonomy is, perhaps, the central long-term goal in the indigenous rights movement, but autonomy is not universally defined. Autonomous indigenous reservations in Australia, Canada, and the United States provide some model, but political power struggles, history of land use, and communications/cultural barriers often complicate negotiations between indigenous communities and federal governments.

The process to implement a state-recognized autonomous zone (Indigenous Territorial Entities, or ETIs) in Colombia has been long and arduous.[95] ETIs are envisioned as regions in which "exploitation of natural resources is contingent upon the consent of the communities where it would take place."[96] According to new Colombian laws, ETIs would be funded with federal money like departments and municipalities are, but development projects "would be directed, organized, and administered" by the indigenous authorities.[97] In 1993, a joint government-indigenous commission initiated a process of public hearings with the purpose of drafting the laws that would establish and regulate the ETIs. Many controversial issues had to be addressed, such as (1) how territories would be demarcated, (2) what would happen to nonindigenous peoples such as campesinos living in predominantly indigenous areas, (3) who would govern territories where two or more indigenous groups subside, and (4) who would control the rights to subsoil natural resources such as oil. (The constitution, based on Roman law, dictates that the subsoil is the property of the state. However, it also guarantees respect for the natural resources of indigenous territories).[98] The implementation of the ETIs has not been supported by the Gaviria or Samper administrations: it is opposed by many local landowners, who are well represented in the Colombian congress.[99] Vice President Jorge Eastman, in his first meeting about the ETIs, told indigenous leaders that he was meeting with them, "but not because we have to take into account what you are going to say. The government has its own autonomy."[100]

Implementing indigenous autonomy elsewhere in Latin America has been extremely difficult as well. In Nicaraugua, for example, Miskitu, Mayagna, and Rama indigenous populations as well as Afro-Nicaraguans living in the North and South Atlantic "Autonomous Regions" have been virtually unable to exercise their autonomous rights. An excessively vague autonomous law, a dysfunctional Autonomous Regional Council, a centralized national government, and an export-oriented economic policy all have contributed to the lack of power for these "autonomous" areas.[101] The situation is similar to indigenous efforts to establish autonomous zones in southern Mexico. EZLN's effort to create autonomous indigenous areas where communities exercise economic, political, and sociocultural self-determination has been met with strong resistance from the Mexican government, which sees the Zapatistas' vision of autonomy as anti-state.

Autonomy as a solution for ensuring indigenous rights to land, resources, and culture therefore must be constructed in such a way that grants explicit and real power to indigenous governing bodies. True autonomy can be realized only when rights include full reign over property, land, and resources. Without resource rights, traditional peoples stand little chance of living in a truly autonomous nation. Rubén Darío Gómez, an anthropologist with the Colombian Interior Ministry's Office of Indigenous Affairs, described the current reality when he asked,

> How do you expect to establish Autonomous Indigenous Territories in areas that are rich in mineral resources like oil when at the same time you are trying to encourage foreign investment in oil development? The major multinationals recognize this contradiction, and are exploiting it completely. And unfortunately, they have the upper hand.[102]

This brings us back to a central question about development. As the Yanomamo people living on the Brazil–Venezuela border explained to World Bank representatives in the 1980s, "Development can have many meanings. Your interpretation of development is material. Ours is spiritual. Spiritual development is as legitimate as material development."[103] Questions about development, then, are fundamentally related to autonomy and the politics of self-determination. Ian McIntosh notes, "In a western political tradition, self-determination is a concept without an ethnic dimension. It is about land and not people. For many Indigenous peoples, self-determination is autonomy, being able to set one's own agenda on one's own land."[104]

In 1995, the United Nations announced an International Decade of the Indigenous Peoples of the World and called on governments to address the problems of native populations. But as Guatemalan Nobel Peace Prize winner and Mayan Indian Rigoberta Menchu noted, "It was not increased government awareness that led to the declaration of the decade, but rather action and campaigns by the indigenous peoples themselves. Governments are not interested, and this must be acknowledged."[105]

Ultimately, more attention needs to be given toward the development of creative community-based economic initiatives that incorporate traditional indigenous beliefs with sustainable ecosystem management. Indigenous groups in the Gran Sabana, for example, are already engaged in ecotourism, agro-ecological management of arable land, traditional medicinal knowledge applications, and the sustainable collection and marketing of nontimber forest products such as fruit, honey, and nuts (see Chapter 3). These projects represent a move away from destructive extractive export industries (oil, mining, logging, energy transport, and so on) and toward locally based development projects that are consistent with traditional indigenous ideologies and methods of social organization. While alternative development schemes are not unproblematic (especially projects like ecotourism that remain dependent on foreigners—see Chapter 3), they do represent a critical tool in the move toward economic self-sufficiency. Of course, projects in which indigenous people are the project designers, decisionmakers, participants, and beneficiaries have been the most successful.

Conclusions: Indigenous Survival in the Twenty-First Century

To finish here, we need to discuss several general themes that emerge from this chapter. First, the national economic policy of a country (as influenced by external economic and political forces) is often an important factor in the introduction of indigenous–developer conflicts. As in the rest of Latin America, in the last twenty years national economic crises have led Colombian and Venezuelan governments to implement structural economic reforms under the supervision of multilateral lending institutions such as the World Bank and the IMF. These reforms, readers know by now, are designed to encourage foreign investment, privatization, and export-oriented industries and have encouraged and sped the penetration of frontier forests by state and multinational developers. In both of our case studies, states (or private developers working in coordination with the state) introduced development conflicts into indigenous territories.

In much of Latin America, prospects for sustainable development remain limited by a climate of war and political violence. According to a World Bank study, 23 percent of countries where at least one-quarter of the economy depends on primary commodities exports (e.g., oil) experience military conflict.[106] By contrast, countries with no primary commodities exports have a less than 1 percent chance of conflict. As Amnesty International Secretary General Pierre Sane notes, "When you combine the two (oil and the military), you are faced with countries that are very difficult to move in the direction of bowing to international pressure."[107] This weakens the hand of indigenous groups seeking to use foreign activists and international treaties to gain rights and protections.

However, in Colombia, political instability has ironically worked to the advantage of the U'wa. Rebel forces, outspokenly opposed to multinational resource extraction, have targeted oil installations near U'wa territory; in response, military and paramilitary units occupied the area. The U'wa have been able to argue successfully that further oil development in the region will inevitably lead to more violence. This climate of violence also jeopardizes the ability of multinational oil companies to do safe and efficient business in the region.

Second, we note that national and international laws protecting the rights of indigenous people are necessary components to effective resistance campaigns but must be accompanied by a broader mobilization. Policy development and legal lobbying are important tools, but these can be easily undermined by local government and business elites. Furthermore, even when indigenous territories are demarcated, indigenous groups cannot prevent oil exploration because subsoil resources are legally owned by the state in most Latin American nations. Indigenous advocates argued that the Colombian Council of State was essentially able to undermine U'wa rights to land, culture, and consultation even though these rights were explicitly guaranteed under the 1991 Constitution. Mexican, Venezuelan, and other Latin American indigenous groups continue struggling to utilize seemingly unenforceable "paper legislation."

Third, foreign-owned, transnational corporate developers (Occidental and Shell in Colombia) are often more vulnerable to indigenous activism than are Latin American state-owned developers (CVG-EDELCA in Venezuela). The U'wa case challenges the notion of the "untouchable corporate giant," while the Pemon case illustrates that state development agencies might be becoming more responsive to the international economic system rather than to a country's own citizens. As global markets expand and poor nations lose the ability to regulate trade, many transnational corporations "have more political and economic power than the nation-states across whose borders they operate."[108] But transnational corporations now have to respond to transnational social movements, which, like themselves, operate across geographical and cultural borders.[109] State developers, in contrast, have no responsibility to the "global public" and are less likely to be influenced by transnational action. We saw in the last chapter that facing criticism from environmentalists and indigenous rights groups abroad, which threatened their access to the World Bank and foreign private banks for funding, Brazil has now attempted to forge ahead with its own funding for the huge dams and roads of the Avança Brasil project.

However, state developers and policymakers often do have a responsibility to foreign corporations. This point was illustrated when an American advisor to the Chase Manhattan Bank sent a letter to the Mexican government saying, "The government will need to eliminate the Zapatistas to demonstrate their effective control of the national territory and security policy."[110] Although the government did attempt to take Chase Manhattan's advice, the Zapatistas and Zapatista-inspired activities, such as the blockage of over sixty oil wells by Chontal Indians in the state of Tabasco in 1996, continue to create an "unstable investment climate" in Mexico.

Fourth, indigenous social mobilizations and the tactics employed by indigenous groups largely depend on the relative openness of their host nation's political system.[111] A NACLA report on Colombia remarks, "In the past, the government would respond to indigenous organizing through the force of its military and police apparatus; over 400 indigenous leaders have been killed in the [indigenous] movement's 25-year history. Today, indigenous activism is met with negotiations and agreements on paper."[112] While the U'wa have not been completely protected from intimidation and violence, it is true that political changes in Colombia (and the accompanying growth in international human rights observer groups) have helped the U'wa publicize their cause. In the case of the U'wa, a lack of significant political support from national government officials, combined with the inability of the Colombian court system to uphold indigenous legal rights, has forced U'wa leaders to focus on voicing their claims to the United Nations, the Organization of American States, and international activists. On the other hand, the Zapatistas have been able to capitalize on the comparative openness of the Mexican state and focus on nationally targeted actions. Direct action, although often met with government force, remains a popular and effective tactic of indigenous groups in Colombia, Venezuela, and Mexico.

Last, organized and effective coalition building and activism on the local, national, and transnational level, by indigenous groups and their allies, increase the likelihood of a group stopping or altering a development project. The evidence suggests that the cross-border links established between U'wa leaders in Colombia and solidarity networks in North America and Europe (and the resulting activism) were key factors in Occidental's decision to reduce the size of their initial contract. These actions included a targeted international legal effort, aggressive public advocacy campaigns, U'wa presence at Occidental shareholder meetings, and the well-publicized threat that Occidental Petroleum could cause the mass suicide of five thousand indigenous people. This is not to say that local actions, such as the U'wa's occupation of a proposed Oxy drill site, are insignificant, but rather that local actions are inherently more effective when part of a broader, transnational effort.

By contrast, the most significant resistance to Decree 1850 and the Guri Powerline in Venezuela has occurred within national borders. Roadblocks, the destruction of electrical towers, and other local direct actions have successfully, albeit temporarily, halted the construction of the powerline. By attracting the attention of government officials and NGOs in Caracas, these tactics have had extralocal implications. However, national actions have failed to effectively pull in significant international support. A powerful international base of support would certainly have strengthened the Pemon case, especially given the potential for binational coordination between Venezuela and Brazil on the Guri Powerline.

Throughout Latin America, globalized economic and communications networks are crossing paths with the survival struggles of aboriginal groups. Aboriginal claims to land, resources, and culture are in direct conflict with the interests of large-scale development projects. For generations, the U'wa have guarded the Samore block, Chiapas Indians have looked after the Lacandon, and the Pemon have stewarded one of the world's biological treasures, the headwaters of the Orinoco River basin. Although the notion of indigenous people as "natural conservationists" has been soundly challenged,[113] in many ways Latin America's indigenous people are environmentalists.[114]

However, we want to acknowledge that the indigenous rights movement and the international environmental movement do not necessarily share the same interests or short-term objectives. Indeed, fundamental conflicts between indigenous and environmental organizers have been well documented and continue to pose major challenges to cross-issue coalition building. We think that the perceived divergence in goals between the two movements poses a challenge only in the short term—long-term issues and goals of both movements tend to be compatible and mutually supporting. As Rafael Pandam, Vice President of the Confederation of Indigenous Nationalities of Ecuador (CONAIE), explains,

> When we indigenous people talk about the environment, we are not just talking about the trees, rivers and butterflies. We are also talking about human beings. Likewise, when we talk of human rights, we are not just talking about the right to free speech. We are talking of the political, economic, social and cultural rights of all peoples.[115]

As the campaign "Protecting Those Who Protect the Earth"—on which the Sierra Club and Amnesty International have teamed up—demonstrates, some environmental groups have realized that helping indigenous communities survive the threats from megadevelopment projects is one of the most effective ways to help protect those corners of the Earth.

Organic farmer and his son proudly displaying their produce, Costa Rica, 1999.
Photo by Nikki Thanos.

CHAPTER 7

Building a Global Civil Society:
Living What We Know

We are all too familiar with an end-of-the-book tendency of readers to sink down into our chairs, let out a groan, and complain that everything discussed in the previous two hundred pages has been of negative and hopeless content, of issues unrelated to our lives or communities. In fact, one of our goals in this book was to avoid simplifying environmental problems into something that can be solved with one checklist improvement plan—we hope that we have been fair in our presentation of environmental problems in Latin America and the daunting complexity of possible solutions. The reality is that these environmental problems *are* complex and *are* laced with ironies and contradictions—yet they are not hopeless and they certainly are not unrelated to those of us who live in the global North. We think that it is especially important for those of us living in privileged societies to recognize the problems of the world, and even more important to recognize our own agency in contributing to global environmental problems and their solutions. While this is not a "50 Ways to Save the Planet" book, we do believe the consumption patterns and lifestyle choices of individuals have real consequences. Still, individual actions are not enough to save the planet. In this final chapter we move from small, easy, individual actions to more transnational, collective, and perhaps more challenging ones. We begin with what readers can actively do, and only after that move to what people in the North can do to work with those in Latin America who are dealing with these social-environmental issues every day.

On fighting apathy, it has been our experience that the more we learn about the environmental crisis in Latin America (or anywhere else for that matter), the more our lives begin to change. When we pull into a gas station we find ourselves thinking, "Was this gasoline taken from rainforest indigenous lands in the Amazon? Under what conditions?" Then sometimes a different line of questions begins: "Do I really need to be driving so much? What are my alternatives? Why don't I have other alternatives? What would be some first steps to creating alternatives?" At the coffee shop and grocery store we often wonder where the products came from. Increasingly, we scan stores for some kind of redeeming label: shade-grown, organic, locally produced, fair trade. Sadly we usually don't find green-labeled products at hand, so similar questions arise. "Where and under what conditions was the stuff in this product extracted from the earth? Where was it processed or assembled? Why is it so difficult to even find that out?" Even when we try to do something nice, like buy our family or friends flowers, we might find ourselves wondering if the flowers were harvested by a young girl working on a plantation in Colombia who was exposed to toxic pesticides.

Shopping for clothes, lumber, transportation, even signing up for household telephone or energy service can become a confusing task if our desire is to do the right thing. But rather than being overwhelmed and merely throwing up our hands, we try to see the effort as a chance to learn about bigger issues and make a bit of difference in this troubled world. Doing so can make the chores of life a lot more interesting. When one person asks at a store about fair trade or green-labeled products, they might be treated as wacko or radical fringe. When two ask, the clerk might ask the manager about them. When a half-dozen ask over the course of a week, the company may wonder if it is at risk of losing market share to others who do have products with these labels.

Fortunately, we don't each have to pull this wagon alone: We (the authors) see this kind of thought process and desire to make the world a better place in a substantial number of people around us, and we see *that* as proof of an emerging consciousness about the impact of daily actions in a globalized world. Interviews with twenty thousand people in twenty nations in 2001 found that about half of consumers were concerned about a firm's social responsibility, and one in six people consciously demand that corporations treat employees fairly, protect the environment, and so on.[1] This was the worldwide average—the fractions were higher in the wealthier countries. Therefore despite our leaders' failure to address the big issues of environment and people's fate around the world, citizens have not given up.

Even when it seems that no one around us cares, history suggests there is real reason for hope. Seeing the dramatic social change that swept over isolated Pacific islands because of war and development—what we would now call globalization—anthropologist Margaret Mead remained optimistic about peoples' ability to choose between destructive and more positive futures. "Never doubt that a small group of thoughtful, committed citizens can change the world," she famously wrote, "indeed, it's the only thing that ever has."[2]

We also think that feeling overwhelmed sometimes is inevitable, even healthy, as consumers begin to trace the ecological footprint (the full environmental and social cost of a given product or service) of their actions.[3] As much as we support fair trade markets, locally grown food, and sustainably harvested wood, we believe that overconsumption itself is part of the environmental crisis—we consumers can't just buy our way out of this problem. Questioning the origins of the products we consume is only the beginning— the real challenge begins when we question the necessity of many of the products themselves. And as with all issues, there are serious equity issues that must be addressed along the way, particularly in the case of conscious consumption—it is a luxury and a privilege to be able to afford many green products on the market. Far from giving something up when we change our consumption patterns, we have found that having a "global conscience" actually helps to create a sense of place and build community at the local level. Building community creates a sense of "belonging," which can be an antidote for the relentless, environmentally devastating, and ultimately unfulfilling desire for more stuff.[4] There are no ads on television for learning to appreciate simpler things, and certainly none for learning how to "be in tune with Nature." These are by no means automatic—people need enjoyable ways to be outside (like gardening, exercising, or wildlife observing, for example), relying as we used to on knowledge of soil, weather, and changes in the ecosystem.

It is difficult to talk in general terms about the "environment in Latin America," and the diversity of topics we've raised in this book demonstrates just how varied and complex environmental problems are in the vast region. Attempting in one slim volume to even open the number of issues we have is a risky venture, and we know that we have omitted terribly important issues, sources, and positions. Although solutions must be local and developed by participatory democratic process, in each chapter of the book we sought to propose some concrete directions for improvement that might be considered. We don't want to bore readers with a long rehash of these issues:

There were many. But globalization has imperiled the very environment upon which Latin American, and ultimately global, society depends. Thus bold and multilevel solutions are needed. What we propose here are some steps in contributing to solutions to these crucial problems. We believe improvement is possible. We don't know if it will be enough, but we cannot afford to take the chance of not trying.

Looking at the Label

During the 1999–2000 academic year, college students across the United States began to look seriously at the labels on their clothing, especially those with their college's logo, to see where they were made. Reports of sweatshop conditions and abuse of workers in Third World factories led them to target the big vendors: Nike, Reebok, Champion, and so on. They began by asking their schools to buy only certified "Sweat-Free" products, as labeled by an independent council of labor and human rights advocates. When some schools refused to do so, students staged a series of high-publicity protests. At school after school, they won. New information became available about where and how our clothes are produced. Some big firms have adopted "codes of conduct" and regularly report on their factories and practices. And millions of people were educated about why it mattered. Millions of dollars of school purchases now ride on favorable certification by these organizations.

Confirming Mead's theory, successful campaigns have been launched by quite small groups of environmentalists to push large purchasers and even nations to buy only certified products, such as tropical hardwoods labeled by the Forestry Stewardship Council, organic vegetables and fruit, or "dolphin-safe" tuna. Mainstream churches across the United States are now buying through the "Interfaith Coffee Program," a self-described "life-centered economic model" that helps cooperatives of small farmers get started and guarantees a minimum price and a premium for organic produce, by dealing directly with the producers and cutting out middlemen, such as purchasers, processors, exporters, brokers, coffee companies, distributors, and stores.[5] Organizations like Bioplanet Network in Mexico City are linking fair trade consumers with local producers' groups who are beginning to diversify from selling raw materials to producing and selling bath and beauty items, flour, cookies, beverage mixes, vanilla extract, and snack foods.[6] But these are still tiny operations that need "capacity building"; training, organizational assistance, loans, market research, advertising, consumer education, and so on.

We've already discussed how *real* green labeling can make a difference in protecting workers and consumers from pesticide poisoning (in Chapter 3), and how they might protect disappearing tropical forests and lead to their renewal. In Chapter 4 we argued that green labels could create ways to push large industrial polluters to far cleaner production techniques. We also have suggested how green labels could be developed in some areas like eco-tourism, and other possibilities for labeling are almost endless.

We have unfortunately seen how some industries have sought to undermine truly independent labeling by creating their own councils that can control and minimize the demands on producers to invest in change. Firms then get these *pale* green labels, without doing much at all of real environmental substance. A great opportunity for change is being lost. This is suggested by our research on the chemical industry's Responsible Care program chronicled in Chapter 4, and it appears to be the case for the ISO 14001 certifications now held by over forty thousand companies in 103 nations. We agree with criticisms of ISO and most other industry standards that they are too weak, especially since they do not specify pollution-reduction levels and lack real verification by truly independent "third parties" to ensure that the firm is actually doing what they say they are doing.[7] The only way for weak labels to be strengthened appears to be for there to be a competing, tougher, independent labeling organization with whom they must compete for legitimacy. Although in the right hands they can guide firms to better environmental performance, in the worst hands or in tough times the "environmental management" guidelines of pale green labels become largely hollow "green marketing." Without real independent watchdog groups running the programs, there is little way for consumers to tell which certified firms are which.

To go one step further, we wish to propose here a new set of labels that include both the social criteria of the sweatshop and human rights movements *and* those that are concerned about a product's environmental impacts. That is, we need ecosocial or "blue-green" labels (blue for blue-collar), so that consumers are not forced to ask for multiple ones. This is the problem with having to ask for "shade-grown, organic, fair trade" coffee. Rather, there should be one, fiercely independent, network of groups that labels only the products that are truly better on social and environmental grounds.

There are some efforts in this direction, especially in Europe, and the fair trade labels often include labor, environment, and community criteria. But to make real independent green labels work, we need to be savvy customers, not fooled by industry greenwash, but able to reward companies who are making real progress and represent truly more sustainable solutions to these crucial environmental problems. This means going online to investigate firms and to read critically the claims of groups on both sides. After this book's bibliography, we have assembled a brief list of Web sites where readers might begin their investigations.

Globalizing Standards of Protection

We spend so much time on consumption and labeling here because today, *corporate* policies, production methods, and buying practices have almost universal influence on the world's environment, workers, and communities. There are at least forty thousand corporations operating internationally (in at least two different countries); the couple hundred largest of those operate *globally*, that is, almost everywhere. These are mighty firms: Global transnationals hold 90 percent of all technology and product patents worldwide and are involved in 70 percent of all world trade.[8] If you were to list the one hundred largest organizations on the planet or the Earth in economic terms, listing countries and their annual GNPs and companies with their annual sales, fifty-one would be firms and forty-nine would be countries.[9] Many politicians fear that these institutions are too large to be controlled by national governments, and therefore hesitate to place strict environmental regulations on them. This issue came up several times in Chapter 2 in discussing the maquiladora industries on the United States–Mexico border. However, as economic geographer Peter Dicken documents, these global firms *are* strongly tied to their headquarter nations, and so should be more controllable than is widely feared.[10] The largest number are headquartered in the United States, Japan, and Europe (ninety-five of the top one hundred global corporations[11]), so these places must be the focus of efforts to bring them under control.

It is too simplistic to say that free trade is bad for the environment—we need a nuanced approach that considers both positive and negative aspects of global trade and the agreements that frame it, such as NAFTA, WTO, and the environmental treaties. Free trade advocates believe that aging and inefficient factories in Latin America from the years of high tariff barriers will be shut down and replaced by competitive and more efficient facilities for exports, and so the region's air and waters might become cleaner. We are uncomfortable accepting that the many uncertainties in this hopeful scenario will come to pass as expected. But one positive hope that we do share is that freer trade is bringing a new sort of global integration, which requires us to develop some level of international standardization of environmental regulations.[12]

The "toxic tour" of the United States–Mexico border we took in Chapter 2 suggested that despite some improvements, the NAFTA treaty is largely failing to improve the environment. Even though it included explicit directives regarding the "harmonization" of environmental protection in Canada, the United States, and Mexico, the environmental side agreement to NAFTA falls seriously short of providing acceptable environmental and health safeguards. The new "border institutions" (BECC, CEC) that were created around the treaty show promise but face a different reality: ridiculously inadequate funding, worrisome public accountability issues, lack of enforcement capabilities, and limited autonomy. In the world of trade pacts, these seem to be well-conceived institutions, but they must be strengthened. The mixed environmental results of NAFTA in the face of the proximity of its border to the massive resources of the United States and the border watchdog groups suggest worse results in the future for other proposed treaties like the extension of NAFTA to the whole hemisphere under the FTAA. The World Trade Organization (WTO) may be the worst of all treaties for assuring environmental protection, since it prohibits nations from excluding imports based on environmental considerations on how they were produced.[13]

NAFTA and the issues at the border suggest that many of the environmental issues that arise under free trade efforts are beyond the factory: The dust and sewage, diarreahal diseases, smog from brick kilns, and exhaust from old cars and trucks are all the result of urban poverty, an issue that will not be addressed as long as Mexico must sell itself as a cheap labor haven. A quarter of a million maquiladora jobs were lost in the year before March 2002, as the United States went into recession and Mexico found it could not compete with China, where workers make 25 cents an hour.[14] Labor unions are realizing they must go global in fighting to keep employers from forever undermining their ability to improve their pay and work conditions.[15] Workers in wealthy nations and in a surprising number of occupations face many of the same problems and insecurities under the global economy. Capitalism is ridden with contradictions that threaten its stability, but it is also tremendously flexible and malleable, so as Mead suggested, positive solutions are possible. The sustainability and social effects of new balances of power between communities, firms, workers, environmentalists, governments, and international institutions will be the result of which of these agents is more effective in confronting the shifting scene.

One new trend suggests the possibility of taming the worst aspects of globalization: the growing series of environmental treaties such as those on ozone protection, climate change, and endangered species. The question is whether they can remove these canyons between laws and enforcement of rich and poor nations, stopping firms from fleeing to or taking advantage of "pollution haven" and "wage ghetto" nations. Can these treaties prevent a "race to the bottom," where, in their desperation to try to attract firms, countries, states, or cities reduce their environmental protection to the level of the worst places?[16]

In some research on these treaties we found that Latin American nations have signed many of them, and not surprisingly, the relatively wealthier Latin American nations have signed more than the poorer countries.[17] But the actual importance of these treaties is currently very unclear, for several reasons. These include the fact that many countries sign and then proceed to flaunt them and because some nations (especially the United States) have been blocking their further progress and because of the weakness of their enforcement and dispute resolution mechanisms.[18]

Even when there are good treaties and Latin American governments *want* to enforce them, some are not *able* to effectively protect their environments in the face of economic crisis and recent pressures to "shrink the state." Critics argue that global integration is not conducive to environmental protection because cutthroat international competition can drive nations to neglect safeguards. Austerity programs and the economic crises associated with the transition to market-centered models of accumulation create a desperation that drives poor people to unsustainable use of their resources.[19] To correct exchange rates, control inflation, and lower tariff barriers, global integration and export orientation have been linked with drastic programs of privatization and "state shrinking" in Latin America. With a few exceptions and some momentary shifts, state shrinking has been the dominant ideology of governments across the region for nearly twenty years. As the state shrinks, respect for the rule of law often weakens as does confidence in and funding for environmental protection agencies.[20] Even if those agencies are well funded in times of austerity (presumably by outside financing), many people may see them as increasingly alien and irrelevant in times of desperate hardship. Desperate times tend to favor short-term thinking, not sustainable societies.

Here is one example from Brazil of the problem of unenforced environmental laws. Brazil's congress adopted one of the world's most progressive constitutions on environment and human rights issues, and recently a tough environmental crimes law, which was later substantially watered down by President Cardoso before he signed it. Still, a new review of the biggest contamination lawsuits in the country since the 1980s shows that no firms involved were ever pursued by the judicial system because of civil or criminal actions.[21] Rather, they receive only fines, which are customarily appealed. Prosecutor José Carlos Meloni Sícoli, of the Center for Assistance to Environmental Prosecutors in São Paulo, makes the comparison: "The legislative arsenal in Brazil is infinitely superior to those in countries like the USA, for example, but the implementation of the law there is light-years more efficient than here." As a result, "Betting on impunity is still very frequent."

Before we can definitely answer the question on whether economic globalization is improving or destroying the environment we simply need better data. In the United States a huge groundswell of activism linking labor unions, communities, and environmentalists pushed for the Community Right to Know Act, which became federal law in 1985, against the tide of a decade of deregulation.[22] This established the Toxic Release Inventory (TRI), which obliges companies to monitor, compute, and report their own data on annual pollution emissions to the air, water, and soil. What we are suggesting here is a "Global TRI." There are some initial efforts in this direction in Mexico and Europe, but little else across the region. Latin Americans almost entirely still lack the right to know about what poisons are around them at work and in their communities. National programs would of course be a valuable start, but to answer our core questions—of whether trade is causing a flight of toxic industries or a "race to the bottom" in enforcement of environmental laws—will require a global standardized Toxic Release Inventory.

Long-term economic growth and social development remains elusive for many Latin American nations, and it is unclear whether the funding from banks and investors will be forthcoming if nations institute more socially and environmentally oriented development projects. Would a nation of small-scale, low-tech eco-social (Curitiba-like) initiatives be able to gain sustained financing? And without foreign financing, what would happen to the domestic economy? Multinational lending institutions are so dominant in Latin America today that there appears to be very little room to resist regional integration efforts. One hopeful sign is that the multilateral lending agencies are increasingly featuring this kind of loans. But the negative edge is the debt that results, the dependence on these outside lenders.

With the demise of many government social programs and substantial public sector employment, most researchers envision greater income inequality and poverty throughout the region. An important question then will be whether income inequality leads to wasteful consumption with greater environmental damage without commensurate social gains.[23] The direct implication of these questions is that too rapid liberalization and "modernization" of the state risk dire environmental crisis. The skyrocketing number of cars in many Latin American cities during the 1990s economic recovery should give us pause: The cities can't handle the traffic.

So what do treaties, global TRI, NAFTA, and state shrinking have to do with the poor tired reader who is feeling overwhelmed by it all and already sinking down into their chair? Individuals can act alone to help important efforts to "tame" globalization, but they would be far more effective if they joined collective efforts. The most basic step is for U.S. citizens to encourage our government to pay what it has promised to support the UN's operating expenses. A key campaign must be to develop and strengthen these international institutions and the treaties and emerging laws they are tasked with enforcing. If we expect nations and firms to comply with these new international standards of protection, some international environmental agency will have to have "teeth" and the financial resources to enforce them. Citizens of the wealthier nations can write letters, support eco-social lobbying groups, or even help organize efforts to pressure their nations to sign and enact strong international agreements on the environment that are supportive of eco-social improvement in Latin American nations. Efforts to develop an international criminal court have important implications for firms and executives attempting to avoid being tried for environmental crimes by staying out of the country. Campaigns to "revise the charter" of extraordinary rights accorded to corporations in national laws need support and development. Again, we provide some places to start in the Online Resources section.

Supporting Victims of Environmental Injustice

For over five centuries centuries now, the plunder of Latin America's people and land served to benefit the foreigners, landowners, entrepreneurs, and government officials who got rich exploiting local resources. As historian Guillermo Herrera said, making off with a continent's natural riches for five hundred years took continual innovations in authoritarianism and relentless oppression of groups with alternative relationships with nature.[24] Millions of Indians have died at the hands of the Spanish, Portuguese, English, Dutch, and French through centuries of enslavement, disease, cultural warfare, and environmental pillaging. As the Indians died, African slaves were dragged by the millions to work Latin America's plantations, build its roads, and supply cargo boats with the commodities that satisfied the fancies of another continent, Europe, and enriched its financiers and kings.

The core argument of this book is that one cannot understand environmental problems and their resolution without dealing with the fundamental issues of economy, inequality, and democracy—in short, the "social structure." For some First World environmentalists, this realization is a relatively new one, and it can feel quite overwhelming. Discovering this fact sometimes leads people back to simplistic approaches to the issues. We believe this can perpetuate unrealistic or even unjust approaches.

Hopefully the information we set forth in this book makes clear that environmental degradation affects people differently, depending upon their race, class, gender, and ethnicity. Like wealthy people all over the world, elites in Latin America experience few of the problems of their poor neighbors. Many of the social/environmental problems we discuss in this book, like unpotable water along the United States–Mexico border, housing shantytowns, and soil erosion in Central America, may not seem that important or even "real" to middle- or upper-class Latin Americans. As we said in Chapter 4, water filters can be purchased. Although smog may be relatively "democratic" in burning the lungs and eyes of all classes who work downtown, the dirtiest factories and smelliest open sewers can be avoided by purchasing a home in a wealthy neighborhood. Undesirable dumps and dangerous factories are simply never sited in wealthy neighborhoods that have high property values and a politically powerful citizenry. Poor farmers and other rural producers' survival is directly endangered as soils wear out or crops fail in drought, a problem from which the rest of the residents are entirely shielded by food purchased from elsewhere.

This argument that environmental risks are unfairly distributed was developed in the 1980s in the U.S. South, where patterns of "environmental racism" and "environmental injustice" in the siting of dumps and polluting factories were documented and a protest movement developed.[25] One strategy of the environmental justice movement in the United States has been to empower those at the bottom of the social ladder so that they can fight the "disproportionate impact" they receive from environmental pollutants (see, for example, the discussion in Chapter 4). Some go further to argue that one of the only ways to drive real environmental improvement is to push the problems up the ladder of social stratification, so that wealthy decision makers share the strain of environmental burdens.[26] The environmental justice movement was explicit in one of its earliest statements that the goal was not merely to shift these pollutants to others, but rather to work for a cleaner world for all.[27] Is it true that only when there is nowhere else to go and nobody else upon which to dump one's waste that radically cleaner options such as "zero discharge" will be considered reasonable? Again, the ability to exploit other groups of humans allows us to continue to treat our place poorly.[28]

So returning to options for concrete actions, a third way to make a difference is to directly support grassroots and umbrella groups inside Latin America working for the environment and social justice. Since the scene shifts continually, to do any of these things wisely, of course, readers should try to stay as informed as they can. Networking listservs and Web sites are out there, and we list a few in the Online Resource section as places to start. Support can mean writing a check, certainly, but commonly these groups are asking first for "solidarity" efforts, like letter-writing to presidents, environment ministers, or corporate directors. Amnesty International pioneered this strategy decades ago, with great impact on outcomes of human rights cases around the world, even in the darkest dungeons of absolute dictatorships. It is now repeatedly used by environmentalists and indigenous rights groups.

Further, we have known many people who have had excellent experiences doing internships or volunteer work with these organizations. Learning Spanish or Portuguese is of course a great first step, but some have gone to Latin America with little or no language ability. The Ecotravels in Latin America Web site has excellent directories of short- and longer-term language schools throughout the region. Subscribers to listservs like the Environment in Latin America Network routinely request suggestions over the list about which groups they should contact for such opportunities. Some send queries along the lines of "who needs a volunteer?," to which local groups around the region respond. Some groups and directories compile many such opportunities. Some groups such as Global Exchange and Witness for Peace do "reality tours" that put participants in direct contact with leaders of important grassroots groups in these countries. Some are focused on particular environmental issues or even particular angles on them, such as women in environmental restoration, organic agriculture, or faith-based organizing on the environment. Many school, church, and other groups send "delegations" down to work together on environmental and social assistance projects. If the projects are well chosen and guided by local needs and decision-making, these groups can help substantially. Certainly the problem doesn't go away because of such aid work, but sometimes enduring links are built that support these grassroots efforts. Often such contact informs strategic advocacy work on one or both sides of the North–South divide. Lives can be changed.

The same can be said of academic programs in the region and of linkages between universities and other schools across the North–South divide. There are semester- and year-abroad programs that focus on culture, social science, and natural science approaches, coming in very different styles:

Some spend most time in classrooms, some on field trip experiences, some get students into original independent or team research projects. (Again, see the Online Resources section.) But less mentioned is the value university faculty and their students from the North would gain with closer links with the region. As International Affairs professor Billie DeWalt said in an excellent testimony to the U.S. Senate in 2000 about why poverty and environmental destruction are linked, U.S. universities can play a much larger role on these issues.[29] "International NGOs have done a relatively good job of establishing linkages with local NGOs. Although there are exceptions, U.S. universities have not developed the same sorts of collaborative research and development linkages for environmental research and policy-making with counterparts in Latin America." If government funding is to flow to support such work, as DeWalt suggests it should, relationships need already to be building. Rather than merely observing these issues from afar and wringing our hands, we need to be engaged. Institutions can be changed.

Finally, a comparative point about engagement with local groups and academics: We have tended too often to take the easiest path. In researching transnational conservation efforts in Chile, Peru, and Ecuador by groups based in the United States, environmental sociologist Tammy Lewis notes a pattern.[30] Conservation groups like World Wildlife Fund and the Nature Conservancy have tended to select nations to assist in the development and protecting of parks much more on the basis of *political* openness than on the actual biodiversity that needs to be protected. They need to show results from their efforts, and working with repressive or difficult regimes is risky in many ways. The result, she points out, is that a very uneven pattern of conservation is developing, and the gap between the ecologically protected and depleted nations is growing starkly. This contrasts with international human rights groups, who seek out the worst places and attempt to raise the bar. The point here is that those with language abilities and experience in the region who are interested in making the most difference may be able to do so in the places about which we hear very little.

Eco-Social Aid and the Direction of Progress

Looking back across the history of Latin America and the five sets of issues in each of the chapters—toxics on the border, pesticides, plantations and protected areas in forests, sewage and foul air in cities, the uncertain fate of the Amazon, and the struggles of indigenous nations in the face of development projects—we return with the view that globalization holds both perils and promise. We could say so in a way more circumspect, but after evaluating this veritable catalog of socio-environmental issues one thing is clear to us: Which way things go will depend on whether the course of development is directed primarily by the needs of the people and the planet or whether the central decisions shaping the future are directed by the needs of multinational corporations, banks, and foreign militaries. In short, will it be globalization from above or below?

Much of the influence in the current global economic system is concentrated in the hands of United States-based and international financial institutions such as private banks, the IMF, and the World Bank. Global decision makers no longer wear crowns, but neither are they elected. Leslie Sklair and others have called them the "transnational capitalist class," the "Wall Street–Washington elite."[31] We can debate the origins of their power, but their influence today is incontestably vast. For example, a bad rating, or even a small shift in a rating, on the credit risk ratings published quarterly by Merrill Lynch analysts in New York City can severely damage a country's ability to get loans for important projects at a good interest rate on good payment terms. Current bank policies set by the World Bank and the IMF constrain the choices of Latin American governments, limiting how they can shape their economies and care for their neediest citizens. The governing board of the World Trade Organization determines a great deal of what measures member nations can take to protect their workers and environment, but these judges are not elected, nor even representative. Our point here is that Latin American economies are very vulnerable to outside forces in a way entirely foreign to most people who live in large, wealthy, politically powerful nations. This is why so many Third World people have responded with fear and protest at this new globalization. Concerted efforts by advocates in the global North and South have often successfully pressured for change in these institutions. Certainly we cannot expect just change in them without coordinated efforts from North and South.

Our studies here convince us that our understanding of current environmental problems and globalization must be firmly rooted in an understanding of *inequality* and how things got this way. Poor nations and the poorest people within them will never be able to address environmental issues without the basics of a decent life. Unlike many policy advisors and politicians who call for states to "get out of the way and allow markets to operate" to drive these improvements, we conclude that markets alone cannot be expected to solve them. Social problems in Latin America have been developing over the course of five centuries largely dominated by conditions of free trade. Let us be clear here: We are not proposing a violent shift to some kind of communism, neither can states alone be expected to solve these profound problems. But alternative economic models, perhaps economies mixing the best of capitalism and socialism—so as to be sure the market serves the people and the environment that sustains them—should not be excluded if nations choose to try them. Even if the U.S. model for growth was environmentally sustainable and economically just it would be preposterous to propose it as the source of an inalterable recipe to be applied everywhere. Given that it is outrageously unsustainable—with 5 percent of the world's population consuming 25 percent of its fossil fuel and creating over 25 percent of its pollution—it is even more outlandish that we do so.

Since Latin American nations experimenting with redirecting development to local needs have so often "run afoul" of the foreign policy of the United States, this is another area where the bulk of our readers can have an impact. U.S. culture has excellent elements and terrible ones: Let us be honest about both, because others certainly recognize them and our credibility falls each time we deny them. Specifically, readers can encourage policymakers and those who make key decisions in financial markets (e.g., mutual fund managers and university trustees who decide on endowment investments) to support nations to try what may be needed to move themselves in a positive direction, whether it is a model we recognize as "democratic capitalism" or not. In fact many, many of the regimes the Unites States has supported over the years have been exceedingly undemocratic and approached "cleptocracies," with military regimes lining their own pockets and those of the economic elites at the expense of the earth and the people.[32] Now, the demands of global investors require only an extremely superficial democracy—a "polyarchy" where every four years the masses get to select from among a few elite members, little different from under the dictatorships.[33]

These are strong words, but terrible deeds have been done in the name of "American interests," when those interests were actually those of a few U.S.-based corporations. In fact, we would argue, those shortsighted, narrow interests now are working against us, as we become aware that social, economic, and environmental problems alike are global. The claim that "What's good for General Motors is good for the United States" probably was never true, but it certainly is not true now. All that's assured now is that what's good for GM might be good for GM. Based on the current need of management in publically traded companies to increase their stock prices, what's good for GM might be good mostly only for the short-term benefit of GM's management or top five shareholders.[34] These firms would have to be deeply reformed to be part of sustainable solutions: the United States should insist upon longer-term corporate thinking. More, we need to develop a foreign policy based on the longer view, one based in the sustainable use of the land inside and outside our borders. The rest of the world and especially Latin America—a region deeply tied to our own—requires that shift in thinking.

Recent models of "mixed economies" in Latin America—Cuba in the late 1990s, Nicaragua in the late 1980s—were hardly successes. In our travels, we visited both and saw their dire problems and surprising successes. But as social scientists we cannot draw firm conclusions from these experiments, since both nations were under relentless attack from an enemy many times their size (the United States), and so were never really given much chance to succeed. Expelled from the U.S. circle, these nations had to turn to a failed and failing project in state-led socialism, the Soviet Union. We believe that "constructive engagement" by the United States, more like that taken by our allies in Europe in their relations with Latin states, would probably have better outcomes. Certainly the U.S.'s hostile policy toward Cuba must be seen as a complete failure if the goal was to unseat Fidel Castro. As we write this the policy has failed for over four decades, yet remains firmly in place.

Rather, like Scandanavia, the United States must support long-range state intervention in Latin American economies to support positive actions by local groups and their national private firms, build an infrastructure based on renewable energy and lower-impact fossil fuels, and encourage active programs to raise the aspirations and chances of the "marginalized" poor. We argue that this policy would better serve the real self-interest of the United States, by securing the peace and avoiding the ecological "natural" disasters causing massive crises that create millions of environmental refugees and require billions of dollars in aid. [35] Rather than waiting for the next Hurricane Mitch, which caused economic collapse that cost billions of dollars to bail out, we should be *reducing the need* for the landless, and those whose land is being lost to erosion and contamination, to migrate illegally across our border.[36] The money for environmental refugees is already being spent: border patrols and services for the millions of illegal migrants from Mexico and the other Central American nations once in the United States cost hundreds of millions of dollars a year. We are arguing here for a new approach to international aid, a bold initiative directed at real eco-social development in the poorer nations of Latin America. This policy must leave room for local actors to make a difference in innovating policy to redirect their own growth. Leadership on foreign policy and aid in most nations is quite narrow; in the case of the United States it is held by those in the Senate

Foreign Relations Committee. This small group can be influenced by advocates who make creative connections from global environmental issues to their local districts and constituents.

There are now decades of speeches, academic and political texts, huge agencies, and the dedicated lives of "aid workers," all of whom set out to help Third World nations overcome the impediments in their societies to "development," to bring our experience and know-how to them. The wealthier nations were industrial and "modern," and this was the condition to be worked toward.[37] That Western-style "development" is good continues to be the deepest assumption underlying the whole operation, and environmental problems with that assumption were never seriously acknowledged, even in the thirty years since the environmental movement took off after the first Earth Day in 1970.

One of the boldest applications of the ecological insights of the last thirty years to the great debate on international development was a 1995 piece by Bob Sutcliff entitled simply "Development after Ecology." In it, he argues bluntly that our whole effort at attempting to make Third World nations like First World ones is heading in exactly the wrong direction. First, he reasons, the developed countries have levels of resource use and contamination that make them the greatest causes of the global environmental crisis, and yet we "still cannot meet the human needs of large sections of our populations."[38] Second, "the globalization of the characteristics of developed countries would surely make the planet uninhabitable." These are virtually incontrovertible facts about which there is wide consensus in the field of environmental science, and mountains of evidence. Yet this fact is ignored systematically by the entire community of economic development planners and academics.

Sutcliff goes one logical step further, where few dare tread, suggesting that our model should be closer in resource use to the poor countries. This model would be "dramatically more sustainable," he argues, than that of the developed countries. Sutcliff continues that there are other ways in which "underdeveloped countries often, if by no means always, offer a better model than developed ones: for instance, the persistence in some place of more sustainable forms of agricultural production and healthier vegetable-based diets which are less costly in resources; there are some examples where common rights are better maintained; and others where mechanisms of social solidarity and redistribution are more intact." Sutcliff suggests that what counts as modern is perhaps turned on its head: We need to learn from those living more sustainably. The conclusion is logical, if amusing to ponder: Perhaps it is we who need the teams of consultants from the poor countries to come give us advice on what to do. They could come from indigenous tribes in the Amazon, from Andean peasants' unions, from artisan fishers, or at least from those in governments who have worked with their communities to create participatory, low-tech, sustainable solutions to urban problems we share.

A new environmental justice movement is growing in Latin America, with the goal of bridging the gap between social justice and environmental groups. This movement is attempting to frame solutions to environmental degradation and inequity: Without giving up on democracy and equity we must build a sustainable society. Experts from the U.S. environmental justice movement were asked to make suggestions based on the North American experience and to provide longer-term links for the movement.[39] Environmentalists from several nations, representatives from labor unions, academics, peasant farmers, and indigenous groups were there; the founding document they created has been endorsed by dozens of groups in an ever-widening network.

It would not be fair to Sutcliff to not follow his argument to his conclusion: Based on all of this, he believes that "sustainable human development is thus a task demanding radical mass political action." Sutcliff defines development as popular participation, democracy, equity, and justice, and argues that the only way we will get there is to make these also the *process* of getting there. The Latin American environmental justice movement has the potential to link those who could work for such change. It also has the potential to serve as a model of participatory democracy for those of us in the wealthier nations.

From quite easy individual actions to complex collective ones, we have laid out a series of things readers—even overwhelmed novices—might do about environmental crises in Latin America. Taking a few of these actions would have many other positive effects, in many other parts of the world (including one's own home). People can consume more consciously, demanding independently labeled products and standard information on risks. These standards in turn require strong international institutions to enforce them, and these need our support.

As the environmental justice movement seeks to do, we can support those at the bottom of society's pile, who are most likely to bear the brunt of risks. We can work with rights and environmental groups to press nations to end cycles of impunity and lack of enforcement of environmental and human rights laws. Study and travel in Latin America and connections between communities and universities across the North-South divide can create lasting bonds and new directions of change. And we need to call for a drastic rethinking of priorities in international aid and finance. Aid needs to support solutions which address social and environmental problems at the same time, along the lines of those which have worked to address depleted soils and deforestation in Central America and urban ills in Curitiba, Brazil. Many specifics are in the chapters, but the core insight is that to make lasting progress on the world's greatest environmental problems, we must address inequality and environmental issues at the same time.

Globalization has imperiled the environment upon which Latin American and global society depends. Working thoughtfully together, we can shape a positive globalization. We cannot afford to take the chance of not trying.

Working thoughtfully together, we can shape a positive globalization.

NOTES

Chapter 1: The Scene, Its Problems and Roots

1. There has been a substantial debate on this issue, as the term was often inaccurately misused. See, e.g., Browder 1988. We return to this issue in Chapters 3 and 5.

2. Karl 1997; Acselrad 2001a.

3. Galeano 1973, p. 24.

4. Bakewell 1984, p. 110.

5. E. G. Galeano 1973, p. 33; Frank 1971.

6. Vitale 1983, p. 74.

7. Bakewell 1984.

8. Bakewell 1984.

9. Bakewell 1984.

10. Dean 1995, p. 42.

11. Dean 1995, p. 51.

12. Crosby 1972, p. 67.

13. Mintz 1985.

14. Padua 2001, p. 5.

15. Crosby 1972, p. 66.

16. Dean 1995, p. 46.

17. Dean 1995, p. 48.

18. Vitale 1983, p. 64.

19. McCartney 1997, p. 49. Sir Walter Raleigh's colony at Roanoke never survived.

20. Bakewell 1984.

21. Padua 2001, p. 3.

22. Curtin 1969; Klein 1999, cited in Padua 2001.

23. Dean 1995.

24. Dean 1995, p. 24; Denevan 1976.

25. Lombardi and Lombardi 1983, p. 20.

26. Wolf 1959.

27. Wolf 1959.
28. Conrad 1984.
29. Cavalcante 1988, cited in Dean 1995, p. 371, n17
30. Dean 1995, p. 28.
31. Dean 1995, pp. 30–31.
32. Dean 1995.
33. Dean 1995, p. 21.
34. Black 1991, p. 246.
35. Burns 1991, pp. 67–68.
36. Burns 1991, p. 71.
37. Burns 1991, p. 73. Guano was bird droppings from coastal rookeries, a potent fertilizer.
38. Burns 1991, pp. 73–74.
39. Wolf and Hansen 1972; Bunker 1985.
40. Prebisch 1950, 1964; Cardoso and Faletto 1979; Frank 1967.
41. World Bank 1992.
42. Much of this explanation comes from Loveman 1979.
43. Orlando San Martín, personal communication, March 12, 1995.
44. Green 1991.
45. Hite 2002. This is especially true outside the official project's boundaries (Becker 1990; Roberts 1992).
46. There is tremendous debate about this point; see Chapter 4.
47. See, e.g., Roberts and Grimes 1997; Talukdar and Meisner 2001; and Chapter 4, this volume.
48. World Bank 1992.
49. Cicantell 1994; Roberts 1992.
50. E.g., Rostow 1960.
51. This is a huge literature that we can only suggest here. For a start on the contrasting positions, see Roberts and Hite 2000.
52. McMichael 2000.
53. For example, see Baran and Sweezey 1968; Frank 1967; see Kay 1998.
54. Valuable reviews of this literature are in Kay 1989, 1998.
55. Wallerstein 1974, 1979; Chase-Dunn 1989. For a review see Shannon 1996.
56. Terlouw 1992; Shannon 1996; Dicken 1998.
57. Evans 1979.
58. Korzeniewicz and Martin 1994; Dicken 1998.
59. 1998 external debt for the region was U.S.$786 billion, while its total GDP was U.S.$2.055 trillion. Tables 21 and 12, World Bank 2001.
60. Faiola 2001.
61. Pearlstein 2001.
62. Blustein 2001.
63. Pearlstein 2001.
64. Pearlstein 2001.
65. E.g., Serbin et al. 1993; Barkin 1995.
66. United Nations Research Institute for Social Development 2000; our estimate is for 2001 based on Internet reports.
67. National Public Radio, November 2001 report.
68. Skidmore 1993; Black 1977, 1986.

69. Schwoch 1992.
70. Herz 1987.
71. This is not to say it is all powerful; there are counterexamples (see, e.g., Skidmore 1993).
72. Dorfman and Mattelart 1975.
73. Roberts 1995c; Kottak 1990.
74. Castro and Acevedo 1989.
75. Power and Roberts 2000.
76. For a recent account, see Fearnside 2001.
77. Barkin 2002.
78. Barber 2001.
79. Nash and Safa 1985; Fernández-Kelly 1989; Gereffi and Korzeneiwitz 1994.
80. Advertisement appearing in the *Washington Post* July 9, 2001.
81. In 1998, 19 percent of Venezuela's exports were manufactures, 82 percent were imports. These 1998 data were from before the spike in oil prices multiplied that nation's oil revenues. World Bank 2001, p. 312.
82. Here the CEPAL data for Mexico's exports in manufactures is 89.9 percent, while the World Bank reports 85 percent. Both are above the World Bank's data for the United States (82 percent) and the "High Income" countries (82 percent; World Bank 2001, table 20, p. 312).
83. These 1998 data are excluding Brazil and Mexico. *CEPAL News*, April 2001, p. 3.
84. *Washington Post*, November 2001.
85. Herrera 2001.

Chapter 2: Pollution Havens on the United States–Mexico Border?

1. Sierra Club presentation, January 2001, Brownsville, Texas.
2. Axtman 2001b.
3. Domingo Gonzalez, personal communication, January 2001.
4. The data vary, since the neural tube defect rate per ten thousand babies in Cameron County, Texas, was 9.08 in 1997 and 19.94 in 1998. This is almost twice the national average (NAFTA Index).
5. *NAFTA Supplemental Agreement*, September 13, 1993—Final Draft.
6. Mader 1997.
7. Leovy 2001b.
8. Ingram and Varady 1996.
9. Southwest Center for Environmental Research and Policy 1999.
10. See, e.g., UCLA statistical volumes on the border.
11. The one-seventh figure is from Ingram and Varady 1996. Hall 1997 lists the difference as in North of the border is more than double that on the Mexican side. The difference appears to lie in the sizes of the areas compared.
12. Leovy 2001.
13. Quote from 1928. Herzog 1990, p. 189.
14. Treaty of Guadalupe Hidalgo, 1848. Online. http://users.dedot.com/mchs/treaty.html.
15. Rylander n.d.
16. Rylander n.d.
17. Rylander n.d.

18. Cañon de Santa Elena and Maderas del Carmen Protected Areas are also on the Mexican side.

19. Knight 2000.

20. Axtman 2001a, b; Knight 2000.

21. Rylander n.d.

22. Rylander n.d.

23. Axtman 2001b.

24. Knight 2000.

25. Axtman 2001b.

26. Axtman 2001b.

27. California Department of Water Resources, Division of Planning and Local Assistance 1994.

28. GEOMarine 2000, pp. 1–3.

29. GEOMarine 2000, pp. 3–19.

30. GEOMarine 2000, pp. 3–20.

31. GEOMarine 2000, pp. 3–20.

32. Dallett 2001.

33. Kolbowski and Treviño 2001.

34. U.S. Geological Survey 2001a.

35. Niiler 2000.

36. Brady et al. 2001.

37. Simon 1997, pp. 205–235

38. Saldaña 1994, 1998.

39. Surfrider Foundation 2002.

40. Rodgers 2001.

41. Commission for Environmental Cooperation 2001.

42. Liverman et al. 1999, p. 615.

43. U.S. Geological Survey 2001b.

44. Ingram and Varady 1996.

45. Fernández-Kelly 1983.

46. The results on this count have fascinating nuances, but ironically many families have used the border as a staging area for work-seeking expeditions into the United States and Canada.

47. Thompson 2001.

48. Thompson 2001.

49. On June 24, 2000, for instance, over twenty members of the independent October 6 Union of auto-assembly workers from Han Young entered a NAFTA meeting hall and were reportedly beaten and dragged away by officials (Lynda Yanz, Maquila Solidarity Network, Marta Ojeda, president of Coalition for Justice in the Maquiladoras, personal communication).

50. Although employees must legally be at least sixteen years of age, it is common for women much younger obtain false documents to work.

51. Seventy percent of maquila workers in Mexico are women (Maquila Solidarity Network).

52. Fernández-Kelly 1983.

53. Corporations often contract out maquila work to smaller companies along the border even though these companies may be fully owned by the "mother" company. Corporate contracting legally distances large companies from liability from smaller (and often "dirtier") operations.

54. Thompson 2001.

55. City of El Paso 2002.

56. Carlsen 1998.

57. Hall 1997, p. 3.

58. 1.3 million Mexicans were employed in maquilas as of January 2000; INEGI 2000.

59. Thanos 2000.

60. Critics call these "neo-liberal reforms."

61. Mexico received U.S.$16 billion in foreign investment in 1999; U.S.$19,045 billion in 1994; U.S.$2,778 billion invested in maquiladora sector in 1999 (INEGI 2000). These numbers can vary tremendously from one year to another.

62. Thompson 2001.

63. See, e.g., Fernández-Kelly 1989; Beneria and Roldan 1989; Wilson 1990.

64. Rocco 2001.

65. Arrillaga 1997.

66. Quoted in Arrillaga 1997. See Feldstein and Singer 1997.

67. Feldstein and Singer 1997.

68. Texas Dept. of Health 1998.

69. Global Trade Watch 1997.

70. National Toxics Campaign data.

71. Bandy 1997.

72. Quoted in Light 1999, p. 4, from a 1996 study in the *International Journal of Occupational and Environmental Health.*

73. O'Neill 1999, EPA average between 1991 and 1996. The 40 percent is from a 1995 report cited in *Global Trade* Watch; the 70 percent is from O'Neill 1999. Williams reports that in 1995 the Mexican Federal Attorney for Environmental Protection asserted that the final disposition of 25 percent, or thirteen thousand tons, of hazardous and toxic wastes produced by the maquiladora industry were not accounted for. Five to six million metric tons of hazardous waste were produced annually (Wilson 1994).

74. Signed in 1983, the La Paz Agreement was more a promise of executive goodwill between presidents Reagan and de la Madrid than a binding environmental treaty. La Paz established a two-hundred-kilometer zone straddling the border as a sort of "neutral ground" and jump-started initiatives to monitor cross-border pollution. Out of the La Paz Agreement grew the Border XXI Program, chartered to establish a basis for cross-border discussion and cooperation. Like the La Paz Agreement, it has no real political authority, but is an important part of maintaining harmonious relations.

75. Perry et al. 1998, cited in Liverman et al. 1999, p. 634.

76. Global Trade Watch 1997.

77. TNRCC 2001; Liverman et al. 1999, p. 611.

78. El Paso, TX; Dona Ana County, NM; Imperial County, CA; San Diego, CA; Douglas, AZ; Nogales, AZ; and Yuma, AZ, all exceeded federal ambient air quality standards.

79. See volume 276, issues 1–3 of *The Science of the Total Environment*, 10 August 2001, and studies funded by the U.S.–Mexican university consortium SCERP, the Southwest Center for Environmental Research and Policy (www.scerp.org). "US-Mexico Border Air Quality Poster Session," SCERP Technical Conference, Las Cruces, NM, November 18, 1999.

80. Simon 1997.

81. Liverman et al. 1999, p. 633.

82. Southwest Center for Environmental Research and Policy 2001.

83. The Carbón II power plant burns "dirty" coal. After criticism on environmental grounds, the World Bank and a U.S. investor withdrew from the project's original plan, but the project was redesigned and built. Visibility 130 miles to the northwest in Big Bend, Texas, can be reduced by up to 60 percnet. See also Rylander n.d.

84. Hart et al. 1999.

85. Keene 1999.

86. Keene 1999.

87. Blackman, Newbold, and Jhih-Shyang 1999.

88. Blackman, Newbold, and Jhih-Shyang 1999.

89. Hogenboom 1998.

90. Simon 1997, p. 210.

91. Metalclad asked for over $100 million in damages and loss of potential business but was awarded $16.7 million (the value of existing property only).

92. Scoffield 2000; also FOE 2000.

93. Gallon 2002; Moyers 2002.

94. Kelly, Reed, and Taylor 2001.

95. Liverman et al. 1999, p. 625.

96. According to its Web site, the CEC was established to address regional environmental concerns, help prevent potential trade and environmental conflicts, and promote the effective enforcement of environmental law.

97. An extremely strong burden of proof falls on the prosecution in all CEC lawsuits. If the prosecution wins, CEC fines are capped at $20 million and are paid by the member government, *not* the polluting industry. There is the possibility of using trade sanctions as part of CEC enforcement, but these can only be used against the United States and Mexico.

98. Hansen 2000.

99. Again, these sanctions cannot be used against Canada—it was granted an exemption during negotiations.

100. Unfortunately, the HAZTRACKS program has not been granted any funding for cleanups, and it often takes at least six months to identify illegal dumpers after a violation has occurred.

101. Graves 1999.

102. Clark-Bellak 1999; Simon 1997.

103. Mumme 1999.

104. Carlsen 1998.

105. Mignella 1997.

106. Salinas-León 1991.

107. Salinas-León n.d.

108. Environmental News Service 2001.

109. Gallagher 2002.

110. See Moody and McGinn 1992; Warnock 1995; Bullard 1993.

111. Garcia-Johnson 2000.

112. Simon 1997, p. 216.

113. Roberts 1998.

114. Institute for Agriculture and Trade Policy 1999.

115. Paterson 1998.

116. Schneider 1999; Bandy 1997.

117. Carruthers n.d.; Bandy 1997, n.d.

118. Sierra Club 2001.

119. Simon 1997, p. 211. Certainly it may be true that a third of the sites they tested were highly contaminated, but to claim that this describes two thousand miles is wild hyperbole.

120. Neumayer 2001.

121. Sprouse and Mumme 1997.

122. Carlsen 1998.

Chapter 3: Green Revolutions, Deforestation, and New Ideas

1. Frank 2002. This account is also based on visits by both authors to banana plantation in Central America.

2. Pallister 1999.

3. Lambrecht 1993b; see also Wright 1990.

4. Smith 2002.

5. Frank 2002.

6. Wargo 1996, p. 165.

7. Smith 2002.

8. "Farming the Garden of Eden" 2000.

9. See, e.g., Paige 1997; Robinson 1996.

10. United Nations Environment Programme 2000.

11. The UN's Economic Commission on Latin America and the Caribbean, among other agencies, has made these projections.

12. Knott and Day 2000. This is about a fifth of the at least 220,000 people a year who lose their lives as agricultural laborers (Gatti 1998).

13. Other figures from 1993 have the WHO reporting that 25 million farmers in developing nations suffering some symptoms of pesticide poisoning per year (Lambrecht 1993a).

14. See, e.g., McMichael 2000.

15. Murray and Hoppin 1992.

16. Kaimowitz 1992; Murray 1994.

17. Faber 1993.

18. Faber 1993; Murray and Hoppin 1992; Murray 1994.

19. Faber 1991, p. 32.

20. Murray and Taylor 2000.

21. World Resources Institute 1996, Tables 11.4 and 10.2.

22. 1996 figure, Benedetti quoted in Ruiz 1999.

23. Faber 1991, p. 32.

24. Murray 1994.

25. Faber 1993.

26. Scanlan 1994.

27. Scanlan 1994.

28. Schemo 1995.

29. Scanlan 1994.

30. Scanlan 1994.

31. Accidental deaths include tragedies like this story from the small town of Tauccamarca, Peru: In 1999, a government-donated milk substitute poisoned forty-four children (twenty-two fatally). Authorities speculate that an insecticide (possibly parathion) intended to kill stray dogs somehow got mixed in with the children's milk (Boyd 1999).

32. Murray 1994.

33. Murray and Taylor 2000.

34. Wesseling et al. 1997.

35. Lash et al. 1996.

36. Magdoff, Foster, and Buttel 2000.

37. Food and Agriculture Organization 2001.

38. Peritore and Galve-Peritore 1995; Nash 2000.

39. Franz 2002a.

40. Cornell University 1999.

41. Arguing that biotechnology is one of the few technologies in which less developed nations could "catch up" are Gonsen 1998; Correa et al. 1996.

42. Peritore 1999.

43. Gupta 1999, 2000.

44. Brush 1998.

45. Quist and Chapela 2001.

46. Lappé, Collins, and Rosset 1996.

47. MacKerron and Cogan 1993, p. 58.

48. Utting 1993, p. 5.

49. Hyde et al. 1996.

50. MacKerron and Cogan 1993. For a more complete analysis of the link between consumption and deforestation, see Vandermeer and Perfecto 1995.

51. Rainforest Alliance, speech at William and Mary, April 2002.

52. E.g., Annis 1992; Redclift 1986, 1999; Hajek 1995; Faber 1993; Rogge and Darkwa 1996; Mink 1993; Kelly and Mwangi wa Gîthînji 1994.

53. See, e.g., Myers 1984, 1993; Stonich 1993.

54. Murray and Barry 1995; Durham 1979; Anderson 1981.

55. Durham 1979; Anderson 1981.

56. See, e.g., Galeano 1971.

57. Galeano 1971.

58. Rudel and Roper 1997a and b.

59. Rudel and Roper 1997a and b, p. 61; see also Rudel 1997. For more on the connection between population growth and deforestation, see Rosero-Bixby and Palloni 1998; Preston 1996.

60. Reardon and Vosti 1993; Vosti and Reardon 1995.

61. Large forests, by contrast, are more affected through road building, state development projects, industry initiatives, and multistakeholder consortiums of actors from different social classes. In essence they find that each theory explains some cases, but we need an even more nuanced understanding to explain bigger trends of deforestation.

62. Boyce 1994.

63. Boza 1999.

64. Ulate 1999.

65. Hünnemeyer, Veloso, and Müller 1997.

66. Lewis 2000.

67. See the fascinating cases and themes in Brandon, Redford, and Sanderson 1998; Bebbington 1996; Vasconez 2001; Armijo 2001; Keck 2001; Ericson and Russell 2001; Wilshusen 2001.

68. Mitchell and Schlanger 1991; Umaña and Brandon 1998.

69. U.S. MAB numbers are from 1996.

70. Barkin 2002.

71. Barkin 2002.

72. See, e.g., Young 1999; Brandon et al. 1998.

73. Lewis 2000.

74. Fisher, Russell, and Ericson 2001.

75. Young 1999; Mumme and Korzetz 1997.

76. See Young 1999, p. 377.

77. Wyckoff-Baird et al. 2000.

78. Cuello, Brandon, and Margoluis 1998.

79. Smallholders were paid as little as two thousand *colones* per hectare, while largeholders got around fourteen thousand (Utting 1993).

80. Steinberg 2001.

81. Mahony 1992.

82. Some estimates placed the late 1990s rate of deforestation in Costa Rica over 5 percent.

83. Umaña and Brandon 1998; Riley 2001; Rohter 1996; Christen 1995.

84. Weinberg 1991.

85. Luth 2000, p. 9.

86. Luth 2000.

87. Luth 2000.

88. Richards 1997, p. 143, cited in Luth 2000.

89. "Colombia Revisited" 2001.

90. Contrast, for example, Vandermeer and Perfecto 1995 and Brandon et al. 1998.

91. Brandon 1998, p. 418.

92. The debate goes well beyond these points; see note 67.

93. Carias 2000.

94. Mader 2000.

95. Pleumaron 1995; Orams 1995.

96. Gould 2000.

97. Gould 2000.

98. "Ecotourism" 1997.

99. Lovejoy 1997.

100. Gould 2000, p. 5.

101. Gould 2000.

102. See Rodriguez 2000.

103. Gould 2000.

104. Padgett et al. 1996.

105. There are several proposals for how to evaluate ecotourism; see, e.g., Orams 1995; Shores 1995.

106. Gould 2000.

107. Scanlan 1994.

108. Wiehl 1990.

109. Lanchin 2001.

110. Thrupp 1995.

111. N. Franz, 2002b.

112. Faber 1993, p. 69.

113. Sierra Club 2000; Leovy 2001; Riley 2001; Cevallos 2001; Turati and Jimenez 2001.

114. EcoExchange, April 2000.

115. However, there has been much work deconstructing the image of "Indian as environmental protector"; see Redford 1991; Fisher 2000.

116. Gonzálvez 1995.

117. AVANCSO/PACCA 1992.

118. This of course isn't always the case, particularly with organic products, as large, multinational corporations begin to penetrate the organic market.

119. Van Bemmelen 1995.

120. Thanos's interview with Rafael Coto 1999.

121. Brown 2001.

122. Diebel 1997.

123. *Coffee* 2002.

124. Inter Press, January 26, 1994.

125. Juan Leon-Vega, interview 2000.

126. The Special Period began in 1989 with the fall of the Soviet Union. Jim Bass reports that unofficially Cuban government officials predict the rapid uptake of pesticides once they become available again (personal communication).

127. Thanos's interview with Luis Sanchez 2000.

128. Thanos, field research 2000.

129. Thanos, field research 2000.

Chapter 4: Hazards of an Urban Continent

1. Michaels 1988; "49 Killed" 2001.

2. Oliveira da Silva 1999; Fleisher 2001.

3. Acselrad and Mello 2000a; Federação Única dos Petroleiros 2000.

4. Roberts's interview with Yacht Club receptionist in September 2001. At her minimum-wage job, Clede must work 120 hours to earn enough money for a basic monthly basket of food for one person. Nearly one in five Brazilian women work as domestic servants, virtually none with a signed contract or benefits, and many earn well below the minimum salary (DIESSE 1997).

5. Johns Hopkins Population Research Program 2001.

6. CEPAL, November 2000, p. 2.

7. *World Resources 1996–1997.*

8. United Nations Research Institute for Social Development 1995, p. 60. These are the region's five megacities according to the Globalization and World Cities Study Group and Network (Parnreiter). There are vastly different estimates for these populations, depending on where one (arbitrarily) draws the line separating these capitals from other nearby agglomerations. The World Bank defines a megacity as any city with more than 10 million inhabitants, although others use figures as low as 4 million (see, for instance, Gilbert 1994). UNDIESA and UNU have spoken of a "general agreement that a megacity is different from an ordinary city," but the specific ways in which megacities distinguish themselves remain undefined (Gilbert 1994, p. 5).

9. Acselrad 2001a.

10. Carriere 1994.

11. Minc 2001.

12. Cited in Rico 2000; statistic is from CEPAL 1994.

13. World Bank 1992, pp. 3–5.

14. World Resources 1996–1997, p. 153.
15. World Resources 1996–1997, p. 21.
16. World Resources 1996–1997, p. 39.
17. Contreras n.d.
18. Contreras n.d., pp. 20–22.
19. See also Projeto Billings Potável por Inteiro n.d.
20. See Hochstetler 1998; Projeto Billings n.d.; Contreras n.d.
21. World Resources 1996–1997, p. 20.
22. World Resources 1996–1997, p. 21.
23. World Resources 1996–1997, p. 40.
24. World Resources 1996–1997, p. 40.
25. World Bank PID 1999; Gonzalez 2000.
26. Pick and Butler 1997; Sequeira 1996.
27. World Resources 1996–1997, Table 8.5.
28. Gilbert 1994, p. 119.
29. Gonzalez 2000.
30. World Bank PID 1999.
31. Gonzalez 2000.
32. World Resources 1996–1997, p. 20.
33. See, e.g., Beck 1992.
34. Sanches 2000.
35. Bullard 1990; Roberts and Toffolon-Weiss 2001.
36. Acselrad 2001a, b, and comments by Barbara Lynch 2000. Roberts attended the first International Colloquium on Environmental Justice in Niterói in September 2001, organized by Selene Herculano, Henri Acselrad, José Padua, and others at the Universidade Federal do Fluminense.
37. World Bank 1993; Tardanico and Larín 1997.
38. CEPAL, September 2000, p. 2.
39. See Heilbronner's excellent invocation of the experience, cited in Sanderson 1999.
40. Jenkins 2000, p. 2.
41. The environmental racism/justice movement and the NIMBY (not in my backyard) groups are important variants.
42. Leff 1986; Viola 1992. This was confirmed for the Brazilian case in interviews with Arturo Deiges (June 19, 1993) and Beth Grimberg (June 21, 1993). For an attempt to look comparatively at this issue across Latin America, see Christen et al. 1998.
43. See Viola 1992, p. 61. Steven Sanderson (interview November 29, 1993) made similar observations.
44. Dunlap et al. 1993.
45. Inglehart 1995.
46. Roberts's interview with Pedro Leitão, June 22, 1993.
47. Dunlap et al. 1993.
48. Gallup/Environics 2002.
49. Environics 2002.
50. I am referring to Inglehart's "post-materialism" hypothesis (e.g., 1995); see, e.g., critiques in Bell 1998, and Mertig and Dunlap 1995, the special issue of *Social Science Quarterly*, and, for Brazil, Anderson 1995; and Bugge 2001b.
51. Gates 1998.
52. Viola 1992; Movimento Ecológico Mater Natura/WWF 1992; Landim 1992.

53. This point is drawn from observations and discussions with several activists and scholars in Brazil in 2001; Looye 2000 also makes this point.

54. Roberts's interview with Flávio de Mattos Franco, World Wildlife Fund, June 22, 1993.

55. Viola 1992, pp. 62–63.

56. Hochstetler 1998.

57. Hochstetler 1998.

58. Martins 2000, 2001.

59. Hochstetler 1998.

60. Gates 1998.

61. Hochstetler 1998; R. Rocco 2001. See Wyckoff-Baird, Kaus, Christen, and Keck 2000 on land conservation and decentralization.

62. Sanches 2000.

63. R. Rocco 2001.

64. R. Rocco 2001.

65. Sanches 2000.

66. R. Rocco 2001.

67. R. Rocco 2001.

68. Looye 2000.

69. Evans 2000.

70. Looye 2000.

71. Looye 2000.

72. Paulo Martins, personal communication, August 7, 2002.

73. Gilbert 1994, pp. 128–136.

74. Gilbert 1996; Kaimowitz 1996.

75. Brandon 1998.

76. Menezes 1996; Rabinovitch and Leitman 1996; Meadows 1995; Kamm 1992; Traicoff 2001.

77. Menezes 1996; Traicoff 2001.

78. Meadows 1995; Traicoff 2001.

79. Traicoff 2001.

80. Meadows 1995.

81. Meadows cites one-eightieth the construction cost (1995); Traicoff cites 0.33% of the cost ($200,000 per kilometer versus $60 million per kilometer; 2001).

82. Traicoff 2001.

83. Taniguchi 1995.

84. Meadows 1995.

85. Kamm 1992.

86. Kamm 1992.

87. Menezes 1996; Kamm 1992.

88. Menezes 1996; Traicoff 2001.

89. Meadows 1995.

90. Meadows 1995.

91. Kamm 1992.

92. Traicoff 2001.

93. McKibben 1995, p. 77.

94. Municipality of Curitiba 2001.

95. "Home Remedies" 1993.

96. Traicoff 2001, pp. 7–8.

97. Moura 2001.

98. Grover, cited in Traicoff 2001.

99. Moura 2001.

100. Logan and Molotch 1987; Gould et al. 1996; Roberts and Toffolon-Weiss 2001.

101. Menezes 1996; Moura 2001; Evans 2000.

102. Moura 2001, pp. 207, 228.

103. Portes 2000.

104. Portes 2000, p. 361.

105. Traicoff 2001, p. 12.

106. Staten 1992; Eisner 1992.

107. Staten 1992.

108. SESI 1991.

109. Staten 1992.

110. SESI 1991a, b; Lemos 1998.

111. Gutberlet 1996.

112. Mishtu Ghosh, personal communication 1995.

113. Roberts 1998.

114. West 1995.

115. Cascio 1996, p. xi.

116. Jenkins 2000.

117. Holusha 1990, p. A2.

118. E.g., Mol and Spaargaren 1993; Mol 1995; Mol and Sonnenfeld 2000; Mol 2001.

119. Hawken, Lovins, and Lovins 1999.

120. Karliner 1997, p. 31.

121. INEM 2002.

122. Sissel 1996; ABIQUIM 1998; Marcelo Kos, Associação Brasileira da Indústria Química, interview with Roberts in October 1998.

123. ICCA 2002; American Chemistry Council 2000. Facing a series of exposés in the press of contamination from the plants the Brazilian organization ABIQUIM is beginning to allow nonindustry people to participate in a "third-party audit" of how well the plants are doing environmentally. They are beginning in 2002 with two state-of-the-art plants in São Paulo state.

124. Greer and Bruno 1996; Karliner 1994, 1997.

125. Associação Brasileira da Indústria Química 1996.

126. Athanasiou 1996, p. 237.

127. Copesul 2002.

128. Karliner 1997.

129. Sissel 2002, p. 63.

130. Roberts 1998.

131. Garcia-Johnson 2000; Jenkins 2000.

132. Guedes 2000.

133. Odegard 2000; Barton 2000.

134. Dominguez 1998.

135. Dasgupta, Hettige, and Wheeler 1997.

136. We compared the South and Southeast to the North, Northeast, and Center-West regions and did focal work at the petrochemical complex at Camaçari in Bahia and the firms around São Paulo.

137. Lemos 1998a, b.

138. CETESB 1992.

139. Lemos 1998a; Thanos interview with Lemos in 2000.

140. Hawken 1994, p. xiii.

141. Kuznets 1955.

142. Hettige, Mani, and Wheeler 1997.

143. See, e.g., Beckerman 1992.

144. See Arrow et al. 1995.

145. Beckerman 1992; Hettige et al. 1992; Reed 1992; World Bank 1992; United Nations Environment Program and the World Health Organization 1992, 1994; Grossman and Krueger 1993, 1995; Holtz-Eakin and Selden 1995; Selden and Song 1995. A special issue of *Ecological Economics* in 1998 addressed the issue, and more recent issues have dozens of pieces on the Environmental Kuznets Curve.

146. Arrow et al. 1995.

147. Roberts and Grimes 1997.

148. Grossman and Krueger 1995.

149. Hettige et al. 1992; Holtz-Eakin and Selden 1995.

150. Roberts and Grimes 1997.

151. Goldemberg 1995; Goldemberg et al. 1985; Grimes et al. 1993; Krebill-Prather and Rosa 1994; Mazur and Rosa 1974; Rosa and Krebill-Prather 1993.

152. Beckerman 1992; World Bank 1992; Grossman and Krueger 1995.

153. See, e.g., Wallerstein 1979; Chase-Dunn 1989.

154. See, e.g., Smith and White 1992; Korzeniewicz and Martin 1994; Gereffi and Korzeniewicz 1994; Gereffi and Wyman 1990; Grimes 1996.

155. Fröbel, Heinrichs, and Kreye 1981; Hettige et al. 1992; Dicken 1998; Moomaw and Tullis 1994.

156. Dicken 1998; Gereffi and Korzeniewicz 1994.

157. Grimes et al. 1993; Roberts 1996b.

158. Grimes et al. 1993.

159. See, e.g., Sayer 1996; Neumayer 2001.

160. Furtado and Belt 2000.

161. Carlos Vainer 2000, remarks at Latin American Studies Association Conference, 2000; Acselrad 2001a, b; Sanches 2000.

Chapter 5: Bio-Splendor, Devastation, and Competing Visions in the Amazon

1. Much on this point can be found in Hecht and Cockburn 1990.

2. The government of Brazil created yet another definition of the region, "Amazonia Legal," in 1953, which contains 4,975,527 square kilometers, only 3,374,000 of which is forest. The remainder is grasslands, covered with water, or deforested.

3. There is considerable debate on the number of species in the Amazon. Norman Myers (1984, 1993) reported that 300,000 plant and animal species from tropical forests worldwide have been identified and cataloged (approximately 15 percent of the total number of species). *Veja*, the largest Brazilian newsweekly, reported 30 percent (July 5, 1989). Other sources estimate over 10 million species live in the Brazilian Amazon.

4. Raven 1988, p. 121, in Wilson 1988; *Amazônia* 1989, p. 74; Reid 1989.

5. Bigarella and Ferreira 1984; Daly and Prance 1989.

6. Myers 1984, pp. 75–79.

7. This is true in Central America's rainforests as well.

8. Bigarella and Ferreira 1984.

9. Colinvaux 1989; Colinvaux, Oliveira, and Bush 1999.

10. Denevan 1976.

11. *Amazônia* 1989.

12. Gentry 1989, p. 394.

13. Undated direct mail membership request from the Rainforest Alliance, signed by Daniel R. Katz, Executive Director, C. 2000.

14. Nepstad et al. 2000. See also Carvalho, Barros, Moutinho, and Nepstad 2001, p. 131.

15. Laurance et al. 2001 and debate responses to the article, at the *Science* Web site.

16. Jacquacu 2001, pp. 58–59.

17. Ministério de Planejamento 2001a.

18. Ministério de Planejamento 2001b.

19. Laurance et al. 2001, supplemental data.

20. Laurance et al. 2001.

21. Laurance et al. 2001, supplemental data.

22. McGrath, Nepstad, and Alencar 2000.

23. Vidal 2001.

24. That study, called the Biological Dynamics of Forest Fragments Project (BDFFP), has been funded for decades by the Smithsonian Institution and the World Wildlife Fund/Conservation Foundation.

25. Vidal 2001.

26. Fox 2001.

27. Ministério de Planejamento 2001c.

28. Silveira 2001.

29. Kirby 2001.

30. IPAM 2000. Also Nepstad et al. 2001; Carvalho et al. 2001.

31. Widely differing estimates of deforestation in the Amazon have all been generated using information from a seemingly objective instrument: the satellite photograph. Each estimate represents a compromise based on the size of the budget and the staff. (Foster Brown, interview, August 1989).

32. Reuters 1999.

33. Recent estimates are that about 19,836 square kilometers were deforested in 2000, the highest level in five years. INPE 2001, cited in Bugge 2001a.

34. Deforestation is also known to be high in Ecuador's Amazon, and Peru is rapidly increasing its deforestation rates. But exact figures for these countries are still lacking.

35. Peters, Gentry, and Mendelson 1989.

36. Of 275 tree species they identified.

37. Anderson and Loris 1992.

38. *London Times* 1989; Lutzenberger 1989.

39. Rainforest Alliance 2002.

40. *Amazônia* 1989, p. 71.

41. IBGE 2001; Laurence et al. 2001. The 2000 census counted 12.9 million inhabitants in the north region of Rondonia, Acre, Amazonas, Roraima, Pará, Amapá, and Tocantins. The number rises to 21.1 million if one includes the bordering states of Maranhão and Mato Grosso.

42. Amazon Alliance conference, June 2001.

43. Hecht and Cockburn 1990.

44. For histories of development in the Amazon in English, see Hemming 1987; Moran 1985; Bunker 1985; Dourojeanni 1988; Padoch 1988; Schmink and Wood 1993; and Hecht and Cockburn 1990.

45. Hecht and Cockburn 1990.

46. Schmink and Wood 1993; Foweraker 1981; Bunker 1985.

47. SUDAM 1968.

48. Katzmann 1975; Reis 1968.

49. Mahar 1989; Moran 1981, 1985.

50. For a quantitative review, see Hecht and Schwartzmann 1988, Table 1. There are also many case studies.

51. Ministério de Fazenda, cited in Margolis 1989.

52. Wood and Schmink 1979; Hecht and Cockburn 1990. The estimate is from Hecht 1985, 1988.

53. Reuters News Service 1999.

54. Pompermeyer 1979, 1984.

55. Browder 1989.

56. Yokomizoâ 1989.

57. Fearnside 1981; Goodland 1985, p. 25; Hecht 1982, 1985; Hecht et al. 1988; Buschbacher 1986.

58. Hecht et al. 1988.

59. Hecht 1985, 1988; *Amazônia* June 5, 1989 p. 90.

60. Instituto Brasiliero de Geografia e Estatística 2001.

61. Cited in Costa 1979, p. 62.

62. Santos 1981, 1986; Galeano 1973; Haines 1989.

63. Santos 1986; CVRD 1987.

64. Santos 1986; Soares 1981, p. 6; Roberts 1992.

65. Santos 1982; Becker n.d.; Soares 1981; Roberts 1992.

66. Soares 1981; Santos 1982.

67. Oliveira Filho 1988.

68. Grupo de Trabalho/SBPC 1981, p. 44.

69. Cagnin 1988, p. 3.

70. On the growth pole strategy, see Bunker 1989; Hite 2002.

71. CVRD n.d.

72. Pinto 1982; Fearnside 1986; Anderson 1991; Hall 1987.

73. Davies de Freitas 1989.

74. Fearnside noted that the World Bank and EEC loans required strict environmental protection (cited in Instituto de Apoio Jurídico Populár, 1989)

75. See Pinto 1982, 1983; Sá 1982; Roberts 1992, 1994, 1995a, b; Browder and Godfrey 1997; Becker 1990, 2000.

76. In Brazil, virtually all gold mining is done by men. In Colombia and in Bolivia, some parts of the work of mining is done by women.

77. Cleary 1990; Schmink and Wood 1993.

78. These points are based on our personal interviews in southeast Pará state in 1989–1990. Excellent accounts can be found in Cleary 1990 and Schmink and Wood 1993.

79. World Resources Institute 2001.

80. Adapted from Hecht and Schwartzmann 1988, p. 16.

81. Fisher 2000.

82. Laurance et al. 2001; supplemental data.

83. Margolis 2000, p. 10, cited in Laurance et al. 2001, supplemental data note 13.

84. Goodland 1985, p. 25.

85. Speech at the Amazon Alliance conference, June 28, 2001, Washington, D.C.

86. Pinto 2001.

87. Eighty percent of Plan Colombia funding is earmarked for military, police, and fumigation; 7 percent for alternative development; 5 percent for human rights; 4 percent for law enforcement; 3 percent for aid to the displaced; and 1 percent for judicial reform.

88. "Mexcla ilegal en fumigaciòn" September 2001.

89. Forero 2001.

90. "Colombia Revisited" 2001

91. "Colombia Revisited" 2001.

92. Knight 2001. Even plan supporters estimate the total number of displaced persons (at the end of the two years) to be around forty thousand people; humanitarian groups estimate many more.

93. Rohter 2000a, b.

94. Darling 1998.

95. Lamus 1997; "Signa protesta en Caqueta" 1996.

96. This is based on including populations in Ciudad Guyana in Venezuela, Iquitos in Peru, Las Yungas in Bolivia, and smaller populations in lowland Ecuador, Peru, and Colombia. The population in the Amazon portions of Guyana, Suriname, and French Guiana probably do not total more than thirty thousand, if Brazilian gold miners are excluded.

97. Roberts 1992.

98. John 2001.

99. Bugge 2001b; World Wildlife Fund 2001.

100. "Brazil Triples Protected Area" 2002. This might have been in response to the 2000 fires and 2001 *Science* articles by Laurance's and Nepstad's groups described earlier.

101. Some excellent proposals are in Nepstad et al. 2002.

102. E.g., Vandermeer and Perfecto 1995.

103. Nepstad et al. 2002.

104. Here we point readers to works in English by Fearnside 2001; Bunker 1985; Schmink and Wood 1993, among others. There are many other works in Portuguese, and for other nations in Spanish.

105. Rone 1992.

106. *Estado de São Paulo*, September 15, 1997, pp. 1 and A8.

107. Emmi 1988.

Chapter 6: Indigenous Peoples, Development Megaprojects, and Internet Resistance

1. Interview with Berito KuwarU'wa on May 31, 1997, in Project Underground 1998a.

2. Interview with Berito KuwarU'wa, on May 4, 1997, in Project Underground 1998a; interviews by Roberts and Thanos at Amazon Alliance conference June 2001.

3. "Sigue Protesta en Caqueta" 2000b.

4. Association of Traditional U'wa Authorities and the Regional Indigenous Council Arauca 2000.

5. Project Underground 2000.

6. Amazon Watch 1999a.

7. U.S. State Department 1995.

8. Rÿser and Korn 1997.

9. Comite Colombia es U'wa (CCEU) 1994.

10. Berman, Seital, and McCann n.d.

11. Author's (Gorman) interview with David Rothschild, September 2000.

12. Roldán 1995.

13. Dudley and Murillo 1998, p. 45.

14. Dudley and Murillo 1998, p. 45.

15. Dudley and Murillo 1998, p. 45.

16. Pratt 2000.

17. "Potential Oil Industry Flashpoint Centers" 1999.

18. Author's (Gorman) interview; anonymous.

19. Amazon Watch 2000a.

20. Amazon Watch 2000b.

21. Whittemore 1992.

22. Kimmerling 1994.

23. Gedicks 2001.

24. Amazon Watch 2000c.

25. Saltani and Hindery 1999.

26. Grimbaldi 2002.

27. Manriquez 2000.

28. Amazon Watch 1998.

29. Moody 1997.

30. Gedicks 2001.

31. Manuel and Posluns 1974; Griggs and Fallon 1992; Rÿser and Korn 1996.

32. Nietschmann 1994.

33. Seton 1999. Petras and Zeitlin 1968 and others in Latin America called this "internal colonialism" three decades ago.

34. Project Underground 1998a, p. 5.

35. Project Underground 1998a, b.

36. Project Underground 1998a.

37. "Potential Oil Industry Flashpoint Centers" 1999.

38. Project Underground 2000; author's (Gorman) interview with David Rothschild, September 2000.

39. The notary who made the transfer official on November 18, 1999, Dr. Daniel Jordan Penaranda, has since been murdered (Project Underground 2000).

40. Mendez 1997.

41. Project Underground 1998b.

42. Mendoza, Del Pilar, and Mendez Moreno 1998, in Project Underground 1998a, b.

43. Marin 1999.

44. Ebaristo 2000.

45. Ebaristo 2000.

46. Although unsubstantiated, the claim indirectly linked the U'wa with a guerrilla group—a suspicion that in Colombia often invokes a violent government counterinsurgency response. In April 1997, Stephen Newton, president of Occidental Colombia, said that the U'wa territory is "the house of Father Perez" (a former priest who at the time was the leader of the ELN) (Marin 1999).

47. Rainforest Action Network/Amazon Watch/Project Underground 2001.

48. Amazon Watch 2001; EcoAméricas 2001.

49. *EcoAméricas* 2001.

50. Cultural Survival 1999.

51. Environment News Service 1997.

52. Amazon Watch 1999a.

53. Soto 2000.

54. Soto 2000.

55. Mining and logging projects in other areas of Bolivar state have resulted in defor-estation, mercury contamination of water and soil resources, and increased rates of disease (Miranda et al. 1998).

56. Miranda et al. 1998.

57. Miranda et al. 1998.

58. Author's (Gorman) interview with Atossa Saltani, November 2000.

59. Cultural Survival 1999.

60. Author's interview with Atossa Saltani, November 2000.

61. Author's interview with Atossa Saltani, November 2000.

62. Native Communities of the Gran Sabana Opposed to Construction of Guri Powerline 2000.

63. Community of Santa Elena de Uairen, electronic communication to José Rafael Leal 2000.

64. Amazon Watch 1999d.

65. Keck 1995.

66. Rucht 1999; Keck and Sikkink 1997.

67. Author's (Gorman) interview with David Rothschild, September 2000.

68. Comité Colombia es U'wa (CCEU) 1998.

69. U'wa Defense Working Group 2000.

70. Wollock 1999; Knol 1999.

71. Donna Lee Van Cott, personal communication.

72. Project Underground 1998b.

73. Amazon Watch 1999b.

74. Amazon Watch/Rainforest Action Network 2000.

75. A spokeswoman for Gore said, "It's a matter that involves the internal policies of another country. [The Vice President] has not made a decision proactively himself to make investments."

76. "Potential Oil Industry Flashpoint Centers" 2000; Rainforest Action Network 2001.

77. Pratt 2000.

78. Valdmanis 2000.

79. Frynas 1997.

80. Colombian government interdepartmental notes taken during meetings with Oxy representatives support this argument (interdepartmental meeting notes between the Ministry of Mines, Interior and the Environment, February 3, 1998, in Project Underground 1998a, p. 25).

81. "Potential Oil Industry Flashpoint Centers" 1999.

82. Amazon Watch 1999c.

83. Global Response 1998.

84. Cultural Survival 1999.

85. Marcos 2001, pp. 22–29.

86. Ross 1996. Mexico has reportedly overtaken Venezuela as the world's sixth-largest oil producer. PEMEX, the state oil company, reported some 125 oil spills in 1995 alone (Chethik 1996).

87. Donna Lee Van Cott, personal communication 2001.

88. The U'wa say that they have known about petroleum beneath their territory for thousands of years. To the U'wa the world was created in layers of earth, water, oil, mountains, and sky. *Ruiria*, the U'wa name for petroleum, is a sacred earth resource that sustains life (Osborn 1982, p. 17).

89. Associación de Cabildos y Autoridades Tradicionales U'wa, INCORA 1997.

90. Murillo 1996, p. 22.

91. International Labour Organization 2001.

92. Author's (Gorman) Interview with David Rothschild, September 2000.

93. Murillo 1996, p. 22.

94. Earth Council for Sustainable Development 1996.

95. Van Cott 2000.

96. Dudley and Murillo 1998, p. 45.

97. Murillo 1996, p. 22.

98. Murillo 1996, p. 22.

99. Donna Lee Van Cott, personal communication.

100. Murillo 1996, p.22.

101. Brooks, 1999.

102. Dudley and Murillo 1998, p. 45.

103. Seton 1999, p. 3.

104. McIntosh 1999, p. 4.

105. Cevallos 1995.

106. Collier 2000.

107. Sane 1996, p. 11.

108. Karliner 1997.

109. Gould, Schnaiberg, and Weinberg 1996.

110. Gedicks 2001, p. 18.

111. Christen et al. 1998.

112. Murillo 1996, p. 21.

113. Redford 1991; Fisher 2000.

114. Netting 1993; Rudel, Bates, and Machinguiashi n.d.

115. Jochnick 1995.

Chapter 7: Building a Global Civil Society: Living What We Know

1. Environics 2001.

2. Institute for Intercultural Studies 2001.

3. See Rees Wackernagel 1996.

4. Bell 1998; Bullfrog Films 1997.

5. Equal Exchange n.d.

6. Nauman 2002.

7. Europe, Brazil, and Chile are adopting third party-verification in late 2002, but it appears that environmental and community members of auditing committees may be routinely outvoted. Sissell 2002a, b.

8. Karliner 1997, p. xiii.

9. Anderson and Cavenaugh 2000. But see De Grauwe and Camerman 2002, who rank countries by value added, not by total sales. This calculation puts corporations as 29 and nations as 71 of the top 100 entities. We believe even this is a startlingly large number, and await more discussion of the most valid way to do these comparisons.

10. Dicken 1998.

11. United Nations Conference on Trade and Devlopment 2001.

12. E.g., Neumayer 2001.

13. There is now a huge literature on this point, and it is a complicated one. See, e.g., Biggs 1993; Karliner 1997; Danaher and Burbach 2000; Neumayer 2001. On the other hand, the WTO approach answers the greatest fears of some Latin American leaders who worry that environmental restrictions on imports will become a new camouflage for protectionism of core markets. See, e.g., Alsogaray 1993; Ominami 1993.

14. Jordan 2002.

15. See, e.g., Bandy and Bickham-Mendez *forthcoming*.

16. There is a substantial debate about this issue; see, e.g., the *Journal of Environment and Development*. This is also called "Downward Harmonization."

17. Roberts 1996a; Roberts and Vasquez 2002.

18. Biggs 1993; Guimaraes 2000; Mastny and French 2002.

19. Barkin 1995; Serbin et al. 1993; Economic Commission on Latin America 2002.

20. Neumayer 2001; Jenkins 2000.

21. Viveiros 2001.

22. Szasz 1993.

23. Sanderson 1993.

24. Herrera 2001.

25. Bullard 1993; Roberts and Toffolon-Weiss 2001.

26. Gould 2001 and others make this point.

27. People of Color Environmental Leadership Summit 1991.

28. The Social Ecology perspective makes a similar argument. See Brulle 2000.

29. DeWalt 2000.

30. Lewis 2000.

31. Sklair 1995.

32. Maguire and Brown 1986.

33. Robinson 1996.

34. "Hooked on Fast Growth" 2001.

35. McConahay 2000.

36. DeWalt 2000.

37. See Roberts and Hite 2000 for some review on this.

38. Sutcliff 1995; also in Roberts and Hite 2000.

39. Roberts attended a founding conference in this effort, organized at the Federal University of Fluminense, in Niterói, near Rio de Janeiro in October 2001.

BIBLIOGRAPHY

Acselrad, Henri. 2001a. "Democratizacão urbana e modernizacão ecológica." *Polilíticas Ambientais* 9 (27): 10–11.

———, ed. 2001b. *A Duracão das Cidades*. Rio de Janeiro: DP&A Editora.

Acselrad, Henri, and Cecília Campello do A. Mello. 2000a. *Trabalho Industrial e Poluicão Ambiental no Rio de Janeiro: Cenas de um Desastre Anunicado*. IBASE/Projeto Meio Ambiente e Democracia. Rio de Janeiro: IBASE.

———. 2000b. *Ambientes de Trabalho, Ambientes de Vida: Capitulos da Poluicão Industrial no Rio de Janeiro*. IBASE/Projeto Meio Ambiente e Democracia. Rio de Janeiro: IBASE.

Alsogaray, María Julia. 1993. "International Trade and the Environment: A View from Argentina." In *Difficult Liaison: Trade and the Environment in the Americas*, ed. by Heraldo Muñoz and Robin Rosenberg, pp. 153–158. New Brunswick, NJ: Transaction.

Amano, Hidetake. 1993. "Globalization of the Economy and the Response of the Japan Development Bank." *Japan 21st* 38 (December): 20–21.

Amazônia. 1989, July 5. Special issue. *Veja* (Brazilian newsweekly).

Amazon Watch. 1998. "Investor Advisories: Camisea Investor Alert." Online. www.amazon-watch.org/megaprojects/camiseaadvisory.html; accessed October 21, 2000.

———. 1999a. "Mega-Projects: Venezuela's Indigenous Peoples Defend Land Against Electrical Transmission Line." Online. www.amazonwatch.org/megaprojects/guripower-line.html; accessed November 13, 2000.

———. 1999b. "Colombian Oil Project on U'wa Land Sparks International Outcry: Two Women Hang Peace Banner from Roof of Colombian Consulate in Los Angeles." October 12. www.amazonwatch.org/newsroom/newsreleases99/oct1299uwaaction.html; accessed November 13, 1999.

———. 1999c. "On Assignment: Amazon Communications Team." Online. www.amazonwatch.org/act-html; accessed November 13, 2000.

———. 1999d. "Venezuelan Indigenous Communities Reaffirm Opposition to Powerline Project Despite Offers of Bribes by Companies. Press Release." October 8. Online.

www.amazonwatch.org/newsroom/newsreleases99/oct0899venpr.html; accessed
    November 13, 1999.
———. 2000a. "Eye on Mega Projects: Tapajos Waterway." Online.
    www.amazonwatch.org/megaprojects/tapajos.html; accessed October 21, 2000.
———. 2000b. "Eye on Mega Projects: The Xingu Dam." Online.
    www.amazonwatch.org/megaprojects/xingudam.html; accessed October 21, 2000.
———. 2000c. "Eye on Mega Projects: Bolivia-Cuiaba Pipeline." Online. www.amazon-
    watch.org/megaprojects/boliviacuiabapipeline.html; accessed October 21, 2000.
Amazon Watch, Project Underground, Rainforest Action Network. 2001. "Colombia's
    U'wa Tribe and Supporters Celebrate Oxy's Failure to Find Oil." August 1. E-mail press
    release.
Amazon Watch/Rainforest Action Network. 2000. "Celebrities Call on Gore to Take Action
    to Save Colombia's U'wa People." August 15. Online. www.amazonwatch.org/news-
    room/newsreleases00/aug1500uwa.html; accessed October 10, 2000.
Ambrus, Steven. 2001. "Air War on Drugs Stokes Anger on Ground." *EcoAméricas,* August,
    pp. 6–8.
American Association for the Advancement of Science (AAAS). 2002. *Atlas of Population
    and Environment.* Berkeley: University of California Press. Also online.
American Chemistry Council. 2000. "ICCA Participating Countries." Online.
    http://www.americanchemistry.com; accessed August 6, 2002.
Anderson, Anthony B. 1990. "Smokestacks in the Rainforest: Industrial Developmpent and
    Deforestation in the Amazon Basin." *World Development* 18 (9): 1191–1205.
Anderson, Anthony B. and Edviges M. Ioris. 1992. "Valuing the Rain Forest: Economic
    Strategies by Small-Scale Forest Extremivists in the Amazon Estuary." *Human Ecology*
    20: 337–369.
Anderson, Dennis. 1990. *Economic Growth and the Environment.* London: Shell.
———. 1991. *Oil, Gas, and the Environment.* Washington, D.C.: Economic Development
    Institute of the World Bank.
Anderson, Jamie Jacobs. 1995. "Urban Environmental Politics in Brazil: Popular Perception
    and Participation." Paper presented at the Latin American Studies Association Congress,
    Washington D.C., September 27–30.
Anderson, Sarah, and John Cavanaugh. 2000. *The Rise of Corporate Power.* Washington,
    D.C: The Institute for Policy Studies.
Anderson, Thomas P. 1981. *The War of the Dispossessed: Honduras and El Salvador, 1969.*
    Lincoln: University of Nebraska Press.
Annis, Sheldon, ed. 1992. *Poverty, Natural Resources and Public Policy in Central America.*
    New Brunswick, NJ: Transaction.
Armijo, Natalia. 2001. "Community Based Conservation in Quintana Roo, Mexico." Paper
    presented at the Latin American Studies Association Meetings, Washington D.C.,
    September 6–8.
Arrillaga, Pauline. 1997. "Parents Say Factories Cause Rash of Birth Defects." *Times-
    Picayune,* June 15.
Arrow, Kenneth, Bert Bolin, Robert Costanza, Partha Dasgupta, Carl Folke, C. S. Holling,
    Bengt-Owe Jansson, Simon Levin, Karl-Goran Maler, Charles Perrings, and David
    Pimentel. 1995. "Economic Growth, Carrying Capacity, and the Environment." *Science*
    268 (April 28, 1995): 520–521.
Associação Brasileira da Indústria Química (ABIQUIM). 1996. *Relatório Anual.* São Paulo:
    Author.

————. 1998. "Responsible Care." Online: http://www.abiquim.org.br/english/resp1.htm; accessed October 20, 1998.

Associación de Cabildos y Autoridades Tradicionales U'wa, INCORA-Gobiernaciones de Boyaca, Santander and North Santander, Instituto de Estudios Ambientales para el Desarollo (IDEADE) Universidad Javeriana, Santa Fe de Bogatá. 1998."Mapa de Teritorios Ancestrales." In *Project Underground*. 1998, p. 21.

Association of Traditional U'wa Authorities and the Regional Indigenous Council Arauca. 2000. "Urgent: Three U'Wa Children Killed During Combined Police and Military Raid." February 11. Online: http://forests.org/archive/samerica/couwabol.htm; accessed Feb. 25, 2000.

Athanasiou, Tom. 1996. *Divided Planet: The Ecology of Rich and Poor*. Boston: Little, Brown and Company.

AVANCSO/PACCA. 1992. *Growing Dilemmas: Guatemala, the Environment and the Global Economy*. Austin, TX: Documentation Exchange.

Axtman, Kris. 2001a. "In Texas, Free Trade Puts Border Colonias in Spotlight." *Christian Science Monitor*, May 10.

————. 2001b. "Low Water Hurts Shrimpers and Farmers." *Christian Science Monitor*, May 21.

Bakewell, Peter. 1984. "Mining in Colonial Spanish America." In *The Cambridge History of Latin America*, ed. Leslie Bethell, pp. 110–152. Cambridge: Cambridge University Press.

Bandy, Joe. 1997. "Reterritorializing Borders: Transnational Environmental Justice Movements on the U.S./Mexico Border." *Race, Gender & Class* 5 (1): 80–103.

———— and Jennifer Bickham Mendez. n.d. "Problems of Democratization for Transnational Civil Society: Coalition and Conflict in Cross-Border Movements." Unpublished.

Baran, Paul, and Paul Sweezy. 1968. *Monopoly Capital*. Hamondsworth: Penguin.

Barber, Benjamin R. 2001. *Jihad vs. McWorld*. New York: Ballantine Books.

Barkin, David. 1995. *Wealth, Poverty, and Sustainable Development*. Mexico City: Editorial Jus.

————. 2002. "Sustainable Regional Resource Management: A Strategy to Create New Beneficiaries from World Trade." Unpublished.

Barton, Jonathan R. 2000. "'Aço Verde': the Brazilian Steel Industry and Environmental Performance." In *Industry and Environment in Latin America*, ed. Rhys Jenkins, pp. 89–120. London: Routledge.

Bebbington, Anthony. 1996. "Organizations and Intensifications: Campesino Federations, Rural Livelihoods and Agricultural Technology in the Andes and Amazonia." *World Development*. 24 (7): 1161–1177.

Beck, Ulhrich. 1992. *Risk Society: Towards a New Modernity*. Newbury Park, CA: Sage Publications.

Becker, Bertha K. 1990. *Amazônia*. São Paulo: Editora Atica.

————. 2000. "Insustainability and Sustainability of Urbanization in Amazonia." Paper presented at the International Sociological Association Research Committee 24 Conference, Rio de Janeiro, August 1–3.

————. n.d. "Gestão do Território e Territorialidade na Amazônia: A CVRD e os Garimpeiros na Província Mineral de Carajás." Mimeo.

Beckerman, Wilfred. 1992. "Economic Growth and the Environment: Whose Growth? Whose Environment?" *World Development*. 20 (4): 481–496.

Bell, Michael M. 1998. *An Invitation to Environmental Sociology*. Thousand Oaks, CA: Pine Forge Press.

Benería, Lourdes, and Martha Roldan. 1987. *The Crossroads of Class and Gender: Industrial Homework, Subcontracting, and Household Dynamics in Mexico City*. Chicago: University of Chicago Press.

Berman, Tressa, Peter Seital, and Anthony McCann. n.d. "Local Empowerment and
    International Cooperation: A Report on the Working Conference, A Global Assessment
    of the 1989 Recommendation on the Safeguarding of Traditional Culture and Folklore."
    Online. www.folklife.si.edu/unesco/; accessed January 12, 2001.
Berry, Albert. 1997. "The Income Distribution Threat in Latin America." *Latin American
    Research Review* 32 (2): 3–40.
Bigarella, J. J. and Ferreira, A. M. M. 1985. "Amazonian geology and the Pleistocene and
    the Cenozoic environments and paleoclimates." In *Amazonia*, eds. G. T. Prance and T.
    E. Lovejoy, pp. 40–71. Key Environments Series. Pergamon Press, New York.
Biggs, Gonzalo. 1993. "The Interrelationship Between the Environment and International
    Trade in Latin America: The Legal and Institutional Framework." In *Difficult Liaison:
    Trade and the Environment in the Americas*, ed. Heraldo Muñoz and Robin Rosenberg,
    pp. 167–204. New Brunswick, NJ: Transaction.
Black, Jan K. 1977. *United States Penetration of Brazil.* Philadelphia: University of
    Pennsylvania Press.
————. 1986. *Sentinels of Empire: The United States and Latin American Militarism.* New
    York: Greenwood.
Blackman, Allen, Steven Newbold, and Jhih-Shyang Shih. 1999. "Benefits and Costs of
    Alternative Pollution Control Strategies for Traditional Brick Kilns in Cd. Juárez,
    Mexico." SCERP workshop.
Blustein, Paul. 2001. "Argentine, Turkey Get Buffeted." *Washington Post*, July 17, p. E1.
Boyce, James. 1994. "Inequality as a Cause of Environmental Degradation." *Ecological
    Economics* 11: 169–178.
Boyd, Stephanie. 1999. "Battle to Halt Pesticides and Save Lives." *The Toronto Star.*
    December 30.
Boza, Mario. 1999. "Biodiversity Conservation in Mesoamerica." In *Managed Ecosystems:
    The Mesoamerican Experience,* ed. L Upton Hatch and Marilyn E. Swisher, pp. 51–60.
    New York: Oxford Press.
Brady, Laura M., Floyd Gray, Mario Castaneda, Mark Bultman, and Karen Sue Bolm.
    2001. "Critical U.S–Mexico Borderland Watershed Analysis, Twin Cities Area of
    Nogales, Arizona and Nogales, Sonora." Online. geopubs.wr.usgs.gov/open-file/of02-
    112/; accessed
Brandon, Carter. 1998. "Cities and Health." *Environment Annual Review*. The World Bank
    Group. Online. www.worldbank.org; accessed August 21, 2000.
Brandon, Katrina. 1998. "Perils to Parks: The Social Context of Threats." In *Parks in Peril*,
    ed. Branson et al., pp. 415–440.
Brandon, Katrina, Kent H. Redford, and Steven E. Sanderson. 1998. *Parks in Peril: People,
    Politics, and Protected Areas.* Washington, D.C.: The Nature Conservancy/Island Press.
Brasil. Ministério do Planejamento e Orçamento. 1997. *Brasil em Números* [Brazil in
    Figures]. Rio de Janeiro: Instituto Brasileiro de Geografia e Estatística.
"Brazil Triples Protected Area of Amazonian Forest." 2002. The News Mexico.com.
    September 7.
Browder, John O. 1988. "The Social Costs of Rain Forest Destruction: A Critique and
    Economic Analysis of the 'Hamburger Debate.'" *Interciencia* 13 (3): 115–120.
Browder, John O., and Brian Godfrey. 1997. *Rainforest Cities: Urbanization, Development,
    and Globalization of the Brazilian Amazon.* New York: Columbia University Press.
Brown, Catherine. 2001. *The Herald* (Glasgow), March 3.

Brush, Stephen. 1998. "Bio-cooperation and the Benefits of Crop Genetic Resources: The Case of Mexican Maize." *World Development* 26 (5): 755–766.

Bugge, Axel. 2001a. "Destruction of Amazon Jungle Hits 5–Year High." Reuters, May 16.

———. 2001b. "Poll-Saving Forest Is Top Priority in Amazon." Reuters, June 8, 2001.

Bullard, Robert D. 1990. *Dumping in Dixie: Race, Class, and Environmental Quality.* Boulder, CO: Westview.

———. 1993. *Confronting Environmental Racism: Voices from the Grassroots.* Boston, MA: South End Press.

Bullard, Robert D., and Beverly Wright, 1992. "The Quest for Environmental Equity: Mobilizing the African-American Community for Social Change." *American Environmentalism: the U.S. Environmental Movement, 1970–1990*, ed. Riley E. Dunlap and Angela G. Mertig, pp. 35–50. Philadelphia : Taylor & Francis.

Bullfrog Films. 1997. *Affluenza.* Video.

Bunker, Stephen G. 1985. *Underdeveloping the Amazon: Extraction, Unequal Exchange, and the Failure of the Modern State.* Urbana: University of Illinois Press.

———. 1989. "The Eternal Conquest." *NACLA Report on the Americas* 23 (1): 17–25.

Bunker, Stephen G. and Paul S. Ciccantell. 1998. *Space and Transport in the World-System.* Westport, CT: Greenwood.

Burgess, John. 2000. "Exportable Commodities Cause Civil Wars, Study Says." *Washington Post*, June 17, p.3-A.

Burns, Bradford E. 1991. "The Continuity of the Colonial Period." In *Black Latin America, Its Problems and Its Promise*, ed. Jan Knippers, pp. 67–88. Boulder, CO: Westview.

Buschbacher, Robert J. 1986. "Tropical Deforestation and Pasture Development." *Bioscience* 36 (1): 22–28.

Cagnin, João Urbano. 1988. "Exploração Econômico da Amazônia: Perspectivas para a Região de Carajás." Mimeo.

California Department of Water Resources, Division of Planning and Local Assistance. 1994. "Bulletin 160–98: California Water Plan Update." Online. http://rubicon.water.ca.gov.

Cardoso, Fernando, and Enzo Faletto. 1979. *Dependencia y desarrollo en América Latina: ensayo de interpretación sociológica.* Mexico City: Siglo XXI Editores.

Carias, Suyapa. 2000. "Mesoamerican Biological Corridor Is Formally Established." *Honduras This Week Online*, July 17. www.marrder.com/htw

Carlsen, Laura. 1998. "Twin Plants: Despite Cries from Critics, the Maquiladora Engine Continues to Rev." *Business Mexico*, November 1.

Carriere, Jean. 1994. "Degradación Medioambiental en América Latina: Un tema que atañe cada vez más a los Latinoamericanistas." *Redial* 5:7–14.

Carruthers, David. n.d. "Environmental Nongovernmental Organizations in the U.S.–Mexican Borderlands." Online. www.borderecoweb.sdsu.edu/NGOWeb.htm; accessed January 10, 2002.

Carvalho, G., A. C. Barros, P. Moutinho, and D. C. Nepstad. 2001. "Sensitive Development Could Protect Amazonia Instead of Destroying It." (Letter) *Nature* 409 (January 11): 131.

Cascio, Joseph. 1996. *ISO 14000 Guide.* New York: McGraw Hill.

Castro, Edna M. Ramos de, and Rosa E. Acevedo Marin. 1989. "Amazônia: Dinámica Política da Divisão Regional do Trabalho." In *Transformação na Divisão Inter-regional do Trabalho no Brasil*, ed. Liana M. Carleial and Maria Regina Nabuco. São Paulo: ANDEC/CAEN/CEOSPLAR.

CEPAL News. April 2000; June 2000; November 2000. United Nations Economic Commission on Latin America and the Caribbean.

CETESB. 1992. *Acao da Cetesb em Cubatão: Situacao em Junho de 1992.* São Paulo: Author.

Cevallos, Diego. 1995. "Indigenous Peoples: Will U.N. Honour Be Mere Lip Service?" Inter Press Service.

Chase-Dunn, Christopher. 1989. *Global Formation: Structures of the World-Economy.* Cambridge, MA: Basil Blackwell.

Chayanov, Alexander V. 1925/1966. *The Theory of Peasant Economy.* Homewood, IL: American Economic Association.

Chethik, Sunita. 1996. "Oil Protesters Attacked." *Earth Island Journal* 11 (2). Online. ww.earthisland.org.

Christen, Catherine. 1995. "Field Scientists and Park Administrators: Environmental Conservation Initiatives in Costa Rica, 1960s–1970s." Paper presented at the 1995 Meeting of the Latin American Studies Association. Washington. D.C.

Christen, Catherine, et al. 1998. "Latin American Environmentalism: Comparative Views." *Studies in Comparative International Development.* 33 (2): 58–87.

Chudnovsky, Daniel, Andrés López, and Valeria Freylejer. 2000. "The Diffusion of Pollution Prevention Measures in LDCs: Environmental Management in Argentine Industry." In *Industry and Environment in Latin America*, ed. Rhy Jankins, pp. 66–88. London: Routledge.

Cicantell, Paul. 1994. "The Raw Materials Route to the Semiperiphery: Raw Materials, State Development Policies and Mobility in the Capitalist World-System." Paper presented at the American Sociological Association Annual Meetings, August, Los Angeles, CA.

Clark-Bellak, Gina. 1999. "The Case of Metales y Derivados." *Borderlines* 7 (10 November): online at: www.us-mex.org/borderline/1999/b1b1/b162case.htm

Cleary, David. 1990. *Anatomy of the Amazon Gold Rush.* Houndmills, Basingstoke, Hampshire: Macmillan, in association with St. Antony's College, Oxford.

Colinvaux, Paul A. 1989. "The Past and Future Amazon." *Scientific American*, May: 102–108.

Colinvaux, Paul A., P. E. De Oliveira, and M. B. Bush. 1999. "Amazonian and Neotropical Plant Communities on Glacial Time-Scales: The Failure of the Aridity and Refuge Hypotheses." *Quarternary Science Reviews* 19 (2000): 141–169.

"Colombia Revisited." 2001. *The Ecologist* 31 (6): 28ff.

Comité Colombia es U'wa (CCEU). 1997. "AbrilU'wa: el ingreso de la petrolera al territorio U'wa, significará el exterminio," *Utopias* V (44, May)

———. 1998. "Project Underground Interview." In Project Underground, p. 29.

Commission for Environmental Cooperation. 1996. "Building a Framework for Assessing NAFTA Environmental Effects: Report of a Workshop Held in La Jolla, California, on April 29 and 30, 1996." Working Paper: Environment and Trade Series.

Commission for Environmental Cooperation (CEC). 2001. *The North American Mosaic: A State of the Environment Report.* Québec: CEC. Online. http://www.cec.org.

Community of Santa Elena de Uairen. 2000. "Comunicado de Santa Elena de Uairen." Electronic Communication to Jose Rafael Leal. August 24. Environment and Latin America Network (ELAN) Listserve; accessed October 21, 2000.

Conrad, Geoffrey W. 1984. In *The Cambridge History of Latin America*, ed. Leslie Bethel. New York: Cambridge University Press.

Contreras Castilho, José. n.d. *História Condensada da Represa Billings.* Mimeo, Municipality of Diadema.

Copesul. 2002. "Ecoeficiência." Corporate environmental report release. Online. www.copesul.com.br; accessed September 14, 2002.

Cornell University. 1999. "Toxic Pollen from Widely Planted, Genetically Modified Corn Can Kill Monarch Butterflies, Cornell Study Shows." Press pelease, May 19. Online. http://www.news.cornell.edu/releases/May99/Butterflies.bpf.html.

Correa, Carlos et al. 1996. *Biotecnología: innovación y producción en América Latina.* Buenos Aires: Universidad de Buenos Aires.

Costa, José Marcelino Monteiro da, ed. 1979. *Amazônia: Desenvolvimento e Ocupação.* Rio de Janeiro: Paz e Terra.

Crosby, Alfred W. 1972. *The Columbian Exchange: Biological and Cultural Consequences of 1492.* Westport, CT: Greenwood Press.

Cuello, César, Katrina Brandon, and Richard Margoluis. 1998. "Costa Rica: Corcovado National Park." *Parks in Peril*, ed. Brandon et al., pp. 143–192.

Cultural Survival. 1999. "Active Voices: Action Alerts: Challenging Deforestation and Ethnocide in the Venezuelan Amazon." Also interview with Andre, Jerrick (Indigenous Federation of the State of Bolivar). Online. www.culturalsurvival.org; accessed November 13, 1999.

Curtin, Philip D. 1969. *The Atlantic Slave Trade, a Census.* Madison: University of Wisconsin Press.

CVRD n.d. "Plano Preliminar do Projeto Ferro Carajás." Vol. I, p. 26. Mimeo.

———. 1987. *Jornal da Serra.* July 31.

Dallett, Nancy 2001. "Moving Waters: The Colorado River and the West." Virtual Exhibit. Online. http://www.movingwaters.org/virtualexh.html.

Daly, Douglas C., and Ghillean T. Prance. 1989. "Brazilian Amazon." In *Floristic Inventory of Tropical Countries*, ed. David G. Campbell, and H. David Hammond. Bronx: New York Botanical Garden, pp. 401–426.

Danaher, Kevin, and Roger Burbach, eds. 2000. *Globalize This! The Battle Against the World Trade Organization and Corporate Rule.* Monroe, ME: Common Courage Press.

Darling, Juanita. 1998. "US War on Drugs Becomes Blurry in Colombia." *Los Angeles Times*, June 3.

Dasgupta, Susmita, Hemamala Hettige, and David Wheeler. 1997. "What Improves Environmental Performance? Evidence from Mexico Industry." Washington: World Bank, Development Research Group Working Paper Series 1877. Online. www.worldbank.org/nipr/work_paper/1877.

Davies de Freitas, Maria de Lourdes. 1989. "State and Corporate Environmental Policies for the Amazon—Experiences Under Carajás Iron Ore Project." Paper presented at the University of Florida, September 1988.

Dean, Warren. 1995. *With Broadaxe and Firebrand: The Destruction of the Brazilian Atlantic Forest.* Berkeley: University of California Press.

"Deforestation Could Push Amazon Rainforest to Its End." June 28, 2001. UniSci Daily News. Online. http://forest.org/archive/brazil/decopush.htm; accessed August 6, 2001.

De Grauwe, Paul, and Filip Camerman. 2002. "How Big Are the Big Multinational Companies?"

Denevan, William M. 1976. "The Aboriginal Population of Amazonia." Unpublished mimeo (UNCTAD website). In *The Native Population of the Americas in 1492*, ed. William M. Denevan, pp. 205–234. Madison: University of Wisconsin Press.

DeWalt, Billie R. 2000. "Testimony to the Subcommittee on Western Hemisphere, the

Peace Corps, Narcotics and Terrorism of the Senate Committee on Foreign Relations—
July 25, 2000." Congressional testimony.

Dicken, Peter. 1998. *Global Shift: The Internationalization of Economic Activity*. 3d ed. New
York: Guilford Press.

Diebel, Linda. 1997. "Ground by Coffee, Practically Enslaved: Workers in Guatemala Pay a
High Price to Help You Get Your Morning Jolt in a Mug." *Toronto Star*, September 28.

DIESSE. 1997. "Cresce a participação da mulher no mercado de trabalho." Online.
http://www.diesse.org.br/esp/es2mar97.html; accessed October 1, 2001.

Dietz, Thomas, and Linda Kalof. 1992. "Environmentalism Among Nation States." *Social
Indicators Research* 26: 353–366.

Dominguez Villalobos, Lilia. 1998. "Control de la contaminacion en la industria de fibras
quimicas en un contexto de apertura economica." Paper presented at the XX Latin
American Studies Association International Conference.

Dorfman, Ariel, and Armand Mattelart. 1975. *How to Read Donald Duck: Imperialist
Ideology in the Disney Comic*. New York: International General.

Dourojeanni, Marc J. 1988. *Amazonia Peruana: Que Hacer?* Unpublished.

Dudley, Steven and Mario Murillo. 1998. "Oil in a Time of War." *NACLA Report on
Chiapas and Colombia*. XXXI (5, March/April) 45.

Dunlap, Riley E., George Gallup Jr., and Alec M. Gallup. 1993. *Health of the Planet: Results
of a 1992 International Environmental Opinion Survey of Citizens in 24 Nations*.
Princeton, NJ: George H. Gallup International Institute.

Durham, William. 1979. *Scarcity and Survival in Central America*. Stanford, CA: Stanford
University Press.

Earth Council for Sustainable Development. 1996. "Legal Frameworks for Indigenous
Rights: Technical Consultation on Indigenous Rights, Environmental Law and
Sustainable Development." San Jose, Costa Rica, June 24–27. Online.
www.ecouncil.ac.cr; accessed January 22, 2001.

EcoAméricas. 2001. "Oxy Decision Elates U'Wa, Depresses Energy Officials." *EcoAméricas*
August, p. 2.

Eco-Exchange. 2000. "Murders in Guatemala Stun Conservationists." *Eco-Exchange: From
the Rainforest Alliance*. April. Online. http://www.rainforest-
alliance.org/programs/cmc/newsletter/apr00–1.html

Economic Commission on Latin America (ECLAC)/CEPAL. 2002. *Globalization and
Development*. Chapter 9: "Globalization and Environmental Sustainability." Santiago:
ECLAC.

"Ecotourism: A Good Trip?" *The Economist*, August 30, 1997, p. 48.

Edelman, Marc. 1995. "Rethinking the Hamburger Thesis: Deforestation and the Crisis of
Central America's Beef Exports." In *The Social Causes of Environmental Destruction in
Latin America*, ed. Michael Painter and William H. Durham, pp. 25–62. Ann Arbor:
University of Michigan Press.

Eisner, Peter. 1992. "Mexico Reels from Explosion." *Newsday*, April 24, p. 2.

Emmi, Marília Ferreira. 1988. *A Oligarquia da Castanha: Crise e Rearticulação*. Belém:
NAEA/UFPA.

Environics International. 2001. "Corporate Social Responsibility Monitor 2001." Online.
www.environicsinternational.com; accessed September 7, 2002.

———. 2002. "The Global Public's Agenda for the World Summit on Sustainable
Development (WSSD)." Press Release, January 31.

Environmental Health Coalition. 1995. "Border Environmental Justice Campaign: Right to Know." Online. www.environmentalhealth.org/rtk.html; accessed November 6, 2000.

Environment News Service. 1997. "Pemon Indians Paralyze Powerlines." May 19. Online. www.envirolink.org/archives/enews/0409.html; accessed November 19, 1999.

———. 2001. "Bush: Opposition to Free Trade Blocks Cleaner Air, Water." May 8. Online at www.ens-news.com.

Ericson, Jenny A., and Vance Russell. 2001. "Multi-Stakeholder and Community Based Coalitions for Conservation: The Nature Conservancy's Experiences in Latin America." Paper presented at the Latin American Studies Association Meetings, Washington, D.C., September 6–8.

Evans, Peter. 1979. *Dependent Development: The Alliance of Multinational, State, and Local Capital in Brazil.* Princeton, NJ: Princeton University Press.

———. 2000. "Sustainability, Degradation, and Livelihood in Third World Cities: Possibilities for State-Society Synergy." In *The Global Environment in the Twenty-First Century: Prospects for International Cooperation,* ed. Pamela S. Chase, pp. 42–63. New York: United Nations University.

Faber, Daniel. 1991. "A Sea of Poison." *NACLA Report on the Americas* 25 (2, September): 31–36.

———. 1993. *Environment Under Fire: Imperialism and the Ecological Crisis in Central America.* New York: Monthly Review.

Faiola, Anthony. 2001a. "Latin Turmoil Spreads." *Washington Post,* July 13, p. E1.

———. 2001b. "Hooked on Fast Growth." *Washington Post,* December 4, 2001.

———. 2001c. "Besieged President Resigns in Argentina: Opposition Party Vows to End Market Policies That Sparked Rioting." *Washington Post,* December 21, 2001; p. A1.

"Farming the Garden of Eden." *The Economist,* March 25, 2000.

Fearnside, Philip M. 1986. "Agricultural Plans for Brazil's Grande Carajás Program: Lost Opportunity for Sustainable Local Development?" *World Development* 14 (3): 385–414.

———. 2001. "Land-Tenure Issues as Factors in Environmental Destruction in Brazilian Amazonia: The Case of Southern Pará." *World Development* 29 (8): 1361–1372.

Federação Única dos Petroleiros. 2000. "Vasamento de Óleo na Baía de Guanabara: Trazendo a Verdade à Tona." *Primeira Mão.* April. Mimeo.

Feldstein, Mark, and Steve Singer. 1997. "The Border Babies: Did Toxic Waste from U.S. Factories Across the Border Damage the Environment of a Texas Town?" *Time,* May 26, p. 72.

Fernández-Kelly, Maria Patrícia. 1983. *For We Are Sold, I and My People: Women and Industry in Mexico's Frontier.* Albany: SUNY Press.

———. 1989. "Broadening the Scope: Gender and International Economic Development." *Sociological Forum* 4 (4): 611–635.

Fisher, Larry, Vance Russell, and Jenny Ericson. 2001. "Coalition Building for Conservation: Latin American Multi-Stakeholder Partnerships." Paper presented at the Latin American Studies Association, Washington, D.C., September 6–8.

Fisher, William H. 2000. *Rain Forest Exchanges: Industry and Community on an Amazonian Frontier.* Washington, D.C.: Smithsonian.

Fleisher, David. 2001. "Brazil Focus," internet newsletter. September 22–28.

Food and Agriculture Organization (FAO). 2001. "Statement on Biotechnology." Online. www.fao.org/biotech/state.htm; accessed December 2000.

Forero, Juan. 2001. "No Crops Spared in Colombia's Coca War." *New York Times,* January 29.

————. "49 Killed in Mudslides and Flooding in Brazil."

2002. *New York Times*, December 27, p. A10.

Foweraker, Joe. 1981. *The Struggle for Land: A Political Economy of the Pioneer Frontier in Brazil from 1930 to the Present Day*. Cambridge: Cambridge University Press.

Fox, Maggie. 2001. "Building Roads Could Destroy Amazon, Report Says." Reuters, January 19.

Frank, Andre G. 1967. *Capitalism and Underdevelopment in Latin America: Historical Studies of Chile and Brazil*. New York: Monthly Review Press.

————. 1971. *Lumpenbourgeoisie: Lumpendevelopment. Dependence, Class, and Politics in Latin America*. New York: Monthly Review Press.

Frank, Dana. 2002. "Our Fruit, Their Labor and Global Reality." *Washington Post*, June 2, p. B5.

Franz, Neil. 2002a. "USDA Figures Show Rise in GM Crop Plantings." *Chemical Week*, April 10, p. 36.

————. 2002b. "Senate Heats Up Debate on POPs Treaty." *Chemical Week*, May 22, p. 37.

French, Hilary. 2000. *Vanishing Borders: Protecting the Planet in the Age of Globalization*. Washington, D.C.: Worldwatch Institute.

Freudenberg, Nicholas, and Carol Steinsapir, 1992. "Not in Our Backyards: The Grassroots Environmental Movement." In *American Environmentalism: The U.S. Environmental Movement, 1970–1990*, ed. Riley E. Dunlap and Angela G. Mertig, pp. 27–37. Philadelphia: Taylor & Francis.

Friends of the Earth (FOE). 2000. "NAFTA Decision Threatens Environment, Group Says." Press release, August 31.

Fröbel, Folker, Jürgen Heinrichs, and Otto Kreye. 1980. *The New International Division of Labor*. New York: Cambridge University Press.

Furtado, José, and Tamara Belt, eds. 2000. *Economic Development and Environmental Sustainability: Policies and Principals for a Durable Equilibrium*. Washington, D.C.: The World Bank Institute.

Galeano, Eduardo H. 1971/English 1973. *Open Veins of Latin America: Five Centuries of the Pillage of a Continent*. New York: Monthly Review Press.

Gallagher, Kevin P. 2002. "Fast Track: Fix It or Nix It." Commentary, Interhemispheric Resource Center. Online. www.us-mex.org; accessed January 23, 2002.

Gallon, Gary. 2002. The Gallon Environment Letter, March 21, 2002. Internet newsletter. E-mail.

Gallop International/Environics International. 2002. "Giving the World's People a Voice at the World Summit on Sustainable Devleopment." Press release, August 29.

Garcia-Johnson, Ronie. 2000. *Exporting Environmentalism: U.S. Multinational Chemical Corporations in Brazil and Mexico*. Cambridge, MA: MIT Press.

Gates, Marilyn. 1998. "Eco-Imperialism? Environmental Policy versus Everyday Practice in Mexico." In *The Third Wave of Modernization in Latin America: Cultural Perspectives on Neoliberalism,* ed. Lunne Phyllips, pp. 155–174. Wilmington, DE: Scholarly Resources.

Gatti, Daniel. 1998. "Environment: Hazardous Waste a High Risk in Latin America." Inter Press Service, March 29.

Gedicks, Al. 2001. *Resource Rebels: Native Challenges to Mining and Oil Corporations*. Cambridge: South End.

Gelbard, Enrique A. 1992. *Changes in Industrial Structure and Performance Under Trade Liberalization the Case of Argentina*. Ottawa: National Library of Canada.

Gentry, Alan. 1989, "Northwest South America (Colombia, Ecuador and Peru)." In

Floristic Inventory of Tropical Countries, ed. David G. Campbell and H. David Hammond, pp. 391–400. Bronx: New York Botanical Garden.

GEO Marine, Inc. 2000, May. *Environmental Assessment of the Effect on San Luis, Arizona by the Proposed Construction of a Wastewater Treatment Plant and Improvements to the Wastewater Collection System for San Luis Rio Colorado, Sonora.* Online. http://www.cocef.org/aproyectos/slrc_EA16may00.pdf.

Gereffi, Gary, and Miguel Korzeniewicz, eds. 1994. *Commodity Chains and Global Capitalism.* Westport, CT: Praeger.

Gereffi, Gary, and Donald L. Wyman. 1990. *Manufacturing Miracles: Paths of Industrialization in Latin America and East Asia.* Princeton, NJ: Princeton University Press.

Gilbert, Alan. 1994. *The Latin American City.* Nottingham: Russell.

———, ed. 1996. *The Mega-City in Latin America.* Tokyo, Japan: United Nations University.

Global Response. 1998. "Protect the Safety of Indigenous Peoples protesting Imitaca Powerline." WorldWide Forest/Biodiversity Campaign News. August 8. Online. www.globalresponse.org; accessed November 13, 1999.

Global Trade Watch. 1997. "NAFTA at 5." Online. www.citizen/trade/nafta/votes/articles.cfm?ID=6473

Goldemberg, José. 1995. "Energy Needs in Developing Countries and Sustainability." *Science* 269: 1058–1059.

Goldemberg, José, Thomas B. Johansson, Amulya K. N. Reddy, and Robert H. Williams. 1985. "Basic Needs and Much More with One Kilowatt Per Capita." *Ambio* 14: 190–200.

Gonsen, Ruby. 1998. *Technological Capabilities in Developing Countries.* New York: St. Martin's Press.

Gonválvez, V. 1995. "La Agricultura Orgánica en Nicaragua." In *Simposio Centroamericana sobre Agricultura Orgánica*, ed. J. Garcia and J. Nagera, San Jose: Universidad Estatal a Distancia.

Gonzalez, Gustavo. 2000. "President's Air Pollution Plan Put to Test." Inter Press Service, April 24.

Gould, Kenneth. 2000. "Sustainability Across Borders? Transnational Ecotourism, Globalism and Place in Western Belize." Paper delivered at the International Sociological Association RC24 symposium on Sustainable Development. Rio de Janeiro, August.

———. 2001. "Environmental Justice from Below." Presentation at the First International Seminar on Environmental Justice, Niterói, Brazil, September.

Gould, Kenneth, Allan Schnaiberg, and Adam S. Weinberg. 1996. *Local Environmental Struggles: Citizen Activism in the Treadmill of Production.* Cambridge: Cambridge University Press.

Graves, Scott. 1999. "Citizen Action and BECC Policymaking." *Borderlines 53* 7 (2, February). Online. www.americaspolicy.org/borderlines/1999/b153/b153becc.html

Green, Duncan. 1991. *Faces of Latin America.* London: Latin America Bureau.

Greer, Jerry, and Kenny Bruno. 1996. *Greenwash: The Reality Behind Corporate Environmentalism.* New York: Apex Press.

Griggs, Richard, and Joseph Fallon. 1992. *The Meaning of Nation and State in the Fourth World.* Kenmore, WA: Center for World Indigenous Studies.

Grimbaldi, James V. 2002. "Enron Pipeline Leaves Scar on South America." *Washington Post*, May 6, p. A1.

Grimes, Peter E. 1996. *Economic Cycles and International Mobility in the World-System: 1790–1990*. Ph.D. dissertation, Johns Hopkins University.

Grimes, Peter E., J. Timmons Roberts, and Jodie Manale, 1993. "Social Roots of Environmental Damage: A World-Systems Analysis of Global Warming," Presentation at the American Sociological Association Annual Meetings, Miami, FL.

Gross, Anthony. 1990. "Amazonia in the Nineties: Sustainable Development or Another Decade of Destruction?" *Third World Quarterly* 12 (3, July): 1–24.

Grossman, Gene M., and Alan B. Krueger. 1993. "Environmental Impacts of a North American Free Trade Agreement." In *The U.S.-Mexico Free Trade Agreement*, ed. P. Garber, pp. 13–56. Cambridge, MA: MIT Press.

———. 1995. "Economic Growth and the Environment." *Quarterly Journal of Economics* 110 (May): 353–377.

Grupo de Trabalho Carajás(GTC)/SBPC. 1982. "Por Que Agora e Desta Forma?" *Ciencia Hoje*. 1 (3): 41–44.

Guedes, Ana. 2000. "Sustainability and Modernization of American and European Transnational Corporations in Brazil." Paper presented at International Sociological Association RC24 Conference, Rio de Janiero, 1–3 August.

"Guerilla aprovecha debate U'wa." *El Tiempo*, February 21, 2000.

Guimaraes, Roberto. 2000. "Brazil and Global Environmental Politics: Same Wine in New Bottles?" Presented at the International Sociological Association Research Committee 24 Conference, Rio de Janeiro, August 1–3.

Gunn, Philip. 1993. "The Tietê Project." Lecture at the University of São Paulo, June 14.

Gupta, Aarti. 1999. "Framing Biosafety in an International Context: The Biosafety Protocol Negotiations." Environment and Natural Resources Program Discussion Paper E-99–10. Cambridge: Harvard University Press.

———. 2000, May. "Governing Trade in Genetically Modified Organisms: The Cartagena Protocol on Biosafety." *Environment* 42: 4.

Gutberlet, J. 1996. *Cubatão: Desenvolvimento, Exclusão Social e Degradação Ambiental*. São Paulo: Editora da USP/FAPESP.

Haines, Gerald K. 1989. *The Americanization of Brazil: A Study of U.S. Cold War Diplomacy in the Third World, 1945–1954*. Wilmington, DE: Scholarly Resources Books.

Hajek, Ernst R., ed. 1995. *Pobreza y Medio Ambiente en América Latina*. Buenos Aires: CIEDLA.

Hall, Anthony. 1987. "Agrarian Crisis in Brazilian Amazonia: The Grande Carajás Programme." *Journal of Development Studies* 23 (4): 522–552.

Hall, Heidi. 1997. "Environmental Cooperation Along the U.S.–Mexican Border: NAFTA and Beyond." Paper presented at the Latin American Studies Association Meeting, April 17–19.

Hansen, Brian. 2000. "Free Trade Is Transforming North America's Environment." Environmental News Service.

Hart, Rebecca, et al. 1999. "Ambient Air Quality and Acute Pediatric Respiratory Illness in the Paso del Norte Airshed." SCERP, the Southwest Center for Environmental Research and Policy (www.scerp.org), "US-Mexico Border Air Quality Poster Session," SCERP Technical Conference, Las Cruces, NM, November 18.

Hawken, Paul. 1993. *The Ecology of Commerce: A Declaration of Sustainability*. New York: Harper Collins.

Hawken, Paul, Amory Lovins, and L. Hunter Lovins. 1999. *Natural Capitalism*. New York: Little, Brown and Company.

Hecht, Susanna B. 1982. "Cattle Ranching Development in the Eastern Amazon: Evaluation of a Development Policy," Ph.D. thesis, University of California, Berkeley.

———. 1985. "Environment, Development and Politics: Capital Accumulation and the Livestock Sector in Eastern Amazonia." *World Development* 13 (6 June): pp. 663–684.

Hecht, Susanna B., and Alexander Cockburn. 1990. *The Fate of the Forest: Developers, Destroyers, and Defenders of the Amazon*. New York: Harper Perennial.

Hecht, Susanna B., and Stephen Schwartzmann. 1988. "The Good, the Bad, and the Ugly: Amazonian Extraction, Colonist Agriculure, and Livestock in Comparative Perspective." Unpublished.

Hecht, Susanna, Anthoney B. Anderson, and P. May. 1988. "The Subsidy from Nature: Shifting Cultivation, Successional Palm Forests, and Rural Development." *Human Organization* 47 (1): 25–35.

Heller, Karen. 1993. "ISO 9000: Stepping-Stone on the Road to a Global Economy: Environmental Standards Take Center Stage." *Chemical Week*, February 10, pp. 30–32.

Hemming, John. 1987. *Amazon Frontier: The Defeat of the Brazilian Indians*. Cambridge, MA: Harvard University Press.

Herrera, Guillermo Castro. 1994. *Los Trabajos de Ajuste y Combate: Naturaleza y Sociedad en la História de América Latina*. Havana: Casa/Colcultura.

———. 2001. "Environmental History (Made) in Latin America." H-Environment Historiography Series. Online. www2.h-net.msu.edu/~environ/historiography/>; accessed April 22, 2001.

Herz, Daniel. 1987. *A história secreta da Rede Globo*. Porto Alegre-RS-Brasil: Tchê!

Herzog, Lawrence A. 1990. *Where North Meets South: Cities, Space, and Politics on the U.S.-Mexico Border*. Austin: University of Texas Press.

Hettige, Hemamala, Robert E. B. Lucas, and David Wheeler, 1992. "The Toxic Intensity of Industrial Production: Global Patterns, Trends, and Trade Policy," *AEA Papers and Proceedings* 82 (May): 478–481.

Hettige, Hemamala, Muthukumara Mani, and David Wheeler. 1997. "Industrial Pollution in Economic Development: Kuznets Revisited." Policy Research Working Paper Series. Washington: World Bank. Online. http://www.worldbank.org/nipr/work_paper/kuznet/index.htm; accessed June 1, 1998.

Hochstetler, Kathryn. 1998. "Neoliberalism, Democratization, and Urban Environmental Politics in Brazil in the 1990s." Paper presented at the Space, Place and Nation Conference, November 20–21, University of Massachusetts.

Hogenboom, Barbara. 1998. *Mexico and the NAFTA Environment Debate*. Utrecht: International Books.

Holtz-Eakin, Douglas, and Thomas M. Selden. 1995. "Stoking the Fires? CO_2 Emissions and Economic Growth." *Journal of Public Economics* 57: 85–101.

Holusha, John. 1990. "Ed Woolard Walks Du Pont's Tightrope." *New York Times*, October 14.

"Home Remedies Are the Best." *The Economist*, April 17, 1993.

Hünnemeyer, Anne-Juliane, Ronnie de Camino Velozo, and Sabine Müller. 1997. *Análisis del desarrollo sostenible en Centroamérica: indicadores para la agricultura y los recursos naturales*. San José, Costa Rica: IICA: BMZ/GTZ.

Hyde, William, Gregory Amacher, and William Magrath. 1996. "Deforestation and Forest Land Use: Theory, Evidence, and Policy Implications." *World Bank Research Observer* 11 (2, August): 223–248.

ICCA. 2002. "ICCA Membership." Online. http://www.icca-chem.org/members.htm; accessed August 6, 2002.

INEGI. 2000. "VI Informe de Gobierno de Ernesto Zedillo, 2000." Online. http://www.epinet.org.

Inglehart, Ronald. 1995. "Political Support for Environmental Protection: Objective Problems and Subjective Values in 43 Societies." *PS: Political Science and Politics* 23 (1): 57–72.

Ingram, H., and R. G. Varady. 1996. "Bridging Borders: Empowering Grassroots Linkages." *Arid Lands Newsletter* (Spring/Summer), p. 39.

Institute for Agriculture and Trade Policy. 1999. "NAFTA Fact Sheet." Online. http://www.corpwatch.org/issues/PID.jsp?articleid=1528; accessed September 7, 2002.

Institute for Intercultural Studies. 2001. "Margaret Mead: An Anthropology of Human Freedom." Web biography. Online. http://www.mead2001.org/biography.html; accessed September 14, 2002.

Instituto Brasileiro de Geografia e Estatística (IBGE). 2001. "Brazilian Census Data Online." Online. www.ibge.gov.br; accessed July 31, 2001; August 31, 2001.

Instituto de Apoio Jurídico Popular. 1989. "Inquerito Civil Programa Grande Carajás." *Informativo* 1.

Inter-American Development Bank—SDS/SOC. 2000. "Occupational Safety in Latin America and the Caribbean: Economic and Health Dimensions of the Problem." SDS/SOC: Technical Working Paper.

International Labour Organization. 2001. "Indigenous and Tribal Peoples: A Guide to ILO Convention No. 169." Online. www.ilo.org/public/english/employment/strat/poldev/papers/1998/169guide/contents.html; accessed January 12, 2001.

IPAM, 2000. "Relatório do Projeto 'Cenários Futuros para a Amazônia.'" June 1, 2000. Online. www.ipam.org.br; accessed August 8, 2001.

Jacquacu, Penelope. 2001. "When Forward Is Backward." *Ecologist* 31 (3, April): 58–59.

Janvry, Alain de. 1981. *The Agrarian Question and Reformism in Latin America*. Baltimore: Johns Hopkins University Press.

Jenkins, Rhys. 2000. *Industry and Environment in Latin America*. London: Routledge.

Jha, Raghbendra, and John Wahlley. 1999, August. "The Environmental Regime in Developing Countries." Bational Bureau of Economic Research. Working Paper 7305.

Jochnick, Chris. 1995. "Amazon Oil Offensive." *Multinational Monitor* XVI. (1–2, January/February) Online. http://multinationalmonitor.org.

John, Liana. 2001. "Quem está Roubando a Amazônia?" *O Estado de São Paulo*, November 30. Online. www.estadao.com.br

Johns Hopkins Population Research Program. 2001. "Hopkins Report: Cities Will Determine Living Standards for Mankind." Press release, June 5.

Jordan, Mary. 2002. "Mexican Workers Pay for Success." *Washington Post*, June 20, p. A1.

Kaimowitz, David. 1990. *Making the Link: Agricultural Research and Technology Transfer in Devloping Countries*. Boulder, CO: Westview Press.

Kaimowitz, David. 1996. "The Political Economy of Environmental Policy Reform in Latin America." In *Development and Change* 27: 43–452.

———. 2002. "Amazon Deforestation Revisited (Review Essays)." *Latin American Research Review*, 37 (2, Spring): 221.

Kamm, Thomas. 1992. "Model City: Urban Problems Yield to Innovative Spirit of a City in Brazil." *Wall Street Journal*, January 10, 1992. p. A1.

Karl, Terry L. 1997. *The Paradox of Plenty: Oil Booms and Petro-States*. Berkeley: University of California Press.

Karliner, Joshua. 1994. "The Environment Industry Profiting from Pollution." *Ecologist* 24 (2): 59–63.

———. 1997. *The Corporate Planet: Ecology and Politics in the Age of Globalization*. San Francisco: Sierra Club.

Katzman, M. T. 1975. "Paradoxes of Amazonian Development in a 'Resource Starved' World." *Journal of Developing Areas* 10: 445–459.

Kay, Cristobal. 1989. *Latin American Theories of Development and Underdevelopment*. New York: Routledge.

———. 1998. "Relevance of Structuralist and Dependency Theories in the Neoliberal Period: A Latin American Perspective." The Hague: Institute of Social Sciences Working Paper Series No. 281.

Keck, Margaret E. 1995. "Parks, People, and Power: The Shifting Terrain of Environmentalism." *NACLA Report on the Americas*, 28 (5, March/April): 36–41+.

———. 2001. "Perspectives from a Political Scientist." Paper presented at the Latin American Studies Association Meetings, Washington D.C., September 6–8.

Keck, Margaret E., and Kathryn Sikkink. 1997. *Activists Beyond Borders: Advocacy Networks in International Politics*. Ithaca, NY: Cornell University Press.

Keene, Frank. 1999. "Ambos Nogales Air Quality Study." (Southwest Center for Environmental Research and Policy) Workshop.

Kelly, Mary. 1993. "NAFTA and the Environment: Free Trade and the Politics of Toxic Waste." *Multinational Monitor* 15 (10): online at www.multinationalmonitor.org

Kelly, Mary, Cyrus Reed, and Lynda Taylor. 2001. "The Border Environment Cooperation Commission (BECC) & North American Development Bank (NADB): Achieving Their Environmental Mandate." Texas Center for Policy Studies Paper, July 2001. Online. www.texascenter.org.

Kelly, Thomas, and Mwangi wa Gîthînji. 1994. "Environmental Degradation and Poverty in Less Industrialized Nations." *Frontera Norte* 6: 77–89.

Kimmerling, Judith. 1994. "The Environmental Audit of Texaco's Amazon Oil Fields: Environmental Justice or Business as Usual?" *Harvard Human Rights Journal* 17 (7–8, Spring): 199–224.

Kirby, Alex. 2001. "Amazon Forest 'Could Vanish Fast.'" June 25, 2001. BBC News Online; http://news.bbc.co.uk; accessed 6 Aug. 2001.

Knight, Danielle. 2000. "Trade Ruling Undermines Environmental Agreements, Warn Conservationists." Inter Press Service, November 21.

———. 2001. "Colombian Governors Protest US Funded Fumigation." Inter Press Service, March 13.

Knol, Ann Schottman. 1999. "Menominee Leader Blames U.S. for Deaths." *Milwaukee Journal Sentinel,* March 7.

Knott, Michelle, and Michael Day. 2000. "Death Crops Up; Farm Worker Protections Not Doing Enough in Developing countries." *San Diego Union-Tribune*, December 13, p. F-1.

Kolbowski, Jens D., and Jorge Treviño, 2001. "Hotel, Motel, Tour & Business Guide to Mexicali." Online. http://www.baha-web.com/mexicali/index.html; accessed 26 Jan. 2002.

Korzeniewicz, Roberto P., and William Martin. 1994. "The Global Distribution of Commodity Chains." In *Commodity Chains and Global Capitalism*, ed. Gary Gereffi and Miguel Korzeniewicz, pp. 67–95. Westport, CT: Praeger.

Korzeniewicz, Roberto Patricio, and William C. Smith. 1996. *Latin America in the World Economy.* Westport, CT: Greenwood.

Kottak, C. P. 1990. *Prime-Time Society: An Anthropological Analysis of Television and Culture.* Belmont, CA: Wadsworth.

Krebill-Prather, Rose L., and Eugene A. Rosa. 1994. "Societal Consequences of Carbon Dioxide Emissions: Impacts to Well Being of Reduced Fossil Fuel Dependence." Presentation at the American Sociological Association Annual Meetings, August, Los Angeles.

Kuznets, Simon. 1955 "Economic Growth and Income Inequality." *American Economic Review* XLV (1): 4–28.

Lambrecht, Bill. 1993a. "Misused Farm Chemicals Poisoning Poor Nations." *St. Louis Post-Dispatch*, October 24, p. 1A.

———. 1993b. "Crop Sprays Leave Residue of Ailments." *St. Louis Post-Dispatch*, December 12, p. 1A.

Lamus, Francisco.1997. "Social Movements of the Amazonian Coca Plantations of Colombia. Rebellions of People Who Survive by Unlawful Ways." Unpublished.

Lanchin, Mike. 2001. "Ex-workers in Nicaraguan Banana Fields Sue U.S. Firms over Illness Linked to Toxic Fumigant." *San Francisco Chronicle*, March 15, p. A14.

Landim, Leilah, ed. 1992. *Sem Fins Lucrativos: As Organizações Não-Governamentais no Brasil.* Rio de Janeiro: Instituto de Estudos da Religião.

Lappé, Francis M. Joseph Collins, and Peter Rosset. 1996. World Hunger: Twelve Myths. Oakland, CA: Institute for Food and Development Policy/Fook First.

Lash, Scott, et al. 1996. *Risk, Environment and Modernity: Towards a New Ecology.* London: Sage.

Laurance, William F., Mark A. Cochrane, Scott Bergen, Philip M. Fearnside, Patricia Delamônica, Christopher Barber, Sammya D'Angelo, and Tito Fernandes. 2001. "The Future of the Brazilian Amazon." *Science* 291 (5503): 438.

Leff, Enrique. 1986. "Notas para un análisis sociológico de los movimientos ambientalistas." In *Política ambiental y desarrollo: Un debate para América Latina*, ed. Marta Cárdenas, pp. 115–126. Bogota: FESCOL/INDERENA.

———. 1998. *Ecología y capital: racionalidad ambiental, democracia participativa y desarrollo Sustentable.* Mexico City: Siglo Veintiuno.

Lemos, Maria Carmen de Mello. 1998a. "The Politics of Pollution Control in Brazil: State Actors and Social Movements Cleaning Up Cubatao." *World Development* 26 (1): 75–87.

Lemos, Maria Carmen de Mello. 1998b. "The Cubatão Pollution Control Project; Popular Participation and Public Accountability." *Journal of Environment and Development.* 7 (1, March): 60–76.

Leonard, H. Jeffery. 1988. *Pollution and the Struggle for the World Product: Multinational Corporations, Environment, and International Comparative Advantage.* Cambridge: Cambridge University Press.

Leovy, Jill. 2001a. "Mexico to Review Activists' Case." *Los Angeles Times*, February 7.

———. 2001b. "Survey Finds a Gulf of Differences Along U.S.–Mexico Border: Study Counters Notion of Transnational Society, as Residents Reflect Their Countries." *Los Angeles Times*, June 3.

Lewis, Tammy L. 2000. "Transnational Conservation Movement Organziations: Shaping the Protected Area Systems of Less Developed Countries." *Mobilization* 5 (1): 105–123.

Light, Julie. 1999. "Engendering Change: The Long, Slow Road to Organizing Women

Maquiladora Workers." *La Linea*. June 26. Online.
www.igc.org/trac/feature/border/women/engendering.html.

Liverman, Diana, et al. 1999. "Environmental Issues Along the United States–Mexico
Border: Drivers of Change and Responses of Citizens and Institutions." *Annual Reveiw
of Engery and Environment* 24: 607–643.

Logan, John R., and Harvey L. Molotch. 1987. *Urban Fortunes: The Political Economy of
Place*. Berkeley: University of California Press.

Lombardi, Cathryn L., and John V. Lombardi. 1983. *Latin American History, a Teaching
Atlas*. Madison: University of Wisconsin Press.

Looye, Johanna W. 2000. "Social Class and the Environment in Greater Rio de Janeiro:
Where Did the Green Go?" Presented to the Latin American Studies Association, March
16–18, Miami, FL.

Lovejoy, Thomas. 1997. "Lessons from a Small Country." *Washington Post,* April 22.

Loveman, Brian. 1979. *Chile: The Legacy of Hispanic Capitalism*. New York: Oxford
University Press.

Low, Patrick, and Alexander Yeats. 1992. "Do 'Dirty' Industries Migrate?" In *International
Trade and the Environment*, ed. Patrick Low, pp. 89–104. World Bank Discussion
Papers. Washington, D.C.: International Bank for Reconstruction and
Development/World Bank.

Luth, Elizabeth. 2000. "Forest Management in Central America: A Case Study Comparison
of Costa Rica and Honduras." Unpublished.

Lutzenberger, Jose A. 1987. "Who Is Destroying the Amazon Rainforest?" *Ecologist* 17
(4/5): 155–160.

MacKerron, Conrad, and Douglas Cogan, eds. 1993. *Business in the Forests*. Washington,
D.C.: Investor Responsibility Research Center.

Mader, Ron. 1997. "Digesting Borderland Environmental News." August. Online.
www.planeta.com

———. 2000. "Latin America's New Ecotourism: What Is It?" June. Online.
www.planeta.com.

Magdoff, Fred, John Bellamy Foster, and Frederick Buttel, eds. 2000. *Hungry for Profit: the
Agribusiness Threat to Farmers, Food, and the Environment*. New York: Monthly Review
Press.

Maguire, Andrew, and Janet Welsh Brown, eds. 1986. *Bordering on Trouble: Resources and
Politics in Latin America*. Bethesda, MD: Adler and Adler.

Mahar, Dennis J. 1989. *Government Policies and Deforestation in Brazil's Amazon Region*.
Washington, D.C.: World Wildlife Fund/Conservation Foundation and World Bank.

Mahony, Rhona. 1992. "Debt-for-Nature Swaps. Who Really Benefits?" *Ecologist* 22 (3,
May/June).

Manriquez, Mercedes. 2000. "Peru: Exploration and Exploitation of Gas of Camisea."
Earth Council on Sustainable Development. Online. www.itpcentre.org/legislation/
english/pen-end.htm; accessed January 22, 2001.

Manuel, George, and Michael Posluns. 1974. *The Fourth World: An Indian Reality*. New
York: Free Press.

Marcos, Subcomandante. 2001. First Declaration of the Lacandon Jungle. January 2, 1994.
Marcos 13. Online: www.ezln.org

Margolis, Mac. 1989. "Amazon Ablaze." *World Monitor*, February, p. 26.

Marin, Monica del Pilar Uribe. 1999. "Where Development Will Lead to Mass Suicide."
Ecologist. 29 (1, January/February): 46.

Martínez Escamilla, Victor Hugo. 1998. *Border Entrepreneurs: Social Networks and Economic Development.* Ph.D. dissertation, Tulane University.

Martins, Paulo R. 2000. "The Sole Central Workers Union (CUT) and the Sustainable Society." Presented at the International Sociological Association Research Committee 24 Conference, Rio de Janeiro, August 1–3.

———. 2001. "Por Uma Política Ecoindustrial." In *O Desafio da Sustentabilidade: Um Debate Socioambiental no Brasil,* ed. Gilney Viana, Marina Silva, and Nilo Diniz, pp. 97–132. São Paulo: Perseu Abramo.

Mastny, Lisa, and Hilary French. 2002. "Crimes of (a) Global Nature." *Worldwatch* 15 (5): 12–23.

Mazur, Allan, and Eugene Rosa. 1974. "Energy and Life-Style." *Science* 186: 607–610.

McCartney, Martha W. 1997. *James City County: Keystone of the Commonwealth.* Virginia Beach: Donning Company/Publishers.

McConahay, Mary Jo. 2000. "No Place to Call Home." *Sierra* (Nov/Dec): 66–72.

McGrath, David G., Daniel C. Nepstad, and Ane Alencar. 2000. "A Cuiabá-Santarém: Ameaça Ecológica ou Caminho da Prosperidade?" Instituto de Pesquisa Ambiental da Amazônia (IPAM). Online. www.ipam.org.br/polamb/cuisant.htm; accessed August 8, 2001.

McIntosh, Ian 1999. "Visions of the Future: The Prospects for Reconciliation." *Cultural Survival Quarterly: World Report on the Rights of Indigenous Peoples and Ethnic Minorities.* Winter, p. 4.

McKibben, Bill. 1995. *Hope, Human and Wild.* Boston: Little, Brown and Company.

McMichael, Phillip. 2000. *Development and Social Change.* 2d ed. Thousand Oaks, CA: Pine Forge Press.

Meadows, Donella. 1995 "The City of First Priorities." *Whole Earth Review.* Spring, pp. 58–60.

Mendez, Edgar. 1997, May 5. "Presentation to Occidental" Project Underground website, Online. www.moles.org/ProjectUnderground/pr_archive/pr00062uwa.html; accessed January 26, 2003.

Mendoza, M., M. Del Pilar, and Edgar Mendez Moreno. 1998. "Communication to Project Underground." *Comité Colombia Es U'wa.* Online. www.moles.org

Menezes, Claudino Luiz. 1996. *Desenvolvimento Urbano e Meio Ambiente: A Experiência de Curitiba.* Campinas, SP: Papirus.

Mertig, Angela G., and Riley E. Dunlap. 1995. "Public Support for New Social Movement Goals: A Cross-National Examination." Paper presented at the American Sociological Association Annual Meetings, August, Washington, D.C.

Messer, Ellen. 1993a. "Anthropology and Human Rights." *Annual Review of Anthropology.* 22: 221–49.

"Mexcla ilegal en fumigaciòn." 2001. *El Espectador,* July 17.

Meyer, Stephen M. 1992. "Environmentalism and Economic Prosperity: Testing the Environmental Impact Hypothesis." Mimeo: Massachusetts Institute of Technology Project on Environmental Politics and Policy.

Michaels, Julia. 1988. "Brazilian Rains Unleash Torrent of Woes." *Christian Science Monitor,* February 24, p. 7.

Mignella, Amy T. 1997. "Cleanup at US-Mexico Border." *Journal of Commerce,* July 7, p. 8A.

Miller, Marian A. L. 1995a. "Globalization and Interdependence: The Third World in the Evolution of Environmental Regimes." International Studies Association Annual Meetings, February 21–26, Chicago, IL.

———. 1995b. *The Third World in Global Environmental Politics*. Boulder, CO: Lynne Rienner.

Minc, Carlos. 2001. "A Ecologia nos Barrancos da Cidade." In *O Desafio da Sustentabilidade: Um Debate Socioambiental no Brasil*, eds Gilney Viana, Marina Silva and Nilo Diniz, pp. 233–250. São Paulo: Editora Fundação Perseu Abramo.

Ministério de Planejamento, Brazil. 2001a. "Avança Brasil." Online. www.abrasil.com.br; accessed August 7, 2001.

———. 2001b. "Banco Japonês Considera Prioridade os Projectos do Programa Brasileiro Avança Brasil para Novos Investimentos de Empresários do País." Online. http://www.planejamento.gov.br; posted April 27, 2000; accessed August 7, 2001.

———. 2001c. "Notícias: Avança Brasil não Prevê Construção de Novas Rodovias." Press release. Online. http://www.planejamento.gov.br; posted January 24, 2001; accessed August 7, 2001.

Mink, Stephen. 1993. "Poverty, Population and the Environment." World Bank Discussion Paper no. 189. Washington, D.C.: The World Bank.

Minkkinen, Petri. 1998. "NAFTA and the Possibility of an Alternative Development Strategy in Mexico." Paper presented at the Latin American Studies Association meeting, September 24–26, 1998, Chicago, IL.

Mintz, Sidney W. 1985. *Sweetness and Power: The Place of Sugar in Modern History*. New York: Viking.

Miranda, Marta, Alberto Blanco-Uribe Q., Lionel Hernández, José Ochoa G., and Edgard Yerena. 1998. *All That Glitters Is Not Gold: Balancing Conservation and Development in Venezuela's Frontier Forests*. Washington, D.C.: World Resources Institute. p. vi.-1

Mitchell, Ellen, and Karen Schlanger. 1991. "The Effect of the Foreign Influence on the Conservation of Costa Rica's Natural Resources." Unpublished honor's thesis.

Mol, Arthur P. J. 1995. *The Refinement of Production. Ecological ModernizationTheory and the Chemical Industry*. Utrecht: Van Arkel.

———. 2001. *Globalization and Environmental Reform: The Ecological Modernization of the Global Economy*. Cambridge, MA: MIT Press.

Mol, Arthur P. J., and David A. Sonnenfeld. 2000. *Ecological Moderization Around the World: Perspectives and Critical Debates*. London: Frank Cass.

Mol, Arthur P. J., and Gurt Spaargaren. 1993. "Environment, Modernity, and the Risk Society: The Apocalyptic Horizon of Environmental Reform." *International Sociology* 8 (4): 431–459.

Molina, D. 1993. "A Comment on Whether Maquiladoras Are in Mexico for Low Wages or to Avoid Pollution Abatement Costs." *Journal of Environment and Development* 2 (1): 221–241.

Moody, Roger. 1997. "The Man with the Golden Arm: Mr. Robert Friedland Goes to Asia." Nostromo Research / Minewatch Asia Pacific. Online. http://www.minesandcommunities.org/Company/friedland1.htm.

Moody, Kim, and Mary McGinn. 1992. *Unions and Free Trade: Solidarity vs. Competition*. Detroit: Labor Notes Book.

Moomaw, William, and Mark Tullis. 1994. "Charting Development Paths: A Multicountry Comparison of Carbon Dioxide Emissions." In *Industrial Ecology and Global Change*, eds. R. Socolow, C. Andrews, F. Berkhout, and V. Thomas, pp. 157–182. New York: Cambridge University Press.

Moran, Emilio. 1981. *Developing the Amazon*. Bloomington: Indiana University Press.

———. 1985. *The Dilemma of Amazonian Development*. Boulder, CO: Westview.

Moura, Rosa. 2001. "Os Riscos da Cidade-Modelo." In *A Duração das Cidades*, ed. Henri Acselrad, pp. 203–237. Rio de Janeiro: DP&A.

Movimento Ecológico Mater Natura. 1992. *Cadastro Nacional de Instituições Ambientalistas.* Curitiba: WWF/Mater Natura.

Moyers, Bill. 2002. "Trading Democracy." Bill Moyers Reports (video). February 20, 2002.

Mumme, Stephen. 1999. "In Focus: NAFTA and the Environment." *Foreign Policy in Focus* 4 (26, October).

Mumme, Stephen P., and Korzetz, Edward. 1997. "Democratization, Politics, and Environmental Reform in Latin America." In *Latin American Environmental Policy in International Perspective*, eds. Gordon J. MacDonald, Daniel L. Nielson, and Marc A. Stern, pp. 40–59. Boulder, CO: Westview.

Municipality of Curitiba. 2001. "Dados Geograficos." Curitiba municipality Web site. Online. http://www.curitiba.pr.gov.br/pmc/a_cidade/index.asp; accessed July 12, 2001.

Murillo, Mario. 1996. "Confronting the Dilemmas of Political Participation." *NACLA Report on Indigenous Movements.* 29 (5): 22.

Murray, Douglas. 1994. *Cultivating Crisis: The Human Costs of Pesticides in Latin America.* Austin, TX: Austin University Press.

Murray, Douglas, and Polly Hoppin. 1992. "Recurring Contradictions in Agrarian Development: Pesticide Problems in Caribbean Basin Nontraditional Agriculture." *World Development* 20 (4): 597–608.

Murray, Douglas L., and Peter L. Taylor. 2000. "Claim No Easy Victories: Evaluating the Pesticide Industry's Global Safe Use Campaign." *World Development* 28 (10): 1735–1749.

Murray, Kevin, and Tom Barry. 1995. *Inside El Salvador.* Albuquerque, NM: Interhemispheric Resource Center.

Myers, Norman. 1984. *The Primary Source: Tropical Forests and Our Future.* New York: W.W. Norton.

———. 1993. "Tropical Forests: The Main Deforestation Fronts." *Environmental Conservation* 20 (1): 9–16.

Nash, June, and Helen Safa. 1985. *Women and Change in Latin America.* South Hadley, MA: Bergin & Garvey Publishers.

Nash, Madeleine J. 2000. "Grains of Hope." *Time,* July 31, pp. 38–46.

Native Communities of the Gran Sabana Opposed to Construction of Guri Powerline. 2000. Electronic Communication to Amazon Alliance. August 12. Environment and Latin America Network (ELAN) Listserv. Online. Accessed October 21, 2000.

Nepstad, D.C., et al. 2000. "Avança Brasil: Cenários Futuros para a Amazônia." Instituto de Pesquisa Ambiental da Amazônia, Belém, Brazil. Online. http://www.ipam.org.br.

———. 2001. "Response to Laurance et al, 'Science and the Future of Amazon Policy.'" *Science,* July 18.

Nepstad, D., D. McGrath, A. Alencar, A. C. Barros, G. Carvalho, M. Santilli, and M. de C. Vera Diaz. 2002. "Frontier Governance in Amazonia." *Science* 295: 629–631.

Netting, Robert McC. 1993. *Smallholders, Householders: Farm Families and the Ecology of Intensive, Sustainable Agriculture.* Stanford, CA: Stanford University Press.

Neumayer, Eric. 2001. *Greening Trade and Investment: Environmental Protection Without Protectionism.* London: Earthscan.

Niiler, Eric. 2000. "River of Hope and Despair." *Boston Globe,* May 2, p. C4.

O'Neill, Kate. 1999. "In Focus: Hazardous Waste Disposal." *Foreign Policy in Focus.* January. Online. www.fpif.org/briefs/vol4/v4N01haz.html

Odegard, Jan Thomas H. 2000. "Economic Liberalisation and the Environment—A Case Study of the Leather Industry in Brazil." In *Industry and Environment in Latin America*, ed. Rhys Jenkins, pp. 121–142. London: Routledge.

Oliveira da Silva, Gláucia. 1999. *Angra I e a Melancolia de Uma Era*. Niterói, RJ: Editora da Universidad Federal Fluminense.

Oliveira Filho, Ladislau Batista de. 1988. *Exploração dos Recursos Minerais da Amazônia Remessa de Valores para outras Fronteiras*. Belém: PLADES/NAES/UFPA.

Ominami, Carlos. 1993. "International Trade and the Environment: A View from Chile." In *Difficult Liaison: Trade and the Environment in the Americas*, eds. Heraldo Muñoz and Robin Rosenberg, pp. 147–151. New Brunswick, NJ: Transaction.

Orams, M. B. 1995. "Towards a More Desirable Form of Ecotourism." *Tourism Management* 16 (1): 3–8.

Osborn, Ann. 1982. "Mythology and Social Structure Among the U'wa of Colombia." Ph.D. thesis, University of Oxford, England.

Padgett, Tim, and Sharon Begley with Joshua Hammer. 1996. "Beware of the Humans." *Newsweek*, February 5, p. 52.

Padoch, C. 1988. "The Economic Importance and Marketing of Forest and Fallow Products in the Iquitos Region." In *Swidden Fallow Agroforestry in the Peruvian Amazon*, eds. William M. Denevan and C. Padoch, pp. 75–89. New York: New York Botanical Garden.

Padua, José A. 2001. "Slavery as a Cause of Environmental Destruction: The Evolution of a Brazilian Intellectual Debate 1786/1888." Unpublished.

Paige, Jeffery M. 1997. *Coffee and Power*. Cambridge, MA: Harvard University Press.

Pallister, Marian. 1999. "Banana Workers Toil in a Pear-Shaped World." *The Herald (Glasgow)*, March 2, p. 13.

"Pastrana hails summit support for Plan Colombia." *El Tiempo*, September 2, 2000.

Paterson, Kent. 1998. "A Movement Blossoms: Cross Border Activism Picks Up Speed." *Borderlines*, October 20.

Pearlstein, Steven. 2001. "U.S. Slowdown Going Global." *Washington Post*, July 18, p. A1.

People of Color Environmental Leadership Summit. 1991. "Principles of Environmental Justice." October. Washington, D.C. Online. www.ejrc.cau.edu.

Peritore, N. Patrick, ed. 1999. *Third World Environmentalism: Case Studies from the Global South*. Gainesville: University of Florida Press.

Peritore, N. Patrick and Ana Karina Galve-Peritore, eds. 1995. *Biotechnology in Latin America*. Wilmington, DE: Scholarly Resources.

Peters, C. M., A. H. Gentry, and R. O. Mendelsohn. 1989. "Valuation of an Amazonian Rainforest." *Nature*, June 29, pp. 655–656.

Peterson, Jack. 1995. "Politics of Paradise." *Business Venezuela* 172 (February): 36–37.

Petras, James, and Maurice Zeitlin. 1968. "Miners and Agrarian Revolution." In *Latin America: Reform or Revolution?* eds. James Petras and Maurice Zeitlin, pp. 235–248. Greenwich, CT: Fawcett.

Pick, James B., and Edgar W. Butler. 1997. *Mexico Megacity*. Boulder, CO: Westview Press.

Pinto, Lúcio Flavio. 1982. *Carajás: O Ataque ao Coração da Amazônia*. 2d ed. Rio de Janeiro: Studio Alpha.

———. 1983. "A Dimensão Social Omitido." *Ciêcia Hoje* 1 (3): 46.

———. 2001. "Rios Obstruídos." *Estado de São Paulo*, June 26.

Pleumaron, A. 1995. "Ecotourism: A New Green Myth in the Third World." Paper presented at a meeting on land management and sustainable use by Third World Network during the third session of the UN Commission on Sustainable Development, New York, April.

Pompermeyer, Malori J. 1979. *The State and the Frontier in Brazil: A Case Study of the Amazon*. Ph.D. dissertation, Stanford University.

———. 1984. "Strategies of Private Capital in the Brazilian Amazon." In *Frontier Expansion in Amazonia*, eds. M. Schmink and C. Wood, pp. 419–328. Gainesville: University of Florida Press.

Portes, Alejandro. 2000. "Neoliberalism and the Sociology of Development: Emerging Trends and Unanticipated Facts." In *From Modernization to Globalization*, eds. J. Timmons Roberts and Amy Hite, pp. 353–368. London: Blackwell.

Portes, Alejandro, and José Itzigsohn. 1997. "The Party or the Grassroots: A Comparative Analysis of Urban Political Participation in the Caribbean." In *Politics, Social Change, and Economic Restructuring in Latin America*, eds. William C. Smith and Roberto Patricio Korzeniewicz, pp. 187–214. Boulder, CO: North-South Center Press.

Portes, Alejandro, Manuel Castells, and Lauren A. Benton, eds. 1989. *The Informal Economy: Studies in Advanced and Less Developed Countries*. Baltimore: Johns Hopkins University Press.

"Potential Oil Industry Flashpoint Centers on OXY's Colombian Rainforest Wildcat." 1999. *Oil and Gas Journal*. November 29, pp. 18–20.

Power, Timothy J., and J. Timmons Roberts. 2000. "The Social Context of Democracy in Brazil." In *Democratic Brazil*, eds. Peter Kingstone and Timothy J. Power, pp. 236–262. University of Pittsburgh Press.

Pratt, Timothy. 2000. "Mutual Funds Employed as Weapon in Environmental Fight." *Washington Post*, February 20.

Prebisch, Raul. 1964. *Dinámica do Desenvolvimento Latino-Americano*. Rio de Janeiro: Ed. Fundo de Cultura (original published 1956).

Preston, Samuel. 1996. "The Effects of Population Growth on Environmental Quality." *Population Research and Policy Review* 15: 95–108.

Project Underground. 1998a. *Blood of Our Mother: The U'wa People, Occidental Petroleum and the Colombian Oil Industry*. Berkeley, CA: Online. www.moles.ore/uwa/u'wa/who1.htm.

———. 1998b. "Chronology." Online. www.moles.org/lwa/crisis/news.html; accessed November 13, 1999.

———. 2000. "The U'wa Struggle Continues: A Chronological Update as of October 2000." October 14. Online. www.moles.org/uwa/crisis/chron99-00.html; accessed October 21, 2000.

Projeto Billings Potável por Inteiro. n.d. "Saiba Como Defender Nossa Agua." 3d ed. Mimeo, Movimento em Defesa da Vida do Grande ABC.

Quist, D. and I. H. Chapela. 2001. "Transgenic DNA Introgressed into Traditional Maize Landraces in Oaxaca, Mexico." *Nature* 414: 541–543.

Rabinovitch, Jonas, and Josef Leitman, 1996. "Urban Planning in Curitiba." *Scientific American*, March, pp. 46–53.

Rainforest Action Network. 2001. "Sanford Bernstein and Occidental Petroleum: A Deadly Partnership." Beyond Oil Campaign News. Online. www.ran.org/ran_campaigns/beyond_oil/oxy/sbernstein.pdf; accessed January 12, 2001.

Rainforest Alliance. 2002. "Smartwood: Practical Conservation Through Certified Forestry." Online. http://www.smartwood.org/features/papers-4.html; accessed September 17, 2002.

Ranis, Gustav. 1989. "Contrasts in the Political Economy of Development Policy Change." In *Manufacturing Miracles: Paths of Industrialization in Latin America and East Asia*, eds. Gary Gereffi and Donald L. Wyman, pp. 207–230. Princeton, NJ: Princeton University Press.

Reardon, Thomas, and Stephen Vosti. 1993. "Links Between Rural Poverty and the Environment in Developing Countries: Asset Categories and Investment Poverty." *World Development* 23 (9): 1495–1506.

Reca, Lucio G., and Ruben G. Echeverría. "Agricultura, Medio Ambiente y Pobreza Rural en America Latina: Situación Actual y Propuestas." In *Agricultura, Medio Ambiente y Pobreza Rural en America Latina*, eds. Lucio G. Reca and Ruben G. Echeverría. 1998. Washington, D.C.: Instituto Internacional de Investigaciones sobre Politicas Alimentarias.

Redclift, Michael. 1986. "Sustainability and the Market: Survival Strategies on the Bolivian Frontier." *Journal of Development Studies* 23 (1): 93–105.

———. 1999. *Sustainability: Life Chances and Livelihoods*. London: Routledge.

Redford, K. 1991. "The Ecologically Noble Savage." *Cultural Survival Quarterly* 15 (1): 46–48.

Reed, David, ed. 1992. *Structural Adjustment and the Environment*. Boulder, CO: Westview Press.

Rees, William, and Mathis Wackernagel. 1996. *Our Ecological Footprint: Reducing Human Impact on the Earth*. Gabriola Island, B.C.: New Society.

Reis, Arthur Cezar Ferreira. 1968. *A Amazônia e a Cobiça Internacional*. Rio de Janeiro: Gráfica Record Editors.

Reisner, Marc. 1986. *Cadillac Desert: The American West and Its Disappearing Water*. New York: Viking.

Reuters News Service. 1999. "Brazil Relaxes Amazon Deforestation Ban." March 25.

———. 2001. "Environmentally Correct Dance Party Set for Amazon." August 2.

Rico, Maria Nieves. 2000. "Desarrollo Sustentable, Manego de Recursos de Agua y Genero." Paper presented at the 2000 Conference of the Latin American Studies Association, Miami, FL.

Riley, Michael. 2001. "Inmate Honored for His Activism." *Houston Chronicle*, February 7.

Roberts, J. Timmons. 1992. *Forging Development, Fragmenting Labor: Subcontracting and Local Response in an Amazon Boomtown*. Ph.D. dissertation, Johns Hopkins University.

———. 1994. "Crisis and Environment [Features: Brazil]." *Hemisphere: A Magazine of Latin American and Caribbean Affairs* 6 (1): 26–30.

———. 1995a. "Subcontracting and the Omitted Social Impacts of Development Projects: Household Survival at the Carajás Mines in the Brazilian Amazon." *Economic Development and Cultural Change* 43 (4): 735–758.

———. 1995b. "Trickling-Down and Scrambling-Up: Informal Sectors and Local Benefits of a Mining 'Growth Pole' in the Brazilian Amazon." *World Development* 23 (3): 385–400.

———. 1995c. "Expansion of Television in Eastern Amazonia." *Geographical Review* 85 (1): 41–49.

———. 1996a. "Predicting Participation in Environmental Treaties: A World-System Analysis." *Sociological Inquiry* 66 (1, February): 38–57.

———. 1996b. "Global Restructuring and the Environment in Latin America." In *Latin America in the World Economy*, eds. Roberto P. Korzeniewicz and William C. Smith. Westport, CT: Greenwood Press.

———. 1998. "Emerging Global Environmental Standards: Prospects and Perils." *Journal of Developing Societies* 14 (1): 144–165.

———. 2001. "Global Inequality and Climate Change." *Society and Natural Resources* 14 (6): 501–509.

Roberts, J. Timmons, and Mary Brook. 1999. "Structural Adjustment, Debt, Poverty and the Environment: A Framework for Rural Interactions." Unpublished.

Roberts, J. Timmons, and Peter E. Grimes. 1997. "Carbon Intensity and Economic Development 1962–1991: A Brief Exploration of the Environmental Kuznets Curve." *World Development* 25 (2): 191–198.

Roberts, J. Timmons, and Amy Hite. 2000. *From Modernization to Globalization: Perspectives on Development and Social Change.* London: Blackwell Publishers.

Roberts, J. Timmons and Erika A. Schaeffer. 2000. "Corporate Environmentalism in Brazil's Chemical Industry: Participation in Responsible Care and ISO14001 Among 619 Firms." Latin American Studies Association XXI International Conference, Miami, March 16–18.

Roberts, J. Timmons, and Melissa Toffolon-Weiss. 2001. *Chronicles from the Environmental Justice Frontline.* Cambridge: Cambridge University Press.

Roberts, J. Timmons, and Alexis A. Vásquez. 2002. "State Environmentalism Revisited: Structural Predictors of Nations' Propensity To Sign Environmental Treaties." Presented at the International Studies Association Annual Conference, New Orleans, March.

Robinson, William. 1996. *Promoting Polyarchy: Globalization, US Intervention, and Hegemony.* New York: Cambridge University Press.

Rocco, Carmen. 2001. Lecture in Brownsville, Texas, February 23, 2001.

Rocco, Rogério. 2001. "Baía de Guanabara, Baía Cidadã." *Tempo e Presença* 317 (May/June): 29–32.

Rodgers, Terry. 2001. "U.S. Settles Suit Over Ocean Sewage at Border: $2 Million to Be Paid for Scientific Studies." *San Diego Union-Tribune.* December 22, p. B-8.

Rodriguez, Arnaldo. 2000. "Kapawi: The Story of an Ecuadorian Ecolodge." June. Online. www.Planeta.com.

Rogge, Mary, and Osei K. Darkwa. 1996. "Poverty and the Environment: An International Perspective for Social Work." *International Social Work* 39: 399–409.

Rohter, Larry. 1996. "Known for Social Programs, Costa Rica Turns to Austerity." *New York Times,* September 30.

———. 2000a. "Latest Battleground in Latin Drug War: Brazilian Amazon." *New York Times*, October 30, p. A1.

———. 2000b. "To Colombians, Drug War Is a Toxic Foe." *New York Times*, May 1.

Roldán, Roque. 1995. "Aproximación historica a la explotación de petroleo en territories indígenas." Tierra Profanada: Grandes Proyectos en Territorios Indígenas de Colombia. Santa Fe de Bogatá: Editolasar y Cia Ltda.

Rone, Jenera. 1992. *The Struggle for Land in Brazil: Rural Violence Continues.* New York: Human Rights Watch.

Rosa, Eugene A., and Rose L. Krebill-Prather. 1993. "Mapping Cross-National Trends in Carbon Releases and Societal Well-Being." Presentation at the American Sociological Association Annual Meetings, August, Miami, FL.

Rosero-Bixby, Luis, and Alberto Palloni. 1998. "Population and Deforestation in Costa Rica." *Population and Environment* 20 (2) 149–185.

Ross, John. 1996. "Is Zapatista Rebellion Rooted in Oil?" *Earth Island Journal.*

Rostow, W. W. 1960. *The Stages of Economic Growth: A Non-Communist Manifesto.* Cambridge: Cambridge University Press.

Rubin, Debra K. 1994. "Firms Gear Up to Think Globally, Link Locally, Focus on Environment." *Engineering News-Record* 232 (February 21): 42.

Rucht, Dieter. 1999. *Social Movements in a Globalizing World.* New York: St. Martin's Press.

Rudel, Thomas. 1997. "Is There a Forest Transition? Deforestation, Reforestation and Economic Development." Paper presented at the 1997 American Sociological Association Meeting in Toronto, Canada.

Rudel, Thomas, and Jill Roper. 1997a. "The Paths to Rain Forest Destruction: Crossnational Patterns of Tropical Deforestation, 1975–90." *World Development* 25 (1): 53–65.

———. 1997b. "Regional Patterns and Historical Trends in Tropical Deforestation, 1976–1990: A Qualitative Comparative Analysis." *Ambio* 25 (3): 160–166.

Rudel, Thomas K., Diane Bates, and Rafael Machinguiashi. 2002. "Ecologically Noble Amerindians?: Cattle Ranching and Cash Cropping among Shuar and Colonist Smallholders in Ecuador." *Latin American Research Review* 37 (1): 144–159.

Rueters. 2001. "Environmentally correct dance party set for Amazon." August 2. Ecosystem 1.0 Web site. Online. www.ecosystem1.org.

Ruiz, Carmelo. 1999. "Agriculture-Puerto Rico: Documenting the Organic Revolution." Inter Press Service, May 11.

Rylander, Carole Keeton. n.d. "Bordering the Future." In *Environment: Common Ground.* Online. www.window.state.tx.us./border/ch09/ch09/html.

Rÿser, Rudolph C., and Leslie E. Korn. 1996. *Indian Self-Government Process Evaluation: Final Report, March 1, 1996.* Olympia, WA: Center for World Indigenous Studies.

Saldaña, Lori. 1994. "Tijuana River: A Controversy Runs Through It." *San Diego Earth Times.* June. Online. http://www.sdearthtimes.com/et0694/et0694s1.html.

———. 1998. "Tackling the Border Sewage Problem." *San Diego Union-Tribune,* February 17.

Salinas-León, Roberto. 1991. "A Mexican View of North American Free Trade." *Foreign Policy Briefing* 9, May 21.

———. n.d. "Green Herrings: NAFTA and the Environment." *The Cato Review of Business and Government.* Online. www.cati.org.

Saltani, Atossa, and Derrick Hindery. 1999. "A World Class Disaster: The Case of the Bolivia-Cuiaba Pipeline: A Report on the Failures of Enron International to Comply Bolivian Environmental Laws and OPIC Loan Conditions in the Construction of the Ipias-Cuibaba Gas Pipeline." *Amazon Watch,* December 8.

Sanches, Manuel A. P. 2000. "Global Elite and Local Citizens: Who Gains with the Guanabara Bay Clean-Up?" Presented at the 2000 Latin American Studies Association International Meeting, Miami, FL.

Sanderson, Stephen K. 1999. *Macrosociology: An Introduction to Human Societies.* 4th ed, New York: Longman.

Sanderson, Steven E. 1993. "International Trade, Natural Resources, and Conservation of the Environment in Latin America." In *Difficult Liaison: Trade and the Environment in the Americas,* eds. Heraldo Muñoz and Robin Rosenberg, pp. 53–78. New Brunswick, NJ: Transaction.

Sane, Pierre. 1996. *Report on Human Rights. Colombia.* London: Amnesty International.

Santos, Breno Augusto dos. 1981. *Amazônia: Potencial Mineral e Perspectivas de Desenvolvimento.* São Paulo: T. A. Queiroz.

————. 1982. "Carajás e o Desenvolvimento Regional." *Revista Brasileira de Tecnologia* 13 (5): 9–18.

————. 1986. "Recursos Minerais." In *Carajás: Desafio Político, Ecológia e Desenvolvimento*, ed. José Maria Goncalves de Almeida. São Paulo: Brasiliense/CNPq.

Santos, Marluze Pastor. 2001. "De Ferro, de Ouro, de Sonho e de Choro, Assim que E!" *Tempo e Presença* 317 (May/June): 33–37.

Sayer, Don. 1996. *Inside ISO 14000: The Competitive Advantage of Environmental Management*. Delray Beach, FL: St. Lucie Press.

Scanlan, David. 1994. "'Kids Are Forever': Banana Workers Sue Companies over Chemical That Left Them Sterile." *Ottowa Citizen*, March 6, p. E3.

Schemo, Diana. 1995. "U.S. Pesticide Kills Foreign Fruit Pickers' Hopes." *New York Times*, December 6.

Schlesinger, Sergio, and Maria Isabel Manzur. 1999. *Exportar é preciso, viver— Mitos do bem-estar alcançado com a exportação de matérias-primas*. Rio de Janeiro: Federação de Orgãos para Assistência Social e Educacional (FASE).

Schmink, Marianne, and Charles H. Wood. 1993. *Contested Frontiers in Amazonia*. Gainesville: University of Florida Press.

Schnaiberg, Allan, and Kenneth A. Gould 1994. *Environment and Society: The Enduring Conflict*. New York: St. Martin's Press.

Schneider, Julie. 1999. "The Internet as a Transboundary Information Resource." Information Services, Latin America (ISLA). Online. http://isla.ige.org/Features/Border/mex7.html.

Scoffield, Heather. 2000. "NAFTA Ruling Raises Environmental Questions." *Toronto Globe and Mail*, September 1.

Selden, T. M., and A. Song. 1995. "Neoclassical Growth, the J Curve for Abatement and the Inverted U Curve for Pollution." *Journal of Environmental Economics and Management* 29: 167–168.

Sequeira, Maricel. 1996. "Environment-Central America: Pollution Reaches Alarming Levels." Inter Press Service, June 14.

Serbin, Andrés, Antonio De Lisio, and Eduardo Ortiz. 1993. "The Environmental Impact of International Trade and Industry: Reflections on Latin America and the Caribbean." In *Difficult Liaison: Trade and the Environment in the Americas*, eds. Heraldo Muñoz and Robin Rosenberg, pp. 127–145. New Brunswick, NJ: Transaction.

Seton, Kathy. 1999. "Fourth World Nations in the Era of Globalisation: An Introduction to Contemporary Theorizing Posed by Indigenous Nations." Center for World Indigenous Studies. Online. http://www.cwis.org/fwj/41/fworld.html.

Shafer, D. Michael. 1994. *Winners and Losers: How Sectors Shape the Developmental Prospects of States*. Ithaca, NY: Cornell University Press.

Shannon, Thomas R. 1996. *An Introduction to the World System Perspective*. 2d ed. Boulder, CO: Westview.

Shores, John N. 1995. "The Challenge of Ecotourism: A Call for Higher Standards." Online. www.planeta.com/planeta/95/0295shores.html.

Sierra Club. 2001. *Make Trade Clean, Green, and Fair: Don't Let the FTAA Trade Away Our Health and Environment*. Interview with Dan Seligman, Center for Labor Studies. Online. http://depts.washington.edu/wtohist/Interviews/Seligman.pdf.

————. 2000. "Rules Against Mexican Environmentalists Convicted of Crimes They Confessed to Under Duress of Torture." Online. www.sierraclub.org/human-rights/mexico/action.asp. Press release. November 9.

"Sigue Protesta en Caqueta." *El Tiempo*, August 13, 1996.

Silveira, Paulo. 2001. "Respone to Lawrence et al." *Science*. Online, May 9.

Simmons, Cynthia. 2001. "Violence in the Amazon: Dynamics and Environmental Effects." Presentation at the Latin American Studies Association, Washington, D.C., September 6–8.

Simon, Joel. 1997. *Endangered Mexico: An Environment on the Edge*. San Francisco: Sierra Club Books.

Simonian, Lane. 1995. *Defending the Land of the Jaguar: A History of Conservation in Mexico*. Austin: University of Texas Press.

Sissell, Kara. 1996. "Brazil Steps Up Environmental Enforcement." *Chemical Week*, November 13, pp. 62–64.

———. 2002a. "Brazil and Chile Begin Third-Party Verification." *Chemical Week*, July 3–10, p. 63.

Skidmore, Thomas E., ed. 1993. *Television, Politics, and the Transition to Democracy in Latin America*. Washington, D.C.: The Woodrow Wilson Center Press.

Sklair, Leslie. 1995. "Social Movements and Global Capitalism." *Sociology* 29: 3.

Slater, Jerome, and Jan K. Black. 1991. "United States Policy in Latin America. In *Latin America: Its Problems and Its Promise*. 2d ed., ed. Jan K. Black, pp. 234–255. Boulder, CO: Westview.

Smith, David A., and Douglas R. White. 1992. "Structure and Dynamics of the Global Economy: Network Analysis of International Trade 1965–1980." *Social Forces* 70: 857–893.

Smith, Jeremy. 2002. "An Unappealing Industry." *Ecologist* 32 (3): 40–41.

Soares, Maria Clara Couto. 1981. "Projeto Carajás: Origens e Desenvolvimento." Mimeo, CNPq/SDI/CTM.

Sorenson, Cynthia. 2001. "Spaces of Frontier Vulnerability." Paper presented at the Latin American Studies Association meetings, Washington, D.C., September 6–8.

Soto, Gioconda. 2000. "Internacional y Diplomacia: Encuentro presidencial en La Casona." *El Nacional* (Caracas, Venezuela), April 6.

Southwest Center for Environmental Research and Policy. 1999. *The U.S.–Mexican Border Environment: A Road Map to a Sustainable 2020*. Border Environment Research Reports. Institute for Regional Studies of the Californias: San Diego State University, San Diego, CA.

———. 1999. "US-Mexico Border Air Quality Poster Session," SCERP Technical Conference, Las Cruces, NM, November 18.

Sprouse, Terry, and Stephen Mumme. 1997. "Beyond BECC: Envisioning Needed Institutional Reforms for Environmental Protection on the Mexico–U.S. Border." Paper presented at the Meeting of the Association of Borderland Scholars, Albuquerque, NM, April 23–26.

"Starbucks: To Drink or Not to Drink." Fall 2002. Special Issue. *Whole Earth Review*.

Staten, Clark. 1992. "Explosions Rip Mexican City, 200 Dead, 600 Injured." Emergency Net News Service, April 22.

Stern, Paul C., Oran R. Young, and Daniel Druckman, eds. 1992. *Global Environmental Change: Understanding the Human Dimensions*. Washington, D.C.: National Academy Press.

Stevens, Candice. 1993. "Organization for Economic Cooperation and Development Framework for the Discussion of Trade and Environment Concerns." In *Difficult*

Liaison: Trade and the Environment in the Americas, eds. Heraldo Muñoz and Robin Rosenberg, pp. 161–166. New Brunswick, NJ: Transaction.

Stonich, Susan. 1993. *"I Am Destroying the Land!" The Political Ecology of Poverty and Environmental Destruction in Honduras.* Boulder, CO: Westview Press.

Superentendência para o Desenvolvimento da Amazônia (SUDAM). 1968. "Amazônia: Desnevolvimento e Ocupação." Mimeo.

Surfrider Foundation. 2002. "Surfrider Mission and Principles." Online. www.surfrider.org/mission.htm.

Sutcliffe, Bob. 1995. "Development after Ecology." In *The North, the South and the Environment: Ecological Constraints and the Global Economy*, eds. V. Bhaskar and A. Glyn. New York: St. Martin's Press.

Szasz, Andrew. 1993. *Ecopopulism: Toxic Waste and the Movement for Environmental Justice.* Minneapolis: University of Minnesota Press.

Talukdar, D. and Meisner, C. M. 2001. "Does the Private Sector Help or Hurt the Environment? Evidence from Carbon Dioxide Pollution in Developing Countries." *World Development* 29 (5): 827–840.

Taniguchi, Cassio. 1995. "Creating an Environmentally Sustainable City: The Curitiba Initiative." *Regional Development Dialogue* 16 (1, Spring): 100–109.

Tardanico, Richard, and Rafael Menjivar Larín, eds. 1997. *Global Restructuring, Employment and Social Inequality in Urban Latin America.* Miami: North South Center.

Tegria, Ebaristo. 2000. "U'wa Leaders Present the Colombian Government with Proof of 'Royal Land Titles' Granted by the King of Spain Colonial." Presentation by U'wa Legal Representative Ebaristo Tegria during the telephone press briefing on September 15, 2000. Online. http://www.amazonwatch.org/newsroom/newsrelease00/sept1500uwa.html

Terlouw, Cornelis P. 1992. *The Regional Geography of the World-System.* Nederlandse Geografische Studies 144. Utrect: Koninklijk Nederlands Aardrijkskundig Genootschap.

Texas Department of Health, Neural Tube Defect Program. 1998. "Neural Tube Defects in Counties on the Texas/Mexico Border." BIOS/Borderlines Web site. Online. www.americaspolicy.org/pdf/bios/neural_tube_defects_texas.pdf.

Texas Natural Resource and Conservation Commission (TNRCC). 2001. "Border Issues." Online. www.tnrcc.state.tx.us/exec/ba/; accessed January 11, 2002.

Thompson, Ginger. 2001. "Fallout of U.S. Recession Drifts South Into Mexico." *New York Times*, December 26, p. C1.

Thrupp, Lori Ann. 1991. "Sterilization of Workers from Pesticide Exposure: The Causes and Consequences of DBCP-Induced Damage in Costa Rica and Beyond." *International Journal of Health Services* 21 (4): 731–757.

———. 1995. *Bittersweet Harvests for Global Supermarkets: Challenges in Latin America's Agricultural Export Boom.* Washington, D.C.: World Resources Institute.

Traicoff, Kristin. 2001. "Environmentalism by Mandate: The Politics of Urban Planning in Curitiba, Brazil." Unpublished.

Turati, Marcela, and Gerardo Jimenez. 2001. "Dan a campesino preso otro premio ambiental." *Reforma*, February 7.

Ulate, Gilbert Vargas. 1999. "Protecting Natural Resources in a Developing Nation: The Case of Costa Rica." In *Managed Ecosystems: The Mesoamerican Experience*, eds. Hatch, L. Upton and Marilyn E. Swisher. New York: Oxford University Press.

Umaña, A., and K. Brandon. 1992. "Inventing Institutions for conservation: lessons from

Costa Rica." Poverty, Natural Resources, and Public Policy in Central America, eds. Katrinia Brandon, Kent H. Brandon, and Steven Sanderson, pp. 85–107. Transaction Publishers. New Brunswick, N.J.

United Nations Conference on Trade and Development (UNCTAD). 2001. *World Investment Report 2001*. New York: United Nations. Online. www.unctad.org.

United Nations Environment Programme. 2000. *GEO-2000. Global Environment Outlook.* Chapter 2: The State of the Environment—Latin America and the Caribbean. Online. www.grida.no/geo2000.

United Nations Environment Programme and the World Health Organization. 1992. *Urban Air Pollution in Megacities of the World.* Cambridge, MA: Blackwell.

———. 1994. "Air Pollution in the World's Megacities." *Environment* 36 (2): 4–13, 25–37.

United Nations Development Program (UNDP). 1999. *Human Development Report 1999.* New York: Oxford University Press.

United Nations Research Institute for Social Development (UNRISD). 1995. *States of Disarray: The Social Effects of Globalization.* London: UNRISD.

U.S. Geological Survey (USAS). 2001a. "Earthshots: Satellite Images of Environmental Change. Imperial Valley, California 1973, 1992." 8th ed., January 12, 2001. Online. http://edcwww.cr.usgs.gov/earthshots/slow/Imperial/Imperial.

———. 2001b. "Angangueo, Mexico 1973, 1986, 2000." Earthshots. Online. http://edcwww.cr.usgs.gov/earthshots.

U.S. State Department. 1995. *Report on Indonesia 1995.* Washington, D.C.: U.S. Department of State. Online. http://usinfo.state.gov/regional/ar/colombia.crop.htm

———. 2001. *The Aerial Eradication of Illicit Crops: Answers to Frequently Asked Questions.* Fact sheet. January 17.

Utting, Peter. 1993. *Trees, People and Power: Social Dimensions of Deforestation and Forest Protection in Central America.* London: Earthscan.

U'wa Defense Working Group. 2000. "Occidental's Oil Project Ignites More Violence Against Peaceful Tribe in Colombia." June 26. Online; accessed October 21, 2000.

Van Bemmelen, C. 1995. "Comercialización de productos orgánicos: El caso de Costa Rica." In *Simposio Centroamericano sobre agricultura orgánica*, eds. Marzo J. Garcia and J. Njera. San José: Universidad Estatal a Distancia.

Van Cott, Donna Lee. 2000. *The Friendly Liquidation of the Past: The Politics of Diversity in Latin America.* Pittsburgh: University of Pittsburgh Press.

Vandermeer, John, and Ivette Perfecto. 1995. *Breakfast of Biodiversity: The Truth About Rain Forest Destruction.* Oakland, CA: Food First.

Vasconez, Sigrid C. 2001. "Putting the Pieces Together: The Future of Locally Based Biodiversity Conservation Efforts." Presented at the Latin American Studies Association meetings, Washington D.C., September 6–8.

Vidal, John. 2001. "Inside Story: Road to Oblivion: The Amazon Jungle Has Long Been Ravaged by Developers." *The Guardian (London)*, June 13.

Viola, Eduardo J. 1992. "O Movimento Ambientalista no Brasil (1979–1991): Da Denúncia e Conscientização Pública para a Institucionalização e o Desenvolvimento Sustentável." In *Ecologia, Ciência e Política*, ed. Mirian Goldenberg, pp. 49–75. Rio de Janeiro: Editora Revan.

Vitale, Luis. 1983. *Hacia Una Hisória del Ambiente en América Latina.* Mexico City: Sociedad.

Viveiros, Mariana. 2001. "Nunca Houve Condenação de Grandes Empresas Crimes Ambientais." *Folha de São Paulo*, December 6.

Vosti, Stephen A., and Thomas Reardon. 1995. *Sustainability, Growth, and Poverty Alleviation: A Policy and Agroecological Perspective.* Baltimore: The Johns Hopkins University Press.

Wallerstein, Immanuel. 1974. *The Modern World System,* vol. 1. New York: Academic Press.

———. 1979. *The Capitalist World Economy.* Cambridge: Cambridge University Press.

Wargo, John. 1996. *Our Children's Toxic Legacy: How Science and Law Fail to Protect Us from Pesticides.* New Haven, CT: Yale University Press.

Warnock, John W. 1995. *The Other Mexico: The North American Triangle Completed.* Montréal: Black Rose Books.

Weeks, John. 1985. *The Economies of Central America.* New York: Holmes & Meier.

Weinberg, Bill. 1991. *War on the Land: Ecology and Politics in Central America.* London: Zed Books.

Wesseling, Catharina, Rob McConnell, et al. 1997. "Agricultural Pesticide Use in Developing Countries: Health Effects and Research Needs." *International Journal of Health Services* 27 (2): 273–308.

West, Karen, 1995. "Ecolabels. The Industrialization of Environmental Standards." *Ecologist* 25: 16–20.

Whittemore, Hank. 1992. "A Man Who Would Save the World." *Parade Magazine,* April 12, p. 4–7.

Wiehl, Lisa. 1990. "Texas Courts Opened to Foreign Damage Cases." *New York Times,* May 25.

Wilshusen, Peter R. 2001. "Beyond Community Conflict and Institutional Disruption: Organizational Practices and the Politics of Local Forest Management in Quintana Roo, Mexico." Presented at the Latin American Studies Association Meetings, Washington D.C., September 6–8.

Wilson, E. O. 1988. "The Current State of Biological Diversity." In *Biodiversity,* ed. E. O. Wilson, pp. 3–18. Washington, D.C.: National Academy Press.

Wilson, Patricia A. 1990. "The New Maquiladoras: Flexible Production in Low Wage Regions." In *New Trends in Industry,* ed. Khosrow Fatemi, pp. 135–158.

Wolf, Eric. 1959. *Sons of the Shaking Earth: The People of Mexico and Guatemala—Their Land, History, and Culture.* Chicago: University of Chicago Press.

Wolf, Eric R., and Edward C. Hansen. 1972. *The Human Condition in Latin America.* New York: Oxford University Press.

Wollock, Jeff. 1999. "Eclipse over Colombia: Events and Cosequences of the Murder of Ingrid Washinawatok and Her Companions." *Native Americans: Akwe'kon's Journal of Indigenous Issues* 16 (2):10–31.

Wood, Charles H., and Marianne Schmink. 1979. "Blaming the Victim: Small Farmer Production in an Amazon Colonization Project." *Studies in Third World Societies* 7: 77–93.

World Bank. 1992. *World Development Report 1992.* New York: Oxford University Press.

———. 1997. *Poverty and Income Distribution in Latin America: The Story of the 1980s.* Technical Paper No. 351. Washington, D.C.: Author.

———. 1999. "Mexico Air Quality II." Loan information. Online. www.worldbank.org/pics/gef/mxge59161.

———. 2001. *World Development Report 2000–2001.* New York: Oxford University Press, p. 312, Table 20.

World Resources Institute. 1996. *World Resources 1996–7.* New York: Oxford University Press.

———. 2001. Earthtrends site. Online. http://earthtrends.wri.org/searchable_db/index.cfm; accessed August 9, 2001.

Worldwatch Institute. 2000. "Chemicals and the Biological Boomerang." Earth Day 2000: A 30–Year Report Card. Online. http://www.worldwatch.org/mag/earthday/chem.html.

World Wildlife Fund (WWF). 2001. "WWF lanca relatório sobre a visão de líderes e povo da Amazônia sobre desenvolvimento e meio ambiente." Press release, June 6. Online. www.wwf.org.br.

Wright, Angus. 1990. *The Death of Ramon Gonzalez: The Modern Agricultural Dilemma.* Austin, TX: University Press.

Wyckoff-Baird, Barbara, Andrea Kaus, Catherine A. Christen, and Margaret Keck. 2000. *Shifting the Power: Decentralization and Biodiversity Conservation.* Washington, D.C.: World Wildlife Fund.

Yanz, Lynda. 2000. "Mr. Fox, Does Mexican Democracy Include Workers?" *Globe and Mail*, August 23.

Young, Emily. 1999. "Local People and Conservation in Mexico's El Vizcaìno Biosphere Reserve." *Geographical Review* 89 (3): 364–390.

Young, Oran 2000. *The Effectiveness of International Environmental Regimes: Causal Connections and Behavioral Mechanisms.* Cambridge, MA: MIT Press.

ONLINE RESOURCES

Latin American Environmental Issues

Brazil & Amazon Resources and Links, by Joseph Domask, Ph.D.
www.geocities.com/RainForest/Canopy/1316

Columbia University's Center for International Earth Science Information
Network (CIESIN)
www.ciesin.org

Online Bibliography for Environmental History of Latin America
www.stanford.edu/group/LAEH

Center for International Policy—a nonprofit educational and research
organization promoting a U.S. foreign policy based on international cooperation, demilitarization, and respect for basic human rights
www.ciponline.org

Environment and Latin America Network listserv and archives
http://csf.colorado.edu/elan

Environmental Portal—providing full text searches of reviewed environmental Internet content, news, links and more
www.Eco-Portal.com

Foreign Policy in Focus—a "think tank without walls" that functions as an international network of more than 650 policy analysts and advocates
www.foreignpolicy-infocus.org

Environment Websites for Latin America, from the University of Texas—LANIC
http://lanic.utexas.edu/la/region/environment/

Information Services Latin America (ISLA)—produces a monthly comprehensive overview of U.S. and British media coverage on Latin America
www.igc.org/isla

Latin American Studies Association—posts academic papers presented at organizational conferences
www.lasa.international.pitt.edu

North American Congress on Latin America—access journal articles online
www.nacla.org

News, articles, and documents on the Amazon from Friends of the Earth—Brazilian Amazonia and Friends of the Earth International
www.amazonia.org.br/english

Planeta.com—a clearinghouse for practical ecotourism around the globe
www.planeta.com

Rainforest Alliance—searchable almanac of current and past conservation projects in Mesoamerica
www.eco-index.org

Washington Office on Latin America (WOLA)—monitors the impact of policies and programs of governments and international organizations
www.wola.org

International Institutions

Border Environment Cooperation Commission—established under NAFTA to help United States–Mexico border communities implement environmental infrastructure projects
www.cocef.org

The Commission for Environmental Cooperation (CEC)—an international organization created by Canada, Mexico, and the United States under the North American Agreement on Environmental Cooperation (NAAEC)
www.cec.org

ECLAC-CEPAL, headquartered in Santiago, Chile—one of the five regional commissions of the United Nations, founded for the purposes of contributing to the economic development of Latin America
www.eclac.org

The Inter-American Development Bank, the oldest and largest regional multilateral development institution—established in December 1959 to help accelerate economic and social development in Latin America and the Caribbean
www.iadb.org

The International Monetary Fund—an international organization of 184 member countries established to promote international monetary cooperation, exchange stability, and orderly exchange arrangements; to foster economic growth and high levels of employment; and to provide temporary financial assistance to countries to help ease balance of payments adjustment
www.imf.org

The United Nations Environment Programme (UNEP), established in 1972—works to encourage sustainable development through sound environmental practices everywhere
www.unep.org

World Bank, founded in 1944—is one of the world's largest sources of development assistance.
www.worldbank.org

The World Trade Organization (WTO)—the only global international organization dealing with the rules of trade between nations
www.wto.org

Industry Groups

Business and industry directories: Latin America, from the University of
Texas at Austin library
www.lib.utexas.edu/benson/bibnot/bn-75.html

LATCO—useful sites for international trade with Latin America
www.latco.org/tools.htm

The Brazilian Chemical Industry Association, ABIQUIM—represents the
Brazilian manufacturers of chemical products
www.abiquim.org.br/english

The International Council of Chemical Associations (ICCA)—a council of
leading trade associations representing chemical manufacturers worldwide
www.icca-chem.org

Environmental and Social Advocacy Organizations with Sites in English

The Amazon Institute of People and Environment, Imazon—a nonprofit
research institution whose mission is to promote sustainable development
in Amazonia through research, dissemination of information, and professional capacity-building
www.imazon.org.br/english

Amnesty International—a worldwide campaigning movement that works to
promote internationally recognized human rights
www.amnesty.org

Action for Community and Ecology in the Region of Central America
(ACERCA)
www.acerca.org

Alliance for Responsible Trade—a national coalition of organizations working for just and sustainable trade policies; also a similar Latin American
coalition, the Alianza Social Continental
www.art-us.org
www.asc-has.org

Amazon Alliance—an alliance between indigenous and traditional peoples
of the Amazon and groups and individuals who share their concern for the
future; argues that the best defense of the Amazon comes through support
of indigenous claims to territory
www.amazonalliance.org

Amazon Watch—works with indigenous and environmental organizations
in the Amazon Basin to defend the environment and advance indigenous
peoples' rights in the face of large-scale industrial development: oil and gas
pipelines, powerlines, roads, and other megaprojects
www.amazonwatch.org

Bank Information Center (BIC)—provides information on the projects,
policies, and practices of the World Bank and other multilateral
development banks
www.bicusa.org

Border Environmental Justice Campaign
www.environmentalhealth.org/border.html

BorderLinks—a not-for-profit organization that conducts travel seminars
focusing on the issues of Mexican border communities
www.borderlinks.org

The Brazilian Landless Workers Movement—the largest social movement
in Latin America.
www.mstbrazil.org

The Center for International Environmental Law (CIEL)—a public interest,
not-for-profit environmental law firm founded in 1989 to strengthen international and comparative environmental law and policy around the world
www.ciel.org

Coalition for Justice in the Maquiladoras—a trinational coalition focusing
on environmental, health, and labor issues in maquila plants, working to
establish the Maquiladora Standards of Conduct
www.enchantedwebsites.com/maquiladora/cjm.html

Co-op America—maintains online Green Pages offering socially/environmentally responsible products, services, and investing
www.coopamerica.org

CorpWatch—a third-party review of corporate practices worldwide
www.corpwatch.org

The Development Group for Alternative Policies—focuses on structural adjustment and international trade liberalization
www.igc.org/dgap

The Economic Policy Institute—a nonprofit, nonpartisan think tank that seeks to broaden the public debate about strategies to achieve a prosperous and fair economy
www.epinet.org

The Ecumenical Program on Central America and the Caribbean (EPICA)
www.epica.org

Environmental Health Coalition—organizes and advocates to protect public health and the environment, especially toxic pollution, focusing on the San Diego/Tijuana region
www.environmentalhealth.org/border.html

Equal Exchange—seeks to balance the inequities found in the conventional coffee trade using internationally recognized fair trade standards
www.equalexchange.com

Fairtrade Labelling Organizations International (FLO)—coordinates the work of national labeling initiatives
www.fairtrade.net

Forestry Stewardship Council—a nongovernmental institution with headquarters in Oaxaca, Mexico, established to set standards for forestry certification programs worldwide and accredit certification organizations that comply with these standards
www.fscoax.org

Maquiladoras at a Glance, from CorpWatch
www.corpwatch.org/issues/PID.jsp?articleid=1528

The Institute for Food and Development Policy, better known as Food First—a member-supported, nonprofit peoples' think tank that highlights root causes and value-based solutions to hunger and poverty around the world
www.foodfirst.org

Fray Bartolome Human Rights Center—facilitates short-term accompaniment in Zapatista communities
www.laneta.apc.org/cdhbcasas/index.html

Friends of the Earth International—a federation of autonomous environmental organizations from all over the world
www.foei.org

Global Exchange—a nonprofit research, education, and action center dedicated to promoting people-to-people ties around the world; includes pages on Cuba, Brazil, Colombia, and Mexico
www.globalexchange.org

Global Response—organizes urgent international letter campaigns to help communities prevent many kinds of environmental destruction at the request of indigenous peoples and grassroots organizations
www.globalresponse.org

Greenpeace—A global organization, focuses on the most crucial worldwide threats to our planet's biodiversity and environment
www.greenpeace.org

The Hemispheric Social Alliance—a forum to facilitate information sharing and strategizing between civil society organizations concerned about free trade throughout the Americas
www.asc-has.org

Human Rights Watch—investigates and publishes research on human rights abuses
www.hrw.org/americas

ILRF—an advocacy organization dedicated to achieving just and humane treatment for workers worldwide
www.laborrights.org

Indigenous Environmental Network
www.alphadc.com/len

Indigenous Peoples Biodiversity Information Network—a mechanism to exchange information about experiences and projects and to increase collaboration among indigenous groups working on common causes related to biodiversity use and conservation
www.ibin.org

The Institute for Agriculture and Trade Policy—promotes resilient family farms, rural communities, and ecosystems around the world
www.iatp.org

International Right to Know—A coalition of more than two hundred environmental, labor, social justice and human rights organizations have joined together to support a legislative proposal that would require U.S. companies to report on the key environmental, labor, and human practices of their overseas operations
www.irtk.org

The Jubilee Network—an international movement calling for the cancellation of the unpayable debt of the world's poorest countries
www.jubileenetwork.org

The Latin America Working Group (LAWG)—a coalition of over sixty religious, human rights, policy, grassroots, and development organizations
www.lawg.org

Mexico Solidarity Network coalition—over eighty organizations focusing on Mexico and the United States
www.mexicosolidarity.org

Oxfam America—since 1970 has worked to alleviate global poverty, hunger, and social injustice
www.oxfamamerica.org

Pachamama Alliance—works to preserve the earth's tropical rainforests by empowering the indigenous people who are its natural custodians
www.pachamama.org

Pesticide Action Network (PAN)—a network of over six hundred participating nongovernmental organizations, institutions, and individuals in over sixty countries working to replace the use of hazardous pesticides with ecologically sound alternatives
www.pan-international.org

Project Underground—exists as a vehicle for the environmental, human rights, and indigenous rights movements to carry out focused campaigns against abusive extractive resource activity
www.moles.org

Rainforest Action Network—since 1985 has been working to protect tropical rainforests and the human rights of those living in and around those forests
www.ran.org

Rainforest Alliance—mission is to protect ecosystems and the people and wildlife that live within them by implementing better business practices
www.rainforest-alliance.org

The Research Foundation for Science, Technology and Ecology—works on biodiversity conservation and protecting people's rights from threats to their livelihoods and environment by centralized systems of monoculture in forestry, agriculture, and fisheries
www.vshiva.net

Responsible Coffee Campaign: Organic, Sustainable, Fair-Traded
www.planeta.com/ecotravel/ag/coffee/campaign/campaign.html

Sierra Club and Amnesty International USA—alliance to push for stronger U.S. support for environmental advocates abroad
www.sierraclub.org/human-rights/amnesty
www.amnestyusa.org/justearth

The Student Environmental Action Coalition (SEAC)—a student-run and student-led national network working to uproot environmental injustices through action and education
www.seac.org

Sunshine Project—focuses on biotechnology and the threat of biological warfare
www.sunshine-project.org

TransFair USA—the only nonprofit certification organization for Fair Trade products in the United States
www.transfairusa.org

United Students Against Sweatshops—an organization of students and community members at over two hundred campuses
www.usasnet.org

Witness for Peace (WFP)—a grassroots coalition of nonviolent activists working to eliminate economic and military violence in Latin America through popular education campaigns and delegations to Mexico, Nicaragua, Cuba, and Colombia
www.witnessforpeace.org

World Social Forum—provides a space where representatives of civil society can come together to democratically debate neo-liberalism and economic globalization
www.forumsocialmundial.org.br/home.asp

Worldwatch—a nonprofit public policy research organization dedicated to informing policymakers and the public about emerging global problems and trends and the complex links between the world economy and its environmental support systems
www.worldwatch.org

World Resources Institute—an environmental think tank that goes beyond research to find practical ways to protect the earth and improve people's lives
www.wri.org

World Wildlife Fund—the largest privately supported international conservation organization in the world
www.wwf.org

INDEX

277